Faith in Hebrews

Victor (Sung Yul) Rhee

Faith in Hebrews

Analysis within the Context of Christology, Eschatology, and Ethics

WIPF & STOCK · Eugene, Oregon

Wipf and Stock Publishers
199 W 8th Ave, Suite 3
Eugene, OR 97401

Faith in Hebrews
Analysis within the Context of Christology, Eschatology, and Ethics
By Rhee, Victor (Sung Yul)
Copyright©2001 by Rhee, Victor (Sung Yul)
ISBN 13: 9781532680779

Publication date 5/8/2019
Previously published by Peter Lang, 2001

To Gloria Yi Soon

CONTENTS

Acknowledgments...xi

Author's Preface xiii

Introduction.. xv

1. Background of Faith in Hebrews 1
   Importance of the Study 1
      Difficulty of Defining "Faith"
         in New Testament...1
      Difficulty in Defining the Concept
         within Hebrews..4
      Lack of Comprehensive Treatment 6
   Method of the Study 12
      Exegesis 12
      Biblical Theology 12
      Chiasm 13
      Alternating Structure 17
         Traditional Method 18
         Patchwork Method..20
         Interweaving (Literary) Method 23

2. Survey of Different Views 29
   Different Views 29
      Ethical View 29
         Proponents of the View 29
         Summary and Evaluation of
            the Ethical View 35
      Eschatological View..39
         Proponents of the View 39
         Characteristics of Faith..45
         Summary and Evaluation...49

Christological View 52
   Christ as the Model of Faith View 52
   Christ as the Object of Faith View 57
   Evaluation of Christological View 59
Summary and Conclusion 62

3. Relationship between 1:1–14 and 2:1–4: Christ's Divinity and the
   Exhortation not to Drift Away 64
   Examination of 1:1–14 65
      Basis for the Literary Unit 65
      Christological Teaching 66
   Examination of 2:1–4 71
      Basis for the Literary Unit 71
      Faith and Christology 72
         Exhortation to Pay Closer Attention (2:1) 72
         The Ground for the Exhortation (2:2–4) 75
   Summary and Conclusion 78

4. Relationship between 2:5–18 and 3:1–4:16: Christ's Humanity and
   the Exhortation to Enter God's Rest 80
   Examination of 2:5–18 80
      Basis for the Literary Unity 80
      Christological Teaching 82
   Examination of 3:1–4:16 84
      Basis for the Literary Unit 85
      Faith and Christology 86
         Jesus as the Object of Faith 86
         Jesus as the Model of Faith 94
         Characteristics of Faith 96
   Summary and Conclusion 99

5. Relationship between 5:1–10 and 5:11–6:20: A Merciful High Priest
   and the Exhortation not to Fall Away 101
   Examination of 5:1–10 101
      Basis for the Literary Unit 102
      Christological Teaching 103
         Qualifications of the Levitical High Priesthood 103
         Qualifications of Christ's High Priesthood 106

Examination of 5:11–6:20 108
    Basis for the Literary Unit 109
    Faith and Christology 112
        Christ as the Object of Faith 112
        Christ as the Model of Faith 126
    Summary and Conclusion...128

6. Relationship between 7:1–10:18 and 10:19–39: Superior High Priest
    and the Warning not to Live in Sin 130
    Examination of the Doctrinal Section (7:1–10:18) 131
        Basis for the Literary Unit......................................131
        Christological Teaching...133
            The High priest after the Order of
            Melchizedek (7:1–28).......................................134
            High Priest of the New Covenant (8:1–13) 141
            Comparison of Sacrifices between
            the two Covenants (9:1–28)...............................144
            Perfect Sacrifice of the New
            High Priest (10:1–18) 148
            Summary of the Christological Teaching.............152
    Examination of the Parenetic Section (10:19–39)................154
        Basis for the Literary Unit......................................156
        Faith and Christology 158
            Exhortation to Continue with Faith (10:19–25) 159
            Consequence of Disloyalty to Christ (10:26–31) 167
            Exhortation to Persevere in Faith (10:32–39)..........171
    Summary and Conclusion...179

7. Relationship between 11:1–40 and 12:1–29: Enduring Faith and
    Danger of Rejecting God's Word 180
    Examination of 11:1–40 181
        Basis for the Literary Unit......................................181
        Teachings on Faith...182
            Middle Section: Interim Comment (11:13–16; H)...........183
            Sarah's Conception and Abraham's Offering up
            of Isaac (11:11–12; G//11:17–19; G')......................187
            Examples of Faith in the Patriarchal Period
            (11:8–10; F//11:20–22 F')..................................190

Examples of Faith Seen through Noah
and Moses (11:7; E//11:23–29; E') 194
Faith Seen from the Principle of Pleasing
God (11:6; D//11:30–31; D') 203
Examples of Triumphs and Sufferings through
Faith (11:4–5; B, C//11:32–38; C', B') 206
Introduction and Conclusion
(11:1–3; A//11:39–40; A') 210
Summary of Chapter 11 220
Examination of 12:1–29 221
Basis for the Literary Unit 221
Faith and Christology 223
Exegesis of 12:1–3 224
Exegesis of 12:4–13 232
Exegesis of 12:14–29 235
Summary of 12:1–29 241
Conclusion 242

8. Summary and Conclusion 243
Summary of the Chapters 243
Chapter One 243
Chapter Two 243
Chapter Three (1:1–14 and 2:1–4) 245
Chapter Four (2:5–18 and 3:1–4:16) 246
Chapter Five (5:1–10 and 5:11–6:20) 247
Chapter Six (7:1–10:18 and 10:19–39) 249
Chapter Seven (11:1–40 and 12:1–29) 250
Conclusion and Implications 252

Bibliography 254

Index of Authors 274

Index of Subjects 276

ACKNOWLEDGMENTS

Estella B. Horning, "Chiasmus, Creedal Structure, and Christology in Hebrews 12:1–2." *Biblical Research* 23 (copyright © 1978). The chiastic structure of Hebrews 12:1–2 is used by permission of the publisher. All rights reserved.

J. P. Meier, "Structure and Theology in Hebrews 1:1–14." *Biblica* 66 (copyright © 1985). The diagram of the ring structure is used by permission of the publisher. All rights reserved.

Victor (Sung-Yul) Rhee, "Chiasm and the Concept of Faith in Hebrews 11," *Bibliotheca Sacra* 155 (copyright © 1998). Reprinted by permission of the publisher. All rights reserved.

Victor (Sung-Yul) Rhee, "Christology and the Concept of Faith in Hebrews 1:1–2:4," *Bibliotheca Sacra* (copyright © 2000). Reprinted by permission of the publisher. All rights reserved.

Victor (Sung-Yul) Rhee, "Christology and the Concept of Faith in Hebrews 5:11–6:20," *Journal of the Evangelical Theological Society* (copyright © 2000). Reprinted by permission of the publisher. All rights reserved.

Victor (Sung-Yul) Rhee, "The Christological Aspect of Faith in Hebrews 3:1–4:16," *Filologia Neotestamentaria* (copyright © 2000). Reprinted by permission of the publisher. All rights reserved.

AUTHOR'S PREFACE

My research for the concept of faith in Hebrews began as a doctoral dissertation presented to the Department of New Testament at Dallas Theological Seminary in May 1996. My doctoral studies at Dallas provided rich background for the development of the ideas in this book. Since the completion of my dissertation, I kept on improving the contents of it by presenting different parts of my work at scholarly meetings, and by publishing them in different journals in the form of articles. As a result, the format and the contents of the book are different to a certain degree from those of my dissertation, but my basic assertions and conclusion remain essentially unchanged.

There are many people who deserve my appreciation for their kind assistance in the publication of this book. I am grateful to the faculty members in the New Testament Department at Dallas Theological Seminary for their dedication in teaching the Word of God. I would like to express my thanks to Dr. Buist M. Fanning and Dr. W. Hall Harris who have guided me in the study of faith in Hebrews as my mentors. Especially, I have a great appreciation to Dr. Fanning who has provided me with the seed thought for developing my thesis on the concept of faith in Hebrews.

I would like to extend my deep gratitude to Talbot School of Theology and Biola University, which granted for me a release time to make the completion of this work possible. My colleagues at Talbot have been a great source of encouragement in completing this book project. Thank you, Dr. Dennis Dirks, for your encouragement and financial consideration in publishing this book. I also would like to thank Dr. Michael J. Wilkins who has been instrumental in guiding me to publish articles in scholarly journals and to publish this book.

There were many people who have read portions of my work, when it was still at the stage of dissertation and journal articles. I would like to thank Dr. Henry Holloman, Dr. Clint E. Arnold, Dr. Walter Russell, Dr. Robert Saucy, Dr. Richard Rigsby, Dr. A. Boyd Luter at Criswell College, Dr. Barry Davis (Multnomah Biblical Seminary), and Dr. David Alan Black (Southeastern Baptist Theological Seminary) for their valuable advice and suggestions.

I also would like to express my special thanks to my friend, Gregory Hillendahl, who has carefully proofread my entire manuscript. I am greatly indebted to him. Finally, my deepest thanks go to my wife Gloria who has constantly encouraged me and prayed for me in completing this book project. My prayer is that God may use this book to draw people to Jesus, the author and perfecter of faith.

Victor (Sung Yul) Rhee
Talbot School of Theology

INTRODUCTION

The concept of faith is important in studying the book of Hebrews because it functions as the "organizing thread" that connects together various themes, such as Christ's sonship, high priesthood, apostasy, Sabbath rest, eschatology, and the new covenant. Although many scholars agree in essence that faith in Hebrews involves moral qualities (e.g., faithfulness and steadfastness), they do not concur on the nature of faith.

Some argue that faith in Hebrews is non-Christological. For example, Erich Grässer argues that it is totally removed from the Christ-event into the ethical category of steadfastness. For him faith in Hebrews is non-Christological because one cannot find phrases, such as "faith in Jesus Christ" or "trust in Jesus." In response to this non-Christological view, some argue faith in Hebrews is Christological in some way. For example, Hamm argues that faith in Hebrews is profoundly Christological, in that Jesus is presented as a model and enabler of Christian faith. However, he falls short of emphasizing that Jesus is the object of faith for believers. Other scholars contend that faith in Hebrews has primarily an eschatological orientation. Even among those who hold the eschatological view, opinions are divided. Some maintain that this eschatological orientation is not temporal, but spatial. Both E. Käsemann and J. W. Thompson hold that eschatology in Hebrews is influenced by the Hellenistic dualism of visible and invisible.

It is my conviction that the concept of faith in Hebrews is both Christologically and eschatologically oriented. The author of Hebrews portrays Jesus as both the model and the object of faith as other books of the New Testament. Although he does not use the Pauline expressions, "faith in Jesus" or "trusting in Jesus," the context makes it clear that faith in Hebrews is based on the work of Christ. I also find that the eschatological outlook in Hebrews is not influenced by the Hellenistic concept of visible and invisible reality, but the temporal orientation of present and future.

To demonstrate that faith in Hebrews is both Christologically and eschatologically oriented, I have taken the following approach. In chapter one, I have described the importance and the significance of studying the concept of faith in Hebrews. In chapter two I have summarized and analyzed different views of faith in Hebrews proposed by many scholars. Then from chapters three through seven I have analyzed the concept of faith utilizing theology, exegesis, and different literary devices, which I believe the author of Hebrews made use of in writing the epistle. In these chapters I have carefully examined the alternating structure of doctrines and pareneses, as suggested by Vanhoye and many other scholars (1:1–14 and 2:1–4; 2:5–18 and 3:1–4:16; 5:1–10 and 5:11–6:20; 7:1–10:18 and 10:19–39; 11:1–40 and 12:1–29). This structure forms the basis for developing my thesis in this book.

In addition, I also find that the author of Hebrews employs the literary device of chiasm in many different parts of the book. It appears that this device is similar to sermon outlines for modern day preaching or lecture outlines for the development of thoughts and ideas. Whenever there is a presence of chiasm in a certain passage, I have attempted to explain the basis for the chiastic structure.

Finally, in chapter eight I have briefly summarized the main points of the book and concluded with my view of faith in Hebrews. I have also suggested some implications of this study by recommending possible areas of further research. I believe that, in Hebrews, one must interpret the ethical aspects of faith in the context of Christology and eschatology to have a proper understanding of the concept of faith as intended by the author of Hebrews.

CHAPTER ONE

BACKGROUND OF FAITH IN HEBREWS

Imagine a beautiful necklace made of pearls. What is holding the small and the large pearls together? It is the string that ties them together. Without the string these pearls would not be able to function as a necklace, however beautiful each component may be. Likewise, there are many important themes in the book of Hebrews, such as the sonship of Christ, the high priesthood of Christ, apostasy, Sabbath rest, and eschatology. Each of these themes is important in itself like each pearl of the necklace. But what is the controlling theme that functions as the thread that connects these various themes together so as to make the book of Hebrews precious like a necklace made of pearls? I believe that it is the concept of faith that organizes these different themes as a unit in Hebrews.

Importance of the Study

The study of the concept of faith in the book of Hebrews is important for at least three reasons: (1) because of the difficulty in defining the term "faith" in the overall context of the New Testament; (2) because of the difficulty in defining the concept within the book of Hebrews; and (3) because of a lack of comprehensive treatment of the concept of faith in Hebrews in current studies of the New Testament.

Difficulty of Defining "Faith" in New Testament

In the New Testament, the word "faith" appears frequently in various forms, sometimes as a noun, other times as a verb or as an adjective. Michel classifies this word group into two categories: (1) πείθομαι group and (2) πίστις group.[1] How frequently do these words appear in

---

[1] O. Michel, "Faith, Persuade, Belief, Unbelief," in *The New International Dictionary of New Testament Theology,* ed. Colin Brown (Grand Rapids: Zondervan Publishing

the New Testament? A careful lexical study indicates that the total occurrences of the πείθομαι group add up to 94 times.[2] Occurrences of the
πίστις group are more frequent in the New Testament. The verbal form
appears 242 times (πιστεύω, 241 times; πιστόω, once); the noun
πίστις occurs 243 times, and the adjective πιστός, 67 times. Thus the
total use of the πίστις group is 552 times. The authors of the New Testament also use the negative forms of the πίστις group to express the
negative aspect of faith. The verb ἀπιστέω occurs 8 times; the adjective
form ἄπιστος, 23 times; and the noun form ἀπιστία, 11 times.[3] The
above analysis reveals that the total number of the word group "faith"
appears 688 times in the New Testament. The frequent occurrences of
the word group clearly indicate that the concept of faith is one of the
major themes in the New Testament. Since the term "faith" is one of the
most commonly used words in the Bible and in Christian circles, many
Christians have a tendency to assume that they know exactly what is
meant by "faith."

However, analyses of the term and the concept of faith reveal that
"faith" cannot be defined in a simple way. The meaning of faith is broad
enough to encompass a variety of senses. For instance, Bultmann well

---

House, 1975), 1:587–606. The following is a list of words Michel includes in each category. (1) πείθομαι group: πείθω (convince, pursuade), πείθομαι (obey, believe),
πέποιθα (be convinced, trust), πεποίθησις (confidence, trust), πειθαρχέω (obey),
πεισμονή (persuasion), ἀπειθέω (be disobedient), ἀπειθής (disobedient), ἀπείθεια
(disobedience), πιθανολογία (persuasive speech); (2) πίστις group: πίστις (faith),
πιστεύω (believe), πίστος (trustworthy, faithful), ἀπιστία (unbelief), ἀπιστέω (disbe-
lieve), ἄπιστος (faithless, unbelieving). He distinguishes the difference of the two categories as follows: "The words dealt with here are basically concerned with that personal
relationship with a person or thing which is established by trust and trustworthiness (including their negation). . . . If this relationship comes about through persuasion or conviction, the verb *peithomai* is used. . . . The words of the *pistis* group denoted originally
the faithful relationship of partners in an agreement and the trustworthiness of their
promises" (1:586–87).

[2] The Greek text is based on Nestle-Aland's Novum Testamentum Graece, 26th
edition. The number 94 is the result of adding all the terms in the πείθομαι group as
indicated by O. Michel.

[3] For the list of the word group πίστις see Rudolf Bultmann, "Πιστεύω κτλ.," in
Theological Dictionary of the New Testament, eds. Gerhard Kittel and Gerhard Frederick, tr. Geoffrey W. Bromiley (Grand Rapids: William B. Eerdmans Publishing Co.,
1968), 6:174–228. This reference will be abbreviated as *TDNT.*

illustrates that the concept of faith in the New Testament includes the following usage: (1) to believe in God's words as recorded in the Scriptures (John 2:22), or believing in Jesus (John 5:46); (2) to obey as shown in Hebrews 11 and Paul's letters (e.g., Rom 1:8; 1 Thess 1:8); (3) to trust in the sense that God will fulfill his promise (Heb 11:11), or to have confidence in God's miraculous power (Mark 11:22–24; Rom 4:17–20); (4) to hope in the future promise of God (Heb 11; Rom 4:18); and (5) faithfulness, namely, the faith in which one must be faithful through endurance and patience (Heb 12:1; 2 Thess 1:4).[4] Bultmann asserts that the reason for this rich variety of meanings of faith in the New Testament is that the Christian usage of this term is a continuation of the Old Testament and Jewish tradition, so that "already in the OT and Judaism 'faith' had become an important term for the religious relationship."[5]

Moreover, many scholars share the opinion that there are different emphases in the use of the term and the concept among the different New Testament authors. Some contend that Paul's concept of faith is different from that of Hebrews. For instance, Ladd observes:

> Faith in Hebrews has a distinctly different emphasis from that in John and Paul. The latter conceive of faith as personal trust and commitment to Jesus that brings union with Christ and therefore salvation. In Hebrews faith is the faculty to perceive the reality of the unseen world of God and to make it the primary object of one's life, in contrast to the transitory and often evil character of present human existence.[6]

Stevens also sees the differences between the use of the concept by Paul and that of the author of Hebrews. He states that in Hebrews "faith is constancy, fidelity, heroic belief in the unseen and the apparently improbable; with Paul it is life-union with Christ."[7] Likewise, Goppelt recognizes the difference of the use between the Synoptic Gospels and Hebrews and argues that, while faith assumed a soteriological function pre-

---

4 Bultmann, "Πιστεύω κτλ.," in *TDNT*, 6:205–8.

5 Ibid., 205.

6 George Eldon Ladd, *Theology of the New Testament*, ed. Donald A. Hagner, rev. ed. (Grand Rapids: William B. Eerdmans Publishing Co., 1974), 630–31.

7 George Barker Stevens, *The Theology of the New Testament* (Edinburgh: T. & T. Clark, 1968), 488.

cisely in the Synoptic Gospels (i.e., the faith that saves was the fundamental living-out of repentance), faith in Hebrews appears as the consequence of repentance.[8] These different opinions indicate that there is no
unanimity in defining the concept of faith in the New Testament. It is
hoped that this study will enhance the reader's understanding of faith in
the New Testament.

Difficulty in Defining the Concept within Hebrews
Furthermore, opinions are divided on the definition of "faith" within
the book of Hebrews. Some scholars consider that the concept of faith in
Hebrews is purely ethical in that Christ is not the content of believers'
faith. For example, Goppelt contends that in Hebrews the Christ-event is
never regarded as the content of faith, even though it was developed
with such depth and thoroughness.[9] In other words, he maintains that in
Hebrews faith does not have a soteriological interest as in the Pauline
epistles and the Gospel of John.[10] He sees that in Hebrews Christ was
the preparer of the way to God and the high priest who interceded for
people before God.[11]

In contrast to the ethical view, there are also those who hold that the
orientation of faith in Hebrews is Christological. For instance, Hughes
emphasizes that in Hebrews Jesus is the perfect model for Christian
faith.[12] He suggests that he is the exemplar of faith because "Jesus *the
pioneer* includes not just an identification of Jesus with the 'many sons,'
but also involves a uniquely pioneering role on their behalf."[13] Hughes
considers that Jesus established the pattern for others to follow as the

[8] Leonhard Goppelt, *Theology of the New Testament*, ed. Jürgen Roloff, trans. John
Alsup (Grand Rapids: William B. Eerdmans Publishing Co., 1981), 2:263.

[9] Goppelt, *Theology of the New Testament*, 2:262.

[10] Ibid.

[11] Ibid., 2:263.

[12] G. R. Hughes, *Hebrews and Hermeneutics*, Society for New Testament Studies
Monograph Series, vol. 36 (Cambridge: Cambridge University Press, 1979), 80.

[13] Ibid.

pioneer of faith.[14] Some scholars go further and suggest that Jesus is not only the model, but also the object of faith for his followers. Leonard contends that the word which God had spoken through his prophets, Christ, and the apostles, has become "the word of hearing" for believers, just as the message given to the Israelites in the wilderness is "the word of hearing" (ὁ λόγος τῆς ἀκοῆς) (4:2).[15] He argues that in Hebrews the word of God, preached and heard, is regarded as the object of faith.[16] Leonard recognizes that the object of faith in this verse is God himself. However, he also argues that it is undeniably false to say that the idea of "faith in Christ" is absent in Hebrews because in 6:1 the author implies that the community has received the elementary doctrine of Christ.[17]

Still others consider that faith in Hebrews is mainly eschatological in its orientation. For example, Barrett contends that the determining factor for the concept of faith in Hebrews is in eschatology.[18] However, within this eschatological framework, there exist three different views. First, some feel that eschatology in Hebrews is primarily forward-looking. For instance, Ellingworth maintains that the entire thrust of Hebrews 11, because of the historical nature of the chapter, has a temporal and forward-looking orientation.[19] Next, others argue that faith in Hebrews carries the notion of both present and future aspects. Barrett, for example, asserts from the study of Sabbath rest that the rest is both present and future in that men enter it, and must strive to enter it.[20] By this

---

[14] Ibid., 85. See also Dennis Hamm, "Faith in the Epistle to the Hebrews: The Jesus Factor," *Catholic Biblical Quarterly* 52 (1990): 270–91. Hamm's argument will be examined in detail in chapter 2.

[15] W. Leonard, *The Authorship of the Epistle to the Hebrews* (London: Polyglott, 1939), 84.

[16] Ibid.

[17] Ibid., 85.

[18] C. K. Barrett, "The Eschatology of the Epistle to the Hebrews," in *The Background of the New Testament and its Eschatology,* Essays in Honor of Charles Harold Dodd, ed. W. D. Davies and D. Daube (Cambridge: Cambridge University Press, 1954), 393.

[19] Paul Ellingworth, *The Epistle to the Hebrews: A Commentary on the Greek Text,* New International Greek Testament Commentary, ed. I. Howard Marshall and W. W. Gasque (Grand Rapids: William B. Eerdmans Publishing Co., 1993), 563.

[20] Barrett, "The Eschatology of the Epistle to the Hebrews," 372.

statement Barrett indicates that the balance between "already" and "not yet" is maintained. Third, some scholars consider that eschatology of Hebrews has to do with a spatial and transcendent reality rather than temporal (i.e., present and future). Thompson, who is one of the proponents of this view, argues that faith in Hebrews is Philonic in that the dualistic contrast between the visible and the invisible realities is maintained.[21] He believes that the author of Hebrews has in mind "a distinctive spatial dualism by which he distinguishes between the material and heavenly world."[22]

This brief survey of the literature already indicates that opinions are divided even among those who hold the eschatological view of faith. Is faith in Hebrews oriented only toward the future, and not the present? Or, is eschatology in Hebrews temporal or spatial? One of the purposes of this book is to discover which eschatological view the author has in mind in the book of Hebrews. The discussion of different views on the concept of faith will be further delineated in the next chapter. The point of this brief treatment is that there is no consensus on the definition of faith in Hebrews among scholars. Indeed, Rissi is right in asserting that the concept of faith in Hebrews is not uniform, but encompasses different aspects.[23] For this reason, I feel that it is necessary to determine the exact meaning of faith used in Hebrews by a careful examination of the passages dealing with this subject.

Lack of Comprehensive Treatment
A survey of the literature on Hebrews reveals that many scholars' treatment of the subject is either too brief or limited to certain aspects of faith in Hebrews.[24] A few examples will suffice to illustrate this point:

---

[21] James W. Thompson, *The Beginnings of Christian Philosophy: The Epistle to the Hebrews*, Catholic Biblical Quarterly Monograph Series 13 (Washington, DC: Catholic Biblical Society of America, 1982), 73.

[22] Ibid.

[23] M. Rissi, *Die Theologie des Hebräerbriefes* (Tübingen: J. C. B. Mohr [Paul Siebeck], 1987), 104.

[24] Probably the only exception is the work done by Erich Grässer, *Der Glaube im Hebräerbrief* (Marburg: N. G. Elwert Verlag, 1965), 1–252. However, I believe that Grässer presents an inadequate view of faith in Hebrews. His thesis is that faith in Hebrews is purely ethical (i.e., it has nothing to do with Christology).

1. Mercado deals with Hebrews 10:37–12:3 extensively by arguing that the discourse on πίστις in this passage bears the mark of a Jewish-Hellenistic homily, that is, it is basically a midrash on the Scriptures.[25] He believes that there are close affinities between Hebrews and Philo in the use of the language of sojourning.[26] He argues that, for the author of Hebrews, the heavenly city "consists in the invisible, eternal, transcendental and unshakable realities, which are at the same time the future realities."[27] For this reason he concludes that the faithful ones of the past in Hebrews were sojourners on earth on the way toward the heavenly fatherland.[28] Although his main purpose is not to define the concept of faith in Hebrews, it is clear that his view of faith is eschatological in nature (i.e., it has a forward-looking aspect). This is not to say that Mercado holds the forward-looking to be the only aspect of faith in Hebrews. In fact, he himself states that "the range of meanings and connections of πίστις in Hebrews is so broad that no other translation will do but faith."[29] Although Mercado is to be commended for embracing different ideas of faith, his treatment of the subject is too brief.[30] Because of this inadequate and selective approach to defining the concept

---

[25] Luis Fidel Mercado, "The Language of Sojourning in the Abraham Midrash in Hebrews 11:8–19: Its Old Testament Basis, Exegetical Traditions, and Function in the Epistle to the Hebrews" (Ph.D. diss., Harvard University, 1967), 64–65.

[26] Ibid., 170–71.

[27] Ibid., 113. Mercado also recognizes the difference between Hebrews and Philo. He states: "Philo conceives of the city as being identical with the intellectual world, but any eschatological perspective is missing. The tradition upon which he builds may originally have been apocalyptic. He uses the language of departure in a metaphorical way to characterize the progress of the soul toward virtue and the heavenly realities" (113). However, Mercado also maintains that there is no direct dependence between Philo and Hebrews (173).

[28] Ibid., 172.

[29] Ibid., 76.

[30] Ibid., 76–80. Mercado considers that faith in Hebrews has the following aspects: (1) it is directed toward God, but not Christ (11:6); (2) it is directed toward God's promises (4:2); (3) it is used synonymously with obedience in 3:7–4:11; (4) faith is almost identical with μακροθυμία (patience) (6:12, 15); and ὑπομονή (endurance) (10:36ff.; 12:1–2); (5) it has a close affinity to hope (11:1). He summarizes all these concepts in less than five pages.

of faith, I am compelled to take a more comprehensive way of defining the term and the function of faith in Hebrews.

2. Gordon devotes his dissertation to the covenantal aspect in Hebrews. While, on the one hand, he has done an extensive work on the sacrifice of Christ and the high priesthood of Christ, he has, on the other hand, made little effort to relate this covenantal theology to the concept of faith.[31] However, he does express his view of faith in Hebrews briefly. For him faith in Hebrews is (1) trust in God (11:1, 17–19, 29f.); (2) hope; (3) positive response to the gospel of Jesus (4:2; 11:6); and (4) obedience (3:18, 19; 1:4–6, 8).[32] In his conclusion, Gordon briefly relates his exposition to the practical exhortation: since Christ has inaugurated the new covenant, believers must turn to him in full confidence and faith to avoid spiritual disaster.[33] In this sense, it can be said that his view of faith in Hebrews is Christologically oriented. As one can see from this analysis, a more comprehensive treatment is needed relating covenantal theology to the concept of faith.

3. Stine's work seems to be attractive for those who want to be engaged in the study of the concept of faith in Hebrews because of the choice of its title.[34] However, Stine focuses his discussion only on the Christological aspect in chapters 1–7. He makes no effort to relate the doctrine of Christ to the theme of faith.

4. Lewis discusses the problem of the Old Testament used in Hebrews, especially in 10:19–12:29, with the structure of the theological thinking of the author of Hebrews.[35] In examining this portion of the passage in Hebrews, he sets out to comprehend the way in which the author of Hebrews employed the Old Testament for Christian faith by scrutinizing how the Old Testament functions in the development of

[31] Victor Reese Gordon, "Studies in the Covenantal Theology of the Epistle to the Hebrews in Light of Its Setting" (Ph.D. diss., Fuller Theological Seminary, 1979), 92–318.

[32] Ibid., 42.

[33] Ibid., 121.

[34] Donald Medford Stine, "The Finality of the Christian Faith: A Study of the Unfolding Argument of the Epistle to the Hebrews, Chapters 1–7" (Th.D. diss., Princeton Theological Seminary, 1964).

[35] Thomas Wiley Lewis III, "The Theological Logic in Hebrews 10:19–12:29 and the Appropriation of the Old Testament" (Ph.D. diss., Drew University, 1965), 5.

thought in 10:19–12:29; especially, in 10:37f., chapter 11, and 12:5–6.[36] His statements in these passages indicate that the author of Hebrews was a theologian of his own time, explicating to the believing community how the Old Testament functions. Lewis asks, "does the possibility of the transformation of the Old Testament lie wholly in the event of the establishment of faith's understanding? Or [sic] does it also lie—and if so, to what extent—in the Old Testament itself?"[37] To this question he answers, "the Old Testament can give clarity for understanding the word of the cross; but at the same time the Old Testament also veils the occurrence of salvation."[38] He further clarifies his statement:

> For this reason the word which proclaims the salvation occurrence must struggle against and overcome the witness of the Old Testament. When the Old Testament witness is overcome, however, it can continue to function. Its function in this case is to hold faith to its way in the world and to keep faith open to the future upon which it is dependent and toward which faith must live.[39]

Lewis has done well in investigating how the Old Testament functions in the concept of faith in Hebrews. Also, he devotes much of his dissertation to discussing the meaning of faith in Hebrews. He even corrects Käsemann's interpretation of faith in Hebrews (i.e., faith as primarily hope and endurance based on the certainty of the future goal), pointing out that "in 12:5–11 the ground of the community's endurance is not specifically the promise of the future world but the word of the cross."[40] Lewis suggests that faith in Hebrews is primarily viewed, not as endurance in hope, but the mode of endurance (i.e., submission to the word of the cross).[41] Although Lewis does not use the expression, "Jesus is the object of faith," his argument implies that Jesus is to be viewed as the object of believers' faith. However, as his choice of the passage indicates (i.e., it is limited mainly to 10:19–12:29), Lewis' treatment of faith

[36] Ibid., 6.

[37] Ibid., 168.

[38] Ibid.

[39] Ibid. Lewis discusses the nature of faith throughout his dissertation, but the section on "Faith and the Men of Israel (11:1–40)" is especially helpful (101–50).

[40] Ibid., 143.

[41] Ibid.

is not extensive enough. Moreover, he is not really concerned about bringing out the ethical aspect of faith (i.e., characteristics of faith).

5. Hurst's definition of faith in Hebrews is broader than many other scholars who express their opinions on the concept of faith. According to him, faith in Hebrews is: (1) faith in Christ (i.e., Christ is not simply viewed as a model of faith, but an object of faith); (2) hope in God's promise (i.e., faith in Hebrews is related to both present and future aspects of eschatology, and not Hellenistic spatial concept of visible and invisible); (3) steadfastness; and (4) trust in God. Hurst attempts to bring together different perspectives of faith proposed by other scholars. His interpretation of faith is that it is Christological as well as eschatological. He does not fail to notice that faith in Hebrews also involves ethical aspects.[42] However, his treatment of faith is quite brief, and a more thorough investigation is necessary.

The above survey illustrates that, although the concept of faith has been examined from certain angles by many scholars, a comprehensive treatment of the concept of faith relating to the major subjects in Hebrews has not been done recently to the best of my knowledge. I believe that a more comprehensive approach is needed to grasp the intended meaning of faith in Hebrews because the concept of faith in Hebrews is related to many other important themes, such as Christ's sonship, Sabbath rest, apostasy, the high priesthood of Christ, eschatology, and the new covenant. For example, the author of Hebrews, while expounding the superiority of Christ (1:1–14), states that in these last days God has spoken to us by his Son (1:2). Then he states that we ought to pay closer attention to the things which have been heard lest we drift away (2:1). Here the concept of faith is expressed positively in terms of προσέχειν ἡμᾶς τοῖς ἀκουσθεῖσιν (to pay attention to what we have heard), and negatively in terms of μήποτε παραρυῶμεν (lest we drift away). This is the author's way of indicating that the concept of faith is related to the sonship of Christ.

Moreover, in the section where the author warns against the apostasy by the theme of Sabbath rest (3:1–4:13), the concept of faith is clearly brought out. The author uses the noun πίστις to indicate that the

---

[42] L. D. Hurst, *The Epistle to the Hebrews: Its Background of Thought,* Society for New Testament Studies Monograph Series 65 (Cambridge: Cambridge University Press, 1990), 119–24.

message they heard did not benefit them because it did not meet with faith (4:2). He also uses the verb πιστεύω to affirm that we who believe are entering that rest (4:3). The author also employs the negative term ἀπιστία twice (3:12, 19) to show that the people of Israel were not able to enter the rest because of their unbelief. Thus it is evident that faith plays an important role in Sabbath rest.

Furthermore, the author of Hebrews relates the high priesthood of Christ and the new covenant to the concept of faith. After the author had a comprehensive treatment of the high priesthood of Christ and the new covenant (7:1–10:18), he proceeds with the exhortation in 10:19–39. The particle οὖν indicates that 10:19–39 is the conclusion of what he has been speaking of in the previous chapters. Ellingworth argues that this particle draws "a conclusion from the whole preceding argument certainly from 8:1, perhaps from 4:14."[43] Why is it that the author spends so much time in his exposition of the high priesthood of Christ? The reason is that he uses this doctrinal section as the basis for his exhortation in 10:19–39. Lindars rightly states concerning the relation between the doctrinal and parenetic sections, "the readers are asked to accept the main argument, because it provides the grounds for understanding what they ought to do in order to cope with their consciousness of sin."[44]

This brief analysis of the relationship between the concept of faith and other related themes seems to support my contention that the concept of faith is intricately related to many other important topics, and therefore, it is almost impossible to determine the author's intended view of faith without paying adequate attention to these related themes. However, because of space limitations, the present study will not deal with the detailed exegesis of all these related topics. It will focus primarily on the Christological and eschatological aspect of faith. It is well known by many scholars that the epistle is written in the alternating genre of doctrine and parenesis. This structure may be illustrated as follows: 1:1–14 (doctrine) and 2:1–4 (parenesis); 2:5–18 (doctrine) and 3:1–4:16 (parenesis); 5:1–5:10 (doctrine) and 5:11–6:20 (parenesis); 7:1–10:18 (doctrine) and 10:19–39 (parenesis); 11:1–40 (doctrine) and

---

43 Ellingworth, *The Epistle to the Hebrews*, 517.

44 Barnabas Lindars, *The Theology of the Letter to the Hebrews* (Cambridge: Cambridge University Press, 1991), 101.

12:1–13:21 (parenesis).[45] By examining each section through lexical, conceptual and literary analysis, I will define what faith is and demonstrate that the concept of faith in Hebrews is both Christologically and eschatologically oriented. In this sense, my approach to the concept of faith in Hebrews is more comprehensive than other works done in the past.

Method of the Study

In order to accomplish the purpose described in the previous section, I will utilize the following methods of study: (1) exegesis, (2) biblical theology, (3) literary device of chiasm, and (4) alternating structure of doctrine and parenesis.

Exegesis

The first method used in this study is exegesis. The English word "exegesis" derives from a Greek word ἐξήγησις, which means "explanation" or "interpretation."[46] The term exegesis in biblical study involves explaining "a text in its historical, cultural, and literary setting with concern for its lexical, grammatical and theological content."[47] Exegesis is the foundational step in defining the concept of faith in Hebrews because it provides the building blocks for biblical theology. I will employ this method consistently in dealing with the passages related to the concept of faith in Hebrews.

Biblical Theology

The second method of this study is biblical theology. Because of the way the author of Hebrews displays the concept of faith throughout the entire epistle, I believe that employing the method of biblical theology is

[45] The basis of employing this methodology will be explained in the following section (i.e., in the "method of the study"). A detailed analysis of these sections will begin from chapter 3 and continue through chapter 7.

[46] Walter Bauer, *A Greek-English Lexicon of the New Testament and Other Early Christian Literature*, 2nd ed., trans. and adapted by W. F. Arndt, F. W. Gingrich, and Frederick W. Danker (Chicago: The University of Chicago, 1979), 276.

[47] D. Bock, "Introduction," in *A Biblical Theology of the New Testament*, ed. Roy B. Zuck and D. Bock (Chicago: Moody Press, 1994), 12.

necessary. What then is biblical theology? A brief discussion will help clarify the method employed in this book. Biblical theology can be defined as "that discipline which sets forth the message of the books of the Bible in their historical setting."[48] Its task is to expound "the theology found in the Bible in its own historical setting, and its own terms, categories, and thought forms."[49] While the task of exegesis is a microscopic examination of each unit of the passage, biblical theology involves analysis and synthesis of the individual contributions of a given writer or given period to the canon's message.[50] Putting it in a different way, it can be said that biblical theology is "the summit, as it were, to which the arduous mountain paths of New Testament exegesis lead, and the vantage point from which one can look back upon them."[51] That is to say that biblical theology "not only gathers the theological conclusions of exegesis, but develops an overview, or better a view of the whole, that stimulates exegesis, and indeed, makes such possible at all."[52] Throughout the discussion of the book I will follow the method stated above and develop a biblical theology of the concept of faith through careful exegesis of the passages related to the issue of faith.

Chiasm

The third method I will employ to develop my thesis in this book is the rhetorical structure of chiasm. I believe that this literary structure is crucial in both the exegesis of individual passages and the biblical theology of faith in Hebrews. This literary device is a means toward more effective communication of messages by authors, and not simply artistry to impress readers.[53] Many scholars have come to recognize the presence and the importance of chiastic structures in the interpretation of

---

[48] Ladd, *Theology of the New Testament,* 20.

[49] Ibid.

[50] Bock, "Introduction," 13.

[51] Goppelt, *Theology of the New Testament,* xxv.

[52] Ibid.

[53] R. E. Man, "The Value of Chiasm for New Testament Interpretation," *Bibliotheca Sacra* 141 (1984): 154.

certain passages in the Bible.[54] This seems to be especially true of Hebrews. Some share the opinion that the entire book of Hebrews was written with a chiastic structure in mind. Two of the chief proponents of a broad chiasm in Hebrews are A. Vanhoye and J. Welch.[55] These scholars differ in the identification of the center and the detailed levels of the chiasm in Hebrews from the literary standpoint. However, one thing both agree upon in their proposals is that they have Christ's high priesthood as the center of the chiasm (e.g., for Welch the center is 8:1–2; for Vanhoye 8:1–9:28).[56] I also find that many small sections of Hebrews are chiastically arranged, which I will demonstrate throughout the book. Recognizing the presence of chiastic structures will clarify some of the ambiguous meanings in certain passages, and strengthen my view that faith in Hebrews is both Christologically and eschatologically oriented.

Because of the importance of this literary device in Hebrews and the ambiguity of the way the term "chiasm" (or chiasmus) is used, it is necessary to define the word more accurately. In addition, the purpose and the criteria of chiasm need to be discussed to justify the use of this literary device in explaining the concept of faith in Hebrews.

To begin with, the first question that needs to be answered is the definition of the term "chiasm." The word derives from the verb χιάζω, which means "to mark with two lines crossing like a χ (chi)."[57] Thus the

[54] Some of the major studies done on the chiasm of the New Testament are: Nils W. Lund, *Chiasmus in the New Testament: A Study in the Form and Function of Chiastic Structures* (Chapel Hill, NC: University of North Carolina Press, 1942; reprint, Peabody: Hendrickson, 1992); Donald R. Miesner, "Chiasmus and the Composition and Message of Paul's Missionary Sermons" (S.T.D. diss., Lutheran School of Theology at Chicago, 1974); John W. Welch, ed., *Chiasmus in Antiquity: Structures, Analyses, Exegesis* (Hildesheim: Gerstenberg Verlag, 1981).

[55] Albert Vanhoye, *La structure littéraire de l'Épître aux Hébreux* (Paris: Desclée de Brouwer, 1976), 240; Welch, "Chiasmus in the New Teatament," in *Chiasmus in Antiquity: Structures, Analyses, Exegesis,* 220.

[56] For the overall chiastic structure of Hebrews see also Albert Vanhoye, *Structure and Message of the Epistle to the Hebrews,* Subsidia Biblica, vol. 12 (Roma: Editrice Pontificio Istituto Biblico, 1989), 40a–b. That scholars differ in identifying the center and different levels of chiasm indicates the need for further study in this area.

[57] H. G. Liddell and R. Scott, *A Greek-English Lexicon: A New Edition Revised and Augmented Throughout with Supplement,* rev. and aug. by Henry Stuart Jones and Roderick McKenzie, 9th ed. (Oxford: Clarendon Press, 1968), 1991.

original Greek term χιασμός denotes "placing crosswise, diagonal arrangement, especially of the clauses of a period, so that the first corresponds with the fourth, and the second with the third."[58] This term is used "in rhetoric to designate an inversion of the order of words or phrases which are repeated or subsequently referred to in the sentence."[59]

However, a survey of the literature on chiasm indicates that the use of the word is not limited to the parallelism of words or phrases; it is also used to refer to an inversion of ideas or concepts in a broad sense. For example, Blomberg's outlining of 2 Corinthians 1:12–7:16 indicates that chiasm is at the conceptual level.[60] Likewise, Luter and Lee take a similar approach in their chiastic outline of Philippians.[61] These examples suggest that the term is used to designate an inversion of concepts and ideas as well as words or phrases in a given passage. In this book, I will use the term in both ways: microscopic level (i.e., words and phrases) and macroscopic level (i.e., ideas and concepts). Employing this device will enhance the understanding of the concept of faith in Hebrews.

What might have been the purpose that the authors of the Bible employed chiasm in their writings? Miesner suggests that there are four functions of a chiastic structure: to promote memory, to elaborate the literary beauty, to clarify meaning, and to aid in recovering the original word.[62] For the purpose of this book the function of clarifying the meaning is the most important reason for employing chiasm. Scholars generally agree that the main idea is usually in the middle of chiasm, and all other thoughts revolve around the center. The importance of the center section may be summarized as follows: (1) the center is always where the turning point takes place; (2) there is often a shift of thought

---

58 Ibid.

59 Nils W. Lund, *Chiasmus in the New Testament,* 31.

60 C. Blomberg, "The Structure of 2 Corinthians 1–7," *Criswell Theological Review* 4 (1989): 8–21.

61 A. Boyd Luter and Michelle V. Lee, "Philippians as Chiasmus: Key to the Structure, Unity and Theme Questions," *New Testament Studies* 41 (1995): 89–101.

62 See Miesner, "Chiasmus," 44–49; also R. E. Man, "The Value of Chiasm for New Testament Interpretation," *Bibliotheca Sacra* 141 (1984): 148–54.

in the center, after which the original trend of thought is continued to the end of the system; (3) in many instances identical ideas which occur at the center are distributed in the extremes.[63] Thus in a given chiastic structure the main emphasis of the passage is more likely to be in the center section. This principle will become evident in the detailed exegesis of the passages in Hebrews. Quite often I find that in Hebrews the references to God, Christ, holding fast to the confidence, or the concept of eschatology are placed in the center section of given passages. It is hoped that detecting the main point in the center position will further support the thesis that faith in Hebrews is both Christologically and eschatologically oriented.

Then what are the criteria for identifying chiastic structures in the passages of the Scriptures? Blomberg suggests a very extensive set of criteria for detecting chiasm in his recent article, "The Structure of 2 Corinthians 1–7."[64] These may be summarized as follows: (1) a problem must exist in determining the structure of the text, in which a more conventional outline fails to explain the passage; (2) a clear example of parallelism must exist between the "halves" of the chiasm even if commentators propose quite different outlines for the text; (3) there should be both verbal (or grammatical) and conceptual (or structural) parallelism in most if not all of the corresponding pairs of subdivisions; (4) the verbal parallelism should not be peripheral or trivial, but should involve central or dominant imagery or terminology; (5) both verbal and conceptual parallelism should include words and ideas which are not regularly found elsewhere within the chiasm; (6) there should exist multiple sets of correspondences between passages opposite each other in the chiasm, as well as multiple members of the chiasm itself. For example, although ABA' or ABB'A' may be considered a chiastic pattern, five or more elements are more likely to imply an intended chiastic pattern; (7) the outline should divide the text at natural breaks which are generally agreed upon even by those who propose very different structures to account for the whole; (8) the center of the chiasm, since it forms the climax, should be a passage worthy of theological or ethical significance; (9) if possible, ruptures in the outline should be avoided. In other words,

---

[63] Lund, *Chiasmus in the New Testament*, 40–41.

[64] Blomberg, "The Structure of 2 Corinthians 1–7," 4–7.

an argument that one or more of the members of the reverse part of the structure have been shifted from their corresponding locations in the forward sequence weakens the case for possible chiasm. Blomberg's nine suggestions for the criteria of chiasm are helpful. Certainly, they will eliminate many purportedly chiastic structures. However, these criteria should not be considered as absolute rules; rather they are to serve as guidelines for identifying chiasm. In the analysis of Hebrews not all these rules may be applied in all the passages. I will use these criteria as helpful guidelines to guard against calling what is not chiasm as chiasm.

Alternating Structure
Lastly, I will employ the alternating design of the doctrinal and parenetic sections which was mentioned briefly in the earlier section of this chapter. Since the examination of the relationship between these alternating sections will be the backbone and the skeleton of the development of this book, a detailed discussion of the basis of the alternating structure is necessary.

A survey of literature indicates that the structure of the epistle is a very complex matter. As Black correctly points out, "in a writing so multifaceted, where topics are foreshadowed and repeated, differences of opinion must inevitably arise regarding the precise divisions of the argument."[65] There is no consensus of opinion regarding the literary structure of Hebrews to this day.[66] Because of its complexity, scholars have different opinions concerning the divisions of the doctrinal and hortatory sections. These different approaches can be classified into three categories: (1) traditional method; (2) patchwork method; and (3) interweaving method.[67] The discussion of these different approaches is

---

65 D. A. Black, "The Problem of the Literary Structure of Hebrews: An Evaluation and a Proposal," *Grace Theological Journal* 2 (1986): 163.

66 This has been well demonstrated by George H. Guthrie, *The Structure of Hebrews: A Text-Linguistic Analysis,* Supplements to Novum Testamentum 78 (Leiden: E. J. Brill, 1994), 3–41. In chapter one Guthrie makes a historical investigation of different views on the structure of Hebrews from the early church Fathers to the modern day. In chapter two he evaluates and summarizes different views set forth by modern scholars on the literary structure of Hebrews.

67 Because of the complicated nature of the literary structure and diverse opinions on this issue, I will limit the discussion of it only for the purpose of proving the Christological aspect of faith.

important because the conclusion drawn from it will be the ground for developing the thesis that the concept of faith in Hebrews is both Christologically and eschatologically oriented.

Traditional Method

To begin with, the traditional view, which is concerned primarily with the content of the epistle, generally divides the epistle into two main sections, namely 1:1–10:18 and 10:19–13:25. The first part (1:1–10:18) is usually called doctrinal, or dogmatic, and the second part (10:19–13:25), either exhortation or parenesis. For example, Brown in his commentary follows this pattern in dividing the book. He divides the entire epistle into two sections: doctrinal (1:1–10:18) and practical (10:19–13:25).[68] Setting forth his central theme for part I as "the superiority of Christianity to Judaism,"[69] he goes on to demonstrate his point as follows: (1) the superiority of Jesus to the angels (1:1–2:18); (2) the superiority of Jesus Christ to Moses (3:1–4:13); the superiority of Jesus to the Aaronical priesthood (4:14–10:18).[70] Brown divides part II into (1) general exhortation and warning (10:19–12:29); (2) particular exhortations (13:1–19), followed by conclusion (13:20–21) and postscript (13:22–25).[71]

More recently, D. Guthrie has also outlined the book in the traditional way in his commentary: he calls the first part, "the superiority of the Christian faith" (1:1–10:18) and the second part, "exhortation" (10:19–13:25). The first part is further divided as follows: God's revelation through the Son (1:1–4), the superiority of the Son to the angels (1:5–2:18), the superiority of Jesus to Moses (3:1–19), superiority of Jesus to Joshua (4:1–13), a superior high priest (4:14–9:14), and the mediator (9:15–10:18). As for the second part (i.e., the exhortation), he divides it into four parts: (1) the believer's present position (10:19–39); (2) faith (11:1–40); (3) discipline and its benefits (12:1–29); and (4) con-

---

[68] John Brown, *An Exposition of the Epistle of the Apostle Paul to the Hebrews,* ed. David Smith (New York: Robert Carter and Brothers, 1862), I:ix–xi; II:the first two pages (no page number is indicated).

[69] Ibid., 1:15.

[70] Ibid., 1:ix–xi.

[71] Ibid., II:the first two pages (no page number is indicated).

cluding advice (13:1–25).[72] Likewise, Kent considers 1:1–10:18 to be the doctrinal discussion, 10:19–13:17 practical exhortation, and 13:18–25 personal instructions.[73] Although he divides 10:19–13:25 into two sections, his division is essentially the same as that of D. Guthrie.[74]

The advantage of the thematic approach is that the divisions are simple and easy to follow. However, this method has some serious weaknesses. First of all, this approach ignores the complex nature of the literary structure of the epistle. It fails to recognize "the letter's obvious stylistic and rhetorical devices, specifically the recurring use of chiasm, hook-words, announcements, etc."[75] Moreover, this method has "a tendency to assimilate Hebrews to a pattern common in Paul's letters to churches by making a single major division between doctrinal teaching and exhortation."[76] It ignores the fact that doctrinal and parenetic sections alternate in relation to each other. In other words, the traditional method fails to explain how these two different genres are operating throughout the epistle, thus weakening the function of faith in each parenetic section which follows the doctrinal exposition.

Lastly, this approach has a tendency to "skew the interpretation of the text as primarily a dogmatic work."[77] Those who follow the tradi-

---

[72] D. Guthrie, *The Letter to the Hebrews*, Tyndale New Testament Commentaries (Grand Rapids: William B. Eerdmans Publishing Co., 1983), 58–59.

[73] Homer A. Kent, *The Epistle to the Hebrews* (Winona Lake, IN: BMH Books, 1972), 28–31. Also for similar approach see P. E. Hughes, *A Commentary on the Epistle to the Hebrews* (Grand Rapids: William B. Eerdmans Publishing Co., 1977), ix–x.

[74] Also see F. Delitzsch, *Commentary on the Epistle to the Hebrews*, trans. T. L. Kingsbury (Edinburgh: T. & T. Clark, 1878), 1:v–vii, II: v–vii. Delitzsch divides the epistle into three parts: (1) the supreme exaltation of the mediator of the New Testament above the angels, above Moses and Joshua, and finally above Aaron (1:1–5:10); (2) the Melchizedekian supra-Levitical character and dignity of our celestial high priest, who, after one self-sacrifice once offered, is now forever royally enthroned (7:1–10:18); and (3) the disposition of mind and manner of life required of us in this time of waiting between the commencement and the perfecting of the work of our salvation (10:19–13:25). Apparently he divides the doctrinal section (1:1–10:18) into two for his own purpose. Nevertheless, his way of outlining falls into the category of the traditional method.

[75] Black, "The Problem of the Literary Structure of Hebrews," 168.

[76] Ellingworth, *The Epistle to the Hebrews*, 52.

[77] Harold W. Attridge, *The Epistle to the Hebrews*, Hermeneia (Philadelphia: Fortress Press, 1989), 14.

tional method consider that Hebrews is centered around one central theme, namely, the superiority of Christ. However appealing it may be, this approach forces the intended meaning of the text at certain points. D. Guthrie, for example, contends that the topic of 1:5–2:18 is superiority of Jesus to the angels. However, a careful look at this section reveals that, although 1:5–14 speaks of the superiority of Christ to the angels, 2:1–4 is the warning against drifting away from Christian faith. Moreover, 2:5–18 is concerned with the humiliation of Jesus during his life on the earth. It has to do with "Christ becoming lower than the angels in order to suffer and die."[78] Moreover, D. Guthrie labels 4:1–13 as superiority of Jesus to Joshua. However, an analysis of this passage indicates that the author's intended meaning is far from the superiority of Jesus to Joshua. It is in the context of Sabbath rest and warning against the failure to enter God's rest. One must note that the name Joshua is mentioned only once (4:8) to prove that the rest is still open for the people of God. Some of these examples clearly indicate that dividing the epistle with the theme of "the superiority of Christ" imposes thoughts other than what the author originally intended to convey.

Patchwork Method
    Some scholars who are not satisfied with the traditional approach analyze the book according to the topics suitable for the sections. This method is properly labeled "the patchwork" approach by David Black.[79] In a sense, this approach is similar to the traditional method because it makes an outline without any concern for the literary structure of the letter. For this reason Ellingworth includes both the "traditional" and the "patchwork" approaches in the category of content-oriented analysis.[80] The major difference between the two approaches is that while the former uses a single concept such as "the superiority of Christ" as the central theme, the latter does not limit itself to a particular theme, but feels free to use different topics appropriate to the sections of the epistle. In other words, those who employ the patchwork approach are "content to follow the chapters and changing themes of the epistle from one aspect

[78] G. H. Guthrie, *The Structure of Hebrews*, 26.

[79] Black, "The Problem of the Literary Structure of Hebrews," 175.

[80] Ellingworth, *The Epistle to the Hebrews*, 58.

to another without submitting every detail to one overriding theory of structure."[81]

For example, Bruce subdivides Hebrews into eight sections without any suggestion for one central theme as follows: (1) the finality of Christianity (1:1–2:18); (2) true home of the people of God (3:1–4:13); (3) the high priesthood of Christ (4:14–6:20); (4) the order of Melchizedek (7:1–28); (5) covenant, sanctuary, and sacrifice (8:1–10:18); (6) call to worship, faith and perseverance (10:19–12:29); (7) concluding exhortation and prayer (13:1–21); (8) postscript (13:22–25).[82] Likewise, Morris in his commentary outlines the book into ten units: (1) introduction (1:1–4); (2) the excellence of Christ (1:5–3:6); (3) the promised rest (3:7–4:13); (4) a great high priest (4:14–5:11); (5) the danger of apostasy (5:12–6:20); (6) Melchizedek (7:1–28); (7) a new and better covenant (8:1–10:39); (8) faith (11:1–40); (9) Christian living (12:1–13:19); (10) Conclusion (13:20–21).[83]

At first glance, it appears that the outlines based on the patchwork method are dramatically different from the traditional approach. However, a careful examination of both Bruce and Morris indicates that this method is simply an elaboration of each major section of the traditional method (i.e., the doctrinal and exhortational sections). The patchwork method has its own weaknesses in outlining the epistle.

To begin with, this approach, as in the case of the traditional method, also has "a tendency to press the argument into a more rigid pattern than is called for by the text itself."[84] For example, Bruce labels 1:1–2:18 "the finality of Christianity." However, his subdivisions (e.g.,

---

[81] Black, "The Problem of the Literary Structure of Hebrews," 175.

[82] F. F. Bruce, *The Epistle to the Hebrews,* New International Commentary on the New Testament (Grand Rapids: William B. Eerdmans Publishing Co., 1964), lxiii–lxiv.

[83] Leon Morris, *Hebrews,* The Expositor's Bible Commentary, ed. Frank E. Gaebelein (Grand Rapids: Zondervan Publishing House, 1981), 12:10–11. Also see Donald Hagner, *Hebrews,* Good News Commentary (San Francisco: Harper & Row Publishers, 1983), vi–viii. Hagner subdivides the book into forty different topics. Some German scholars also take the patchwork approach. See Herbert Braun, *An die Hebräer,* Handbuch zum Neuen Testament (Tübingen: J. C. B. Mohr [Paul Siebeck], 1984), 14:1–485; Hans Weiß, *Der Brief an die Hebräer,* Kritisch-exegetischer Kommentar über das Neue Testament 15 (Göttingen: Vandenhoeck & Ruprecht, 1991), 7–10.

[84] Ellingworth, *The Epistle to the Hebrews,* 52.

Christ better than the angels [1:5–14]; the humiliation and glory of the
Son of man [2:5–9]) do not support his first subtitle, "the finality of
Christianity."[85] The subtitle of 3:1–4:13 as "the true home of the people
of God" also imposes his own idea on the text. The question to ask here
is, "does the author intend to expound the true home of the people of
God?" It appears that the passage is not doctrinal, but exhortational. In
other words, the passage does not teach about the true home but exhorts
the hearers to move on toward that true home.[86]

Next, the patchwork approach cannot explain the complex nature of
the literary structure of Hebrews. Both the traditional and patchwork
approaches "have failed to produce agreement for the simple reason that
the author composes like a musician intertwining one theme with another."[87] One of the literary devices the author frequently employs is the
use of repetition. Throughout the epistle the author introduces a theme
and then leaves it, only to pick it up at a later point in the argument.[88]
For example, the concept of Jesus being the high priest appears for the
first time at 2:17 (πιστὸς ἀρχιερεύς). The author continues with the
exhortation in 3:1 with the theme of high priesthood. Then he moves
away from this theme, and continues with it in 4:14–5:10 (the word
ἀρχιερεύς is used four times [4:14, 15; 5:5, 10]). Again, the author dis-
continues the discussion of this theme until it appears at 6:20. Since the
repeated use of the same theme is in various parts of the epistle, it would
be a dilemma for the conceptual method to determine where the section
on Christ's high priesthood should begin.[89] Furthermore, the patchwork
approach does not account for a change of genre in certain sections of
the book. For example, although both 1:4–2:18 and 3:1–4:13 contain a
teaching about the superiority of Christ, one must realize that 3:1–4:13 is
hortatory in nature; there has been a change in genre.[90]

---

[85] Bruce, *The Epistle to the Hebrews*, lxiii.

[86] G. H. Guthrie, *The Structure of Hebrews*, 28.

[87] J. Bligh, "The Structure of Hebrews," *The Heythrop Theological Journal* 5
(1964): 171.

[88] G. H. Guthrie, *The Structure of Hebrews*, 27–28.

[89] Ibid., 28.

[90] Ibid.

Third, unlike the traditional method which interprets Hebrews with the main theme of the superiority of Christ, the patchwork approach does not consider that there is any clearly defined thread of thought that governs the entire epistle of Hebrews.[91] As discussed in the above, there are many features of language and style that imply a much closer relationship between the author's idea and the structure of his writing.[92] There may be some merit to this patchwork approach because certain blocks of the passages in Hebrews can be organized into recognizable themes.[93] However, the disadvantage of this approach is that the outline is achieved "at the expense of a procedure which cannot commend itself as being in accordance with the principles of scientific criticism."[94]

Interweaving (Literary) Method

Since the traditional and patchwork methods are insufficient in explaining the overall composition and the theme of Hebrews, many scholars in recent years have researched the problem of unity from the literary standpoint. However, a survey of the study on the literary structure reveals that the subject matter is so complex that it could alone be a topic for another book. I will discuss the literary structure only for the purpose of separating the doctrinal sections from the parenetic sections. This will be done by examining Vanhoye's analysis of the literary structure of Hebrews. The result of this finding will then be the basis for examining the relationship between the doctrinal and parenetic sections in chapters three through seven.

Vanhoye, in his monograph *La structure littéraire de l'Épître aux Hébreux*, first published in 1963 and revised in 1976, discusses the literary structure of Hebrews. Synthesizing the earlier work of scholars, he proposes five literary devices employed by the author to mark the beginning and the end of the unified sections in the book of Hebrews.[95] They are: (1) the announcement of the subject (announce du sujet), which prepares for the development of the theme to be introduced; (2)

---

[91] Black, "The Problem of the Literary Structure of Hebrews," 175.

[92] Ibid., 176.

[93] G. H. Guthrie, *The Structure of Hebrews*, 28.

[94] Black, "The Problem of the Literary Structure of Hebrews," 176.

[95] Vanhoye, *La structure*, 37.

hook words (mots-crochets), which mark the end of the section and the
beginning of a new development; (3) change in genre, which alternates
between exposition and exhortation; (4) characteristic terms, which are
repeated within the section to bring out distinctive aspect; and (5) inclusions (or *inclusio*), that is, the bracketing of the section by repeating the
term or formula at the beginning and the end of the section.[96] Recognizing the presence of these literary devices enables one to have an objective means for determining the beginning and end of a unit of discourse.[97] By carefully observing these devices, Vanhoye proposes the
following symmetrical outline, with alternation of the genre between
exposition and exhortation. His outline can be summarized as follows.[98]

a	1:1–4	Introduction	
I	1:5–2:18	The name very different from that of the angels	Doctrine
II A	3:1–4:14	Jesus, faithful	Parenesis
B	4:15–5:10	Jesus, compassionate high priest	Doctrine
III p	5:11–6:20	Preliminary exhortation	Parenesis
A	7:1–28	Jesus, high priest according to the order of Melchizedek	Doctrine
B	8:1–9:28	Came for fulfillment	Doctrine
C	10:1–18	Cause of an eternal salvation	Doctrine
f	10:19–39	Final exhortation	Parenesis
IV A	11:1–40	The faith of the men of old	Doctrine
B	12:1–13	The necessary endurance	Parenesis
V	12:14–13:19	The peaceful fruit of justice	Parenesis
z	13:20–21	Conclusion	

This analysis helps the readers realize that the author of Hebrews
intricately designed the structure of the book so as to alternate doctrine
and parenesis.[99] The author was able to write the epistle this way because he was a masterful writer, and because he was able to make use of

[96] Ibid.

[97] William L. Lane, *Hebrews 1–8*, Word Biblical Commentary (Dallas: Word
Books, 1991), lxxxvii.

[98] Vanhoye, *La structure*, 59.

[99] The term "parenesis" is synonym for "exhortation."

structuralizing techniques which came to him from his Jewish Hellenistic education.[100]

Vanhoye is to be recognized for his significant contribution for the study of the literary analysis in Hebrews. However, an examination of his approach reveals that there are some difficulties which need to be reconsidered. To begin with, there is an inherent disadvantage of working with structure only without much consideration of the flow of the content. Swetnam brings out this point well:

> But worthy as this attention to form is, there is a concomitant danger which should not be overlooked: if form is too much divorced from content it can lead to a distortion of content, not a clarification. That is to say, the discovery of form is an arduous undertaking, and if this undertaking is attempted in complete independence of content it can well result in error as to the form.[101]

Because of the overemphasis on the form of the letter itself, Vanhoye's approach obscures the dynamic, developmental qualities of the book in its effort to concentrate on the static architecture of the discourse.[102]

In addition, Vanhoye's analysis of the architecture is forced and artificial in certain sections.[103] For example, Vanhoye argues that 7:11–19 is a unit because it forms an inclusion by τελείωσις (v. 11) and ἐτελείωσεν (v. 19),[104] labeling it "insufficiency of the old priesthood and replacement by different priesthood.[105] However, a careful analysis of 7:11–19 shows that it does not explain why the levitical priesthood was ineffectual, but describes in what sense Christ is a priest after the order of Melchizedek.[106] What initially appears to be a unit by the verbal pattern turns out to be a misleading guide to the structure of the book of Hebrews.[107]

---

[100] Vanhoye, *La structure,* 19.

[101] James Swetnam, "Form and Content in Hebrews 1–6," *Biblica* 53 (1972): 369.

[102] Attridge, *The Epistle to the Hebrews,* 16.

[103] Ibid.

[104] Vanhoye, *La structure,* 129.

[105] Ibid., 137.

[106] Bligh, "The Structure of Hebrews," 173.

[107] Ibid.

26   CHAPTER ONE

The artificial nature of Vanhoye's scheme can also be detected in his
device called announcement of the subject (announces du sujet). If the
author of Hebrews had this device originally in mind, then it should be
readily distinguishable to the readers. But some of the signposts Vanhoye suggests are not easy to recognize because it stands in the vicinity
of other objects which look much more like signposts.[108] Bligh argues:

> Who, for example, would suspect at first, second, or even third reading that the
> phrase καρπὸν εἰρηνικὸν . . . δικαιοσύνης in 12:11 indicates a major division
> in the argument? Why should he not pick on 12:16, since 12:16a announces the
> subject of 13:1–6 and 12:16b announces the subject of 12:1–18?[109]

Bligh's statement indicates that there is much subjectivity involved in
deciding the divisions of the announcement of the subject. As Swetnam
correctly states, it would take a most alert mind on the part of the reader
to notice the literary devices, such as the announcement of subjects and
the resumption of subjects.[110]

On the other hand, some scholars feel that the devices and the outcome of Vanhoye's investigation are convincing, even if they acknowledge some difficulties in the detailed analysis of his approach. For example, Black, advocating Vanhoye's work, states:

> I would venture to suggest that expositors of Hebrews would profit immensely
> from the thoughtful contribution of Vanhoye. If it does not enjoy the status of
> absolute certainty (and what theory does?), it should nonetheless be studied as
> a viable alternative to the more traditional interpretation.[111]

Lane, also, in his commentary, does not hesitate to admit his indebted-
ness to Vanhoye for the outline of the epistle: "I am eager to acknowledge my own reliance upon the work of Vanhoye, even when the analysis of the literary structure that I propose differs from his own."[112]
Likewise, Ellingworth, following the division suggested by Vanhoye,

---

[108] Ibid., 174.

[109] Ibid.

[110] James Swetnam, "Form and Content in Hebrews 7–13," *Biblica* 55 (1974): 346.

[111] Black, "The Problem of the Literary Structure of Hebrews," 174.

[112] Lane, *Hebrews 1–8*, lxxxvii; For outline see cii–ciii.

speaks of its advantages: "on the one hand, it points to features which lie clearly present on the surface of the text, while on the other hand it avoids pressing the material into a thematic grid which may not faithfully represent the intentions of the author."[113]

I am also inclined to believe that Vanhoye's alternating division of doctrine and parenesis needs to be taken seriously. However, his outline needs some modification. First of all, Vanhoye's first doctrinal section (1:5–2:18) is actually a combination of two doctrinal sections (1:5–14; 2:5–18) and a parenetic section (2:1–4) in between.[114] For this reason I will separate these two doctrinal sections to clarify the relationship between the doctrine and the parenesis in this passage (1:5–2:18). Vanhoye's introduction (1:1–4) will also be incorporated into the first doctrinal section (1:5–14). Next, Vanhoye's parenetic section 3:1–4:14 needs to be modified. Vanhoye contends that this passage continues to 4:14 instead of ending at 4:13 because 3:1–4:14 forms a unit by way of inclusion with the words ἀρχιερεύς and ὁμολογία in 3:1 and 4:14.[115]

However, it appears that the parenesis continues through 4:16. This is supported by the conjunction γάρ in verse 15, which is a further explanation of why one must hold fast the confession. Thus it seems more plausible to consider that verse 15 is the continuation of the thought in verse 14. Moreover, οὖν in verse 16 indicates that it is the conclusion of verses 14 and 15, which suggests that 4:14–16 cannot be divided. Furthermore, the author continues with a word of exhortation in verse 16 (i.e., to draw near to the throne of the grace of God). Because of these reasons, it seems better to regard 3:1–4:16 as a parenetic unit as opposed to 3:1–4:14. Third, for the sake of convenience, I feel justified in classifying Vanhoye's sections III A, B, C as one doctrinal section (i.e., 7:1–10:18). Finally, the parenetic sections IV A and V (i.e., 12:1–13 and 12:14–13:19) and the conclusion (13:20–21) will be put together and

---

113 Ellingworth, *The Epistle to the Hebrews*, 58.

114 Although Vanhoye's broad outline indicates that 1:5–2:18 is labeled as a doctrinal section, his detailed breakdown of this section shows that he views 2:1–4 as parenetic section within the larger doctrinal passage (see Albert Vanhoye, *La structure*, 85).

115 Ibid., 87, 104.

regarded as one parenesis.[116] This reconstruction can be illustrated as follows:

1:1–14 (exposition)	2:1–4 (exhortation)
2:5–18 (exposition)	3:1–4:16 (exhortation)
5:1–5:10 (exposition)	5:11–6:20 (exhortation)
7:1–10:18 (exposition)	10:19–39 (exhortation)
11:1–40 (exposition)	12:1–13:21 (exhortation)

This modified outline will be the basis for analyzing the relationship between the doctrinal and parenetic sections for examining the concept of faith in Hebrews. In summary, the intent of this book is to define the concept of faith and its function (i.e., its relationship to Christology and eschatology) in Hebrews. I will examine the alternating sections of doctrine and parenesis in the epistle to accomplish this purpose. In the process of examining each alternating section, I will apply the methods of exegesis, theology, and literary devices, including chiasm.

---

[116] In the actual analysis I will limit the discussion of the parenetic section of 12:1–13:21 to 12:1–29 only. It is my opinion that 13:1–25 is the conclusion of the epistle. See J. C. Fenton, "The Argument in Hebrews," *Studia Evangelica* 7 (1982): 175.

CHAPTER TWO

SURVEY OF DIFFERENT VIEWS

In this chapter, I will summarize and analyze different views of faith proposed by many scholars. Summarizing different views on the concept of faith in Hebrews is not an easy task because many variations exist even among those who hold similar views. A close examination of the literature indicates that the variant opinions are caused by different interpretations of the author's orientation of faith in Hebrews. One's understanding of the orientation of faith determine, to a greater or lesser degree, how one defines the characteristics of faith in Hebrews. Basically, three different views are observed on the orientation of faith: (1) the ethical view; (2) the eschatological view; and (3) the Christological view. In the following section, I will analyze these three different views of faith and show how the interpretations of the orientation of faith affect the way one understands the concept of faith in Hebrews.

Different Views

Ethical View
Generally speaking, the proponents of the ethical view tend to de-emphasize the Christological orientation of faith. They argue that in Hebrews Jesus is not presented as the content (or the object) of faith. Some are willing to go so far as acknowledging Jesus as the model of faith, but not as the content of faith. To facilitate the understanding of this view, I will summarize the work of some of the prominent scholars who hold it.

Proponents of the View
Erich Grässer. In his book *Der Glaube im Hebräerbrief,* Grässer expounds the ethical view in detail.[1] He points out that with Paul, faith has

---

[1] Erich Grässer, *Der Glaube im Hebräerbrief* (Marburg: N. G. Elwert Verlag, 1965), 1–252. I find the following works to be extremely helpful in grasping an overall understanding of Grässer's book: G. R. Hughes, *Hebrews and Hermeneutics,* Society for

an unbreakable relationship with the salvation event, which is Christ himself; for Paul, faith is always faith in Christ (e.g., Col 2:5; Gal 2:16; 3:22; Rom 3:22; Phil 3:9).[2] On the other hand, Grässer argues that faith in Hebrews is not directed to Christ in any way. According to him, the specific Christological notion of faith finds no continuation either in the reflective sense of Paul or unreflective Synoptic sense.[3] Grässer believes that faith in Hebrews is transformed from a soteriological, personal reference of "faith in Christ" into an ethical category of steadfastness (Standhaftigkeit).[4] For Grässer, faith in Hebrews "has nothing to do with the indicative/imperative tension of the Pauline response to the gospel. It is not a relationship, but a conviction and a way of behaving accordingly—a moral quality, a virtue among other virtues."[5]

What is the basic motive of Grässer for advocating the de-Christologized ethical view? How does he explain his view? The answer to these questions lies in his understanding of eschatology in Hebrews. Grässer considers that the eschatological paradox of "already" and "not yet" is dissolved into the purely temporal scheme of indefinite time in the future. It is called ἐπίλοιπος χρόνος (the remaining time), which is considered the period of testing of faith.[6] Thus, according to Grässer, the tension between "already" and "not yet" is relaxed, and the interval of time (zwischen) is transformed into the time of waiting,[7] namely, into the spatial concept similar to that of Philo.[8] Because of the delay of the parousia "the existential meaning of faith, characteristic of an earlier period, yields, as time goes by, to the treatment of faith as a virtue ap-

New Testament Studies Monograph Series, vol. 36 (Cambridge: Cambridge University Press, 1979), 75–100, 137–42, 173–83, 193–96; C. F. D. Moule, "Review of Grässer, *Der Glaube im Hebräerbrief*," *Journal of Theological Studies n.s.* 17 (1966): 148–50; Gerhard Dautzenberg, "Der Glaube im Hebräerbrief," *Biblische Zeitschrift* 17 (1973): 161–77.

2 Ibid., 65–66.

3 Ibid., 79.

4 Ibid., 63.

5 Moule, "Review of Grässer, *Der Glaube im Hebräerbrief*," 148.

6 Ibid., 171.

7 Ibid., 190.

8 Ibid., 144.

propriate to a situation where the parousia is no longer expected soon."[9] For this reason Grässer concludes that the author of Hebrews is "the theologian on the doorstep of the primitive Christianity to the post-apostolic time."[10] Another issue is whether or not the author of Hebrews shows evidence of originality in setting forth faith in terms of the ethical category. Grässer considers that Hebrews does not bear the mark of originality as such. He sees that the author of Hebrews adopted and applied the ideas traditionally handed down in later Hellenistic Judaism, especially in the LXX and Philo. To begin with, Grässer contends that אמן in the Old Testament is translated into the word with the stem πιστ– in the LXX, which, in turn, was adopted by the author of Hebrews. The point is that, since the basic meaning of אמן is "being firm," the faith word group (πιστίς, πιστεύειν, πιστός) in Hebrews must signify "firmness" or "steadfastness."[11] Moreover, Grässer believes that it is impossible to comprehend the concept of faith in Hebrews without a proper understanding of Hellenistic Judaism in Alexandria, especially that of Philo. He argues that Philo offers ample analogies that facilitate the understanding of Hebrews through the spatial concept. For example, Grässer points out that both Hebrews and Philo employ a metaphorical world expression, namely, a distinction between the visible-transient world and the invisible-eternal heavenly world.[12] Thus he states, "the decisive and conveying concept for the eschatological outline is not a temporal one, but a transcendent space."[13] In this frame of reference, he argues that the unfailing way of entry from this world to that world is faith.[14]

[9] Moule, "Review of Grässer, *Der Glaube im Hebräerbrief,*" 148.

[10] Grässer, *Der Glaube im Hebräerbrief,* 184. "Der Autor des Hb ist damit der Theologe auf der Schwelle vom Urchristentum zur nachapostolischen Zeit."

[11] Ibid., 79.

[12] Ibid., 144.

[13] Ibid., 174. Grässer argues that this spatial idea is applicable to the following concepts: rest (3:11, 18; 4:1, 3, 5, 10, 11), world to come (2:5), age to come (6:5), heavenly homeland (11:14), heavenly city (11:10, 16; 12:22: 13:14), heavenly Jerusalem (12:12), inheritance (11:8), things hoped for and things not seen (11:1), reward (10:35; 11:26), unshakable kingdom (12:28), things which cannot be shaken (12:27), promises (11:13, 39).

[14] Ibid., 144.

How, then, does Grässer define the concept of faith in Hebrews?
Grässer contends that the factor that marks out the Christian way of conduct is firmness without any reference to Christ as the content of faith.
He believes that this is a clear indication of Philonic influence in the
way the author of Hebrews uses the idea of faith. He asserts that no one
has explained the real essence of faith in Hebrews with such intensity as
Philo. For this reason Grässer concludes that πίστις (faith) and βεβαιό-
της (firmness) are synonyms.[15]

Barnabas Lindars. In his volume, *New Testament Theology: The
Theology of the Letter to the Hebrews,* Lindars also brings out the ethical
view of faith. After having expounded the high priesthood and the sacrifice of Jesus, he states that faith is "the proper response to the sacrifice
of Christ and can be regarded as the human side in the new covenant."[16]
He believes that the exposition of the sacrifice of Christ in 7:1–10:18 is
the preparation for the exhortation that follows in 10:19ff. Lindars considers that 10:19–21 is the summary of the argument on atonement in
7:1–10:18, and on this basis the writer of Hebrews exhorts the readers to
draw near (10:22). In this sense, faith can be described as the reception
process, without which the gospel of reconciliation through the atoning
sacrifice of Christ remains merely theoretical and unassimilated.[17] Lindars' close association of the exhortation section (10:19–39) to Christ's
priesthood and his sacrifice might mislead the readers into thinking that
his view of faith has Jesus as the object of believers' faith.

However, he is quick to point out that the author of Hebrews does
not use 'faith' to denote the content of Christian belief. In interpreting
Hebrews 12:1–3, Lindars rightly states that Jesus is the pioneer and perfecter of faith because he alone inaugurated the fulfillment of God's eschatological plan of salvation and carried it through in his own person.
For this reason Lindars views Jesus as the ultimate example of faith, not
as the content or the object of faith.[18] By explaining Jesus simply as the
model of believers' faith, he tends to minimize the Christological aspect

---

[15] Ibid.

[16] Barnabas Lindars, *The Theology of the Letter to the Hebrews* (Cambridge: Cambridge University Press, 1991), 108.

[17] Ibid.

[18] Ibid., 109, 112–13.

of faith in Hebrews to a certain degree, and instead, emphasizes the ethical aspect. This point is clearly brought out in the statement: "Hebrews agrees that faith is the proper response to God's act of salvation through Christ, but he sees it as a moral quality which should be constantly expressed in Christian living."[19]

Based on these premises he proceeds to define the concept of faith in terms of a moral quality of firmness, fidelity, and reliability as in normal biblical usage. He asserts that since keeping faith with his people is one of the attributes of God, the same quality is required of all the Christians. For example, according to Lindars, the faithfulness of Moses and Jesus (3:1–6) are examples of human faithfulness. For this reason he does not see that the author of Hebrews uses "faith" to denote the content of Christian belief, nor does he consider that Hebrews shows any knowledge of Paul's specialized use of faith, namely, "justification by faith."[20]

Harold Attridge. Attridge is another scholar who holds an ethical view of faith in Hebrews. He asserts that, although a Christological referent is characteristic of early Christian literature, it is not by all means universal. Attridge considers that the Christological referent (i.e., Christ as the content of faith) is lacking in Hebrews because its understanding of faith is in continuity with a certain type of tradition.[21] Then which tradition is most likely to have influenced Hebrews' concept of faith? Attridge recognizes that there is a close affinity in the concept of faith between Philo and Hebrews. He points out that in both writings faith is closely related to the virtue of hope. For example, he observes that both writers begin their discussions with a definition of the virtue in question and proceed to list examples of hope's power using the figure of anaphora. He also points out that Philo concludes his reflection with athletic imagery as in Hebrews.[22]

Now, do these similarities automatically warrant direct dependence of Hebrews on Philo? Attridge does not think so. To prove his point he

[19] Ibid., 110.

[20] Ibid., 109.

[21] Harold W. Attridge, *The Epistle to the Hebrews,* Hermeneia Commentary (Philadelphia: Fortress Press, 1989), 313.

[22] Ibid., 306.

brings out some important differences. One difference is that "while Philo uses general types of hopeful people, money lenders, glory seekers, athletes, and philosophers, Hebrews lists particular individuals and episodes taken from scripture."[23] Attridge observes another difference: while faith in God is regularly contrasted with faith in created things in Philo, it is contrasted with rejection of God's promise in Hebrews. He points out that the eschatological component of faith in Hebrews is far more pronounced than that of Philo.[24]

Because of these differences Attridge concludes that there is no direct literary dependence between Hebrews and Philo. He considers that the similarities are due to the common tradition available both to the author of Hebrews and Philo, and both relied upon it.[25] Thus it can be said that the background of Hebrews does not go back to Philo. Instead, Attridge argues that the author of Hebrews was influenced by the OT concept of faith (i.e., אמן concept). He asserts that "faith for Hebrews is something that is necessary for hopes to come true and that puts its possessor in touch with what is most real, though it be hidden."[26] For this reason he suggests that faith in Hebrews is to be understood in terms of affective and behavioral terms, namely, it is equivalent to fidelity, trust, and obedience in relationship between human beings and Yahweh. Therefore, Attridge concludes that Paul's concept of faith as the content of the kerygma or the gospel message is quite lacking in Hebrews.[27] Nevertheless, he believes that faith in Hebrews is developed within the Christological framework in that Jesus is the example of believers' faith.[28]

---

[23] Ibid.

[24] Ibid., 313.

[25] Ibid., 306, n. 11.

[26] Ibid., 308.

[27] Ibid., 311–14.

[28] Ibid., 314. Attridge states, "Despite the absence of a christological referent, Hebrews' understanding of faith is clearly developed within a christological framework. The faith to which the addressees are here called is both made possible and exemplified by the 'perfecter of faith' (12:2), at whose exaltation hopes have begun to be realized and things unseen proved."

Summary and Evaluation of the Ethical View

The above analysis indicates that the interpretation of faith in Hebrews for Grässer, Lindars, and Attridge lacks a Christological aspect, in the sense that Christ is the content or the object of faith as in the Pauline or Synoptic writings. Of the three, Grässer holds a more extreme view than Attridge and Lindars, in that faith in Hebrews is completely non-Christological. For Grässer faith in Hebrews has nothing to do with Christ, neither as the model nor as the content of faith; it is simply a moral character of steadfastness. However, Attridge and Lindars indicate that, although Christ is not viewed in terms of the object of faith, they both consider Jesus as the model and the example of faith for believers. In this respect, the views of both Attridge and Lindars are Christologically oriented to a certain degree. But I contend that they do not go far enough in their Christological interpretation of faith. In Hebrews, Christ is depicted not only as the exemplar of faith, but also the object of faith for believers. This point will be further developed later in this chapter.

As for the characteristics of faith, they all concur in viewing faith as an ethical, moral quality of steadfastness, fidelity, and reliability. It appears that these ethical qualities are an inseparable part of the concept of faith in Hebrews whether one's interpretation of faith is Christologically or non-Christologically oriented. As for the influence of faith in Hebrews, Grässer contends that the author of Hebrews is largely influenced by the LXX, and especially by Philo. Attridge also acknowledges that some similarities exist between Hebrews and Philo; however, he also notices striking differences between the two. Thus he concludes that the concept of faith in Hebrews is derived from the אמן concept in the Old Testament.

At this point I feel that it is important to have a more in-depth discussion of Grässer's concept of faith. Grässer has done a great service in bringing to light the differences of faith between the Pauline literature and Hebrews. Indeed, in Hebrews the ethical aspect of faith cannot be denied. Certainly, faith embodies an aspect of steadfastness. However, one needs to ponder which concept of faith is normal in the New Testament. When Grässer suggests that the Pauline concept of faith (i.e., soteriological aspect) is replaced by the ethical category in Hebrews, he clearly indicates that this Christological aspect of faith is a normative interpretation in the early church.[29]

Yet, a careful study of the Pauline epistles and Synoptic Gospels reveals that the idea of faith is broad enough to include other aspects. An examination of the concept of faith in the Synoptic Gospels indicates that, in addition to the meaning of having Jesus as the object of faith, faith has the following senses. First, it has the idea of believing in God or Christ who is the almighty, self-revealing and beneficent toward humanity, particularly toward the worshipers (Matt 8:13; 21:22; Mark 5:36; 9:23; 15:32; Luke 8:12–13, 50).[30] This aspect of faith is different from the soteriological meaning of trusting in Jesus. Second, faith is related to the miracle stories (e.g., Matt 8:10; Mark 2:5; 5:34).[31] What is the meaning of faith in these instances? These verses reveal that faith is trusting in the mission of Jesus and his power to deliver from trouble."[32] They also indicate that faith is not used in the Christological sense, namely, trust in Jesus for one's salvation.

Moreover, an investigation of the Pauline letters also confirms that the concept of faith is not uniformly used in a Christological way. Bultmann declares:

> At the outset, it may be simply said that "faith" is the condition for the receipt of "righteousness," taking the place of "works," which in the Jewish view constitute that condition. It may also be simply said at the outset such "faith" is the acceptance of the Christian message—following a usage that developed in the missionary enterprise of Hellenistic Christianity.[33]

[29] Gerhard Dautzenberg, "Der Glaube im Hebräerbrief," 174.

[30] E. C. Blackman, "Faith, Faithfulness," in *The Interpreter's Dictionary of the Bible*, ed. George Arthur Buttrick (New York: Abingdon Press, 1962), 2:222–34.

[31] O. Michel, "Faith, Persuade, Belief, Unbelief," in *The New International Dictionary of New Testament Theology*, ed. Colin Brown (Grand Rapids: Zondervan Publishing House, 1975), 1:587–606. Also Dautzenberg, "Der Glaube im Hebräerbrief," 174–75. He believes that the concept of faith in the Synoptic tradition (i.e., Q and miracle stories) is not Christological. He also notices that there are only two passages in Matthew (18:6; 27:34) which express the Christological notion of faith.

[32] Ibid., 599–600. This reference will be abbreviated as *NIDNTT*.

[33] Rudolf Bultmann, *Theology of the New Testament*, trans. Kendrick Grobel (New York: Charles Scribner's Sons, 1951), 1:314.

He maintains that this Christological notion of faith is given a characteristic and decisive stamp by Paul himself.[34] However, he also brings out other aspects of faith. First, faith is obedience. Bultmann correctly takes the phrase ὑπακοὴ πίστεως (obedience of faith) as the genitive of apposition, and understands it as "obedience, which is faith" (Rom 1:5).[35] He argues that the reason is that "the message which demands acknowledgment of the crucified Jesus as Lord demands of man the surrender of his previous understanding of himself, the reversal of the direction his will has previously had."[36] Second, faith is the hope that points toward the future (e.g., Gal 3:11; Rom 1:17; 6:8). Third, faith is confidence in the sense that hope which is based on grace does not disappoint (Rom 5:5), namely, since we have such a hope (2 Cor 3:12), we also have such confidence (3:4).[37] Fourth, Paul's notion of faith also includes faith as a charismatic gift. For example, his mention of faith in 1 Corinthians 12:9 is in the context of the spiritual gifts. Therefore, faith in this verse must be understood as one of the spiritual gifts. Certainly, justifying faith is not meant here, because "it is distinct from 'the utterance of wisdom' and 'the utterance of knowledge' which are mentioned previously (1 Cor 12:8)."[38] A brief study of the Pauline literature and the Synoptic Gospels clearly demonstrates that there are many different strands of faith in these writings. Thus one cannot dogmatically assert that the Christological notion of faith is the normative interpretation in primitive Christianity as Grässer does. Consequently, it cannot be said that faith in Hebrews is ethically oriented in the sense that it is removed from the Christ-event due to the delay of the parousia.

Then how does one account for the ethical aspect of faith in Hebrews? One possible explanation for this question is that it is probably due to the influence of the Old Testament. For example, Bultmann suggests that the rich Christian use of the concept of faith is probably due to

[34] Ibid.

[35] Ibid.

[36] Ibid., 1:315.

[37] Ibid., 1:322–23.

[38] Michel, "Faith, Persuade, Belief, Unbelief," in *NIDNTT,* 1:602.

the Old Testament and Jewish tradition.[39] Dautzenberg also, criticizing Grässer's view that the author of Hebrews has de-Christologized the Christologically oriented concept of faith, argues that the ethical aspect of faith in Hebrews is developed essentially from the traditional Jewish notion of faith (i.e., faithful, or fidelity), rather than the later amputation of certain concepts of faith from the Pauline writings or the Synoptic Gospels. He indicates that such a theological engagement is missing both in Hebrews and in the writings of the post-apostolic time referred to by Grässer for the purpose of comparison.[40]

Another explanation for the phenomenon of the ethical orientation of faith in Hebrews may have to do with the eschatological nature of faith. Hughes rightly points out that πίστις words are used only in parenetic sections in Hebrews.[41] He observes that "this section of the letter consistently views salvation as a future entity, something which the congregation does not yet have within its grasp and which, in their complacency, its members may yet perfectly well lose."[42] Therefore, the emphasis of faith in Hebrews is on faithfulness and the determination to be steadfast as the antidotes to such dangerous lassitude, not because of the author's theological intention to de-Christologize the concept of faith.[43] Hughes sheds further light on this point:

> Because the believing-maintenance of their 'confession of hope' (10:23; cf. 3:6 and 4:14) is, in the last analysis, the measure of their estimation of God's dependability (11:11: 'By faith . . . since she reckoned him to be faithful who had promised' is especially clear and should be regarded as definitive rather than exceptional), words such as 'perseverance' (ὑπομονή) or 'steadfastness' (ὑπόστασις) should not too quickly be taken as clear indices 'of the transformation of faith into behavior.'[44]

---

[39] Rudolf Bultmann, "Πιστεύω κτλ.," in *Theological Dictionary of the New Testament*, ed. Gerhard Kittel and Gerhard Frederick, tr. Geoffrey W. Bromiley (Grand Rapids: William B. Eerdmans Publishing Co., 1968), 6:205.

[40] Dautzenberg, "Der Glaube im Hebräerbrief," 174.

[41] Hughes, *Hebrews and Hermeneutics*, 139.

[42] Ibid.

[43] Ibid.

[44] Ibid., 79.

Therefore, he insists that it would be more in line with the author's intention to describe the ethical aspect of faith as "believing faithfulness," namely, faith which results in certain behavioral and character qualities as opposed to viewing it as a de-Christologized ethical element.[45] This brief interaction with Grässer shows that his thesis needs to be reconsidered from different angles.

Eschatological View

Some scholars also express the opinion that faith in Hebrews is primarily eschatological. Does faith in Hebrews contain both present and the future aspects of eschatology? Or, does it reflect only the future aspect? Or, does the author of Hebrews employ the Philonic concept to indicate that faith in Hebrews is the transcendent reality rather than the temporal future reality? In this section, I will summarize the works of some of the prominent scholars who hold an eschatological view of faith, followed by an analysis of the different views on eschatology.

Proponents of the View

Richard Longenecker. Longenecker claims that the orientation of faith in Hebrews is mainly futuristic. For example he points out from the faith of Abraham that faith in Hebrews has the "forward-looking aspect."[46] Longenecker asserts that imitating Abraham's faith necessarily involves having a forward orientation of life (11:10, 13–16, 13:14).[47] Because of future orientation of faith, he points out that "they should not be looking back, whatever their reverses and whatever their difficult circumstances, but they should be looking forward and moving forward with God."[48]

Ernst Käsemann. Likewise, Käsemann takes an eschatological approach to the concept of faith. Before discussing Käsemann's view of faith, it seems necessary to have some knowledge of his motif to appre-

---

[45] Ibid.

[46] Richard N. Longenecker, "'The Faith of Abraham' Theme in Paul, James and Hebrews: A Study in the Circumstantial Nature of New Testament Teaching," *Journal of the Evangelical Theological Society* 20 (1977): 207–10.

[47] Ibid., 208.

[48] Ibid., 209.

ciate his view of faith. He presents the principal motif in Hebrews as the
Gnostic journey of the wandering people of God. This wandering motif
is clearly seen by the way he designs his book: he begins with 3:7–4:13
as a point of departure, rather than beginning with chapters 1–2.[49] According to Käsemann, the wandering itself is the basic posture of the
bearer of the revelation, and the people of God as bearers of the revelation.[50] The incorporation into the fellowship of the people of God is essential in this wandering because "in union with Christ's companions is
their life, faith, and progress on the individual's way of wandering."[51] In
other words, Käsemann asserts that the author of Hebrews presents the
believing community as a type of Israel during the time of trials in the
wilderness, and wandering as the characteristic model of the community's existence.[52] Käsemann also believes that the motif of the wandering people of God is unfolded clearly from 10:19 to the closing section of the letter.[53] For example, he uses several verses to illustrate his
point: (1) the author's exhortation to go outside the camp with Jesus and
bear the abuse (13:13) and the reference to "the city which is to come"
(13:14); (2) the reference to the "cloud of witnesses" who are described
as wandering toward the city of God (11:8ff., 13ff., 24ff.); (3) Mount
Zion as the goal of faith's wandering.[54]

It is in this context of the Gnostic journey of the wandering people
of God that Käsemann discusses the concept of faith. His concept of
faith is closely related to the ἐπαγγελία (promise) and to eschatology.
Recognizing the identical nature of εὐαγγελίζεσθαι and the reception
of the ἐπαγγελία (4:2,6), he states that *"in a constitutive and fundamental way the divine revelation in Hebrews bears the character of*

---

[49] Ernst Käsemann, *The Wandering People of God: An Investigation of the Letter to
the Hebrews,* trans. Roy A. Harrisville and Irving L. Sandberg (Minneapolis: Augsburg
Publishing House, 1984), 17.

[50] Ibid., 20.

[51] Ibid., 23.

[52] Thomas Wiley Lewis III, "The Theological Logic in Hebrews 10:19–12:29 and
the Appropriation of the Old Testament" (Ph.D. diss., Drew University, 1965), 13.

[53] Käsemann, *The Wandering People of God,* 22.

[54] Ibid., 23.

promise and thus is purely eschatological in nature."[55] Käsemann realizes that the author of Hebrews is familiar with the idea of the eschatological event which has already taken place. However, he contends that
the present aspect of eschatology is not emphasized. He argues that if
God's speaking occurs with the arrival of the Son "in these last days"
(1:2), or "at the consummation of the age" (9:26), then believers also
have tasted the heavenly gift and the powers of the coming age (6:4f.).[56]
For this reason he believes that the eschatological orientation of Hebrews is evidently governed by an expectation of the future, as the emphasis of the concept of promise (ἐπαγγελία) precisely shows.[57]

At first glance it appears that Käsemann's eschatology has a temporal orientation. However, an examination of his writings reveals that his
frame of eschatology is spatially oriented. Käsemann believes that Hebrews' concept of the future as a sphere of what is not visible here and
now is influenced by Hellenistic philosophy. He states, *"The future of
faith may in no way appear as a continuation of the earthly present."*[58]
In other words, it is an eschatological posture, and its future is ushered
in by God as relief from and the end of, indeed as the catastrophe (cf.
12:26ff.) of, the earthly present. For Käsemann faith has nothing to do
with the world of appearance, but belongs to the sphere of signs and
wonders (11:33ff.).[59] He notices, with the statement of "the conviction
[or proof] of the things not seen" in 11:1, that there is a barrier that cannot be overcome between the present and the future world; the only way
to bridge the gap between the two worlds, that is, from changeableness
to unchangeableness is through faith, which is bound to the word of
God.[60]

A brief analysis of Käsemann's view clearly indicates that his view
of faith is eschatological; it has forward-looking emphasis. For him eschatology in Hebrews is entirely future; the present aspect is not emphasized. Moreover, Käsemann's scheme of eschatology is not based on the

[55] Ibid., 26.

[56] Ibid.

[57] Ibid., 27.

[58] Ibid., 41.

[59] Ibid., 40.

[60] Ibid., 41.

temporal orientation of the present and the future, but on the spatial orientation of visible and invisible, similar to that of Philo's transcendent
reality.

James W. Thompson. Thompson's view of eschatology is similar to
that of Käsemann in that he considers the invisible concept of faith in
Hebrews to be spatially oriented. He compares the concept of faith in
Hebrews with that of Plato, Philo, and the book of Maccabees. He sees
that the concept of faith in Hebrews and that in the philosophy of the
Hellenistic period are incompatible with each other.[61] He finds many
important differences between Hebrews and Philo. For instance, Thompson recognizes that the book of Hebrews has a future expectation which
is absent in Philo. He points out that Hebrews has not denied the early
Christian expectation of the return of Christ (9:27; 10:25; 10:36–39) and
that ἐλπιζομένων (things hoped for) in 11:1 points to the expectation of
a final eschatological event.[62]

However, Thompson indicates that the book of Hebrews also has
much in common with Philo in that both writers have employed Platonic
epistemological categories to describe faith.[63] To be more specific,
πίστις (faith) for both Philo and Hebrews entails living as a stranger on
earth and 'seeing' a better reality. He believes that the writer of Hebrews
shares the dualistic distinction between the phenomenal and invisible
worlds.[64] For example, the distinction between the visible and the invisible is seen in 11:27 which speaks of ἀόρατον ὡς ὁρῶν (as seeing
him who is invisible). Moreover, he argues that the expression "of things
not seen" (οὐ βλεπομένων) in 11:1 is equivalent to such terms as "that
which may not be touched" (οὐ ψηλαφωμένος) (12:18), "immovable"
(ἀσάλευτος) (12:28), and "not made with hands" (οὐ χειροποίητος)
(9:11), which are the words used negatively to indicate the distinction

---

[61] James W. Thompson, *The Beginnings of Christian Philosophy: The Epistle to the
Hebrews,* Catholic Biblical Quarterly Monograph Series 13 (Washington, DC: Catholic
Biblical Society of America, 1982), 53.

[62] Ibid., 73.

[63] Ibid., 80. Thompson does not believe that there is literary dependence between
Hebrews and Philo. He considers that "both writers have taken a category which was
relatively unimportant in Greek philosophy and employed it within the framework of
Greek metaphysics."

[64] Ibid.

between the two spheres of reality.[65] Therefore, Thompson concludes that faith in Hebrews involves the recognition of both the future reality and the proof and realization of the metaphysically superior and stable reality.[66] He states, "while the author does not deny the traditional eschatological categories, his interest is heavily influenced by Platonic dualism."[67] This is the underlying presupposition for Thompson's view of faith.

Thompson attempts to demonstrate his point through the exegesis of chapter 11. To begin with, he notices that πίστις (faith) in 11:1 is described in such a way to indicate the author's philosophical training.[68] He observes that ὑπόστασις and ἔλεγχος are key words in unlocking the meaning of faith in Hebrews. Then what is the meaning of ἔλεγχος? Thompson follows Büchsel and defines ἔλεγχος as a "proof" or "persuasion" in the objective sense.[69] As for the meaning of ὑπόστασις, he realizes that this is a term that has been problematic to many scholars. Considering the basic meaning of ὑπόστασις as "to stand under," he suggests that "the word thus was used in a metaphorical sense for reality."[70] He argues that the parallel meaning of ἔλεγχος as "proof" and the usage elsewhere in the epistle (1:3; 3:14) supports the translation of ὑπόστασις as "reality." Then what is reality? Thompson states that it signifies something that is found in those things which are hoped for and invisible, not in those things which are present and visible. For this reason he interprets ὑπόστασις as invisible, transcendent reality. He consid-

---

65 Ibid., 73. I have corrected Thompson's spelling mistake of a Greek word from ψηλαφημένος to ψηλαφωμένος. Also, his way of linking οὐ to ψηλαφωμένος seems to be incorrect. Instead, οὐ is to be connected to προσεληλύθατε. Thus the translation of 12:18a should be "you have not come to what may be touched" rather than "you have come to what may not be touched."

66 Ibid.

67 Ibid., 75.

68 Ibid., 71.

69 Ibid., 70. Friedrich Büchsel, "ἔλγχος," in *Theological Dictionary of the New Testament*, ed., Gerhard Kittel, tr. Geoffrey W. Bromiley (Grand Rapids: William B. Eerdmans Publishing Co., 1964): 2:476.

70 Thompson, *The Beginnings of Christian Philosophy*, 71.

ers that this interpretation is also consistent with Philo and Middle Platonism.[71]

However, Thompson argues that faith in Hebrews is not only a reality, but also a realization. He points out that 11:1 is parallel to the thought in 10:34, in which the community faces the issue of faith and endurance. He suggests that, with the expression "knowing that you yourselves have a better possession (κρείττονα ὕπαρξιν) and an abiding one" (10:34), the church has survived the struggle of faith in the same way as the heroes of chapter 11. He argues that a better possession is obviously the transcendent heavenly world and parallel to ὑπόστασις (reality) in 11:1. Thus in 10:34 the church lives by its knowledge (γινώσκοντες) of the better possession.[72] Furthermore, Thompson suggests that the author's use of the words such as "knowing" (11:3), "remembering" (11:22), and "seeing" (11:13, 26) in chapter 11 is a clear indication that faith (πίστις) is a realization of the transcendent reality. Thus for him faith is not only a reality and proof, but also a knowledge and perception of the unseen world.[73]

Barnabas Lindars. Lindars, who holds the ethical view, also brings out the eschatological aspect in his view of faith in Hebrews. He asserts that the translations of ὑπόστασις into either "nature" or "confidence" in Hebrews derives from the literal meaning of "foundation." Based on this premise, he argues that in Hebrews 11:1 "faith is the foundation of a positive attitude towards the future, which cannot yet be experienced but has to remain a matter of hope."[74] Lindars believes that the word ἔλεγχος is synonymous with ὑπόστασις, and has the basic meaning of "testing." Thus he believes that "faith tests the unseen things by acting as though they were present and visible."[75]

Lindars' scheme of eschatology has both present and future aspects. This is clearly brought out in the statement:

[71] Ibid.
[72] Ibid., 72.
[73] Ibid.
[74] Lindars, *Theology*, 111.
[75] Ibid.

It should now be clear that the response of faith has two sides of it, and both are brought out in the splendid conclusion in 12:18–29. On the one hand it is a matter of living in the present in the light of the future, because the completion of God's plan of salvation has already been reached in the person of Jesus, though it still waits to be completed in us at the parousia.[76]

However, his overall emphasis on eschatology is futuristic. He defines faith as "a frame of mind in which we confidently make trial of what is promised in the future."[77] In referring to the exemplars of faith in chapter 11, Lindars notices that each person acted in faith by looking for a promise concerning the future at a time when it was impossible to see the outcome.[78] Even in the example where there is an immediate fulfillment (11:13–16), Lindars rightly points out that it is not the fulfillment of the promise in its deepest sense, because that final fulfillment belongs to the age to come.[79]

Characteristics of Faith

Then what are the characteristics of faith according to the eschatological view of faith? *First of all, those who take the eschatological orientation of faith emphasize an aspect of endurance.* A question is asked as to how the transcendent reality and the future eschatological hope affect the way believers live on this earth. Käsemann suggests that this realization of an invisible future causes believers to become confident wanderers on this earth.[80] The fact that they are wanderers implies that they will also suffer the indignities of the alien, and they are exhorted to endure the sufferings while they are taking a journey through this phenomenal world.[81]

Käsemann believes that the concept of faith in Hebrews carries an aspect of "obedience" as the Pauline letters do (e.g., Rom 1:5). Thus

---

[76] Ibid., 115.

[77] Ibid., 111.

[78] Ibid.

[79] Ibid., 113.

[80] Käsemann, *The Wandering People of God*, 44.

[81] Thompson, *The Beginnings of Christian Philosophy*, 77.

faith in Hebrews means obedient submission to the word which is revealed (e.g., 3:7ff.).[82] He further elaborates this point:

> The precise concern of that passage was also the coordination and Word and
> the constancy of their union (4:2). Thus by treating in parallel the ἀπιστία of
> 3:12, 19 and the ἀπείθεια of 3:18; 4:6, 11, and by linking παράβασις and
> παρακοή in a hendiadys in 2:2, Hebrews no less than Paul describes the nature
> of faith as obedience.[83]

However, Käsemann observes that this obedience of faith undergoes
a shift in Hebrews. He notes that "in the same section in 3:7ff., the admonition to the obedience of faith is replaced by the formula 'holding
fast our first ὑπόστασις to the end' (3:6, 14)."[84] Putting it another way,
he argues that this formula is directly related to μακροθυμία (patience)
(6:12, the infinitive is used in 6:15) or ὑπομονή (endurance) (10:36;
12:1). Moreover, he observes that these terms are used in juxtaposition
with the term πίστις (faith) (6:12; 10:35ff.), which suggests that faith is
identical to μακροθυμία or ὑπομονή. Thus, according to Käsemann,
faith is defined as persistent endurance by holding fast to what was
promised in assurance of the future.[85]

Thompson, likewise, following Käsemann's idea of a confident
wanderer on the earth, presents the characteristic of faith in terms of endurance. He considers 10:32–39 to be a unit in structure, and asserts that
the call to live by faith in 10:39 is based on the memory of former days
in 10:32–34, which states that at times believers were publicly exposed
to abuses and sufferings, and at times, partakers of those who suffered.[86]
Thompson correctly points out that the μέν . . . δέ constructions of
10:33–34 give details of the παθήματα in 10:32.[87] Since suffering is in
the overall background of the concept of faith, he insists that ὑπομένω
(to endure) and ὑπομονή (endurance) (10:32–34, 36) are the dominant

---

[82] Käsemann, *The Wandering People of God*, 37.

[83] Ibid., 38.

[84] Ibid.

[85] Ibid.

[86] Thompson, *The Beginnings of Christian Philosophy*, 62.

[87] Ibid., 64.

words that are closely related to παρρασία (confidence) (10:35) and πίστις (faith) (10:39).[88]

Thompson also notices the contrast between πίστις (faith) and ὑποστολή in 10:39. The meaning of ὑποστολή, according to Bauer, is "shrinking," or "timidity."[89] Thompson suggests that it is equivalent to "apostasy" in 3:12 and to "deliberate sin" in 10:26. Thus he draws an inference that πίστις means steadfastness. Summing up all the discussion in 10:19–39, he asserts that faith is closely related to endurance (ὑπομονή) and confidence (παρρησία), signifying the steadfastness of the one who, despite suffering and disappointment, maintains his or her orientation toward God.[90]

Moreover, Thompson stresses the importance of accepting the role of the strangers in the pilgrimage on the earth. He points out that one of the major characteristics of those who were on their pilgrimage in 11:1–40 and 12:1–3 was the acceptance of suffering.[91] Furthermore, Thompson notes that "the community's sufferings, which are also mentioned in 12:4–11, indicate that the readers shared the precarious existence in relation to the society which is mentioned in other NT literature."[92] He suggests that this is an exhortation for the addressees to accept the sufferings they were facing in their Christian walk. Thus Thompson concludes that faith in Hebrews can be defined as "endurance."

The second characteristic of faith, which is closely related to endurance, is hope. For example, Käsemann, in considering the aspect of perseverance, argues that faith also involves hope (11:1; 6:11; 10:22).[93] He states, "in Hebrews the obedience of faith is fulfilled when, in trusting the divine promise, one is willing to be led patiently through the present time of suffering into the heavenly future."[94] Käsemann notices: "For

---

[88] Ibid., 62.

[89] Walter Bauer, *A Greek-English Lexicon of the New Testament and Other Early Christian Literature*, 2nd ed., trans. and adapted by W. F. Arndt, F. W. Gingrich, and Frederick W. Danker (Chicago: The University of Chicago, 1979), 847.

[90] Thompson, *The Beginnings of Christian Philosophy*, 68.

[91] Ibid., 77.

[92] Ibid., 62.

[93] Käsemann, *The Wandering People of God*, 39.

[94] Ibid.

Paul, the paradox of faith lies in the witness of the word of the crucified as salvation; for Hebrews it consists in the choice of a transcendent future over earthly delight for the sake of the Word alone, despite the waiting and suffering attached to that future in the immanence of the present."[95]

Likewise, Thompson believes that faith in Hebrews is closely related to hope. For example, he observes that "full confidence of hope" in 6:11 is "full confidence of faith" in 10:22.[96] He also argues that the term "hope" (ἐλπίς) in 3:6 (cf. 3:14), 6:18, and 10:23 is indistinguishable from "faith" (πίστις) because it is related to the unwavering stability of believers made possible by the exaltation of Christ (6:18–19).[97] Thompson further illustrates the connection of faith to hope from chapter 11. He points out that Noah's building of the ark after being warned concerning the things not yet seen (11:7), Sarah's attitude of considering him faithful who had promised (11:11), Abraham's act of offering Isaac (11:17), and Moses' attitude of looking toward the reward (11:6), are indications that faith in Hebrews involves hope which has a forward-looking aspect.[98]

The third aspect of faith has to do with confidence in God's promise. Käsemann believes that πίστις and παρρησία are closely related to each other in meaning. What is the meaning of παρρησία? In response to some scholars who claim it to have a subjective meaning such as joyfulness in approaching God, Käsemann sees that there is also an objective meaning in this word.[99] He argues that since καύχημα in 3:6 is something objective, παρρησία, which is used in the same verse, also has an objective character. "One 'has' (10:19) παρρησία not merely as a subjective attitude, but as an appropriation of something already given. One holds it fast, not merely by holding on as a believer, but by clinging to the presupposition of faith in the promise."[100] For this reason Käse-

---

[95] Ibid.

[96] Thompson, *The Beginnings of Christian Philosophy*, 72.

[97] Ibid.

[98] Ibid., 73.

[99] Käsemann, *The Wandering People of God*, 43.

[100]Ibid.

mann concludes that faith is a confident wandering as seen from the examples of Abraham, Isaac, Jacob, Moses in chapter 11.[101]

Summary and Evaluation

A detailed examination of different models of the eschatological view discloses that all four scholars have one thing in common, namely, they all consider that faith in Hebrews has a futuristic orientation. The general tendency of these scholars is that although they recognize the present aspect of eschatology (i.e., "already"), their emphases are more on the future aspect. The discussion of the present aspect is either minimized or ignored. Both Käsemann and Thompson believe that the author of Hebrews is influenced by the Hellenistic philosophy of invisible reality. They consider that the futuristic aspect of faith has no continuity with the earthly present.

Thompson calls these "Platonic epistemological categories" a dualistic distinction between the visible and invisible world, or a distinction between realization and reality. What he means by "realization" is that which can be known and remembered and seen at the present time. This is equivalent to the present aspect in the temporal eschatological model of present and future. Thompson defines "reality" as that which is not found in the present and visible things. That is, it is an invisible transcendent reality. With this framework of eschatology, the proponents of the spatial dualism define faith as hope and endurance. Thus these characteristics of faith are the means to bridge between the visible and invisible world.

However, one needs to question whether or not the concept of faith is influenced by the Hellenistic philosophy of the spatial concept of visible and invisible world (or, the Philonic concept of dualism according to Thompson). It is doubtful whether the author of Hebrews is directly dependent upon Hellenistic philosophy. It is certainly true that the author of Hebrews expresses his eschatology in terms of visible and invisible things (e.g., 11:1, 3, 27). But do these references permit one to conclude that Hebrews is influenced by Hellenism? Williamson undertakes a thorough investigation on this issue.[102] He contends that Philo nowhere

---

[101] Ibid., 44.

[102] R. Williamson, *Philo and the Epistle to the Hebrews* (Leiden: E. J. Brill, 1970), 309–85.

suggests that faith is the assurance of the things hoped for as stated in Hebrews 11:1, nor does he indicate that faith is that which gives substance to hope.[103] To be more specific, Williamson, on the one hand, acknowledges that for both Philo and Hebrews faith is solidarity, namely, absolute, unwavering certainty of God's reality, which is an elementary constituent of faith, without which no other aspect of faith can be developed.[104] On the other hand, he argues that the main focus of the author of Hebrews is on the ability of faith to turn hope from something that is fearful into something that is full of confident expectation, namely, the capacity of faith to give substance to our hope.[105] Thus Williamson demonstrates that there is no direct Hellenistic influence on Hebrews.

Likewise, Hurst maintains that the idea of hoping for the future fulfillment of God's promise does not derive from Hellenistic philosophy, but from Judaism.[106] He points out that the alleged interpretation of the definition in Hebrews 11:1 as the Hellenistic influence is misleading, because the rest of the chapter is entirely Jewish in nature (i.e., promise and fulfillment). He maintains that viewing faith in Hebrews as insight into the heavenly world has been blown out of proportion.[107]

Thus it is clear that eschatology set forth by the author of Hebrews is not based on Philo's spatial idea of the invisible world, but on the Jewish understanding of the temporal idea. The following evidence further supports this thesis. First, the author's decision to follow an existing pattern of historical recapitulation is an indication that his main concern in this chapter is temporal.[108] Second, the specific reference in 11:7, "things not yet (μηδέπω) seen" suggests the possibility that "things not seen" in

---

[103] Ibid., 340.

[104] Ibid., 341.

[105] Ibid.

[106] L. D. Hurst, *The Epistle to the Hebrews: Its Background of Thought*, Society for New Testament Studies Monograph Series 65 (Cambridge: Cambridge University Press, 1990), 120.

[107] Ibid.

[108] Paul Ellingworth, *The Epistle to the Hebrews: A Commentary on the Greek Text*, New International Greek Testament Commentary, ed. I. Howard Marshall and W. W. Gasque (Grand Rapids: William B. Eerdmans Publishing Co., 1993), 562.

v. 1 should be understood as referring to things not yet visible during the present age of faith, not to things invisible of themselves in this world.[109] Third, more specifically, the author's mention of "city" in 11:16 is expressed in terms of the temporal, not the spatial idea. It is identified as the heavenly country, an object of forward-looking desire on the part of believers. Likewise, God's role as builder and maker (v. 10) is understood temporally as the one who has prepared a city for believers.[110]

Thus far, the discussion has been centered around whether the eschatology of Hebrews is spatially or temporally oriented. The evidence indicates that the temporal idea is more convincing. It is primarily future-oriented because it is closely related to hope and God's promises.

However, it is also to be realized that in Hebrews the present aspect of eschatology (i.e., the idea that eschatological events have taken place already) is as evident as in any other part of the New Testament.[111] For example, the author of Hebrews states that those who have believed are still entering the rest (4:3), which is hinted by the use of the present tense (εἰσερχόμεθα [we are entering]). Ellingworth argues that the verb εἰσερχόμεθα should be understood "as an emphatic equivalent of the future tense."[112] However, the immediate context clearly militates against the futuristic view of this verse. The author of Hebrews specifically mentions in 4:1 that there remains the promise to enter the rest of God. Moreover, the author's use of "today" in 4:7 suggests that the rest still remains open to those who hear his words by faith.[113] Furthermore, verse 9 also indicates that there still remains (ἀπολείπεται) a Sabbath rest for the people of God. Consequently, Hebrews 4:3 is "more than

---

[109] Ibid.

[110] Ibid., 563. This temporal idea will be more fully developed in the discussion of Hebrews 11:1–40 in chapter 7.

[111] C. K. Barrett, "The Eschatology of the Epistle to the Hebrews," in *The Background of the New Testament and its Eschatology,* Essays in Honor of Charles Harold Dodd, ed. W. D. Davies and D. Daube (Cambridge: Cambridge University Press, 1954), 393.

[112] Ellingworth, *The Epistle to the Hebrews,* 246.

[113] Barrett, "The Eschatology of the Epistle to the Hebrews," 367.

proleptic enjoyment of what God has promised."[114] It is to be noted that in both verses (i.e., 4:3, 9) the present tenses are used by the author. These tenses are to be regarded as a true present, because God's promise is predicated upon reality, and believers are now enjoying the rest referred to in the quotation of Psalm 95:11.[115] A brief survey and evaluation of the eschatological view reveals that Hebrews is not dependent on the Hellenistic idea of spatial dualism, or the Philonic concept of visible and invisible world. Rather, the author of Hebrews depends on the Jewish temporal idea of eschatology. The eschatological orientation of Hebrews has not only the future, but also the present aspect. In this eschatological frame faith functions as the bridge to connect the two aspects together, namely, "trust in God who is invisible (11:6, 27) is inevitably linked to trusting in God's promise for the future."[116] The characteristics of faith as "hope," "endurance," and "confident trust in God's promise" needs to be understood within the eschatological frame of present and future.

Christological View
    In response to the ethical view of faith in Hebrews, many scholars express the opinion that the concept of faith in Hebrews is indeed Christologically oriented. A survey of the literature indicates that this Christological view can be divided into two subgroups: (1) "Christ as the model of faith" view and (2) "Christ as the object of faith" view.

Christ as the Model of Faith View
    To what extent is the concept of faith in Hebrews Christologically oriented? Some feel that, although Hebrews does not present Jesus as the object of faith, Christ is depicted as the model of believers' faith. In this section, I will examine and evaluate Dennis Hamm's Christological view. Hamm argues that the concept of faith in Hebrews is profoundly Christological, in that "Jesus is presented as a model and enabler of

---

[114] William L. Lane, *Hebrews 1–8*, Word Biblical Commentary (Dallas: Word Books, 1991), 99.

[115] Ibid.

[116] Hurst, *The Epistle to the Hebrews*, 121–22.

Christian faith and, in some ways, even as object of faith"[117] when one examines the language and imagery of the letter consistently. How does he support his argument for the Christological view? *Argument from 12:1–2.* To begin with, Hamm considers that Hebrews 12:1–2 is one of the key passages that brings out the Christological aspect of the concept of faith. He presents Jesus as the model and enabler of faith by employing Horning's work on the chiastic structure of Hebrews 12:1–2. Horning lays out the structure of the passage as follows:

Τοιγαροῦν καὶ ἡμεῖς,
(Therefore we,)
  A τοσοῦτον ἔχοντες περικείμενον ἡμῖν νέφος μαρτύρων
    (having seated around about us such a cloud of witnesses),
    B ὄγκον ἀποθέμενοι παντα καὶ τὴν εὐπερίστατον ἁμαρτίαν
      (setting aside every weight and clinging sin . . .)
      C δι' ὑπομονῆς (with patient endurance . . .)
        D τρέχωμεν τὸν προκείμενον ἡμῖν ἀγῶνα
          (let us run the race that is set before us . . .)
          E ἀφορῶντες εἰς τὸν τῆς πίστεως ἀρχηγὸν καὶ
            τελειωτὴν Ἰησοῦν (keeping our eyes on Jesus the pioneer
            and perfecter of the faith)
          D' ὃς ἀντὶ τῆς προκειμένης αὐτῷ χαρας (who for the joy
            that was set before him . . .)
        C' ὑπέμεινεν σταυρὸν (patiently endured a cross . . .)
      B' αἰσχύνης καταφρονήσας (despising shame . . .)
    A' ἐν δεξιᾷ τε τοῦ θρόνου τοῦ θεοῦ κεκάθικεν (and is seated at the
      right hand of the throne of God).[118]

In this chiastic structure, Horning points out that the first half of the chiasm (i.e., A to D) is focused on "us" while the second half (D' to A') is on "Jesus."[119] Hamm follows Horning's observation and suggests that "the structure of the parallel members of the chiasm highlights the par-

---

117 Dennis Hamm, "Faith in the Epistle to the Hebrews: The Jesus Factor," *Catholic Biblical Quarterly* 52 (1990): 272.

118 E. B. Horning, "Chiasmus, Creedal Structure, and Christology in Hebrews 12:1–2," *Biblical Research* 23 (1978): 41. I have rearranged Horning's proposed chiasm slightly differently for a better visualization. I have also supplied the Greek text of Heb 12:1–2. The translations are Horning's.

119 Ibid., 40–41.

allel in content between the faith-race of Jesus, and the faith-race of disciples."[120] He asserts that in this sense Jesus is depicted as the exemplar and the facilitator of faith.[121]

Argument from 13:7. Hamm also considers that 13:7 is another key verse that supports his view of Jesus as the model of faith. Hebrews 13:7 states, "Remember your leaders those who spoke to you the word of God, considering the outcome of their life, imitate their faith." Hamm considers that this verse has a Christological implication. How does this exhortation support the view that faith in Hebrews is Christologically oriented? Hamm argues for its Christological implication by studying the immediate context of verse 7. He makes note of the fact that in verse 5 the readers are exhorted to keep a lifestyle that is free from the love of money (ἀφιλάργυρος) and that the exhortation is based on God's promise which states, "I will never leave you; I will never abandon you." He asserts that this is an allusion to Deuteronomy 31:6, 8, where Moses urges the people to be strong and courageous, reminding them of God's presence as they cross over into the promised land. He also observes that this thought is further enforced by the quotation of Psalm 117:6 (LXX). The context here speaks of God's presence to deliver in the past (v. 5), and in the present and the future (v. 6).[122] From these arguments Hamm contends that the exhortation in Hebrews 13:5 is Christologically motivated.

Next, Hamm argues for the Christological view of faith from the phrase "Jesus Christ is the same yesterday and today and forever" in 13:8. He considers that this verse is a hinge that relates to what precedes and what follows. He states:

Catching up the language of LXX Ps 101:27 applied to the Son at Heb. 1:12, which contrasts the Son's divine permanence with the transiency of the created heavens, the assertion of his eternal permanence and identity serves here

---

[120] Hamm, "Faith in the Epistle to the Hebrews," 280.

[121] Ibid., 287. Hamm also has a good discussion on the meaning of ἀρχηγός and τελειωτής. I will interact with his view in Chapter Seven.

[122] Ibid., 275.

SURVEY OF DIFFERENT VIEWS 55

clearly as a contrast to the "various and strange" (*poikilais kai xenais*) teachings by which they are not to be swept away.[123]

Moreover, he argues that verse 8 also serves to further motivate the readers to take courage and to imitate the faith of the leaders (vv. 6–7). He maintains that the faith of the former leaders which the readers should imitate is "the faith which trusts perseveringly in God and his Son simply because the God who has proven trustworthy in the past remains so for the future, and the Son (at God's right hand) shares in that permanent trustworthiness.[124] The analysis of Hamm's interpretation on both 12:1–2 and 13:7 shows that his view of faith in Hebrews is indeed Christologically oriented in that in both passages Jesus Christ is clearly brought out as the enabler and the model of faith for believers.

Characteristic of faith. What, then, is the characteristic of faith in Hebrews according to this view? Hamm draws an inference from his Christological view that faith is obedience. He indicates that although the words for obedience, ὑπακούω and ὑπακοή, are used only three times, they tie together the faith-response of Abraham, Jesus, and Christians.[125] First of all, Abraham's faith is described as obedience in 11:8. When he was called, he obeyed by leaving for a place which he was to receive as an inheritance. Second, the structure in Hebrews 5:6–10 draws attention to the parallelism between the obedience of the human Jesus (expressed as εὐλαβεία) and that of believers (ὑπακούωσιν). Third, the parallel idea between the response of Jesus and that of Christians is confirmed at Hebrews 12:28, in which εὐλαβεία is described as the kind of worship which pleases God.[126]

Moreover, Hamm emphasizes that this obedience is the obedience from the heart. Calling attention to the new covenant in Chapter 10, he states:

In the *pesher* on LXX Psalm 39 and Jeremiah 31, we saw that such obedience is the fruit of that covenant in Jesus, and that such obedience is the fruit of that covenant in the hearts of believers, in whom the law is written (chap. 10). The

[123] Ibid.

[124] Ibid., 276.

[125] Ibid., 289.

[126] Ibid.

heart-obedience called for in Psalm 95 is facilitated by the covenant foretold by
Jeremiah 31 and established by Jesus' own heart-obedience.[127]

He argues that just as Jesus learned the heart-obedience during his
earthly existence, believers ought to follow his pattern, namely, to be
obedient to this divine initiative.[128]

Summary of "Model of Faith" View. According to Hamm, faith in
Hebrews is not ethically oriented as set forth by Grässer, but Christologically oriented: Jesus is both the exemplar and the facilitator of
faith, and in some sense the object of faith. For this reason, believers are
exhorted to follow their leader (i.e., Jesus Christ). In this sense, faith is
obedience, especially heart-obedience. However, although Hamm suggests that Jesus could be viewed as the object of faith, he does not emphasize this point throughout his article.

I feel that this aspect is a weakness of Hamm's view. The overall
structure of Hebrews and the context imply that Jesus Christ is not only
the exemplar of faith, but also the object of faith. This can be seen from
the fact that the doctrinal sections (1:1–14; 2:5–18; 5:1–10; 7:1–10:18;
11:1–40) are followed by the hortatory sections (2:1–4; 3:1–4:16; 5:11–
6:20; 10:19–39; 12:1–13:21).[129] All the doctrinal sections (except for
11:1–40) focus on either the sonship or the high priesthood of Christ.
Based on these teachings the author admonishes the readers to remain in
faith with words, such as "hold fast our confession" (cf. 3:1; 4:14;
10:23), "hold firm the confidence" (3:6, 14; 10:35), and "realize the full
assurance of hope" (6:11). Thus it may be said that Christ is implicitly
depicted as the object of faith throughout the book. Moreover, in Hebrews 1:8 one can see that Jesus is called God by the Father, and the angels worship him. This is another indication that Jesus is to be viewed as
the object of faith for his followers.

---

[127] Ibid.

[128] Ibid., 276.

[129] Schoonhoven also believes that Hebrews has the alternating structure of doctrines and parenenses. However, his understanding of the structure is slightly different
from mine. See Calvin R. Schoonhoven, "The Analogy of Faith and the Intent of Hebrews," in *Scripture, Tradition and Interpretation,* E. F. Harrison Festschrift, ed. W. W.
Gasque and W. S. Lasor (Grand Rapids: William B. Eerdmans Publishing Co., 1978),
109.

Christ as the Object of Faith View

In response to the view that Jesus is described only as the model of faith, some scholars argue that in Hebrews Jesus is depicted as the content of faith as well as an example of faith. One of the proponents of this view is M. R. Miller. In this section, I will examine and evaluate his arguments.

Miller contends that the hortatory use of faith set forth by many scholars has misled some to interpret it in terms of exhortation such as obedience, hope, and endurance because these hortatory definitions can be conceived of as a man's virtue or power.[130] He shares a similar opinion with Hamm in that the concept of faith in Hebrews is Christologically oriented in Hebrews 11:1–12:2. He argues that faith in Hebrews is pointedly Christological when one considers the author's development of the teaching on Christ's high priestly ministry, and the exhortation to enter the throne of grace with confidence based on that ministry (4:14–16; 10:19–25).[131]

While Hamm's position is that the author of Hebrews has portrayed Jesus as the model and enabler of faith, Miller goes one step further and asserts that in Hebrews the idea of Jesus being the object of faith is implied throughout the book even if the phrase πίστις εἰς Χριστόν (faith in Christ) is not used.[132] Miller argues that even though the word "faith" is used with reference to God in Hebrews (6:1; 11:6), the background of these verses is the teaching of chapter one, in which Christ is referred to as God in contrast to the angels.[133]

---

[130] M. R. Miller, "Seven Theological Themes in Hebrews," *Grace Theological Journal* 8 (1987): 131–40.

[131] Ibid. 133

[132] Ibid.

[133] Ibid. Also Bultmann, "Πιστεύω κτλ.," in *TDNT*, 6:208–209. Bultmann argues that faith in God is equivalent to faith in Christ in the New Testament, "in contrast to those who do not yet know the one God, who do not yet believe in Him, who have first to 'believe' in Him in the sense of acknowledging His existence" (208). For example, he maintains that just as πίστις . . . πρὸς τὸν θεόν (1 Thess 1:8) is a description of the Gentile conversion from idols to the one God as a result of proclaiming faith in Christ, so the expression in Hebrews 11:6 is used in this sense. He also indicates that one of the first principles of Christianity, along with μετάνοια ἀπὸ νεκρῶν ἔργων (repentance from dead works), is πίστις ἐπὶ θεόν (faith in God). His implication here is that there is no difference between "faith in God" and "faith in Christ" (209).

Miller observes that this object of faith is expressed in terms of the word of promise (6:12), which is equivalent to the word of God in Pauline terminology. Thus he concludes that "with the personal object (Christ) and the promise in mind it is best to understand faith in Hebrews (indeed, throughout Scripture as a whole) in the general sense of trust."[134] So according to Miller believing (or trusting) in the word of promise in Hebrews is identical to trusting in Jesus Christ in Pauline sense. He applies this definition of faith to Hebrews 11:1–12:2. In this passage, "faith may be defined as an attitude of trust by which the believer sees the unseen and thereby sets his hope on the divine promise."[135] He also applies this to sufferings in Hebrews, indicating that the key to enduring hardship is faith, which is "a confident trust in God's promise that 'He shall come and not delay' (10:37), looking to the Pioneer and Perfecter of faith to lead them on to their final perfection."[136]

Miller has done well in setting forth the idea that the object of faith in Hebrews is explained in terms of the word of promise. Nonetheless, the analysis of Miller's view raises some objections. It has already been pointed out that Miller uses Hebrews 6:1 and 11:6 to argue that the reference to "God" is related to Jesus. It is indeed true that in chapter one Jesus is referred to as the creator (1:3, 10), and more explicitly, as God (1:8, 9). In the book of Hebrews, the word θεός is used 63 times. Out of these uses only two verses specifically designate Jesus as God (1:8, 9). The other references to θεός has to do with God the Father (e.g., 2:4, 9; 4:4; 6:7; 7:1; 10:12; 12:2). More specifically, the verses which Miller uses to support his Christological view of faith (6:1; 11:6) also designates God as God the Father, not Jesus the Son. In 6:1 the author of Hebrews clearly makes a distinction between Christ and God. For this reason the phrase "faith toward God" (πίστεως ἐπὶ θεόν) suggests that the object of faith is not Jesus, but God the Father. Likewise, the immediate context of 11:6 indicates that the reference to God is not Jesus, but God in the Old Testament sense.

Miller also has a tendency to interpret the faith of the Old Testament men and women of faith as if they understood the revelation of the

---

[134] Miller, "Seven Theological Themes in Hebrews," 133.

[135] Ibid., 134.

[136] Ibid.

new covenant. He correctly sees that faith in Hebrews 11:1–12:2 is an attitude of trust to see the unseen, and to set one's hope on the divine promise. However, he goes on to state:

> The elders trusted that they would eventually be 'brought to completion' and qualified to enter their heavenly fatherland, that is, the presence of God. They therefore anticipated the work of Christ as High Priest which would make that entrance possible for them. They 'saw the unseen' both in terms of time (the future event of the cross) and of space (looking to heaven they considered themselves strangers on earth). Inasmuch as they looked to God, they also looked to Jesus who is the eternal God.[137]

This statement suggests that the Old Testament saints mentioned in chapter 11 knew of the cross of Jesus. It is true that the author of Hebrews states that Moses considered the abuse he received in Egypt as suffering for the Christ (11:26). However, it is an overstatement for one to assume that all the Old Testament men and women of faith had a clear comprehension of the new revelation as Miller contends. His interpretation of 11:1–12:2 needs to be looked at from a different perspective. It appears that Miller has made an overstatement out of his zeal to prove that Jesus is indeed the object of faith in Hebrews.

Evaluation of Christological View

I am inclined to believe that in Hebrews Jesus is not only the model of faith, but also the object of faith, as in any other book of the New Testament. In interpreting Hebrews 12:1–3, Westcott argues that the idea of Jesus being the object of faith, namely, the faith of each individual Christian, or the substance of the Christian creed, is unknown to this passage. Instead, he prefers the interpretation that Jesus is the perfect example of faith which one ought to imitate.[138] More specifically, he explicates:

> He too looked through the present and the visible to the future and the unseen. In His human Nature He exhibited Faith in its highest form, from first to the last, and placing Himself as it were at the head of the great army of heroes of

---

137 Ibid.

138 B. F. Westcott, *The Epistle to the Hebrews: A Historical and Theological Reconsideration* (London: Macmillan, 1889), 395.

faith, He carried faith, the source of their strength, to its most complete perfection and to its loftiest triumph.139

In like manner, Ellingworth holds that in 12:2 faith should be understood, not as an acceptance of a series of catechetical propositions, but
as a quality of persistent attachment to Christ.140

Yet, it seems almost impossible to ignore the high degree of content
brought into the author's depiction of Jesus and the cardinal importance
it has in his call for faith among his readers.141 It is important to recognize that in Hebrews Jesus is conceived as the model of faith in face of
the agonies of flesh-and blood-conditioned life (12:1).142 But, at the
same time, I perceive that this "model" interpretation falls short of the
intended meaning of the author of Hebrews.

The author's intention of depicting Jesus as the content of faith can
be seen in various ways. To begin with, the idea of "confidence" shows
that Jesus is the object of faith. The author indicates that Christ's work
of high priesthood is related to the Christian confidence (3:6, 4:16,
10:19, 10:35).143 In 3:1–6 the author exhorts the readers to consider Jesus, the apostle and high priest of our confession. This passage compares
the faithfulness of Moses with that of Christ. In this context "holding
fast the confidence" naturally refers to holding fast the faithfulness of
Christ as the high priest. Moreover, the phrase "whose house we are"
(οὗ οἶκος ἐσμεν ἡμεῖς) implies Christ's Lordship over the believing
community.144 In the same way, the Christian confidence is also related
to the high priesthood of Christ in 4:14–16. The expression, "let us,
therefore, with confidence, draw near to the throne of the grace of God
(v. 16)," is not the language of imitating Christ, but of worshipping God
through the high priesthood of Christ. Hebrews 10:19 and 10:35 also
uses the word "confidence" (παρρησία) without direct reference to the
high priesthood of Christ. However, one must realize that these exhorta-

139 Ibid.
140 Ellingworth, *The Epistle to the Hebrews*, 640.
141 Hughes, *Hebrews and Hermeneutics*, 85.
142 Ibid.
143 Hurst, *The Epistle to the Hebrews: Its Background of Thought*, 119.
144 Ellingworth, *The Epistle to the Hebrews*, 210.

tions are based on the work of the high priesthood, which the author expounded in Hebrews 7:1–10:18. As Lane correctly points out, "the unique character of His personal sacrifice and achievement is not forgotten."[145] In this sense, the high priesthood of Christ is the content of the Christians' confidence. Thus it can be said that Jesus is the object of faith for believers.

The reference to Jesus being the object of faith can also be detected from the author's use of the word ὁμολογία (confession), which is found three times in Hebrews (3:1; 4:14; 10:23). Neufeld believes that the verbs κρατεῖν (4:14) and κατέχειν (10:23), both of which have the meaning of "to hold fast," support the conclusion that ὁμολογία refers to a specific formula or confession of faith known to the author and his readers.[146] His finding permits one to regard that ὁμολογία does not simply refer to the act of confession, but to the content of Christian faith.[147] In 3:1 the reference to ὁμολογία "prepares for the presentation of Jesus as the exalted Son who presides over God's household in v. 6."[148] In 4:14 the author is more specific about the content of faith. He mentions that the content of the confession is "Jesus, the Son of God." Throughout the epistle, the title Son "embraces the concepts of the Logos, the High Priest, and the incarnate Christ. The sonship of Christ expresses his unique function as mediator and sacrifice between God and man, as the agent in creation, and as the transcendent Son of God."[149] In 10:23 the author speaks of "holding fast the confession of our hope." The word "hope," which is more specific than "faith," "gives distinctness to special objects of faith to be realized in the future. Hope gives a definite shape to the absolute confidence of faith."[150] Hope in Hebrews always refers to an objective content, consisting of present and future

---

[145] William L. Lane, *Hebrews 9–13*, Word Biblical Commentary (Dallas: Word Books, 1991), 412.

[146] Vernon H. Neufeld, *The Earliest Christian Confessions* (Leiden: E. J. Brill, 1963), 134.

[147] Ellingworth, *The Epistle to the Hebrews*, 199.

[148] Lane, *Hebrews 1–8*, 74.

[149] Neufeld, *The Earliest Christian Confessions*, 135–36.

[150] Westcott, *The Epistle to the Hebrews*, 323.

salvation. More specifically, in 10:23, it refers to an objective reality related to the priestly ministry of Christ. [151]

An examination of the three passages containing ὁμολογία indicates that it signifies the essential faith of believers, that is, the element which joins the author with the readers.[152] In this respect the idea that Jesus is the content of faith is not lacking in Hebrews. An evaluation of some of the important passages in Hebrews clearly reveals that faith in Hebrews is indeed Christological. The author of Hebrews describes Jesus as the enabler and the model of faith as Hamm has shown in his article. At the same time, the idea of Jesus being the object of faith is imbedded throughout the epistle, although it is not expressed with Pauline terminology.

Summary and Conclusion

A survey of the concept of faith in Hebrews reveals that the meaning of faith depends largely on one's orientation of faith in the book. The ethical view contends that Jesus is removed from being the content and the object of faith. Grässer holds that faith in Hebrews is merely an ethical category of moral quality, namely, steadfastness. Other proponents of the ethical view, although not as radical as Grässer, hold that Jesus is not viewed as the object, but the model of faith. In this sense, faith is defined as the absolute moral quality, such as steadfastness, fidelity, and trustworthiness.

The proponents of the eschatological view believe that faith in Hebrews is intimately related to eschatology. An examination of the text in Hebrews points out that what is seemingly a spatial idea (i.e., the Hellenistic dualism of visible and invisible) actually derives from the Jewish concept of the temporal idea. Faith in Hebrews has the "forward-looking" aspect, not in the spatial, but in the temporal sense. It is also important to realize that this temporal idea is not merely related to the future only; it also has the present aspect. In short, it can be said that faith in Hebrews has both present and future aspects.

---

[151] Lane, *Hebrews 9–13*, 288.

[152] Neufeld, *The Earliest Christian Confessions*, 137.

It is also evident that faith in Hebrews is Christological. In Hebrews Jesus is to be viewed not only as the model of faith, but also the content and the object of faith for believers. The argument for Christ being the object of faith can be summarized as follows: (1) the alternating structure of Hebrews between doctrine and exhortation is a clear indication that the author's exhortation to hold on to faith is based on the redemptive work of Christ; (2) Hebrews' reference to "holding fast the confidence" (3:6; 4:16; 10:19; 10:35) is based on the work of Christ's high priesthood; (3) the author's use of the word "cross" (12:2b) suggests that it is based on the work of Christ's high priesthood in 7:1–10:18; (4) the author's use of the word ὁμολογία (3:1; 4:14; 10:23) is not merely an act of confession, but has to do with the objectivity of faith, namely, the content of Christian faith. The above evidence clearly indicates that Christ is not only the model of faith, but also the object of believers' faith.

I consider that both Christology and eschatology is crucial in defining the concept of faith in Hebrews. It is my belief that the author of Hebrews portrays Jesus as both the model and the object of faith. Moreover, the eschatological orientation of faith in Hebrews is not a spatial, but a temporal one. To be more specific, eschatology in Hebrews involves both the present and the future. The concept of faith in Hebrews should be scrutinized within the framework of Christology and eschatology to understand rightly the author's intended view of faith.

However, it is also to be realized that one cannot totally ignore the contributions made by the proponents of the ethical view. The importance of the ethical dimension of faith should not be minimized because these are the very characteristics of faith. They include steadfastness, fidelity, perseverance, hope and confidence in God's promise, obedience, and reliability. These qualities are true characteristics of faith in Hebrews and must be discussed in the context of the author's intended view of Christology and eschatology. In the following chapters I will further demonstrate this point by a detailed exegesis of the key passages relevant to the issue of faith in Hebrews.

CHAPTER THREE

RELATIONSHIP BETWEEN 1:1–14 AND 2:1–4:
CHRIST'S DIVINITY AND THE EXHORTATION
NOT TO DRIFT AWAY

In chapter one I have argued that the author of Hebrews arranged the contents so as to alternate the doctrinal and the parenetic sections. These adjoining sections of doctrine and parenesis are inter-related, "with specific points of contact between them, and having similar implications with regard to theological meaning and to the inherent mutual relationship of 'faith' and 'action.'"[1] What is the author's purpose of expounding the teachings on Christ in the doctrinal sections? I believe that his intention is to set forth Jesus as the content of faith (i.e., faith in Christ). The author uses faith-related words more frequently in the parenetic sections than in the doctrinal sections.[2] This suggests that the author employs both doctrines and exhortations to encourage believers to remain in faith. In other words, the stylistic alternation between doctrines

---

[1] Kenneth Leroy Maxwell, "Doctrine and Parenesis in the Epistle to the Hebrews, with Special Reference to pre-Christian Gnosticism" (Ph.D. diss., Yale University, 1953), 350.

[2] *Faith-related words used in the parenetic sections:* ἀπιστία—unfaithfulness (3:12, 19); κατέχω—to continue to believe (3:6, 14; 10:23); ἀνέχομαι—to accept, to receive (13:22); ἀκούω—to accept, to listen to (3:7, 15, 16; 4:2, 7; 12:19); παραρρέω—to drift away from belief (2:1); ἀποστρέφω—to cause to turn away from (12:25); παραφέρω—to lead astray (13:9); ἀκλινής—without wavering (10:23); πείθω—to trust in (6:9; 13:17–18); ὑπόστασις—trust, confidence, assurance (1:3; 11:1); πιστεύω—to believe in, to trust (4:3); πιστός—faithful, trustworthy (3:2, 5; 10:23); πίστις—faith (4:2; 6:1, 12; 12:2; 13:7); βέβαιος—trustworthy (3:14; 6:19); ἀθετέω—to reject (10:28); ἀπειθέω—to refuse to believe (3:18). *Faith-related words used in the doctrinal sections:* ἀκούω—to accept, to listen to (2:1, 3); ἀρνέομαι—to refuse to agree to (11:24); πείθω —to trust in (2:13); πιστεύω—to believe in, to trust (11:6); πιστός—pertaining to trusting (2:17; 11:11); πίστις—faith (chapter 11); βέβαιος—trustworthy (2:2; 9:17); ἀπειθέω—to refuse to believe (11:31). These words are taken from J. P. Louw and Eugene A. Nida, ed., *Greek-English Lexicon of the New Testament based on Semantic Domains*, 2 vols (New York: United Bible Societies, 1988), 365–79.

and pareneses implies that Jesus is to be considered the object of faith as in other books of the New Testament. It is precisely this point that I will demonstrate from this chapter on.

To accomplish this purpose the alternating sections of doctrine and parenesis will be examined with the following questions in mind. The doctrinal section will answer the questions: (1) what is the basis for the literary unit? and (2) what is the Christological teaching that the author intends to convey?; in the parenetic section: (1) what is the basis for literary unit? and (2) what is the relationship between the Christological teaching in the doctrinal section and the exhortation to be faithful in the parenetic section? In addition, the basis for the literary unit of this alternating section will be discussed.

Examination of 1:1–14

Basis for the Literary Unit
The first doctrinal section of 1:1–14 can be sub-divided into two parts: 1:1–4 and 1:5–14. An examination of the first part (1:1–4) reveals that it is to be regarded as a unit. The main idea of the passage is, "God has spoken by his Son (1:1–2a)." This can be illustrated as follows:

1:1   Πολυμερῶς καὶ πολυτρόπως πάλαι (in many portions and in many ways in the old)

ὁ θεὸς λαλήσας τοῖς πατράσιν ἐν τοῖς προφήταις (God, after having spoken to the fathers in the prophets),

1:2a   ἐπ᾽ ἐσχάτου τῶν ἡμερῶν τούτων
ἐλάλησεν ἡμῖν ἐν υἱῷ (in these last days he has spoken to us in his Son).[3]

The author also indicates by means of the relative pronouns (ὅν, οὗ in 1:2–3) and the participles (ὤν, φέρων in 1:3; γενόμενος in 1:4) that 1:2b–4 is a further description about the Son. The Greek construction shows that, while God is the implied subject, the Son becomes the central figure in 1:2b, and the subject of the relative clauses in 1:3–4. This means that the Son is the functional subject of 1:2b–4. Thus it may be said that 1:1–4 forms a sub-unit in 1:1–14.

---

[3] I have included my own translation of the passage for clarification.

The second part (1:5–14) forms a unit by the literary device of inclusion. Vanhoye illustrates the inclusion between 1:5 and 1:13 as follows:

> For to which of the angels did he ever say,
>   Thou art my Son . . . (1:5, quotation of Psa 2:7)
> But to which of the angels has he ever said:
>   Sit at my right hand . . . (1:13, quotation of Psa 110:1).4

He argues that the resemblance of 1:13–14 with 1:5–6 constitutes an inclusion which marks the conclusion of the paragraph.5 Then in what way is 1:5–14 related to 1:1–4? First, 1:4 and 1:5 are connected together by the hook word (mot-crochet), angels (ἀγγέλων).6 Moreover, the conjunction γάρ indicates that 1:5–14 is a further explanation of what the author spoke of in 1:1–4, specifically verse 4 which mentions that the Son inherited a more excellent name than the angels. These clues indicate that 1:1–4 and 1:5–14 are structurally related to each other. Therefore, it is reasonable to consider that 1:1–14 is to be regarded as a literary unit. This section as a unit sets forth the Christological teaching which is the basis for the exhortation in 2:1–4.

Christological Teaching

As discussed in the previous section, Hebrews 1:1–14 may be subdivided into two parts, each emphasizing a different aspect of Christology: (1) finality of revelation through the Son (1:1–4); and (2) superiority of Christ to the angels (1:5–14). To begin with, the Christological teaching on "the finality of God's revelation through the Son" is already demonstrated from the sentence structure of 1:1–4. This grammatical structure, coupled with the contrast between the prophets and the Son, indicates that the author has clearly in mind the finality of God's revelation through his Son. Then how does the author describe the Son, who is the functional subject of 1:2b–4? He does so by pointing out eight facts about the Son for the purpose of bringing out his greatness and showing

---

4 Albert Vanhoye, *La structure littéraire de l'Épître aux Hébreux* (Paris: Desclée de Brouwer, 1976), 74.

5 Ibid. "La ressemblance de 1,13–14 avec 1,5–6 constitue une inclusion qui marque la fin du paragraph."

6 Ibid., 53.

why the revelation given in him is the highest that God can give.[7] The Son is depicted as: (1) having been appointed heir of all things, (2) the agent in creation, (3) the reflection of God's glory, (4) the representation of God's nature, (5) upholder of the world, (6) purifier of sins, (7) the one who is exalted at the right hand of the majesty on high, and (8) the one whose name is greater than the angels.

The concentric symmetry of 1:1–4, moreover, elaborates the Christological aspect more clearly. A detailed observation of this passage shows that it forms a unit by chiasm at the conceptual level.[8] This may be illustrated as follows:[9]

A Πολυμερῶς καὶ πολυτρόπως πάλαι ὁ θεὸς λαλήσας τοῖς πατράσιν ἐν τοῖς προφήταις ἐπ' ἐσχάτου τῶν ἡμερῶν τούτων ἐλάλησεν ἡμῖν ἐν υἱῷ (Long ago God spoke to our ancestors in many and various ways by the prophets, but in these last days he has spoken to us by a Son) (1:1–2a),

   B ὃν ἔθηκεν κληρονόμον πάντων (Whom He appointed heir of all things) (1:2b)

      C δι' οὗ καὶ ἐποίησεν τοὺς αἰῶνας (Through whom He also created the worlds) (1:2c)

         D ὅς ὢν ἀπαύγασμα τῆς δόξης καὶ χαρακτὴρ τῆς ὑποστάσεως αὐτοῦ (He is the reflection of God's glory and the exact imprint of God's very being) (1:3a),

      C' φέρων τε τὰ πάντα τῷ ῥήματι τῆς δυνάμεως αὐτοῦ (and he sustains all things by his powerful word) (1:3b),

---

[7] F. F. Bruce, *The Epistle to the Hebrews*, New International Commentary on the New Testament (Grand Rapids: William B. Eerdmans Publishing Co., 1964), 3.

[8] Lane calls this "the concentric symmetry of the period." Although his use of the terminology is different, he clearly expresses conceptual chiasm by this phrase. See William L. Lane, *Hebrews 1–8*, Word Biblical Commentary (Dallas: Word Books, 1991), 6–7. The periodic style is an artistically developed prose with a considerable number of clauses and phrases built into a well-rounded unity. See A. T. Robertson, *A Grammar of the Greek New Testament in the Light of Historical Research* (Nashville: Broadman Press, 1934), 238 (§ 458), 242 (§ 464).

[9] The English text that accompanies the Greek text is from the New Revised Standard Version (NRSV). Lane has shown a similar chiastic structure. For the difference see Lane, *Hebrews 1–8*, 6–7.

Β' καθαρισμὸν τῶν ἁμαρτιῶν ποιησάμενος ἐκάθισεν ἐν δεξιᾷ τῆς μεγα-
λωσύνης ἐν ὑψηλοῖς (When he had made purification for sins, he sat
down at the right hand of the Majesty on high) (1:3c),

Α' τοσούτῳ κρείττων γενόμενος τῶν ἀγγέλων ὅσῳ διαφορώτερον παρ' αὐτοὺς κεκληρονόμηκεν ὄνομα (having become as much superior to angels as
the name he has inherited is more excellent than theirs) (1:4).

The center section (D) shows the Son's relationship to God in his
preexistent state: he is the reflection (ἀπαύγασμα) of God's glory and
the exact representation of his being (χαρακτὴρ τῆς ὑποστάσεως αὐτοῦ). Sections C and C' further describe the Son's relationship to the
universe: he is the direct agent of the creation and the one who is holding the world together. The words "created" (ἐποίησεν) (C) and "sus-
tain" (φέρων) (C') indicate parallelism in thought. Sections B and B' express that God's appointment of his Son as heir of the world is equated
with sitting down at the right hand of the majesty on high. When did
God appoint Jesus heir of all things? The reference to "purification of
sins" in B' indicates that the appointment of the Son as heir took place
with the exaltation of Christ.[10] Finally, the outer sections (A and A') are
parallel in thought. Section A implies that the Son is superior to the
prophets in the Old Testament. The contrast between the old and the new
era by the temporal indicators, "long ago" (πάλαι) and "in these last
days" implicitly suggests that God's revelation given to the new era
through the Son is superior to that given to the old era through prophets.[11] The corresponding section (A'), which is more explicit in describing the greatness of the Son, indicates that the Son is greater than the
angels. The above analysis indicates that this superior Son, who is the
reflection of God's glory and the exact representation of his being, who
is now enthroned at the right hand of God, is the one through whom God
has revealed his final revelation.

---

10 O. Michel, *Der Brief an die Hebräer,* 12th ed. (Göttingen: Vanderhoeck and Ruprecht, 1966), 103.

11 Herbert W. Bateman IV, "Jewish and Apostolic Hermeneutics: How the Old
Testament Is Used in Hebrews 1:5–13" (Ph.D. diss., Dallas Theological Seminary,
1993), 352–54.

The second part of the passage (1:5–14) emphasizes the superiority of the Son to the angels. The author has already announced in the previous section (1:1–4) that the Son is superior both to the prophets and the angels. In 1:5–14 this theme of superiority of the Son to the angels is further developed. The author does it by making three rounds of contrast between the Son and the angels. In the first round (1:5–6) the superiority of the Son is argued from the standpoint of his position: the Son is the begotten of God, and all the angels are commanded to worship him. In the second round (1:7–12) the description of the Son is more vivid. After having mentioned the angels as winds and flaming fire (1:7), the author goes on to describe the Son's characteristics in 1:8–12: the Son's throne is eternal (1:8); he loves justice (1:9); he is the creator (1:10); and the Son himself is eternal (1:11–12). In the third round (1:13–14) the emphasis is placed on the role of the Son and the angels. The Son is commanded to sit at the right hand of God (1:13), but the angels are described as the ministering spirits for those who will inherit salvation (1:14). By these three rounds of argument the author indicates that the Son is superior to the angels in his position, attributes, and role.

Then what is the relationship between 1:1–4 and 1:5–14? A comparison of these two passages reveals that they are thematically related to each other. The general consensus among scholars is that 1:5–14 is the scriptural proof of the Christological statements the author has made in 1:2b–4. In this section the author cites a catena of seven Old Testament passages to demonstrate that Jesus is the exalted Son. Meier suggests that the Christological points in both 1:2b–4 and 1:5–14 are designed as a ring structure of moving back and forward, using the exaltation of the Son as the beginning and the final point. He asserts:

> In each case, the train of throught begins with Christ's exaltation (1,2b; 1,5-6), moves back to creation (1,2c; 1,7), moves 'farther back' to preexistence, divinity, and eternal rule (1,3a; 1,8bc), moves forward again to creation as well as governance and guidance of creation (1,3b; 1,10-12), moves all the way up to exaltation again (1,3d; 1,13), and draws a final conclusion comparing Christ's exalted status to the angels' inferior role (1,4; 1,14).[12]

---

[12] J. P. Meier, "Symmetry and Theology in the Old Testament Citations of Heb 1:5–14," *Biblica* 66 (1985): 523.

Meier's point can be illustrated as follows:[13]

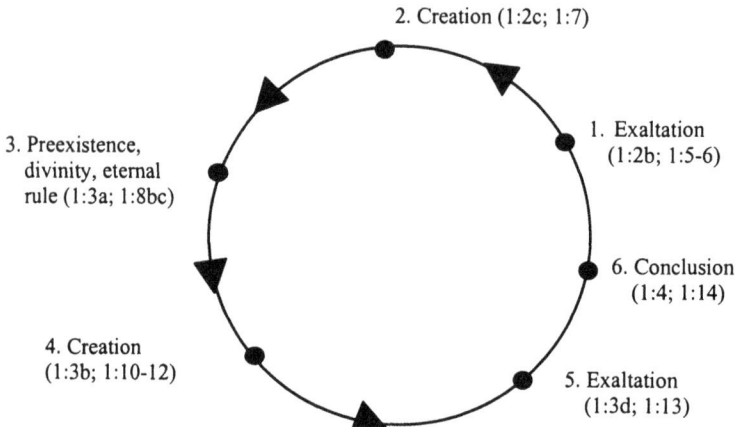

2. Creation (1:2c; 1:7)

1. Exaltation (1:2b; 1:5-6)

3. Preexistence, divinity, eternal rule (1:3a; 1:8bc)

6. Conclusion (1:4; 1:14)

4. Creation (1:3b; 1:10-12)

5. Exaltation (1:3d; 1:13)

This diagram shows that, even with the absence of one to one correspondence between 1:2b–4 and 1:5–14, there is a general agreement of themes between the two passages.[14] An examination of the doctrinal section of 1:1–14 clearly indicates that the teaching of Christology is strongly emphasized. The author sets forth the theme that God has spoken his final revelation through his Son, who is exalted at the right hand of God. The exalted Son is greater than the angels. This Christological teaching is reinforced by the catena of seven Old Testament Scriptures.[15] The significance of the exposition of Christology in this section will become evident in the discussion of the parenetic section in 2:1–4.

---

[13] This construction is based on Meier's ring structure in 1:2b–4. See J. P. Meier, "Structure and Theology in Hebrews 1:1–14," *Biblica* 66 (1985): 189.

[14] Meier points out that the reference to the Son's purification in 1:3c finds no correlation in the catena of OT quotations (1:5–14). This fact indicates that the symmetry lacks one to one correspondence. See Meier, "Symmetry and Theology," 523.

[15] For a detailed discussion of the Old Testament quotations in Hebrews 1:5–14 see Bateman IV, "Jewish and Apostolic Hermeneutics," 350–93.

Examination of 2:1–4

Basis for the Literary Unit

The author signals a change of genre from doctrine to parenesis by διὰ τοῦτο (2:1). Although the literary device of inclusion is not used in this section to define the limit of the passage, 2:1–4 forms a literary unit by conceptual chiasm similar to that of 1:1–4. This may be illustrated as follows:[16]

A Διὰ τοῦτο δεῖ περισσοτέρως προσέχειν ἡμᾶς τοῖς ἀκουσθεῖσιν, μήποτε παραρυῶμεν (Therefore we must pay greater attention to what we have heard, so that we do not drift away from it) (2:1).

B εἰ γὰρ ὁ δι᾽ ἀγγέλων λαληθεὶς λόγος ἐγένετο βέβαιος καὶ πᾶσα παρά-βασις καὶ παρακοὴ ἔλαβεν ἔνδικον μισθαποδοσίαν (For if the message declared through angels was valid, and every transgression or disobedience received a just penalty) (2:2a),

C πῶς ἡμεῖς ἐκφευξόμεθα τηλικαύτης ἀμελήσαντες σωτηρίας (how can we escape if we neglect so great a salvation?) (2:2a).

B' ἥτις ἀρχὴν λαβοῦσα λαλεῖσθαι διὰ τοῦ κυρίου ὑπὸ τῶν ἀκουσάντων εἰς ἡμᾶς ἐβεβαιώθη (It was declared at first through the Lord, and it was attested to us by those who heard him) (2:3),

A' συνεπιμαρτυροῦντος τοῦ θεοῦ σημείοις τε καὶ τέρασιν καὶ ποικίλαις δυ-νάμεσιν καὶ πνεύματος ἁγίου μερισμοῖς κατὰ τὴν αὐτοῦ θέλησιν; (while God added his testimony by signs and wonders and various miracles, and by gifts of the Holy Spirit, distributed according to his will) (2:4).[17]

In this proposed chiastic structure, the outer sections (A and A') may be considered parallel; while section A stresses an importance of paying closer attention to what the readers have heard, section A' explains the reason for it; it is because the message they heard was confirmed by God with signs and miracles. Sections B and B' show parallelism by the idea of confirmation: while B speaks of the confirmation of the message spoken through the angels in the old covenant, B' describes the confirmation

16 Vanhoye also considers that this passage is chiastically structured. See Vanhoye, *La structure,* 76.

17 The English translation used is NRSV.

of the message to the readers by the Lord and those who heard him (i.e., λαληθεὶς and βέβαιος in B and λαλεῖσθαι and ἐβεβαιώθη in B' indicate parallelism). The center section (C) shows what his main point is in this passage: how shall we escape if we neglect so great a salvation? By placing this warning in the middle of the chiastic structure, the author implies that the readers cannot escape if they neglect the message they heard in the new covenant period. A more detailed analysis will be dealt with in the following section. The main emphasis of the discussion in this section is that 2:1–4 forms a literary unit by conceptual chiasm and functions as an exhortation for the readers to remain in faith.

Faith and Christology

Then what is the purpose of setting forth this first exhortation (2:1–4) immediately after the doctrinal section? The structure and the content of the passage suggest that the author intends to exhort believers not to drift away from Christian faith by way of employing the Christological teaching he has just expounded in 1:1–14. A careful examination of this parenetic section (2:1–4) is necessary to determine how it is Christologically oriented. This section may be divided into two parts: (1) exhortation to pay closer attention to what they heard (2:1) and (2) the reason for the exhortation (2:2–4).

Exhortation to Pay Closer Attention (2:1)

It may be recalled from chapter two that Grässer's view of faith in Hebrews is ethically oriented. In commenting on Hebrews 2:1 Grässer argues that faith in this verse has an ethical element. He observes that the concept of faith is not described with such phrases as "repenting in the name of Jesus" (Acts 2:38) or "believing in the name of the Lord Jesus for salvation" (Acts 16:31)," but "to pay attention to what they heard."[18] Grässer contends that the Christological notion of faith is replaced through the theological reflection as an anchor (6:19) to which a Christian must hold fast. Therefore, he concludes that faith in Hebrews should be regarded as στάσις.[19]

---

[18] Erich Grässer, *Der Glaube im Hebräerbrief* (Marburg: N. G. Elwert Verlag, 1965), 215.

[19] Ibid.

Grässer's ethical interpretation of faith in 2:1 leaves no room to consider Jesus as the object of faith for believers because faith is entirely removed from the Christ-event. However, a close examination of 2:1 in relation to the doctrinal exposition of 1:1–14 suggests that Jesus is to be viewed as the object of faith. For the purpose of demonstrating this point, three important words and phrases in this verse will be considered.

First of all, the Christological implication of this passage may be observed from the expression "for this reason" (διὰ τοῦτο). What does this phrase refer to? It may be either inferential (i.e., it looks back to the previous reference; usually translated "therefore") or appositional (i.e., it looks forward to the following statement; translated "namely").[20] In the immediate context the use of the phrase appears to be inferential in that it refers back to what the author discussed in 1:1–14. It denotes that the matters connected by this phrase are inherently related.[21] However, it is not clear exactly from which verse(s) the author draws his inference. Spicq suggests that διὰ τοῦτο goes back to 1:14, in which the author indicates that the angels are the ministering spirits for service, having been sent because of those who are about to inherit salvation. According to Spicq, the significance of διὰ τοῦτο is that since the angels are for the service of Christians, the latter ought to take heed to their responsibilities.[22] But this suggestion is misleading. The language used in 2:1–4 (e.g., all the more, lest we drift away, how shall we escape) are too strong to be considered to refer to 1:14. Rather, it is more likely that διὰ τοῦτο goes back to the entire chapter one, and more specifically to 1:1–2. The phrase τοῖς ἀκουσθεῖσιν (what has been heard) in 2:1 is a strong support for this suggestion. It agrees with the "presentation of revelation in the exordium as the spoken utterance of God. Revelation is a word to be heard."[23] Moreover, the clause "which was first spoken through the Lord" in 2:3 indicates that διὰ τοῦτο should be related to

[20] Walter Bauer, *A Greek-English Lexicon of the New Testament and Other Early Christian Literature*, 2nd ed., trans. and adapted by W. F. Arndt, F. W. Gingrich, and Frederick W. Danker (Chicago: The University of Chicago, 1979), 181.

[21] Maxwell, "Doctrine and Parenesis," 388.

[22] C. Spicq, *L'Épître aux Hebreux* (Paris: Gabalda, 1952), 2:24.

[23] Lane, *Hebrews 1–8*, 37.

1:1–2. Since God has spoken to us by his Son in these last days, and the Son is superior to the angels, we ought to pay all the more closer attention to what we have heard.[24] The author's use of διὰ τοῦτο suggests that the parenetic section of 2:1–4 is Christologically motivated (i.e., it is based on the finality of the revelation in the Son).

Next, the Christological implication of this passage may be noted from the verb δεῖ. This impersonal verb can be translated "it is necessary," "one must or has to,"[25] This word denotes "the character of necessity or compulsion in an event."[26] At times it is used to express the general will of God (Luke 15:32; 18:1; Acts 5:29; 20:35), or decree and the plan of God (Acts 1:21; 19:21; 23:11; 23:11; Rev 1:1).[27] In other words, δεῖ "expresses a logical imperative."[28] Together with διὰ τοῦτο this word emphasizes that since Christ is greater than the angels, "it follows logically that the revelation delivered through the Son must be regarded with the utmost seriousness."[29] The reason that author relates these connotations explicitly to 1:1–14 is to emphasize the importance of soteriology, eschatology, and superior revelation of God and his will in the Son.[30]

Third, the infinitive προσέχειν strengthens the Christological implication of 2:1. This verb means, "to pay attention to," "to give heed to."[31] Maxwell suggests that the word προσέχειν has, as a nautical term, the thought that "there is a 'way,' a 'course,' which the hearers have already embarked upon, which is to be followed to its destination."[32] Thus with this word the author clearly indicates that it is neces-

---

[24] Harold W. Attridge, *The Epistle to the Hebrews*, Hermeneia Commentary (Philadelphia: Fortress Press, 1989), 64.

[25] Bauer, *Lexicon*, 173.

[26] Walter Grundmann, "δεῖ, δέον ἐστί," in *Theological Dictionary of the New Testament*, ed. Gerhard Kittel, tr. Geoffrey W. Bromiley(Grand Rapids: William B. Eerdmans Publishing Co., 1964), 2:21.

[27] Ibid., 22.

[28] Lane, *Hebrews 1–8*, 37.

[29] Ibid.

[30] Maxwell, "Doctrine and Parenesis," 340.

[31] Bauer, *Lexicon*, 714.

[32] Maxwell, "Doctrine and Parenesis," 341.

sary for believers to pay attention to the message all the more. Then what is the content of the message that the author exhorts the addressees to pay attention to? It has already been mentioned that the following phrase ἡμᾶς τοῖς ἀκουσθεῖσιν (what we have heard [NASB]) goes back to 1:1–2 and indicates that "what is heard comprises the entirety of the Christian message, the word that has been proclaimed 'in a Son.'"[33] Lane observes that προσέχειν (to pay attention to) is "analogous to the cognate κατέχειν in 3:6, 14; 10:23, where the hearers are urged to *hold fast to* their confession of faith, without which the goal of salvation cannot be reached."[34] The implication of the verb is that "the community had grown lax in their commitment to Christ and were neglecting the Christian message."[35] For this reason the author is urging them to pay closer attention to what they heard, so that they may not drift away. Here, the author's exhortation to pay closer attention involves more than listening to the words; it involves the action of holding fast to what they had believed in the beginning.

An examination of some of the key words in 2:1 demonstrates that 1:1–14 and 2:1 are structurally and thematically related to each other. The author intends to encourage the readers to continue in faith by reminding them of the Christological teachings which he expounded in 1:1–14. In other words, in Hebrews the doctrine necessarily leads to exhortations, and exhortations are based on the doctrines.[36] In this sense, it may be said that Jesus is viewed as the object of faith for believers, even if it is not expressed with phrases, such as "faith in Jesus" or "believe in Jesus."

The Ground for the Exhortation (2:2–4)

After the author has stated the imperative of paying attention to what they heard, he proceeds to explain the reason for such an exhortation (2:2–4). The conjunction γάρ functions as a link between 2:1 and 2:2–4, giving a further support for the necessity of paying closer attention to

---

33 Attridge, *The Epistle to the Hebrews*, 64.

34 Lane, *Hebrews 1–8*, 37.

35 Ibid.

36 N. A. Dahl, "A New and New Living Way: The Approach to God according to Hebrews 10:19–25," *Interpretation* 5 (1951): 401–12.

what they heard. To substantiate his call to pay closer attention (2:1), the author employs an *a fortiori* literary device, which is an argument from the lesser to the greater (*a minori ad majus*).[37]

The lesser situation is indicated by the protasis in verse 2, which is the reception of the word of God through the angels under the old covenant.[38] The word spoken through the angels is reminiscent of 1:1, which states that God has spoken of the old in many and various ways. It appears that in 2:2 the author illustrates one aspect of many and various ways God spoke of old to our fathers by the prophets, namely, the word spoken through the angels.[39] The word βέβαιος, often with reference to λόγος, generally means "firm," "sure," "well-grounded."[40] However, this meaning does not make sense in this verse. Schlier points out that this term is also used in a technical sense to mean "valid," "effective," "forceful."[41] It was a legal term denoting the confirmation of the transaction between a buyer and a seller,[42] which implies serious obligations between the two parties.[43] In the context of Hebrews 2:1–4 βέβαιος has this meaning. Here, "the word is used in the sense of judicial validity or confirmation in reference to the Old Testament law."[44] The passage suggests that the lesser situation was rebellion against the word which was given to Moses through the angels. The Old Testament clearly indicates that those who rebelled received a just retribution (cf. Num 14:20–45). The author exhorts the readers with the knowledge of the Torah,

---

[37] Herbert Braun, *An die Hebräer*, Handbuch zum Neuen Testament (Tübingen: J. C. B. Mohr [Paul Siebeck], 1984), 48.

[38] George H. Guthrie, *The Structure of Hebrews: A Text-Linguistic Analysis*, Supplements to Novum Testamentum 78 (Leiden: E. J. Brill, 1994), 62.

[39] Maxwell, "Doctrine and Parenesis," 343.

[40] H. Schlier, "βέβαιος κτλ.," in *Theological Dictionary of the New Testament*, ed. Gerhard Kittel, trans. Geoffrey W. Bromiley (Grand Rapids: William B. Eerdmans Publishing Co., 1964), 1:600.

[41] Ibid.

[42] A. Fuchs, "βέβαιος," in *Exegetical Dictionary of the New Testament*, ed. Horst Balz and Gerhard Schneider (Grand Rapids: William B. Eerdmans Publishing Co., 1990), 1:211.

[43] Attridge, *The Epistle to the Hebrews*, 65.

[44] Fuchs, "βέβαιος," 1:211.

reminding them that the rejection of God's word by the wilderness gen-
eration brought about severe punishment.[45] Then what is the greater situation in this argument? It is the great
salvation which was spoken by the Lord first, and confirmed by those
who heard him as described in the apodosis (2:3–4). The fact that "there
is Scriptural precedent for God's punishment in the lesser situation offers a basis for there being even greater punishment if rejection of God's
word takes place in the 'greater' situation."[46] The author's rhetorical
question "how shall we escape if we neglect so great a salvation?" implies that there is absolutely no escape.[47] In other words, all the eschatological terrors and the judgment will certainly fall on him who
turns away from the Son.[48] This is the urgent warning for the readers not
to be indifferent to, nor fail to stay on course, nor to neglect such a great
salvation which was declared and attested to them. This is the author's
way of encouraging the readers to continue with the faith Jesus Christ.

However, as Grässer has correctly pointed out, the author of Hebrews does not explicitly state that the readers must hold fast to Jesus as
the object of faith. Instead, they are reminded to pay attention to the
message spoken by the Lord. Does it necessarily lead one to conclude
that faith in Hebrews is removed from the Christ-event as Grässer argues? Or, did the author of Hebrews intentionally transform the Pauline
or Synoptic use of faith into the ethical category of steadfastness?
Grässer's objection may be answered in two ways.

First, one needs to ponder whether Paul's or the Synoptic notion of
faith (i.e., soteriological aspect of faith) was normative in the early
church. When Grässer suggests that the Pauline concept of faith was replaced by the ethical category in Hebrews, he clearly indicates that this
Christological aspect of faith was a normative interpretation in the early
church.[49] It has already been revealed from the earlier chapters that there

---

[45] G. H. Guthrie, *The Structure of Hebrews*, 62.

[46] Ibid.

[47] D. Guthrie, *The Letter to the Hebrews*, Tyndale New Testament Commentaries
(Grand Rapids: William B. Eerdmans Publishing Co., 1983), 81.

[48] Maxwell, "Doctrine and Parenesis," 343.

[49] Gerhard Dautzenberg, "Der Glaube im Hebräerbrief," *Biblische Zeitschrift* 17
(1973): 174.

were many different strands of faith in these writings. A careful study of the Pauline epistles and Synoptic Gospels reveals that the idea of faith is broad enough to include other aspects.[50]

Second, an examination of both the Synoptic Gospels and the Pauline literature indicates that accepting the word of Jesus is directly related to faith in Jesus, even if the message was spoken by someone other than Jesus himself. For example, listening to the word of Jesus and acting upon it are considered as being obedient to Jesus himself (Matt 7:21–27; Luke 6:46–49). Trusting the word of Jesus is equated with believing in the authority of Jesus (Matt 8:5–13). Accepting the word of Jesus preached by the apostles is identified as believing in Jesus (Acts 4:4; Rom 10:8–9; Eph 1:13; 1 Tim 1:5). These examples clearly demonstrate that receiving the message of the gospel is directly related to Jesus himself. In other words, receiving the message of Jesus is another way of showing trust and allegiance to him. It is to be noted that "paying attention to what has been spoken by the Son and those who heard him (i.e., the apostles and other eyewitnesses) in Hebrews 2:1 is not very much different from the references to responding to the word of Christ in the Synoptic Gospels and the Pauline letters. In Hebrews the author's call to pay closer attention to the message they once heard is another way of exhorting the readers to continue to trust in Jesus. In this sense, faith in Hebrews is not removed from the Christ-event. In Hebrews Jesus is regarded as the object of faith for believers even if faith is expressed differently.

Summary and Conclusion

A thorough examination of Hebrews 1:1–2:4 imparts much insight into the concept of faith in Hebrews. Analyses of 1:1–14 and 2:1–4 reveal that they are intricately related to each other both structurally and thematically. That is, the doctrinal exposition (1:1–14) and the practical exhortation (2:1–4) "are related generally and specifically in literary construction, generally and specifically in points of contact of ideas, and generally and specifically in theological thought."[51]

[50] See Chapter One, 2–3; Chapter Two, 36–37.

[51] Maxwell, "Doctrine and Parenesis," 349.

The phrase διὰ τοῦτο (for this reason) in 2:1 looks back to the entire passage in 1:1–14. The author indicates that since God has spoken through his Son, and the Son is superior to the angels, we must pay closer attention to what has been heard. The author also employs an *a fortiori* argument to warn against neglecting the salvation which was spoken first by the Lord and confirmed by those who heard. This is an urgent call to hold fast the faith which they had when they first believed. Moreover, throughout 2:1–4, the author intentionally employs faith related words (e.g., "it is necessary," "to pay attention," "to drift away," "to neglect," "salvation") to exhort believers to stand firm in faith, even if the word "faith" is not mentioned. Furthermore, the author's exhortation to pay closer attention to the spoken word is his own way of expressing Jesus as the object of faith.

It is true that in Hebrews faith is not expressed in terms of "faith in Christ" or "to believe in Jesus" as in the Pauline literature. But this does not mean that faith in Hebrews is replaced by a mere ethical category of steadfastness or endurance as the proponents of the ethical view contend. An analysis of Hebrews 1:1–2:4 reveals that the Christological aspect of faith is not lacking. The author presents abundant evidence throughout the alternating section of doctrine and parenesis that Jesus is portrayed as the object of faith for believers. This point will become more evident in the following chapters.

CHAPTER FOUR

RELATIONSHIP BETWEEN 2:5–18 AND 3:1–4:16:
CHRIST'S HUMANITY AND THE EXHORTATION
TO ENTER GOD'S REST

After a brief exhortation not to drift away in 2:1–4, the author of Hebrews proceeds with the second exposition of the doctrine of Christ in 2:5–18, followed by the parenesis in 3:1–4:16. In this second major alternating structure of doctrine and parenesis, I will continue to examine the basis of the literary unit for each section and discuss the concept of faith. The purpose of examining the doctrinal section is to determine what aspect of the Christological teaching is emphasized. In the parenetic section I will examine how this Christological teaching affects the way one understands the concept of faith in Hebrews.

Examination of 2:5–18

This section is the continuation of the thought mentioned in 1:14, in which the author indicates that the angels are the ministering spirits sent for those who are about to inherit salvation. In 2:5 the author expresses the same thought in a different way: he (God) did not subject the world to come to the angels. As Guthrie rightly states, it is an emphatic way of stating the underlying supposition that "the world which is to come" (1:14) has been submitted to the Son.[1]

Basis for the Literary Unity

What structural clues does the author suggest to indicate that 2:5–18 forms a literary unit? To begin with, the literary device of inclusion by the word "angels" (2:5 and 2:16) suggests that this section forms a unit. Vanhoye observes that the phrase οὐ γὰρ ἀγγέλοις (not to angels)

---

[1] George H. Guthrie, *The Structure of Hebrews: A Text-Linguistic Analysis*, Supplements to Novum Testamentum 78 (Leiden: E. J. Brill, 1994), 63.

(2:5) and Οὐ γὰρ δήπου ἀγγέλων (surely not to angels) (2:16) marks the limit of the passage.[2] However, I contend that the unit does not stop at 2:16, but continues to 2:18. The conjunction ὅθεν in 2:17 is inferential, in that it sums up the argument which he began from 2:10.[3] Moreover, the conjunction γάρ in 2:18 indicates that it explains why Jesus had to be humanlike in all aspects in 2:17; because he himself was tempted in that which he has suffered, he is able to help those who are tempted. Thus it is reasonable to consider that 2:17–18 is the continuation of the inclusion marked by ἀγγέλων in 2:16.

Next, the subdivision of 2:5–9 is marked by inclusion with the word "angel" (ἄγγελος, vv. 5, 9). The term ἄγγελος occurs five times in Hebrews 2 (vv. 5, 7, 9, 16). That the author does not use the word between 2:10 and 2:15 indicates that he wants to make 2:5–9 as the subunit. In addition, the use of ὑποτάσσω (to subject) in 2:5 and 2:8 indicates that the word also functions as an inclusion to indicate the subdivision. Third, 2:10–18 is connected to 2:5–9 by the particle γάρ in 2:10, "which introduces a statement implying the solidarity between the Son of God and the sons who are being led by God to their heritage."[4]

Fourth, a comparison of the ideas expressed in 2:10–13 and 2:14–18 indicates that 2:10–18 should be considered a sub-unit of 2:5–18. The expressions, "those who are sanctified" (ἁγιαζόμενοι, v. 11), "brethren" (ἀδελφοί v. 12), and "children" (παιδία, v. 13), are repeated in a chiastic manner in 2:14–18: "children" (παιδία, v. 14), "brethren" (ἀδελφοί, v. 17), and "those who are tempted" (πειραζομένοι).[5] In addition, ὤφειλεν (he had to be) in 2:17 corresponds to ἔπρεπεν (it was fitting) in 2:10, which means that the author further explains in 2:17 the thought he developed in 2:10 (i.e., it was proper to perfect the author of

[2] Albert Vanhoye, *La structure littéraire de l'Épître aux Hébreux* (Paris: Desclée de Brouwer, 1976), 78.

[3] Paul Ellingworth, *The Epistle to the Hebrews: A Commentary on the Greek Text,* New International Greek Testament Commentary, ed. I. Howard Marshall and W. W. Gasque (Grand Rapids: William B. Eerdmans Publishing Co., 1993), 180.

[4] William L. Lane, *Hebrews 1–8,* Word Biblical Commentary (Dallas: Word Books, 1991), 53.

[5] O. Michel, *Der Brief an die Hebräer,* 12th ed. (Göttingen: Vanderhoeck and Ruprecht, 1966), 158.

salvation).[6] The above analysis suggests that the doctrinal section of 2:5–18 is to be considered a literary unit with two subdivisions: (1) humiliation and glory of humanity (2:5–9) and (2) solidarity of the Son with humanity (2:10–18).[7]

Christological Teaching

In this second doctrinal section the author expounds yet another Christological aspect. In 1:1–14 it was revealed that the focus was on Christ's superiority to the angels and his exalted state. In 2:5–18 the emphasis is switched to the humanity of Christ. How does he develop this theme?

First of all, the author begins the section on humiliation and glory of humanity (2:5–9) with the quotation of Psalm 8:5–7 [LXX] and the interpretation of it. A question is asked whether or not the quotation of Psalm 8 in 2:6b–8a is to be regarded as a messianic (Christological) psalm. Opinions are divided among scholars in this matter. Some scholars consider that Psalm 8 is a Christological psalm. For example, Bruce identifies "the son of man" in Psalm 8 with the "one like unto a son of man" in Daniel 7:13, who receives from the Ancient of Days "an everlasting dominion, which shall not pass away."[8] He argues that ever since Jesus spoke of himself as the Son of Man, this expression came to have a messianic connotation beyond its etymological force for Christians, including the author of Hebrews.[9] Likewise, Moffatt contends that "'Hebrews' has no room for the notion of Christ as the ideal or representative Man, as is implied in the messianic interpretation of αὐτῷ in v. 8."[10]

Others, on the other hand, believe that the quotation of Psalm 8 is not Christological, but has a direct application to humanity as a whole.

---

[6] J. Moffatt, *A Critical and Exegetical Commentary on the Epistle to the Hebrews,* The International Critical Commentary (Edinburgh: T. & T. Clark, 1924), 37.

[7] Swetnam suggests a chiastic structure in 2:10–18. See James Swetnam, *Jesus and Isaac: A Study of the Epistle to the Hebrews in Light of the Aqedah.* Analecta Biblica 94 (Rome: Pontifical Biblical Institute Press, 1981), 131. If Swetnam's suggestion is correct, it strengthens the view that 2:10–18 forms a literary sub-unit of 2:5–18.

[8] F. F. Bruce, *The Epistle to the Hebrews,* New International Commentary on the New Testament (Grand Rapids: William B. Eerdmans Publishing Co., 1964), 35.

[9] Ibid.

[10] Moffatt, *Hebrews,* 23.

They argue that Jesus is the representative fulfillment of the destiny of humankind as a human being. For example, Lane observes that υἱὸς ἀνθρώπου is anarthrous in Psalm 8 [LXX]. For this reason he argues that the author of Hebrews did not find a Christological title in the designation. Lane contends that the author of Hebrews cites Psalm 8:5 because he desires the readers to understand that Jesus fulfilled the vocation intended for humankind in a representative sense.[11] He continues, "the quotation of Ps 8 may readily be applied to Jesus without finding in the vocabulary an implied reference to the Son of Man Christology of the Gospels."[12] Likewise, Caird asserts that the quotation in 2:6–8 is to illustrate that "man has been destined by God to a glory excelling that of the angels and that this destiny has been achieved by Christ, both individually and representatively, as the pioneer of man's salvation who came to lead many sons into their destined glory."[13] Hurst also argues:

> since Ps. 8 in its original setting was a psalm concerning the glory of man in God's original intention, and since it was not considered 'Messianic' in the LXX or in rabbinic Judaism, one might normally take Jesus in 2:8 as proleptically fulfilling what is as yet unfulfilled for man, that is, he represents man in the ideal state for which he was created, a state identified as 'glory.'[14]

It appears that the non-messianic view is more likely to be what the author has in mind. The expression "now we do not yet see all things being subjected to him" in 2:8b indicates that it has a reference to humankind as a whole. In addition, the author clearly points out that the quotation has its fulfillment in Jesus in 2:9a (i.e., but now we see Jesus who has been made lower for a little while, was crowned with honor and glory through suffering). Furthermore, the reference to ὑπὲρ παντός (for all) in 2:9 strengthens the view that Christ's role in this passage is a representative one.[15] In this sense, one can see that Jesus identifies him-

---

11 Lane, *Hebrews 1–8*, 47.

12 Ibid.

13 G. B. Caird, "The Exegetical Method of the Epistle to the Hebrews," *Canadian Journal of Theology* 5 (1959): 49.

14 L. D. Hurst, "The Christology of Hebrews 1 and 2," in *The Glory of Christ in the New Testament: Studies in Christology in Memory of George Bradford Caird*, ed. L. D. Hurst and N. T. Wright (Oxford: Clarenden Press, 1987), 153.

15 Ibid.

self with humankind in his destiny. This passage should not be regarded as a digression but an indispensable part of developing Hebrews' Christological and parenetic program.[16] While the emphasis of 1:1–14 was on the exaltation of Christ, the focus of 2:5–18 is on the humiliation of Christ. In other words, the author indicates that incarnation is the prerequisite for the Son (i.e., Jesus) to be in solidarity with the sons (i.e., believers) and to be able to help them.[17]

Next the theme of the humanity of Christ is emphasized through the idea of solidarity between the Son and humankind (2:10–18). This solidarity is demonstrated in at least three ways: (1) in calling believers "brothers and sisters" (2:10–13); (2) in identifying himself with the humanity in flesh and blood (2:14–15); and (3) in identifying himself with humanity by offering help in temptation (2:16–18). Through the exposition of 2:5–18, the author emphasizes that Jesus is qualified to become a merciful and faithful high priest because of his identification with humanity (2:17–18). This point will become evident in the exposition of the parenetic section (3:1–4:16).

Examination of 3:1–4:16

Now the author shifts once again to the genre of exhortation from 3:1, which he continues to the end of chapter 4. The change of genre can be detected by the change of the topic from the earthly life of Jesus (2:5–9) and the solidarity of Son to the sons (2:10–18) to the author's entreaty to consider the faithfulness of Jesus.[18] Moreover, the change of the subject from "the Son" in 2:10–18 to "believers in the community" in 3:1 also points out that there is a change of genre from the doctrine to the exhortation.[19]

[16] Harold W. Attridge, *The Epistle to the Hebrews,* Hermeneia Commentary (Philadelphia: Fortress Press, 1989), 69.

[17] G. H. Guthrie, *The Structure of Hebrews,* 64.

[18] Ibid., 65.

[19] Ibid.

Basis for the Literary Unit

There are some clues which may indicate that 3:1–4:16 forms a unit. First of all, it is indicated by the literary device of inclusion. For example, the author uses ἀρχιερεύς (high priest) in 3:1 and 4:14. The reference to Ἰησοῦς (Jesus) is also used in both verses. More importantly, the section forms an inclusion by ὁμολογία (confession) in 3:1 and 4:14.[20] Thus it is very likely that there is a literary unit between 3:1–4:14. Vanhoye contends that, due to inclusion by ὁμολογία, the unit should end at 4:14.[21] However, I believe that it continues through 4:16. As Guthrie correctly states, "the closing element of an inclusion need not occur a the very end of the unit which it marks."[22] The conjunction γάρ in 4:15 suggests that it is the continuation of 4:14. In addition, οὖν in 4:16 indicates that it is a conclusion of 4:14–15. Therefore, 3:1–4:16 should be taken as a unit.

Next, the literary unit of 3:1–4:16 is supported by other structural keys between the subsections of the passage. For example, 3:7–11 (i.e., warning not to harden heart) is connected to 3:1–6 (i.e., faithfulness of Jesus as the high priest) by διό (3:7). There is no connective between 3:11 and 3:12, but the context makes it obvious that 3:12–19 is the exhortation in light of the negative example of Israel in 3:7–11. The conjunction οὖν in 4:1 probably looks back to 3:19. In 3:19 the author states that they (Israel) were not able to enter (the rest) because of unbelief. In 4:1 he exhorts the addressees to be fearful lest they be too late to enter his rest. In this sense, οὖν in 4:1 can be taken as the conclusion of 3:12–19. One may note that 4:1–11 forms an inclusion by κατάπαυσις (rest) (4:1, 11) and 4:12–16 is connected to 4:11 by γάρ. Thus it can be safely concluded that the author intended the entire passage of 3:1–4:16 to be a parenetic unit which follows 2:5–18.

Then what are the structural clues which denote that 3:1–4:16 is related to 2:5–18? To determine the relationship between the two passages, one needs to examine the force and the significance of ὅθεν in 3:1. It is a conjunction that connects the preceding arguments to the dis-

---

20 Vanhoye, La structure, 87.

21 Ibid., 104.

22 G. H. Guthrie, The Structure of Hebrews, 78.

cussion that follows.[23] In the immediate context the particle refers back to 2:17–18. Specifically, ἀδελφοί in 3:1 and 3:12 looks back to ἀδελφοῖς in 2:17. The term ἅγιοι (3:1) corresponds to οἱ ἁγιαζόμενοι (2:11). More importantly, the author's exhortation to consider the high priest of our confession (3:1) clearly goes back to faithful high priest in 2:17. Since 2:17–18 is the conclusion of the exposition of the humanity of the Son in 2:5–16, one can draw the inference that ὅθεν in 3:1 goes back to the entire 2:5–18.

Then what is the significance of establishing that 3:1–4:16 should be taken as a literary unit, and that this parenetic section relates back to the doctrinal section in 2:5–18? My contention is that 3:1–4:16 is an exhortation to be faithful (i.e., a warning not to fail to enter God's rest), and it is based on the Christological teaching, namely, his identification with the humanity as a true human, who is qualified to become a merciful and faithful high priest (2:17–18).

Faith and Christology

Having demonstrated the literary relationship between 2:5–18 and 3:1–4:16, the next step is to proceed with the examination of 3:1–4:16 to ascertain how faith is related to Christology. It is true that this section is also important for other subjects, such as Sabbath rest, eschatology, and apostasy. However, the main concern for this section is to discuss the Christological implication of faith. The discussion will be done under the following subheadings: (1) Jesus as the object of faith; (2) Jesus as the model of faith; (3) and characteristics of faith.

Jesus as the Object of Faith

What are the proofs which may suggest that Jesus is the object of faith in 3:1–4:16? This may be demonstrated from the following aspects: (1) the meaning of ὁμολογία (3:1); (2) the phrase "confidence and pride of hope" (3:6); and (3) the reference to the "word of God" (3:7–4:16).

The meaning of ὁμολογία. First, Jesus being the object of faith may be detected from the meaning and the nature of ὁμολογία (confession). The author begins chapter three with an exhortation to consider the apostle and high priest of our confession (3:1). How are these words re-

---

[23] G. W. Buchanan, *To the Hebrews*, Anchor Bible 37 (Garden City, NY: Doubleday & Company, Inc., 1972), 54.

lated to the concept of faith? Do they point to Jesus as the object (or the content) of faith? To answer this question, one must determine the meaning of ὁμολογία. The term is also used in two other places in the epistle (4:14; 10:23). Does "our confession" refer to the subjective act of confession or the objective content of Christian faith? Opinions are divided on this issue among scholars.

On the one hand, Delitzsch asserts that ὁμολογία denotes the confession or profession of faith made by Christians, namely, the act of the believing church or person, and not simply a creed or formulary.[24] Taking both ἀπόστολος and ἀρχιερεύς as the substantive, he argues that Jesus is the subject of our confession in the sense that he is sent from God to bring us the message of salvation and became a high priest to accomplish it.[25] Manson also, understanding ὁμολογία in this sense, translates the verse as "Jesus, whom in our confession we acknowledge to be our Apostle and high priest."[26]

On the other hand, other scholars believe that ὁμολογία has the objective sense, namely, it is a fixed confession formula. For example, Gyllenberg asserts that the meaning of confession is used not in a subjective but an objective sense. Thus, according to him, ὁμολογία is considered to be synonymous to πίστις (faith).[27] Likewise, Käsemann states that it would be easiest to understand 3:1 as an allusion to a fixed confession of the community in which the title of *apostle*, along with *high priest,* had assumed a place.[28]

It is difficult to determine which view is more in line with the author's intended meaning. On the one hand, the language used by the author in association with ὁμολογία indicates that it is more likely to be used in the objective sense. In 3:1 the verb κατανοέω (3:1) means, "to

---

[24] F. Delitzsch, *Commentary on the Epistle to the Hebrews,* trans. T. L. Kingsbury (Edinburgh: T. & T. Clark, 1878), 1:155.

[25] Ibid., 1:155.

[26] William Manson, *The Epistle to the Hebrews: A Historical and Theological Reconsideration* (London: Hodder And Stoughton, 1951), 52.

[27] Rafael Gyllenberg, "Die Christologie des Hebräerbriefes," *Zeitschrift für systematische Theologie* 11 (1934): 672.

[28] Ernst Käsemann, *The Wandering People of God: An Investigation of the Letter to the Hebrews,* trans. Roy A. Harrisville and Irving L. Sandberg (Minneapolis: Augsburg Publishing House, 1984), 168.

notice," "to observe carefully," "to contemplate."²⁹ The author uses
κρατέω in 4:14, which means to "hold fast (to)" someone or something
so as to remain closely united to it or him.³⁰ In other books of the New
Testament κρατέω refers to observance of the Christian tradition, which
was laid down as binding (2 Thess 2:15; 6:18; Rev 2:13, 25; 3:11).³¹ In
10:23, with the use of ὁμολογία, the author employs the verb κατέχω,
which means "to hold fast," "to retain faithfully."³² In Luke 8:15 the
word κατέχω is used in the sense of "guarding the tradition."³³ What do
these words reveal about the nature of ὁμολογία? They seem to indicate
that it refers to some form of objective confession known to the author
and his readers. On the other hand, however, since the author nowhere in
the letter specifically indicates the exact nature of the confession, it may
be too much of an assumption to assert that ὁμολογία refers to "a firmly
outlined, liturgically set tradition by which the community must
abide."³⁴ It is possible that "the writer was simply challenging them to
continue their confession of Christ in the general sense of maintaining
their open allegiance to him."³⁵

From this brief discussion one can see the difficult nature of the
problem. I feel that the meaning of ὁμολογία should not be either/or,
but both/and. The term appears to be ambiguous enough to imply that
the two interpretations belong together; Jesus whom we confess

²⁹ Walter Bauer, *A Greek-English Lexicon of the New Testament and Other Early Christian Literature*, 2nd ed., trans. and adapted by W. F. Arndt, F. W. Gingrich, and Frederick W. Danker (Chicago: The University of Chicago, 1979), 415.

³⁰ Ibid., 448.

³¹ G. Braumann, "κράτος," *The New International Dictionary of New Testament Theology*, ed. Colin Brown (Grand Rapids: Zondervan Publishing House, 1978), 3:716–18.

³² Bauer, *Lexicon*, 423.

³³ Ibid.

³⁴ O. Michel, "ὁμολογέω κτλ.," in *Theological Dictionary of the New Testament*, ed. Gerhard Friedrich, tr. Geoffrey W. Bromiley (Grand Rapids: William B. Eerdmans Publishing Co., 1967), 5:215.

³⁵ David Peterson, *Hebrews and Perfection: An Examination of the Concept of Perfection in the 'Epistle to the Hebrews,'* Society for New Testament Studies Monograph Series 47 (Cambridge: Cambridge University Press, 1982), 229.

creedally is also the one whom we confess publicly.[36] This means that, no matter which view one holds, the author uses ὁμολογία to emphasize that Jesus is the content (or the object) of faith for believers. That is, the reason why the author employs this word in his exhortation to remain in faith is to emphasize that Jesus is the object of believers' faith.

This leads to another question. What, then, is the nature of the confession (ὁμολογία)? That is, what is the content of the confession to which they were exhorted to hold fast? Although Jesus was certainly important to the confession, the limit and entire content of it are not known.[37] However, the overall context implies that the community's confession of Jesus as the Son of God involved considering the prominence of the title "Son" in Hebrews (e.g., 1:2, 4, 5; 2:6; 4:14).[38] This may well have been an echo of the ὁμολογία.[39] More specifically, the phrase "the apostle and high priest of our confession" in 3:1 provides further insight on the nature of ὁμολογία. The phrase could be considered one of the confessional titles or the summary of the content of the confession in the early Christian community. In what way is Jesus the apostle (ἀπόστολος)? This word occurs only once with reference to Jesus in the whole New Testament. For this reason it is difficult to ascertain the exact meaning of it. If one takes the basic meaning of the word, then Jesus is the apostle in a sense that he was sent by God. However, the word could carry a deeper meaning. One needs to ask why the author brings together ἀπόστολος and ἀρχιερεύς in 3:1. Do these words have any Christological implication?

To answer this question one needs to consider the larger context which describes Jesus as "the apostle and high priest." In 1:1–14 the author has expounded the divine aspect of Jesus; he is the Son through whom God has spoken, who is exalted at the right hand of God. Then he includes a short parenetic section of 2:1–4, which exhorts the readers not to drift away from the Christian faith. Afterward, in 2:5–18 the author

---

[36] P. E. Hughes, *A Commentary on the Epistle to the Hebrews* (Grand Rapids: William B. Eerdmans Publishing Co., 1977), 129.

[37] Buchanan, *To the Hebrews*, 80–81.

[38] Attridge, *The Epistle to the Hebrews*, 108.

[39] Vernon H. Neufeld, *The Earliest Christian Confessions* (Leiden: E. J. Brill, 1963), 135.

returns to the doctrinal section. Here, the focus is on the humiliation of Christ. This passage describes the doctrine of the Son's solidarity with humanity through incarnation.

I am inclined to believe that the phrase "the apostle and high priest" (3:1) is the summary statement of the two doctrinal sections as described above. It has already been mentioned that the term ἀρχιερεύς refers back to 2:5–18, which describes the humanity of Jesus (i.e., the humiliation and glory of the Son). This is seen from the use of the word ὅθεν in 3:1. The author indicates that Jesus is qualified to become a merciful and faithful high priest (2:17–18). This thought leads to the possibility that the word "apostle" (ἀπόστολος) might even go back to 1:1–14, which emphasizes the exalted state of Jesus. Although the word is not found elsewhere in Hebrews, the verbal form is used in 1:14, in which the angels are referred to as ministering spirits sent (ἀποστελλόμενα) for service.[40] This verbal-noun correlation connotes that the author even looks back to 1:1–14 with the use of ἀπόστολος in 3:1.

If this suggestion is correct, then the author's implication is this: Jesus, in his exalted state, became greater than the angels. Just as the angels are sent out by God for service, Jesus is also sent out by God for greater service. 3:1–6 further indicates that Jesus, as the Son, is even greater than Moses in the matter of the house of God. Thus the overall context indicates that ἀπόστολος points to Jesus' divinity as opposed to his humanity.[41] Jesus is both the apostle and the high priest in that he is sent by God to make it possible for humanity to have access to God.[42] The two terms in 3:1 have a significant Christological implication: Jesus is both divine and human. In this sense, ἀπόστολος and ἀρχιερεύς can be considered the summary statement about Jesus which the author expounded in 1:1–2:18. Thus it can be said that the exhortation to consider Jesus, the apostle and high priest of our confession (3:1), is to emphasize that Jesus is the object (or the content) of faith for believers.

The phrase "confidence and pride of hope." Next, Jesus being the object of faith can also be demonstrated from the statement "if we hold

---

[40] C. Spicq, *L'Épître aux Hebreux* (Paris: Gabalda, 1952), 2:65. Swetnam also argues that the reference to ἀπόστολος in 3:1 corresponds to ἀποστελλόμενα in 1:14. See James Swetnam, "Form and Content in Hebrews 1–6," *Biblica* 53 (1972): 370.

[41] Swetnam, "Form and Content in Hebrews 1–6," 370.

[42] Ellingworth, *The Epistle to the Hebrews*, 199.

firm the confidence and the pride that belong to hope" in 3:6b. It is interesting to note that 3:1–6 is chiastically arranged, which can be schematized as follows:[43]

A Ὅθεν, ἀδελφοὶ ἅγιοι, κλήσεως ἐπουρανίου μέτοχοι, κατανοήσατε τὸν ἀπόστολον καὶ ἀρχιερέα τῆς ὁμολογίας ἡμῶν Ἰησοῦν (Therefore, brothers and sisters, holy partners in a heavenly calling, consider that Jesus, the apostle and high priest of our confession) (3:1),

   B πιστὸν ὄντα τῷ ποιήσαντι αὐτὸν (who was faithful to the one who appointed him) (3:2a),

      C ὡς καὶ Μωϋσῆς ἐν [ὅλῳ] τῷ οἴκῳ αὐτοῦ (just as Moses also was faithful in all God's house) (3:2b).

         D πλείονος γὰρ οὗτος δόξης παρὰ Μωϋσῆν ἠξίωται, καθ' ὅσον πλείονα τιμὴν ἔχει τοῦ οἴκου ὁ κατασ- κευάσας αὐτόν· (Yet Jesus is worthy of more glory than Moses, just as the builder of a house has more honor than the house itself) (3:3).

         D' πᾶς γὰρ οἶκος κατασκευάζεται ὑπό τινος, ὁ δὲ πάντα κατα- σκευάσας θεός (For every house is built by someone, but the builder of all things is God) (3:4).

      C' καὶ Μωϋσῆς μὲν πιστὸς ἐν ὅλῳ τῷ οἴκῳ αὐτοῦ ὡς θεράπων εἰς μαρτύριον τῶν λαληθησομένων (Now Moses was faithful in all God's house as a servant, to testify to the things that would be spoken later) (3:5),

   B' Χριστὸς δὲ ὡς υἱὸς ἐπὶ τὸν οἶκον αὐτοῦ· οὗ οἶκος ἐσμεν ἡμεῖς (Christ, however, was faithful over God's house as a son, and we are his house) (3:6a),

A' ἐάνπερ τὴν παρρησίαν καὶ τὸ καύχημα τῆς ἐλπίδος κατάσχωμεν (if we hold firm the confidence and the pride that belong to hope) (3:6b).

In this proposed structure the center sections (D and D') show parallelism by the words οἶκος (house) and κατασκευάζω (to build). Sections C and C' complement each other in that both describe Moses: C' is a further explanation of C. Sections B and B' are parallel with each other

---

43 Bligh also believes that 3:1–6 is arranged chiastically. However, my proposed scheme is slightly different from his. See J. Bligh, *Chiastic Analysis of the Epistle to the Hebrews* (Heythrop: Athenaeum, 1966), 4. NRSV was used for English translation.

in that both describe the faithfulness of Jesus: B' is a further explanation of B. Sections A and A' show parallelism by the word "consider" (κατανοήσατε) (3:1) and "hold firm" (κατάσχωμεν) (3:6). Both terms express similar concepts. This brief comparison suggests that the author arranged 3:1–6 chiastically.

The main concern for this discussion is the relationship between A and A'. The chiastic construction shows that "if we hold fast the confidence and the hope" in 3:6b is parallel to "consider Jesus, the apostle and high priest of our confession in 3:1b." In other words, the conditional clause in 3:6b is a further amplification of "considering the messenger and the high priest of our confession" (3:1b). It speaks of the behavior or virtue of believers who confess Jesus as the object of faith.

In the Greek world the term παρρησία (confidence) denotes the sign of the freedom of speech in a political sense.[44] In the Septuagint and Hellenistic Jewish literature it is used in reference to open access toward God or free and joyful standing before God.[45] This sense of confident openness toward God is carried over to the New Testament, including Hebrews. For example, in 4:16 the word refers to the confident access to the throne of the grace of God. However, in 10:35 it has the sense of "a public demonstration of Christian commitment."[46] In 3:6 the meaning of the term is ambiguous, perhaps denoting both one's devotion to Christ and the outward demonstration of faith in Christ. In this sense, the author's exhortation to hold fast the confidence may be understood as his way of exhorting the readers not to forsake their faith in Jesus whom they believed. Thus for the author of Hebrews Jesus is considered the object of faith.

The next phrase in 3:6b, τὸ καύχημα τῆς ἐλπίδος (the boast of hope), also brings out the nature of faith in Jesus. I take the word "hope" (ἐλπίδος) to be a genitive of content, which means that ἐλπις does not refer to one's act of hoping, but an object for which one hopes.[47] This

---

[44] H. Schlier, "Παρρησία, παρρησιάζομαι," *Theological Dictionary of the New Testament*, ed. Gerhard Friedrich, tr. Geoffrey W. Bromiley (Grand Rapids: William B. Eerdmans Publishing Co., 1967), 5:871–72.

[45] Ibid., 875–76.

[46] Attridge, *The Epistle to the Hebrews*, 112.

[47] Ellingworth, *The Epistle to the Hebrews*, 212.

idea is consistent with the use of ἐλπίς in other books of the New Testament. One of the essential features of New Testament hope is that it is always centered on Christ and God.⁴⁸ Specifically, the content of ἐλπίς is defined as salvation (1 Thess 5:8), righteousness (Gal 5:5), resurrection (1 Cor 15:52ff.; Acts 23:6; 24:15), eternal life (Titus 1:2; 3:7), seeing God and being conformed to his likeness (1 John 3:2).⁴⁹ In Hebrews the word ἐλπίς is used five times in the noun form (3:6; 6:11, 18; 7:19; 10:23). It is not immediately clear what the object of hope is in these verses. However, the phrase "he who promised" in 10:23 indicates that the content of hope has to do with the promise of God.

As for the content of hope in 3:6, the context of 3:1–6 suggests that it refers to the faithfulness of Jesus. The parallel thought between A (3:1) and A' (3:6b) in the chiastic structure implies that the object of hope mentioned in 3:6b is the high priesthood of Christ. Therefore the expression "holding fast the confidence" and "the pride of hope" in 3:6 is the author's way of showing that Jesus, our apostle and high priest, is the object of faith in Hebrews, even though it is described in terms of Christian conduct.

The reference to the word of God. Lastly, the idea of Jesus being the object of faith may be seen from the reference to take heed to the word of God (3:7–4:16). In 3:7a the author exhorts the readers not to harden their hearts when they hear his voice. This exhortation is followed by the negative example of unbelief of the wilderness generation in the Old Testament (3:7b–11) (cf. Psa 95:7–11; Exod 15:23; 17:7; Deut 6:6; Num 14:21–23). This passage indicates that the wilderness generation was not able to enter the rest because they did not hearken to the voice of God (3:11). One may notice that the idea of not listening to God's voice is equated with "an unbelieving heart," "falling away from the living God" (3:12), "deceitfulness of sin" (3:13), and "unbelief" (3:19). For the author of Hebrews, "not listening to the word of God" is analogous to "not having faith in God." Putting it differently, obedience to the word of God has to do with entering into God's rest. It is in this context that the reference to the word of God in 4:12 needs to be interpreted. This

⁴⁸ E. Hoffmann, "ἐλπίς," in *The New International Dictionary of New Testament Theology,* ed. Colin Brown (Grand Rapids: Zondervan Publishing House, 1986), 2:242.

⁴⁹ Ibid.

verse is further support of the potentially destructive power of God's word which the author emphasized in 3:7–4:11.[50]

Then what is the evidence which may indicate that the reference to the word of God is related to faith in Christ? A detailed analysis of the context reveals that it has to do with the Christian message. For example, the word of God is expressed in terms of "hearing his voice" (3:7) and "good news came to us" (ἐσμεν εὐηγγελισμένοι, literally we have been evangelized) (4:2). Moreover, 1:1–2 clearly supports the idea that the word of God is the message which God has spoken by his Son. Furthermore, in 2:1–4 the author maintains that the word of God is the very Christian message which the readers encountered when they first believed. Here, taking heed to the word of God is described in terms of "paying closer attention to what we have heard" (2:1). More specifically, the message of God's word is closely related to the message of salvation which was first spoken by the Lord and then attested to the readers by those who heard him (i.e., Jesus) (2:3). Thus it may be said that disobeying the voice (or the word) of God is equivalent to not receiving the message of salvation which they heard when it was proclaimed to them. In this sense, one can see that the exhortation to take heed to God's word is another way of encouraging the readers to believe in the message of salvation which God brought about through his Son Jesus Christ. Thus it is clear that the author's appeal to consider the apostle and high priest of our confession, to hold fast the confidence and the boast of the hope, and to take heed the word of God are different ways of expressing Jesus as the object of faith.

Jesus as the Model of Faith

Up to this point my main concern was to prove that Jesus is to be considered an object of faith for believers, even if this idea is not stated in terms of "faith in Jesus" or "believing in Christ." Another issue which should not escape one's notice in 3:1–6 is that Jesus is also viewed as the model of faith. In 3:1b–2 the author exhorts the readers to consider Jesus who was faithful (πιστός) to the one who appointed him as Moses was in his (God's) house.[51] An examination of the passage confirms that

---

[50] Ellingworth, *The Epistle to the Hebrews*, 260.

[51] The word πιστός can mean either "faithful or "trustworthy." For the meaning of "faithful" see Lane, *Hebrews 1–8*, 76; Mary Rose D'Angelo, *Moses in the Letter to the*

Jesus is not only the object of faith, but also the model of faith for his followers.[52] This may be demonstrated in two ways.

First of all, the structural relationship between 2:17–18 and 3:1–6 suggests that Jesus is the model of faith for believers. The theme of high priesthood is officially announced in 2:17, in which the author states that Jesus became a merciful (ἐλεήμων) and a faithful (πιστός) high priest. The author proceeds to delineate two aspects of Jesus' high priesthood in 3:1–5:10. However, he does so in an inverted order. That is, the author explains the faithful aspect of the high priest in 3:1–6, followed by the urgent need for the hearers to remain faithful (3:6b–4:13). Then he takes up the merciful aspect of Jesus' high priesthood (4:14–5:10).[53] Thus it is clear that the overall emphasis of 3:1–6 is on Jesus' faithfulness as the high priest. In this context the author's admonition to consider Jesus corresponds to his exhortation to imitate the faithfulness of Jesus.

Next, the theme of Jesus being the model of faith is also supported by the comparison between the faithfulness of Jesus and that of Moses. It has already been pointed out that 3:1–6 is arranged as a chiastic structure. This construction shows that the author reinforces his emphasis on the contrast between the faithfulness of Jesus and that of Moses by way of repetition. The argument of this passage can be divided into three phases. Firstly, the author exhorts the readers to consider Jesus, who is the apostle and high priest of our confession, who was faithful to the one who appointed him (3:1–2).[54] Secondly, he draws a contrast by a general analogy of the builder of a house and the house itself (3:3–4). Thirdly, he provides an exegetical ground for the analogy (3:5–6).[55] That is, while Moses was faithful as a servant, Jesus was faithful as a

---

Hebrews, Society of Biblical Literature Dissertation Series 42 (Missoula, MT: Scholars Press, 1979), 74–75; for the meaning of "trustworthy" see Ellingworth, *The Epistle to the Hebrews,* 202; Dennis Hamm, "Faith in the Epistle to the Hebrews: The Jesus Factor," *Catholic Biblical Quarterly* 52 (1990): 282. Either one of the translations makes a good sense in the context and does not affect the author's intended purpose for this section.

52 For the view that Jesus is the example of faith see Hamm, "Faith in the Epistle to the Hebrews," 270. Hamm points out that in Hebrews Jesus is portrayed as both the model and the enabler of faith.

53 Lane, *Hebrews 1–8,* 68.

54 G. H. Guthrie, *The Structure of Hebrews,* 65.

55 Attridge, *The Epistle to the Hebrews,* 104.

Son. The implication for this comparison is that Jesus is worthy of more glory than Moses as described in 3:3. For this reason the author exhorts the readers to consider the faithfulness of Jesus all the more (3:1). This is supported by the particle γάρ, which clearly indicates that 3:3–6 goes back to κατανοήσατε (consider) in 3:1. The comparison between Moses and Jesus is the faithfulness in the *service* in God's house. Because of this emphasis on *service*, the author's exhortation to consider Jesus should be understood in terms of imitating the faithfulness of Christ. Thus it is evident that the analogy of Jesus and Moses further supports the thesis that Jesus is to be viewed as the model of faith for the readers.

Characteristics of Faith
        Up to this point I have been concerned with the orientation of faith in 3:1–4:16, namely, that Jesus is both the object and model of faith. In this section an emphasis will be placed on discovering the characteristics of faith in 3:1–4:16. To begin with, faith is defined as *faithfulness or trustworthiness*. In 3:1–6 the author compares the faithfulness of Moses and Jesus in his exhortation to consider Jesus. The phrase "in his whole house" in 3:5 suggests that the term πιστός should be understood as "faithful" or "trustworthy." In other words, in 3:5–6 the author compares the difference between the faithfulness of Moses and that of Jesus: while Moses was faithful (πιστός) in all God's house as a servant, Jesus was faithful as Son in his house. Thus faith can be defined as trustworthiness to the things of God. Next, faith is defined as *steadfastness*. This characteristic can be observed in the author's exhortation to hold fast the confidence and the pride of hope (3:6b), to hold fast the beginning of the confidence firm until the end (3:14).
        The third characteristic of faith, which is the foremost important one in this parenetic section, is *obedience*. What evidence is there to prove that faith involves obedience in 3:12–4:16? It can be observed from the way the author combines the themes of faith and obedience.
        Firstly, the relationship of faith to obedience may be observed from Israel's negative example of disobedience in the wilderness (cf. Num 13–14) in 3:7–11. The author of Hebrews quotes Psalm 94 [LXX] to emphasize that the Israelites were not able to enter God's rest because they had failed to obey the word of God. The concept of disobedience is expressed in terms of hardening of the heart in response to God's word (3:7–8). The word παραπικρασμός (3:8), which means "revolt" or "re-

bellion," also signifies the Exodus disobedience.[56] The word δοκιμασία (v. 9) is subject to different interpretation. It may have a negative sense, denoting the time of temptation in the wilderness. However, it may also describe the attitude opposite to the radical faith which one can display in response to the word of God.[57] In other words, δοκιμασία refers to unbelief mixed with mistrust and doubt.[58] In this sense, this word is closely related to disobedience. In addition, the expressions "they go astray in their heart" and "they have not known my way" (v. 10) indicate the act of disobedience of the Israelites. Thus it can be said that the entire emphasis of 3:7–11 is on disobedience of God's voice by the people of Israel. Through the example of disobedience, the author implies that faith entails obedience to the word of God.

Secondly, the relationship of faith to obedience may be detected from the reference to ἀπιστία *(3:12, 19).* Vanhoye observes that 3:12–19 forms a unit by inclusion, which is indicated by ἀπιστία and βλέπω in 3:12 and 3:19.[59] The focal point of the discussion is on ἀπιστία. What is the purpose of the author using ἀπιστία by way of inclusion? His intention is to stress the importance of faith by the use of this negative term. Then in what sense does the author use the word ἀπιστία in both 3:12 and 3:19? This word could mean either "unfaithfulness" or "unbelief."[60] The context in Hebrews indicates that the word is used in the sense of "unbelief." For example, in 3:12 the phrase "to fall away from the living God" indicates that ἀπιστία has the significance of "unbelief." This expression refers to the condition of those who do not believe, not of those who are unfaithful to God as believers. Likewise, the words such as σκληρύνω (to harden) (3:15), παραπικρασμός (rebellion) (3:15), παραπικραίνω (to be rebellious) (3:16) suggest that ἀπιστία should be understood as "unbelief" rather than "unfaithful."

---

[56] Bauer, *Lexicon,* 621.

[57] O. Hofius, *Katapausis. Die Vorstellung vom endzeitlichen Ruheort im Hebräerbrief* (Tübingen: J. C. B. Mohr (Paul Siebeck), 1970), 213, n 797.

[58] Ibid.

[59] Vanhoye, *La structure littéraire,* 94–95.

[60] Bauer, *Lexicon,* 501.

Then in what way is the reference to "evil heart of unbelief" in 3:12 related to the concept of obedience? It is to be noted that this phrase recalls "hardening of the heart" in 3:8. The author implies that an evil heart is similar to hardening of the heart, which was clearly an act of disobedience by Israelites in the wilderness. The word ἀπιστίας may be taken as a genitive of description, in which case the phrase "evil heart of unbelief" (καρδία πονηρὰ ἀπιστίας) can be understood as a heart characterized by unbelief. By its close association with disobedience, the author clearly shows that "faithlessness involves not simply passive disbelief, but active resistance to God's will."[61] In other words, ἀπιστία does not denote simply a lack of faith as believers, but a refusal to believe.[62] In this sense, it may be said that faith has the characteristic of obedience.

Thirdly, the phrase "deceitfulness of sin" (ἀπάτῃ τῆς ἁμαρτίας) in 3:13 clearly reveals the author's intention to relate faith to obedience. Again, the word σκληρύνω reminds the readers that the "deceitfulness of sin" is none other than the act of rebellion in the wilderness (cf. 3:7–11). It refers to the hardening of the heart against the promise of God (3:13f. 4:1).[63] A careful observation of 3:12–13 suggests that this idea is expressed in a chiastic structure. This can be illustrated as follows:

A Βλέπετε, ἀδελφοί, μήποτε ἔσται ἔν τινι ὑμῶν καρδία πονηρὰ ἀπιστίας ἐν τῷ ἀποστῆναι ἀπὸ θεοῦ ζῶντος (Take care, brothers and sisters, that none of you may have an evil, unbelieving heart that turns away from the living God.) (3:12),

   B ἀλλὰ παρακαλεῖτε ἑαυτοὺς καθ' ἑκάστην ἡμέραν (But exhort one another every day) (3:13a),

   B' ἄχρις οὗ τὸ σήμερον καλεῖται (as long as it is called "today") (3:13b),

A' ἵνα μὴ σκληρυνθῇ τις ἐξ ὑμῶν ἀπάτῃ τῆς ἁμαρτίας (so that none of you may be hardened by the deceitfulness of sin) (3:13c).

---

61 Attridge, *The Epistle to the Hebrews*, 116.

62 Michel, *Der Brief an die Hebräer*, 187.

63 Käsemann, *The Wandering People of God*, 44.

This construction enables one to understand that the "deceitfulness of sin" (A') in 3:13 is another way of expressing an "evil heart of unbelief" (A) in 3:12. Thus the "deceitfulness of sin" refers to the act of disobedience, which is also equivalent to unbelief (ἀπιστίας).

Fourthly, the relationship between faith and obedience can also be observed from the commentary on Psalm 95:7–11 in 3:15–19. The exhortation in 3:15–19 is based on the negative example of Israel in the wilderness (3:7–11); the repetition of the quotation from Psalm 95:7–11 suggests that 3:15–19 is the continuation of the theme discussed in 3:7–11. The author raises a series of three rhetorical questions in 3:16–18: (1) who were rebellious when they heard? (3:16); (2) against whom was he provoked for forty years? (3:17); and (3) against whom did he swear that they will not enter his rest? The answers to these questions refer to the same people. They are those who came out of Egypt (3:16), sinned in the wilderness (3:17), and disobeyed (3:18). Through the repetition of these questions and answers the author re-emphasizes the incident of disobedience in the wilderness. The theme of faith in 3:18–19 is discussed in the context of disobedience. The context makes it clear that those who were disobedient were not able to enter God's rest because of unbelief. In this sense, one may conclude that unbelief involves disobedience.

Fifthly, the interrelationship between faith and obedience can be traced through in the exhortation to enter God's rest (4:1–16). In 4:2 the author indicates that although the good news was proclaimed to that generation (εὐηγγελισμένοι), it did not benefit them because they did not mix it with faith. Then in 4:6 he points out that those who formerly heard the good news (οἱ πρότερον εὐαγγελισθέντες) were not able to enter because of disobedience (ἀπείθειαν). The author also exhorts the readers not to fall into the same example of disobedience in 4:11, which is a clear reference to the rebellion in the wilderness. These verses indicate that unbelief (ἀπιστία) is a synonymous term for disobedience (ἀπειθεία). Thus it is reasonable to conclude that the concept of faith in 3:7–4:16 involves obedience to the word of God.

Summary and Conclusion

A close analysis of 2:5–18 and 3:1–4:16 demonstrates that faith in Hebrews is not removed from Christ as some scholars insist. Faith in Hebrews has Jesus as the object of faith for believers, even if it is not expressed in terms of "faith in Christ." The doctrinal section (2:5–18), which emphasizes the humanity of Christ, is the basis for the exhortation to enter God's rest in the parenetic section (3:1–4:16). This is the author's implicit argument that Jesus is the object of faith for believers. Moreover, the evidence for the Christological orientation of faith in 3:1–4:16 is abundant. The reference to confession (ὁμολογία) demonstrates this point, whether the word is understood subjectively or objectively. More specifically, the words "apostle" (ἀπόστλος) and "high priest" (ἀρχιερεύς) imply the divine and human aspects of Jesus. This is the author's way of indicating that Jesus is to be regarded as the object of faith. The phrase "holding fast to the confidence and the pride of the hope" is another way of expressing Jesus as the object of faith. This study also reveals that the "voice of God" or "the word of God" refers to the Christian message; faith in Jesus is described in terms of "taking heed to the word of God."

An examination of this passage also reveals that Jesus is portrayed as the model of faith. The author of Hebrews points out that Jesus was worthy of more glory than Moses because, while Moses was faithful as a servant, Jesus was faithful as a Son. The overall emphasis of the passage is clearly on the faithfulness of Jesus. For this reason believers are exhorted to consider this Jesus, who was the apostle and the high priest of our confession, and faithful to the one who appointed him. As for the characteristics of faith in 3:1–4:16, the author expresses them in different ways: faith involves faithfulness, steadfastness, and obedience. Among these, the most important aspect of faith in this passage is the quality of obedience to the word of God. However, these characteristics are not merely ethical elements, as some contends. These qualities of faith revolve around Jesus being the object and the model of faith. Therefore, it may be concluded that faith in Hebrews in 3:1–4:16 is based on Christology.

CHAPTER FIVE

RELATIONSHIP BETWEEN 5:1–10 AND 5:11–6:20:
A MERCIFUL HIGH PRIEST AND THE EXHORTATION NOT TO FALL AWAY

The author again changes the literary genre from parenesis (3:1–4:16) to exposition (5:1–10). The theme of high priesthood which is developed in 5:1–10 is already announced in 4:14–16. However, the difference between the two passages is that while 4:14–16 speaks of holding fast to the confession and coming to the throne of the grace of God by the readers based on the high priesthood of Christ, 5:1–10 describes the appointment of Jesus to the office of high priesthood.[1] In this section the relationship between the doctrinal (5:1–10) and parenetic section (6:1–20) will be examined to demonstrate that faith in Hebrews is Christologically oriented. In the parenetic section the characteristics of faith will also be explored.

Examination of 5:1–10

It has already been revealed from the previous discussion that the author mentioned the dual aspects of Christ's high priesthood in 2:17, namely, a merciful and faithful high priest. These two characteristics are further expounded in 3:1–5:10. The latter (i.e., faithful high priest) is explained in 3:1–6, while the former (i.e., merciful high priest) is elaborated in 5:1–10.[2] These two facets show both divine and human elements of the high priesthood of Christ, each with different purpose: "the point of the exhortation based on Christ's divinity is Christ's faithfulness; the

---

[1] George H. Guthrie, *The Structure of Hebrews: A Text-Linguistic Analysis*, Supplements to Novum Testamentum 78 (Leiden: E. J. Brill, 1994), 69.

[2] To be more precise, the first aspect of Christ's high priesthood begins from 4:14. I consider that 4:14–16 forms a transition between 3:1–4:13 and 5:1–10.

point of the exhortation based on Christ's humanity is Christ's mercy."[3]
In this section I will first establish the basis for the literary unit for 5:1–
10, followed by the author's intended Christological teaching in this passage.

Basis for the Literary Unit
What clues does the author present to indicate that 5:1–10 forms a
literary unit? To begin with, the word "high priest" (ἀρχιερεύς) used in
5:1 and 5:10 reveals that this passage forms a unit by inclusion. Next,
the overall structure of 3:1–5:10 also reveals that 5:1–10 forms a unit.
As pointed out previously, the theme of Jesus being a *merciful* and
faithful high priest was announced in 2:17. These two aspects of high
priesthood of Jesus were delineated in 3:1–5:10 in an inverted order.
First, he explains the faithful aspect in 3:1–6, followed by the exhortation not to be disobedient to the word of God (3:7–4:16). Then in 5:1–10
he comes back to his discussion on the high priesthood of Jesus and explicates the merciful aspect. In this sense, it seems logical to consider
5:1–10 as a self-contained unit. Third, the unity of 5:1–10 can also be
detected from the chiastic structure at the conceptual level, which can be
illustrated as follows:[4]

> A The earthly high priest is appointed to make offerings for sins (5:1).
> B The earthly high priest is able to deal gently with the sinners because he is
>   also beset with weaknesses (5:2–3).
> C The earthly high priest must be appointed by God (5:4).
> C' The heavenly high priest is also appointed by God, but as Son and after
>   the order of Melchizedek (5:5–6).
> B' The heavenly high priest can sympathize with humanity because He experi-
>   enced the human weaknesses (5:7–8).
> A' The heavenly high priest became the source of eternal salvation after the order of
>   Melchizedek (5:9–10).

In this proposed structure the center of the chiasm is contrasted by the
humanity of the levitical high priesthood (C) and Christ's high priesthood (C'). The sections above C (i.e., ABC) describe the characteristics

---

[3] James Swetnam, "Form and Content in Hebrews 1–6," *Biblica* 53 (1972): 383.

[4] Lane has identified basically the same chiastic arrangement as mine. See William
L. Lane, *Hebrews 1–8*, Word Biblical Commentary (Dallas: Word Books, 1991), 111.

of the levitical high priesthood, and the sections below C' (i.e., C'B'A'), Christ's high priesthood. This type of chiastic arrangement is called "the law of the shift at the center." In this literary device there is often a change in the trend of thought at the center, and an antithetic idea is introduced. This thought is resumed and continued until the end of the chiasm.[5] The passage in consideration (5:1–10) fits the description of the above criterion for chiasm. For this reason it is reasonable to consider that 5:1–10 is arranged in a mirror image. The above structural marks clearly demonstrate that 5:1–10 should be regarded as a literary unit.

Christological Teaching
Then what Christological doctrine does the author set forth in 5:1–10? As I have explained briefly above, the purpose of this passage is to demonstrate that Jesus is the merciful high priest. In 4:14–16 the author has already announced that Jesus is the high priest who can sympathize with our weaknesses because he was tempted in every aspect like us, yet without sin. In order to prove how Jesus as the high priest is able to sympathize with the weaknesses of his followers, the author first describes the qualifications of high priests in the Old Testament (5:1–4), then specifically gives Christ's qualifications as high priest (5:5–10).

Qualifications of the Levitical High Priesthood
To bring out the author's emphasis on the compassionate high priesthood of Jesus, a brief discussion of the qualifications of the levitical high priesthood is necessary. Although 5:1–4 does not provide an exhaustive list of the characteristics of the Old Testament high priest, it focuses on the qualifications relevant to the theme of Christ as high priest.[6] Then what are the qualifications of the levitical high priest? To be more specific, how many qualifications of a high priest are mentioned

---

[5] Nils W. Lund, *Chiasmus in the New Testament: A Study in the Form and Function of Chiastic Structures* (Chapel Hill, NC: University of North Carolina Press, 1942; reprint, Peabody: Hendrickson, 1992), 41.

[6] David Peterson, *Hebrews and Perfection: An Examination of the Concept of Perfection in the 'Epistle to the Hebrews,'* Society for New Testament Studies Monograph Series 47 (Cambridge: Cambridge University Press, 1982), 81.

in 5:1–4? There are three major parallel qualifications between the
earthly high priest and the heavenly high priest.[7]
The first qualification of a high priest has to do with the atonement
of sins of people. In 5:1 the author states that every high priest is appointed for the things of God. The purpose of this appointment is indicated by ἵνα in 5:1b., namely, it was to offer gifts (δῶρα) and sacrifices
(θυσίας) for sins. Although recognizing that the same offering could be
called either "gifts" or "sacrifices" under different circumstances, Westcott argues that when "gifts" and "sacrifices' are used together, the former refers to the meal offering and the latter the bloody offering.[8] However, this distinction seems unnecessary. The phrase should be understood "as a general description of the offering over which the high priest
officiated."[9] For example, in 8:3–4 the terms are used interchangeably.
In 8:3 the phrase "gifts and sacrifices" (δῶρά τε καὶ θυσίαι) is used in
the same manner as in 5:1. Yet, in the next verse the author of Hebrews
uses only "gifts" to refer to "gifts and sacrifices" in 8:3. This is also
supported by the immediate context of 8:3–4, which indicates that both
"gifts and sacrifices" and "gifts" refer to the sacrificial system under the
old covenant. Moreover, in 11:4 the words δῶρον and θυσία are used
separately, which refer to the same referent, namely, the offering of
Abel. Thus it is clear that the expression "gifts and sacrifices" is the
general reference to the offering under the Old Testament system. Furthermore, in 9:9 it appears that "'gifts and sacrifices' together are related

---

[7] For the proponents of three items of qualifications, see Harold W. Attridge, *The
Epistle to the Hebrews*, Hermeneia Commentary (Philadelphia: Fortress Press, 1989),
142–54; Peterson, *Hebrews and Perfection*, 81–96, 234 n. 79. For the proponents of two
items of qualifications, see F. F. Bruce, *The Epistle to the Hebrews*, New International
Commentary on the New Testament (Grand Rapids: William B. Eerdmans Publishing
Co., 1964), 88. Bruce sees that only two qualifications are discussed: "A high priest must
be *(a)* able to sympathize with those whom he represents, and *(b)* divinely appointed to
his office"; J. Moffatt, *A Critical and Exegetical Commentary on the Epistle to the Hebrews*, The International Critical Commentary (Edinburgh: T. & T. Clark, 1924), 61.

[8] B. F. Westcott, *The Epistle to the Hebrews: A Historical and Theological Reconsideration* (London: Macmillan, 1889), 118.

[9] P. E. Hughes, *A Commentary on the Epistle to the Hebrews* (Grand Rapids: William B. Eerdmans Publishing Co., 1977), 175.

by implication to the removal of sin."[10] The phrase, "which cannot make perfect the conscience of worshipper" (9:9), is a clear reference to the expiation of sins. This is supported by 9:14, which states, "how much shall the blood of Christ . . . cleanse our conscience from dead works to serve the living God." A brief examination of the terms θυσίαι and δῶρα indicates that they are used to refer to the entire offering system under the old covenant, and their purpose is for the removal of sins.

The second qualification of a high priest is expressed in 5:2–3. It is possible that the adverbial participle δυνάμενος (being able to) (5:2) may modify καθίσταται (appointed) in 5:1. But the clause seems to function as an independent sentence, suggesting another qualification of a high priest, that is, he is able to deal gently with those who are igno-rant and led astray. The word μετριοπαθεῖν (to deal gently) is derived from the adjective μετριοπαθής, which denotes the one who knows how to moderate one's passion.[11] Thus the verbal form means, "to exer-cise moderation in emotions or passions."[12] This word study suggests that one of the qualifications of being a high priest is to be able to mod-erate the feelings of other people. The reason is that he himself is also beset with weakness (5:2). Because of his weakness he is bound to offer sacrifices, not only for the people but also for himself (5:3).

The third qualification of a high priest is that he must be called by God (5:4). In the extra-biblical literature the word "honor" (τιμή) is used at times to denote the designation of an office.[13] The context in Hebrews 5:4 indicates that the word is used in this sense. Thus "honor" refers to the office of high priest. It is a well-known fact that the office of high priesthood for Aaron and his descendants is divinely appointed (Exod 28:1; Num 3:10; 18:1). The construction of the participle "being called" (καλούμενος) is difficult to comprehend. Ellingworth suggests that verse 4 should be understood as follows:

10 Paul Ellingworth, *The Epistle to the Hebrews: A Commentary on the Greek Text,* New International Greek Testament Commentary, ed. I. Howard Marshall and W. W. Gasque (Grand Rapids: William B. Eerdmans Publishing Co., 1993), 274.

11 W. Michaelis, "μετριοπαθέω," in *Theological Dictionary of the New Testament,* ed. Gerhard Friedrich, tr. Geoffrey W. Bromiley (Grand Rapids: William B. Eerdmans Publishing Co., 1967), 5:938.

12 Ibid.

13 Josephus, *Antiquities of the Jews* 3.8.1; 12:42.

οὐχ ἑαυτῷ τις λαμβάνει τὴν τιμὴν (anyone does not take the honor for himself)

ἀλλὰ   (λαμβάνει τὴν τιμήν) (but [he takes the honor])

καλούμενος ὑπὸ τοῦ θεοῦ (when he is called by God).[14]

With this reconstruction one can easily understand that καλούμενος can be taken as an adverbial participle indicating time. Thus the meaning of 5:4 can be paraphrased as, "and one does not assume the honor of the office of high priesthood for himself, but one receives it when one is called by God just as Aaron was." The office of the high priesthood is possible only by divine appointment. This point is also supported by the word καθίστημι in 5:1, which means "to ordain," or "to appoint."[15] The passive voice indicates that every high priest is appointed by God.

Qualifications of Christ's High Priesthood

The qualifications of the earthly high priest according to 5:1–4 are: (1) to offer sacrifices for the sins of people; (2) to be able to deal gently with sinners; and (3) to be appointed by God. Then what is the point of the discussion on these qualifications? An analysis of 5:1–10 reveals that the author relates these qualities to Christ's high priesthood. However, he does so in an inverted order. In this passage the author also brings forth the contrast between the earthly and the heavenly high priesthood.

First, after having discussed the qualification that one must be called by God (5:4), the author points out that Christ, likewise, did not glorify himself in becoming a high priest: he also had to be appointed by God (5:5). The word οὕτως in 5:5 refers to what precedes (5:1–4) and indicates that there is a parallel between the appointment of the levitical priesthood and Christ's priesthood. This divine appointment is further explicated by the citation of Psalm 2:7 and 110:4 in 5:5–6. However, the quotation of the Psalms also suggests that there are differences between

---

[14] Ellingworth, *The Epistle to the Hebrews*, 279. The above structure is a slight modification of Ellingworth's structural layout. The Greek words in parenthesis is added to show that they are not in the Greek text. The English translation is mine.

[15] Walter Bauer, *A Greek-English Lexicon of the New Testament and Other Early Christian Literature*, 2nd ed., trans. and adapted by W. F. Arndt, F. W. Gingrich, and Frederick W. Danker (Chicago: The University of Chicago, 1979), 390.

the appointment of the earthly and the heavenly high priests. Psalm 2:7 was already quoted by the author in 1:5, in which it is used with reference to the exalted Son. The reemergence of Psalm 2:7 in 5:5 has the function of recalling the argument of 1:1–14, and emphasizes the absolute superiority of the Son's priesthood over the levitical priesthood. Likewise, the quotation of Psalm 110:4 in 5:6 shows the difference between the levitical priesthood and Christ's priesthood. In certain places when καθώς is followed by καί, it has the sense of simple comparison (e.g., 1 Thess 5:11). But in 5:6 the conjunction is used in a normative sense. For this reason καθώς should not be translated as "the same as," but "according as."[16] This translation allows one to see that the author's implicit intention is to show the difference between the levitical high priesthood and Christ's high priesthood. Indeed, the contrast is that, while the levitical priesthood is temporary in nature, Christ's office of high priesthood is eternal; also, Christ's order of priesthood is not according to the levitical system, but according to the order of Melchizedek. It is clear that, with the citation of Psalm 110:4, the author asserts implicitly the discontinuity and the superiority of the Christ to Aaron, although he defers the interpretation of the text until 7:1–25.

Next, in 5:7–8 the author applies the second qualification of the levitical high priest (5:2–3) to Christ. Just as the earthly high priest understands the weaknesses of humanity, Jesus, the heavenly high priest, can also identify himself with humankind because he himself experienced human weaknesses while he was on earth. Just as the levitical high priest was obligated to bring offerings for the sins of people (5:1b, 3), Jesus also offered prayer and entreaty to the one who is able to save him from death (5:7a). The verb προσφέρω is used consistently in these verses to compare the offerings of the earthly high priest and that of Jesus. However, the author also points out that there is a difference between the earthly and heavenly high priest. According to verse 3, the levitical high priest had to offer sacrifices for his own sins as well as for those of the people. But in verse 7 the author implies that Jesus did not have to make an offering for himself because he was without sin. The participial clause εἰσακουθεὶς ἀπὸ τῆς εὐλαβείας (having been heard because of his godly fear) is reminiscent of 4:15, which states that Jesus was

---

16 Albert Vanhoye, *La structure littéraire de l'Épître aux Hébreux* (Paris: Desclée de Brouwer, 1976), 237.

tempted in all aspects as we are, yet without sin. Moreover, the reference to the perfect obedience to the will of God in 5:8–9a indicates that Jesus did not have to make a sin offering for himself.

Third, as a way of completing the chiastic arrangement of 5:1–10, the author applies the first qualification of the earthly high priesthood (5:1) to Christ in 5:9–10 (i.e., the qualification of atoning for the sins of people). However, his emphasis is more on the contrast between the two offices. This contrast is already mentioned in 5:5–6 by way of quotations from Psalm 2:7 and 110:4 (i.e., temporary nature of earthly high priest-hood vs. eternality of Christ's high priesthood; levitical order vs. Melchizedekian order). In 5:9 the author reiterates the eternality of Christ's high priesthood by stating that Jesus became the source of eternal salvation. He also restates that the order of Christ's high priesthood is according to the order of Melchizedek (5:10), which he further develops in 7:1–10:18.

In conclusion, the Christological teaching in 5:1–10 may be summarized as "Christ who is the merciful high priest." The author presents this teaching by comparing and contrasting the qualifications of the levitical high priesthood and Christ's high priesthood. The similarities between the two are: (1) both offer sacrifices for the sins of the people; (2) both are able to deal gently with the sinners; and (3) both are appointed by God. The contrast between the earthly high priest and heavenly high priest are: (1) while the levitical high priesthood is transient, Christ's high priesthood is eternal; (2) the order of the earthly priesthood is based on the levitical sacrificial system, but the heavenly high priest-hood is after the order of Melchizedek; and (3) the levitical high priest also had to offer sacrifices for his own sins; Jesus, the heavenly high priest did not have to because he was without sin.[17]

Examination of 5:11–6:20

According to Vanhoye, 3:1–5:10 constitutes the second major part in his scheme of dividing the book of Hebrews. He considers that 5:11–6:20 is related, not to the previous doctrinal section (i.e., 5:1–10), but to

---

[17] For the discussion on the qualification of high priesthood see also David John MacLeod, "The Theology of the Epistle to the Hebrews: Introduction, Prolegomena and Doctrinal Center" (Th.D. diss., Dallas Theological Seminary, 1987), 342–46.

what follows (7:1–10:39), which is the third major part.[18] Thus for Van-hoye, 5:11–6:20 is the preamble paragraph to the third major part. Van-hoye's division of the book suggests that the second section ended, not by parenesis, but by doctrine. Moreover, in his scheme, the parenesis (i.e., 5:11–6:20) is presented before the doctrinal section in 7:1–10:18. His suggestion implies that 5:11–6:20 is the only exception in the author's pattern of alternating doctrine and parenesis. However, it seems more natural to consider that a parenesis follows an exposition.[19] The phrase περί οὗ in 5:11 indicates that the parenetic section of 5:11–6:20 belongs to 5:1–10 rather than 7:1–10:19. In other words, 5:11–6:20 is the continuation of the Christological teaching which he expounded in 5:1–10. In this parenesis the author exhorts the readers to remain in faith by warning them of the danger of remaining in spiritual immaturity. As with the other parenetic sections, I will first establish the basis for the literary unit, and then examine the relationship between faith and Christology.

Basis for the Literary Unit

The author provides some clues to indicate that 5:11–6:20 forms a literary unit. To begin with, the transitional nature of the passage sug-gests that it is to be regarded as a unit. In 5:10 the author has just men-tioned that Jesus was given the title of high priest after the order of Mel-chizedek. Then in 5:11 he begins with περὶ οὗ, which signals that he wishes to address this issue further.[20] The next phrase "there is much to say" (πολὺς ἡμῖν ὁ λόγος) supports this idea. However, with the ex-pression καὶ δυσερμήνευτος λέγειν (and it is hard to say), the author implies that he is about to make a transition in the subject matter. The expression "since you have become dull in hearing" shows why it is dif-

---

[18] Vanhoye, *La structure,* 54–55, 114, 124.

[19] Swetnam, "Form and Content in Hebrews 1–6," 385.

[20] The antecedent of the relative pronoun οὗ is ambiguous because the form itself can be either masculine or neuter. As neuter it could refer to the entire subject matter of the high priesthood after the order of Melchizedek. For example, Moffatt translates the phrase as "on this point," which points to the fact of high priesthood (Moffatt, *Hebrews,* 68). Or, as masculine, it may refer to Melchizedek or Christ. In this verse the antecedent seems to be Melchizedek (5:10), rather than Christ (5:5) because it is closest to the rela-tive pronoun.

ficult for him to explain. In other words, the author tells the readers that he has much to say concerning him (i.e., Melchizedek) but it is difficult to say because they have become dull of hearings (5:11).[21] Thereafter, in 5:12–6:20, the author warns the readers not to fall away from faith based on the Christological doctrine which he explained in 5:1–10. Finally, after having restated the high priesthood after the order of Melchizedek in 6:20 (cf. 5:10), he comes back to the discussion of Melchizedek in 7:1–3.[22] The demonstrative pronoun οὗτος and the specific mention of the name "Melchizedek" in 7:1 further support the thesis that 5:11–6:20 is a transitional passage. Because of these reasons 5:11–6:20 is to be considered a unit.

Next, the literary unit of 5:11–6:20 may be observed from the sub-units of the passage. The literary devices employed in this parenetic section indicates that it is divided into two parts: (1) 5:11–6:12 and (2) 6:13–20. The author's use of νωθροί (dull or sluggish) both in 5:11 and 6:12 gives a clue that 5:11–6:12 forms a unit by inclusion. Lane observes that this word occurs only here (5:11; 6:12) in Hebrews and nowhere else in the New Testament, and suggests that its literary function corresponds to the use of ἀπιστία (unbelief) in 3:12 and 3:19 and shows the limit of the paragraph.[23] In addition, the unity of 5:11–6:20 is also confirmed by the subsection of 6:13–20. In this passage the author's concern is to show God's faithfulness to his declarations and the confidence which such faithfulness should afford Christians (6:17–20).[24] Vanhoye observes that there is a change of literary genre in 6:13–20. He argues that this section no longer speaks of exhortation, but is an exposition of firmness in response to the divine promises.[25] However, the context clearly reveals that there is a close connection between 6:12 and 6:13. The conjunction γάρ indicates that verses 13–15 are the continuation of verse 12. The purpose of 6:13–15 is to give an example of faith and patience to the recipients of the letter from the life of Abraham. The

---

[21] Here, the conjunction καί has an adversative force.

[22] Bruce, *The Epistle to the Hebrews*, 106. See also Ellingworth, *The Epistle to the Hebrews*, 299.

[23] Lane, *Hebrews 1–8*, 134.

[24] G. H. Guthrie, *The Structure of Hebrews*, 110.

[25] Vanhoye, *La structure*, 121.

author's implication is clear: just as Abraham received from God the confirmation of the promise of numerous descendants after having patiently endured the test, so the readers should be ready to exercise faith and patience to receive what they hope for. [26]

Moreover, verse 16 is also related to verse 17 by another explanatory conjunction γάρ. In verses 16–20, the author continues to explain God's faithfulness to his declarations by showing his faithfulness to Abraham's descendants. This point is clearly seen from the use of the word ὀμνύω (to swear) (6:13 [twice], 16) and ὅρκος (oath) (6:16, 17). Then what is the basis of the oath in this passage? It appears that the author has Psalm 110:4 in mind, which he introduced in Hebrews 5:6. The reference to "mediating with an oath to show the unchangeableness of his will" (6:17) is an allusion from Psalm 110:4a, which states, "the Lord has sworn and will not change His mind" (NASB). This thought is more fully expressed in 7:21. This type of literary device, in which the exhortation utilizes semantic material from the related expositional discussion, is referred to as semantic borrowing.[27] Why then does the author employ this literary device? I am convinced that he intends to exhort the readers to remain in faith based on the exposition of the Christological teaching in 5:1–10. At the same time the author intends to lead further into the discussion of the Melchizedekian high priesthood of Christ. In this passage Psalm 110:4 is alluded to show that, through these unchangeable deeds (i.e., his purpose and oath), we may have encouragement (6:18). This is clearly the call to move on to maturity by imitating those who inherit God's promises through faith and patience.[28] Since there is a direct correlation between the doctrine in 5:1–10 and the parenesis in 5:11–6:20, it can be said that the concept of faith in 5:1–6:20 is Christologically oriented. That is, for the author of Hebrews, Jesus is regarded as the object and the model of faith for believers. This point will be further delineated in the following section.

[26] James Swetnam, *Jesus and Isaac: A Study of the Epistle to the Hebrews in Light of the Aqedah.* Analecta Biblica 94 (Rome: Pontifical Biblical Institute Press, 1981), 184–85.

[27] G. H. Guthrie, *The Structure of Hebrews,* 140–41.

[28] Ibid., 111.

Faith and Christology

In addition to the structural relationship between 5:1–10 and 5:11–
6:20, the conceptual analysis also indicates that faith in Hebrews is Christologically oriented. In this section some of the terms and phrases will
be examined to demonstrate that Christ is viewed as both the object and
the model of faith. At the same time the characteristics of faith will also
be examined. However, because of the nature of the discussion the characteristics of faith will not be treated separately; it will be undertaken
along with the discussion of faith's relationship to Christology.

Christ as the Object of Faith

Some argue that the idea of Jesus being the object (or, content) of
faith is absent in 5:11–6:20. For example, Grässer asserts that the term
σπουδή in 6:11 has an ethical sense of "earnest striving" or "being eager." He considers that σπουδή has become an irrevocable Christian
command. Grässer also understands πίστις καὶ μακροθυμία in 6:12 as
hendiadys, namely, faith which is patience.[29] He believes that the two
terms should not be regarded as the mode of acquiring salvation, but as
steadfastness (i.e., Standhaftigkeit).[30] For this reason Grässer concludes
that faith in Hebrews has no specific Christological element, namely,
Jesus is not the object of faith.[31]

Grässer has done well in pointing out the ethical aspect of faith in
this passage. Indeed, faith is depicted as steadfastness in 6:11–20. However, an exploration of the context in 5:1–6:20 indicates that Christ is
not removed from faith. Rather, the structural relationship between 5:1–
10 and 5:11–6:20 clearly shows that the ethical quality of steadfastness
is not detached from Christ, but intimately related to him. Moreover, a
detailed exegesis of the parenetic section (5:11–6:20) suggests that Jesus

---

[29] The term hendiadys is defined as the coordination of two ideas by καί, in which
one is dependent on the other. In the New Testament this device is used to avoid a series
of dependent genitives. See F. Blass, F. Debrunner, and R. W. Funk, *Grammar of the
New Testament and Other Early Christian Literature*, trans. R. W. Funk (Chicago: The
University of Chicago Press, 1961), 228 (§ 442).

[30] Erich Grässer, *Der Glaube im Hebräerbrief* (Marburg: N. G. Elwert Verlag,
1965), 28.

[31] Ibid., 35.

is portrayed not only as the imitator of faith, but also as the object of faith for believers.

What are the proofs which may substantiate the claim that Jesus is portrayed as the object of faith? The author's Christological aspect of faith can be demonstrated from the following three different aspects: (1) the meaning of the phrase "the beginning principles about God's oracles," (2) the warning passage, and (3) the relationship of faith to the word of God.

First of all, the Christological reference to faith in 5:11–6:20 can be observed from the phrase "the beginning principles about God's oracles" (τὰ στοιχεῖα τῆς ἀρχῆς τῶν λογίων τοῦ θεοῦ) in 5:12.[32] The context suggests that the term στοιχεῖον has the meaning of "fundamental principles," or "letters of the alphabet, ABC's."[33] In other words with use of στοιχεῖον the author of Hebrews has in mind the fundamental Christian doctrines which they received when they first believed. This is supported by the use of ἀρχή (beginning) in Hebrews. For example, in 3:14, he uses ἀρχὴν τῆς ὑποστάσεως (the beginning of the confidence) to refer to the confidence or trust which the recipients began when they first became Christians.[34] More specifically, in 6:1 the author uses ἀρχή to refer to the fundamental doctrines concerning Christ. Thus it is clear that the phrase "the beginning principles about God's oracles" in 5:12 is equivalent to the expression "the beginning teaching about Christ" in 6:1.[35]

---

[32] The genitive τοῦ θεοῦ in 5:12 needs to be taken as the objective genitive (i.e., the oracles about God) because the author of Hebrews speaks of the oracles which God has already spoken through his messengers.

[33] Bauer, *Lexicon*, 768–69.

[34] P. E. Hughes, *A Commentary on the Epistle to the Hebrews* (Grand Rapids: William B. Eerdmans Publishing Co., 1977), 152.

[35] It is more appropriate to understand the genitive τοῦ Χριστοῦ in 6:1 as the objective genitive (i.e., the word about Christ) rather than the subjective genitive (i.e., the word which Christ spoke) because the author of Hebrews refers to the message which was spoken through the Lord (2:3). For the view that takes the phrase as the subjective genitive see J. C. Adams, "Exegesis of Hebrews vi.1f.," *New Testament Studies* 13 (1967): 382.

114   CHAPTER FIVE

The immediate context also supports the idea that both phrases are identical. The phrase "the beginning principles of the oracles of God" is related to milk (γάλακτος) in 5:12b, both of which belong to the spiritual infant (5:13). On the other hand, in 5:14 the author indicates that solid food belongs to the mature. Based on this analogy, the readers are exhorted to move on to maturity by leaving the elementary doctrine of Christ (τὸν τῆς ἀρχῆς τοῦ Χριστοῦ λόγον) (6:1). Evidently, Christian maturity is contrasted with the elementary doctrine of Christ in 6:1. For this reason, it is reasonable to consider that the phrases "the beginning principles of the word of God" in 5:12 and "the beginning teaching about Christ" in 6:1 are synonymous to each other in meaning.

Then what is the content of the elementary doctrine of Christ? The grammatical construction of 6:1 suggests that the six elements described in 6:1b–2 are further descriptions of the elementary doctrine of Christ mentioned in 6:1a. The main verb φερώμεθα (let us move on) in 6:1 is accompanied by two adverbial participles, ἀφέντες (having left) and καταβαλλόμενοι (laying down). These participles are parallel in thought because the expression "not laying again the foundation of repentance from dead works and of faith upon God, teaching on baptisms and laying on of hands, resurrection of the dead and eternal judgment" is a further description of the phrase "having left the elementary doctrine of Christ" in 6:1a. [36]

It is true that the author of Hebrews does not express faith in terms of "faith in Christ" or "believing in Jesus." However, this does not necessarily mean that 6:1b–2 has no reference to Christ. The discussion of the phrases "the beginning principles about the word of God" and "the beginning teaching about Christ" clearly demonstrates that they refer to the fundamental doctrines of Christ which the readers received when they were first introduced to Christianity. In this sense, it may be said that Christ is construed as the object and the content of Christian faith in Hebrews even if the author does not use the phrase "faith in Christ."

[36] For a different view see Adams, "Exegesis of Hebrews vi.1f.," 379–80. Adams argues that the six items mentioned in 6:1b–2 do not have any reference to Christianity, but they are part of the faith of Jews. The reason is that there is no reference to phrases such as "faith in Christ" or "believe on the Lord Jesus Christ." He asserts that the author's use of "faith in God" in 6:1 is the proof that it is the faith held commonly by Jews, and not by Christians.

Next, the Christological reference to faith in 5:11–6:20 can also be detected from the warning passage in 6:4–8. In order to determine the relationship between faith and Christology, a detailed study of 6:4–8 is necessary. To begin with, the complex sentence structure of 6:4–6 can be visualized as follows:[37]

6·4 'Αδύνατον γὰρ (For it is impossible)
    τοὺς ἅπαξ (1) φωτισθέντας (those who have been enlightened once)
    (2) γευσαμένους τε τῆς δωρεᾶς τῆς ἐπουρανίου (and those who have tasted of the heavenly gift)
    καὶ
    (3) μετόχους γενηθέντας πνεύματος ἁγίου (and those who have become partakers of the Holy Spirit)
6·5   καὶ
    (4) καλὸν γευσαμένους θεοῦ ῥῆμα δυνάμεις τε μέλλοντος αἰῶνος (and those who have tasted good word of God and the powers of age to come)
6·6   καὶ
    (5) παραπεσόντας (and those who have fallen away),

πάλιν ἀνακαινίζειν εἰς μετάνοιαν (to renew again to repentance [i.e., those who are mentioned above]),
    (6) ἀνασταυροῦντας ἑαυτοῖς τὸν υἱὸν τοῦ θεοῦ (because they crucify again the son of God against themselves)
    καὶ
    (7) παραδειγματίζοντας (and because they publicly put [him] to shame).

The above structural layout reveals that ἀνακαινίζειν in verse 6 functions as an epexegetical infinitive to the adjective 'Αδύνατον (i.e., "it is impossible to renew"). The participles in (1) through (5) ought to be classified as substantival participles because they are introduced by the article τούς and connected to each other by a simple connective series, τε . . . καὶ . . . καὶ . . . καί.[38] Some English translations regard παραπεσόντας (having fallen away) in (5) as an adverbial participle,

<hr/>

[37] I have supplied my own translation of this passage for a better understanding of the text. I have intentionally used redundant phrases with an attempt to bring out the author's intent.

[38] J. A. Sproule, "Παραπεσόντας in Hebrews 6:6." *Grace Theological Journal* 2 (1981): 328.

rendering it as a conditional sentence.[39] However, the above structure clearly shows that the fifth participle is also governed by the article τοὺς, and therefore, it should be taken as a substantival participle. These participles, as accusatives, function as direct objects of the infinitive ἀνακαινίζειν (to renew). As for the participles in (6) and (7), they are to be categorized as adverbial participles, both expressing the cause for the impossibility of renewing to repentance.

Then what evidence does the author provide in 6:4–8 which may support the idea that Jesus is considered the object of faith in Hebrews? An examination of this passage indicates that the warning against the apostates itself points to Jesus as the object of faith. This may be observed from the following aspects: (1) the characteristics of the apostates; (2) the impossibility of repentance by the apostates, and (3) the consequences for the apostates.

1. The characteristics of the apostates. The above grammatical analysis shows that those who are impossible to be renewed to repentance have four characteristics.[40] First, according to verse 4, they are the ones who have been enlightened once (ἅπαξ φωτισθέντας). Conzelmann suggests that, although not fully developed, the word is used in Hebrews to refer to baptism.[41] Likewise, Käsemann asserts that with the adverb ἅπαξ (once) the participle φωτισθέντες (having been enlightened) in 6:4 *"is related to a concrete action that can only be Baptism."*[42] However, the use of the term φωτίζειν (to enlighten) in Hebrews suggests that it refers to the spiritual enlightenment associated with salvation. In Hebrews the word occurs twice (6:4; 10:32). The reference to "the contest of sufferings" described in 10:32–33 indicates that the verb

[39] NIV translates verse 6, "if they fall away." RSV translates it, "if they then commit apostasy." On the other hand, NASB and NRSV translate, "and then have fallen away."

[40] For the purpose of this discussion I have combined (2) and (4) into one category because the same verb γεύομαι is used in both phrases.

[41] Hans Conzelmann, "φῶς κτλ.," in *Theological Dictionary of the New Testament,* ed. Gerhard Friedrich, tr. Geoffrey W. Bromiley (Grand Rapids: William B. Eerdmans Publishing Co., 1974), 9:355.

[42] Ernst Käsemann, *The Wandering People of God: An Investigation of the Letter to the Hebrews,* trans. Roy A. Harrisville and Irving L. Sandberg (Minneapolis: Augsburg Publishing House, 1984), 187.

φωτίζειν in 10:32 is more than simply the ritual of baptism; it has to do with reception of the message of salvation (irrespective of the genuineness of the reception). This is further supported by the phrase "after having received the knowledge the truth" (10:26).[43] In other words "having been enlightened" (10:32) is equated to having received the knowledge of the truth (10:26). Likewise, in 6:4 the use of φωτίζειν (to enlighten) along with the idea of "having tasted the heavenly gifts and the good word of God" (6:4, 5) and "having been made partakers of the Holy Spirit" (6:4) suggests that it implies a deeper spiritual teaching after initial enlightenment. Thus it seems clear that the word φωτίζειν does not refer to the baptismal ritual, but the reception of the knowledge of salvation.[44]

The second characteristic of those who are impossible to be renewed for repentance is described as having tasted (γευσαμένους) the heavenly gift (6:4) and the good word of God and the world to come (6:5).[45] The word "to taste" (γεύομαι) occurs 15 times in the New Testament (12 times outside Hebrews; 3 times in Hebrews). The usage outside of Hebrews can be divided into two categories. First, the word has the meaning of "experiencing" in a metaphorical sense (e.g., Matt 16:28; Mark 9:1; Luke 9:27; John 8:52; 1 Pet 2:3). Second, it is used in a physical sense to refer to "tasting slightly" (e.g., Matt 27:34; John 2:9) or "eating" in the sense of ingesting (Luke 14:24; Acts 10:10; 20:1; 23:14; Col 2:21). In Hebrews the verb γεύομαι is used to mean, "to taste" in a metaphorical sense. The issue at stake in Hebrews 6:4–6 is whether the author of Hebrews uses the word "to taste" in the sense of "tasting slightly" or "ingesting fully." Nicole argues that in 6:4–5 the word refers to taking a small amount of food or drink to determine whether it is suitable.[46] He suggests that the term is used in the sense of making a trial or

43 Ellingworth, *The Epistle to the Hebrews*, 320.

44 With the expression "reception of the knowledge of salvation" I am not suggesting that these individuals had a genuine conversion experience. I believe that it is possible for someone to come to the point of receiving the knowledge of salvation without necessarily going through a genuine conversion experience.

45 I have decided to discuss the characteristics mentioned in vv. 4–5 as one category because γεύομαι (to taste) occurs in both verses.

46 R. Nicole, "Some Comments on Hebrews 6:4–6 and the Doctrine of the Perseverance of God with the Saints," in *Current Issues in Biblical and Patristic Interpreta-*

experiment. However, the author's use of the term seems to imply more than a simple tasting. For example, in 2:9 the author mentions that Jesus tasted death for all. This does not mean that Jesus had a near death experience, but he experienced death in its entirety. Moreover, the spiritual experiences of those who are described in 6:4–6 indicates that the tasting is not a superficial, but an authentic one. The author indicates in verse 4 that these individuals have tasted the "heavenly gift" which is an image for the salvation bestowed in Christ.[47] In addition, in verse 6, they are described as having tasted "the good word of God" and "the power of the age to come." The former recalls God's word, which is so prominent in the first four chapters of Hebrews. The latter recalls the manner in which the message of salvation was confirmed among the readers (2:4).[48]

The above analysis clearly suggests that γεύομαι in verse 4–5 does not means "to eat" (or "to drink") for the purpose of merely "tasting," but "to experience to the full."[49] Apparently, the individuals mentioned in these verses have tasted in full the knowledge of salvation which was available to them through faith in Jesus Christ.[50] Thus it may be said that the verb "tasting" signifies an experience that is real and personal.[51]

The third characteristic of those who are impossible to be renewed for repentance is that they have become partakers of the Holy Spirit (v. 4). Lane suggests that the Holy Spirit has to do with the heavenly gift (namely, the reality of personal salvation) mentioned earlier.[52] However,

---

tion, ed. G. F. Hawthorne (Grand Rapids: William B. Eerdmans Publishing Co., 1975), 360.

[47] O. Michel, *Der Brief an die Hebräer,* 12th ed. (Göttingen: Vanderhoeck and Ruprecht, 1966), 242.

[48] Attridge, *The Epistle to the Hebrews,* 170.

[49] Ellingworth, *The Epistle to the Hebrews,* 320.

[50] The context of 6:4–8 implies that these people willfully rejected salvation in light of the privilege of having tasted the knowledge of salvation in full. This refers to the sin of deliberate rejection of Christ after receiving the knowledge of truth mentioned in 10:26.

[51] P. E. Hughes, "Hebrews 6:4–6 and the Peril of Apostasy," *Westminster Theological Journal* 35 (1972–73): 141.

[52] Lane, *Hebrews 1–8,* 141.

the conjunctions in vv. 4–6 (τε . . . καὶ . . . καὶ . . . καί) indicate that the descriptions of the individuals in these verses are to be considered different characteristics of the apostates. This means that "partaking of the Holy Spirit" cannot be equated with the "heavenly gift." These people tasted not only the heavenly gift, but also became partakers of the Holy Spirit.

Then in what sense were they partakers of the Holy Spirit? It appears that the partaking has to do with the distribution of the spiritual gifts. In Hebrews 2:4 the author indicates that the distribution of the Holy Spirit is one of the ways that God confirmed the message which was spoken by the Lord and by those who heard from him. In other words, the distribution of the Holy Spirit was regarded as the mark of the Christian community.[53] This leads one to speculate the possibility that these individuals were closely associated with the believing community. The expression "partakers of the Holy Spirit" does not necessarily mean that they have received the Holy Spirit as true believers do. They were partakers in a sense that they have witnessed the confirmation of the gospel which was accompanied by the distribution of the Holy Spirit. Moreover, the phrase "partakers of the Holy Spirit" may also refer to the benefits they had received from the ministry of the apostles which were accompanied by signs and wonders and various miracles.

The fourth characteristic of those who are impossible to be renewed to repentance is that they have fallen away (παραπεσόντας), even though they had such great spiritual blessings (v. 5). The word παραπίπτω appears only here in the New Testament, and therefore, it is difficult to ascertain its exact meaning. However, in the Septuagint the word is used to refer to a culpable mistake or sin.[54] The verb is used to express an attitude reflecting deliberate rejection of God (Ezek 14:13; 15:8; 18:24; 20:27; 2 Chr 26:18; 28:19; 29:6; 30:7; Wis 6:9; 12:2). This idea is carried over to Hebrews and clearly means either to fall away or commit apostasy, which is equivalent to "falling away from the living God" (ἀποστῆναι ἀπὸ θεοῦ ζῶντος) in 3:12.

---

[53] Attridge, *The Epistle to the Hebrews,* 170.

[54] W. Michaelis, "παραπίπτω, παράπτωμα," in *Theological Dictionary of the New Testament,* ed. Gerhard Friedrich, tr. Geoffrey W. Bromiley (Grand Rapids: William B. Eerdmans Publishing Co., 1968), 6:170.

120										CHAPTER FIVE

The analysis of the characteristics of the apostates indicates that they are the ones who deliberately rebelled against God, and chose not to believe after they had been enlightened by the word of God. Hughes expresses this point well, "it is a sin committed, not in ignorance, but in the face of knowledge and even experience of the truth—not the sin of those who are 'ignorant and wayward' (5:2) but of those who 'sin deliberately after receiving the knowledge of the truth (10:26).'"[55] These characteristics suggest that the warning in 6:4–8 has a soteriological significance.[56]

2. *The impossibility of repentance by the apostates*. The author points out that, for these apostates, there is no possibility of being restored to repentance (6:6).[57] What is the reason for this impossibility? It is explained by two participles following the infinitive "to renew" (ἀνακαινίζειν). The first reason for the impossibility is indicated by the

55 P. E. Hughes, "Hebrews 6:4–6 and the Peril of Apostasy," 148.

56 The issue of whether those who are mentioned in Heb 6:4–6 are genuine believers or not is indeed a difficult matter to resolve. I tend to hold that this passage refers to those individuals who were only professing believers (i.e., those who did not have a genuine conversion experience). It appears that they have been brought to a place of repentance for salvation. They were enlightened by receiving the knowledge of truth. But instead of placing their faith in Christ, they willfully rejected the salvation in Christ (cf. Heb. 10:29). If one understands the warning passages in Hebrews this way, then the sin of the apostates may be similar to that of the blasphemy against the Holy Spirit in the Gospels (i.e., the willful rejection of Jesus as the Messiah [cf. Matt 12:32; Mark 3:29]) and the sins committed by the false prophets in 2 Peter 2:20–22. I chose not to discuss different views on the warning passages because of space limitations. *For the view that it refers to professing believers see* P. E. Hughes, "Hebrews 6:4–6 and the Peril of Apostasy," 137–55; Nicole, "Some Comments on Hebrews 6:4–6," 355–364; Stanley D. Toussaint, "The Eschatology of the Warning Passages in the Book of Hebrews," *Grace Theological Journal* 3 (1982): 67–80; *For the view that it refers to genuine Christians who will lose their reward see* J. B. Rowell, "Exposition of Hebrews Six: 'An Age-Long Battleground'" *Bibliotheca Sacra* 94 (1937): 321–42; T. K. Oberholtzer, "The Warning Passages in Hebrews. Part 3 (of 5 parts): The Thorn-Infested Ground in Hebrews 6:4–12," *Bibliotheca Sacra* 145 (1988): 319–28; Randall C. Gleason, "The Old Testament Background of the Warning in Hebrews 6:4–8," *Bibliotheca Sacra* 155 (1998): 62–91.

57 It is sometimes asked how a person can become an apostate if he/she was not a believer from the beginning. It appears that the word has to do with the perception of a person by other believers. In 6:4–6, these individuals are described as the apostates (i.e., those who have fallen away) because other believers including the author assumed that they were part of the believing community, but their action showed that they were not. In this sense the word "apostates" is used.

participle ἀνασταυροῦντας. The verb ἀνασταυρόω occurs only here in the New Testament. In extra-biblical Greek, the prefix ἀνά, when used with the verb σταυρόω, does not have the sense of "again" but "up." Thus the word ἀνασταυρόω simply means "to crucify."⁵⁸ For this reason some commentators suggest that the word in 6:6 simply has the meaning of "to crucify."⁵⁹ However, an examination of the context suggests that ἀνασταυρόω means "to crucify again." One may observe that the emphasis of 6:1–6 is on the word πάλιν (again). This word is used in 6:1 to warn the readers not to lay the foundation again (πάλιν) of the elementary teaching concerning Christ. In 6:6 the author also indicates that it is impossible for these apostates to be restored again (πάλιν) to repentance. Moreover, the characteristics of the apostates described in 6:4–6 presuppose that they had come to have the knowledge of the crucified Lord. Thus it is reasonable to understand ἀνασταυρόω as "to crucify again."

The second reason for the impossibility of renewal for those apostates is expressed by the second participle παραδειγματίζοντας. This verb, which occurs only here in the New Testament, means "to expose to public obloquy."⁶⁰ In other words, the author of Hebrews indicates that the apostates expose the Son of God to public humiliation by rejecting him. Verse 6 implies that those who forsake their faith in Jesus Christ "in reality join forces with those who crucified Christ and brought him into contempt as criminal. Thus apostasy is tantamount to shaming Christ, and therefore brings such serious results."⁶¹ It is clear that the reasons for the impossibility of repentance by the apostates have to do with the rejection of Christ himself. In this sense, faith in Hebrews is as Christological as that of the Synoptic Gospels and the Pauline writings. The author of Hebrews clearly portrays Jesus as the object of faith through unbelief by the apostates.

⁵⁸ Josephus *Vit.* 420; *Bell.* 2:306; 5:449; *Ant.* 2:73; 11:246.

⁵⁹ For example, Moffatt, *Hebrews,* 79; Attridge, *The Epistle to the Hebrews,* 171.

⁶⁰ H. Schlier, "παραδειγματίζω," *Theological Dictionary of the New Testament,* ed. Gerhard Kittel, tr. Geoffrey W. Bromiley (Grand Rapids: William B. Eerdmans Publishing Co., 1964), 2:32.

⁶¹ A. Mugridge, "Warnings in the Epistle to the Hebrews: An Exegetical and Theological Study," *Reformed Theological Review* 46 (1987): 77.

3. The consequences for the apostates. The warning against the apostasy is further illustrated in 6:7–8. The sentence structure of these verses may be diagrammed as follows:[62]

6·7   γῆ γὰρ ἡ (1) πιοῦσα τὸν ἐπ' αὐτῆς ἐρχόμενον πολλάκις ὑετόν (for the ground that drinks the rain which often falls upon it)
καὶ
(2) τίκτουσα βοτάνην εὔθετον ἐκείνοις δι' οὓς καὶ γεωργεῖται (and brings forth vegetation useful to those for whose sake it is also tilled),
μεταλαμβάνει εὐλογίας ἀπὸ τοῦ θεοῦ ([the ground] receives a blessing from God).

6·8   ἐκφέρουσα δὲ ἀκάνθας καὶ τριβόλους (but if it yields thorns and thistles),
ἀδόκιμος καὶ κατάρας ἐγγύς, ἧς τὸ τέλος εἰς καῦσιν (it is worthless and close to being cursed, and it ends up being burned).

In this diagram one can see that the subject of both v. 7 and v. 8 is γῆ (ground). The contrast here is between the land which is fruitful and the land which is unfruitful (i.e., blessing vs. curse). In these verses the author of Hebrews employs an agricultural parable to speak of the fate of those who fall away. The descriptions of the apostates as having produced "thorns" and "thistles," and their fate being "worthless" and "cursed" and "burned" clearly indicate what God will do with the apostates. That vv. 7–8 is related to vv. 4–6 is evident from the author's use of γάρ in v. 7, which shows that it is a further description of the consequences for the apostates. The final outcome of re-crucifying Christ by apostasy is burning in the fire in the eschatological sense. The author of Hebrews expresses himself with such a stern warning to plead with his readers not to abandon Christ.[63]

The description of the characteristics of the apostates, the impossibility of renewing the apostates to repentance, and the severity of the judgment against the apostates indicate that faith, in Hebrews, is highly Christological. In this passage (6:7–8) the idea of faith in Jesus is expressed in negative terms. Just as the act of unbelief (or deliberate rejection) by people caused Jesus to be crucified according to the Gospels, so

---

[62] The translation of Greek text is based on the NASB with a slight modification.

[63] R. Williamson, *Philo and the Epistle to the Hebrews* (Leiden: E. J. Brill, 1970), 246.

the act of apostasy among some members of the Christian community of Hebrews will cause Jesus to be crucified again. This exegetical finding certainly supports my contention that the author of Hebrews considered Jesus as the object and the content of faith.

Lastly, the Christological aspect of faith can be noticed from faith's relationship to the word of God.[64] In 6:13–20 the idea of Jesus being the object of faith is depicted in terms of the word of God. In this passage the author relates God's oath to fulfill his promises to believers' steadfastness to hold on to the promise of God. At this point it seems appropriate to bring out the author's emphasis on steadfastness. In 6:12 the author exhorts the readers not to become dull but become imitators of those who through faith and patience (διὰ πίστεως καὶ μακρπθυμίας) inherit the promises. The particle καί in 6:12 may be used epexegetically and be translated "faith, that is, patience."[65] Or, it could be an example of hendiadys, meaning, "persevering faith."[66] In either case "faith" and "perseverance" are related to each other and μακροθυμία brings out an aspect of what faith is. This idea can be supported from the use of μακροθυμέω (to wait patiently) in 6:15. For the author of Hebrews, faith involves perseverance or steadfastness.

In order to demonstrate the persevering aspect of faith, the author of Hebrews employs Abraham's example of steadfastness in verses 13–15 to show that Abraham obtained the promise of God by waiting for it patiently (μακροθυμήσας). The reference to "obtaining the promise" in 6:15 is more likely to refer to Abraham's receiving back of Isaac from the "dead" in the land of Moriah (Gen 22) rather than to the birth of Isaac. A comparison of the citation in 6:15 with the Septuagint's translation of Gen 22:17 shows that the author of Hebrews closely follows

---

[64] I am fully aware that this is a less obvious point than the previous ones I discussed to argue for the Christological aspect of faith. However, I find that the author of Hebrews implicitly sets forth the Christological aspect of faith by the concept of the word of God.

[65] James H. Moulton, *A Grammar of New Testament Greek*, vol. 3, *Syntax*, by Niegel Turner (Edinburgh: T. & T. Clark, 1963), 335.

[66] Grässer, *Der Glaube im Hebräerbrief*, 28; Ellingworth, *The Epistle to the Hebrews*, 333.

the LXX version of Gen 22:17.[67] Moreover, the description of "God swearing by himself" in 6:13 corresponds to Genesis 22:16 rather than God's initial promise in Genesis 12. Thus the author's point is that Abraham reaffirmed the divine approval by waiting patiently for God's promise.

Then what was Abraham's object of faith? The context indicates that it was his faith in God's promise. The notion of God swearing by himself signifies that he is bound to his word by his character and provides the guarantee that excludes doubt and affirms the abiding validity of the promise.[68] Thus Abraham's belief was in the God who was able to fulfill what he had promised, specifically, what he had promised him (i.e., to Abraham). In other words, Abraham's behavior of steadfastness itself is an indicator of a responsiveness to God and to his word.[69] In this sense, it can be said that the promise of God and his faithfulness to keep his word were the very object of Abraham's faith (cf. Rom 4:20–21). Putting it another way, Abraham's faith was faith in God himself.

Here in this passage faith is expressed in terms of believing in God's promise and his ability to fulfill it. It has also been observed from the previous discussion that the author uses the expressions "oracles of God" (5:12) and "faith toward God" (6:1) in place of the expressions, such as "faith in Jesus Christ" and "trust in Jesus." Do these expressions necessarily warrant that faith in Hebrews is removed from Christ and his work? In what ways are these phrases related to the Christological aspect of faith? These questions can be answered in two ways.

First, an examination of other New Testament writings shows that describing the Christian faith in terms of faith in God is not unique to the author of Hebrews. This idea is also used by other authors of Scriptures to refer to an acceptance of Christian proclamation. For example, in 1 Thessalonians 1:8 the conversion of the Thessalonians is described in terms of "faith in God" (πίστις πρὸς τὸν θεόν). This faith in God is further elaborated in verses 9–10 as "turning from idols to serve a living and true God (v. 9) and "waiting for his Son (i.e., Jesus) from heaven (v.

---

[67] Swetnam, *Jesus and Isaac*, 184. Attridge observes that the author follows Genesis 22:17 with a slight modification (*The Epistle to the Hebrews*, 179).

[68] Lane, *Hebrews 1–8*, 151.

[69] G. R. Hughes, *Hebrews and Hermeneutics*, Society for New Testament Studies Monograph Series, vol. 36 (Cambridge: Cambridge University Press, 1979), 79.

10)." Likewise, in Acts 20:21, Luke uses "repentance toward God" and "faith in our Lord Jesus" side by side (see also 1 Pet 1:21). Thus it is evident that the idea of "faith in God" can be a synonymous phrase for "faith in Jesus Christ." Bultmann succinctly states this point as follows:

> Whereas in the OT and Judaism (except in propaganda) faith is required as the appropriate attitude to the God who has long since made Himself known as whose existence cannot be doubted, the primitive Christian kerygma brings the message that there is one God, and with this it also brings the message about Jesus Christ His Son, and about what God has done and will do through Him. Acceptance of this kerygma is πιστεύειν.[70]

Second, the context of Hebrews 5:11–6:8 plainly indicates that the description of faith in terms of faith in God or God's promise is none other than faith in Christ himself. It may be recalled from the previous discussion of 5:11–6:2 that the phrase "the beginning principles about the oracles of God" (5:12) is identical to "the elementary doctrine of Christ" (6:1). Moreover, it was also revealed that the six elements described in 6:2–4 are a further elaboration of the elementary doctrine of Christ in 6:1a. In this sense, the author's description of "faith toward God" in 6:1 is to be regarded as "faith in Christ." Furthermore, a careful exegesis of 6:4–6 makes it evident that the author's concept of faith is related to Christ. I have already pointed out in the previous discussion that the characteristics of these apostates have to do with the rejection of Christ. More specifically, by the author's use of the two participial clauses in 6:6—the crucifying again of the Son of God and the putting of him to open shame—the author intends the readers to understand that the phrase "having tasted the good word of God" in 6:5 has Christological implications. For this reason rejecting the word of God may be equated to rejecting the salvific work of Christ. Thus it may be concluded that, for the author of Hebrews, having God or God's words as the object of faith is equivalent to having Jesus as the object of faith.

In summary, the above analysis shows the evidence that faith in Hebrews is not removed from Christ; it has Jesus as the object of faith as in the Pauline epistles. For the author of Hebrews "the beginning principles

---

[70] Rudolf Bultmann, "Πιστεύω κτλ.," in *Theological Dictionary of the New Testament,* ed. Gerhard Kittel and Gerhard Friedrich, tr. Geoffrey W. Bromiley (Grand Rapids: William B. Eerdmans Publishing Co., 1968), 6:174–228.

of the word of God" is another way of stating "the beginning teaching about Christ." The characteristics and consequences of the apostates indicate they are the ones who deliberately reject Christ. The author's expressions of "the word of God" and "faith toward God" are equivalent to "faith in Christ." In this sense, faith in Hebrews is Christologically oriented.

Christ as the Model of Faith

An examination of Hebrews 5:11–6:20 also reveals that Jesus is construed not only as the object of faith, but also as the model of faith. Again, going back to 6:11–12, the author of Hebrews admonishes the readers to demonstrate the same eagerness in the work and the love which they showed by serving the saints (v. 11). The purpose of this exhortation is indicated by the ἵνα clause in verse 12: "that you may not be sluggish, but imitators of those who through faith and perseverance inherit the promises."[71] The concept of imitating faith runs throughout 6:12–20. It has already been revealed from the discussion of "faith's relationship to the word of God" that the purpose of 6:13–15 is to illustrate that Abraham is one of those who inherited the promises by faith and perseverance. Another purpose for the inclusion of the illustration about Abraham in 6:13–15 may be that the author wants the readers also to imitate the steadfastness of Abraham. This idea is supported by the argument in 6:17–18. These verses continue with the discussion of the irrevocable nature of God's oath which he spoke in Genesis 22:16–17. However, the emphasis is on Christians who are designated as the heirs of the promise.[72] The purpose of God intervening with an oath is for believers to have strong encouragement to hold fast the hope that lies ahead of them (v. 18). In other words, the reason why the author of Hebrews connects 6:13–15 and 6:16–18 with the theme of an oath is to show the need for believers to imitate Abraham's persevering faith. As Lane states, "the unchanging purpose of God provides a strong reason for emulating the trust and steadfastness of Abraham."[73]

---

[71] NASB translation.

[72] Lane, *Hebrews 1–8*, 152.

[73] Ibid.

Then how does the emulation of Abraham's faith relate to the believers' imitation of Christ? This relationship may be observed from the link between 6:18 and 6:19. In 6:18 the author mentions that believers have fled for safety to lay hold of the hope set before them. The idea of hope goes back to Abraham's faith in waiting patiently for God's promise, as seen in 6:13–15. As Abraham hoped for what God had promised him, so do the believers in the new covenant hope for that which is set before them. What is the believers' hope? It is explained in 6:19. In this verse the relative pronoun ἥν (which) takes ἐλπίς (hope) as its antecedent, which in turn is related to εἰσερχομένην (i.e., one which enters). This may be illustrated as follows:[74]

6·18   κρατῆσαι τῆς προκειμένης ἐλπίδος· (to lay hold of the hope set before us)
6·19   ἥν ὡς ἄγκυραν ἔχομεν τῆς ψυχῆς ἀσφαλῆ
        τε καὶ βεβαίαν (which we have as an
        anchor of the soul, both sure and steadfast)
        καὶ
        εἰσερχομένην εἰς τὸ ἐσώτερον τοῦ καταπε-
        πετάσματος (one which enters within the veil).

This diagram allows one to see that it is hope that enters within the curtain in the heavenly sanctuary where Jesus has already entered as forerunner by becoming a high priest according to the order of Melchizedek.[75] The implication is that hope penetrates behind the curtain and it is by this hope that we believers draw near to God (7:19).[76] The word πρόδρομος is used only here in the New Testament. In classical Greek the term was used in the sense of going before by running.[77] Apparently, the author of Hebrews has this sense in mind in 6:20. In the present context the term has the idea that Jesus is the model of faith for his followers. Thus the author's exhortation to have strong encourage-

---

[74] The translation is a slight variation of NASB.

[75] Grammatically speaking, it is possible to take the antecedent of the participle εἰσερχομένην as ἄγκυραν. If this is what the author had in mind, then v. 19 is to be translated "the anchor which enters within the veil." This is the view held by Attridge (see Attridge, *The Epistle to the Hebrews*, 178, 183–84). On the other hand, Lane prefers to take ἐλπίδος (hope) as the antecedent of εἰσερχομένην (Lane, *Hebrews 1–8*, 153).

[76] Lane, *Hebrews 1–8*, 153–54

[77] Herodotus 7.203; 9.14; Polybius, *Hist.* 12.20.7.

ment to hold fast (κρατέω) this hope (v. 18b) suggests that believers ought to imitate the act of Jesus in entering inside of the curtain. It is also to be noted that the author uses the verb εἰσέρχομαι (to enter) both in verses 19 and 20. However, the author uses the aorist tense with reference to Jesus (εἰσῆλθεν), but the present tense with reference to believers (εἰσερχομένην). The implication is clear: "in hope, believers may now enter where Jesus has already entered in reality, namely, into the heavenly sanctuary."[78] Thus the author's exhortation to follow the steadfastness of Abraham is equivalent to having persistent faith in Christ. In the author's mind imitating those who inherit the promises (6:12) is equivalent to imitating Christ. In this sense, in Hebrews Jesus is to be considered the model of faith for which believers ought to emulate.

Summary and Conclusion

A careful examination of 5:1–6:20 reveals that faith in Hebrews is very much Christological. The concept of faith in Hebrews is not to be defined solely in terms of Jesus being the model and enabler of faith as Hamm suggests. In Hebrews Jesus is also portrayed as the object of faith for believers. Phrases such as "the beginning principles of the word of God" in 5:12 and "the beginning teaching about Christ" in 6:1 suggest that Christ is the content (or the object) of faith. Moreover, in the analysis of 6:4–8, the characteristics of those who fall away, the reasons for their impossibility to be renewed again, and the final consequence of the apostates clearly indicate that the initial faith of the apostates has to do with faith in Jesus. Thus it can be said that the concept of faith expressed in 6:4–8 is parallel to Paul's idea of trusting Jesus as one's Savior. This passage also demonstrates that Jesus is the model of faith for believers as Hamm has correctly pointed out. The author of Hebrews depicts Jesus as being the model of faith in two ways: (1) by exhorting the readers to imitate Abraham's trust and his steadfastness (note: following the example of Abraham is equivalent to believing in the promise of God, which, in turn, is also identical to persevering faith in Jesus) and (2) by reminding the readers that Jesus is our forerunner (πρόδρομος) who en-

---

[78] Ellingworth, *The Epistle to the Hebrews,* 347.

tered inside the curtain. The author exhorts the readers to enter the curtain, as Jesus did.

As for the characteristics of faith, the author shows that faith involves the quality of steadfastness. However, unlike Grässer's contention, this quality of faith is not merely an ethical element; it is based on the attributes of God (i.e., God is not unjust to forget your work and the love which you showed . . . [6:10]) and on the promise of God. The apostle Paul, moreover, also uses this aspect of faith to refer to Christian faith. Therefore, it may be concluded that faith in 5:1–6:20 is based on Christology. In Hebrews, Jesus is regarded both as the object and the model of faith for believers.

CHAPTER SIX

RELATIONSHIP BETWEEN 7:1–10:18 AND 10:19–39:
SUPERIOR HIGH PRIEST AND THE WARNING NOT TO LIVE IN SIN

In the long doctrinal section of 7:1–10:18 the author emphasizes the doctrine of the high priesthood of Jesus, which is one of the dominant themes that runs through the book of Hebrews.[1] This theme was implied already in 1:3 with the phrase "after having made purification of sins" and officially announced in 2:17: Jesus had to be like his brethren in all respects, in order that he may become a merciful and faithful high priest. These two aspects of Christ's high priesthood are further developed in 3:1–5:10 in reverse order: a faithful high priest (3:1–6) and a merciful high priest (4:14–5:10). Then in 6:20 the theme of the high priesthood of Christ is again announced. This verse notes that Jesus went inside the curtain by having become a high priest after the order of Melchizedek. In 7:1–10:18 the author delineates this theme in great detail. The explanatory particle γάρ in 7:1 indicates that he intends to conclude the long parenetic section of 5:11–6:20 and resume the discussion of the high priesthood of Christ.[2] The emphasis of this doctrinal section is to make a contrast between Christ's high priesthood after the order of Melchizedek and the levitical high priesthood.[3] The author employs this

---

[1] This is evident from the occurrences of the words ἀρχιερεύς and ἱερεύς. The word ἀρχιερεύς occurs 17 times in Hebrews. Eleven times it is used to refer to Christ (2:17; 3:1; 4:14; 4:15; 5:1; 5:5; 5:10; 6:20; 7:26; 8:1; 9:11; 9:25; 13:11); six times, to refer to the levitical high priests (7:27; 7:28; 8:3; 9:7; 9:25). The word ἱερεύς is used 14 times in Hebrews. It is used twice in reference to Melchizedek (7:1; 7:3); six times, in reference to the levitical priesthood (7:11; 7:14; 7:20; 7:23; 9:6; 10:11); six times, in reference to Christ (7:15; 7:17; 7:21[x2]; 8:4; 10:21).

[2] B. F. Westcott, *The Epistle to the Hebrews: A Historical and Theological Reconsideration* (London: Macmillan, 1889), 170.

[3] William L. Lane, *Hebrews 1–8*, Word Biblical Commentary (Dallas: Word Books, 1991), 111.

Christological teaching on high priesthood to discuss what faith entails in the parenetic section (10:19–39).

It has already been made evident from the previous chapters that faith in Hebrews is Christologically oriented (i.e., Jesus is viewed as the object and the model of faith). In this chapter I will continue to examine 7:1–10:18 and 10:19–39 to establish the relationship between Christology and the concept of faith. In each section I will establish the basis for the literary unit, followed by the discussion of the Christological teaching.

Examination of the Doctrinal Section (7:1–10:18)

Basis for the Literary Unit

The unity of the doctrinal section 7:1–10:18 is evident from both the structural clues and the conceptual ideas. An observation of Hebrews 7 reveals that it is divided into two major parts by inclusion. The first part (7:1–10) forms a unit by the name "Melchizedek" in verse 1 and 10. The unity of the second part (7:11–28) is indicated by the noun "perfection" (τελείωσις) in verse 11 and the verb "to perfect" (τελειόω) in verse 28.[4] These two main sections are connected by the particle οὖν, which shows that the author draws an inference from 7:1–10 that the high priesthood after the order of Melchizedek would not be necessary if perfection is through the levitical high priesthood. Moreover, an inclusion by ἱερεύς (priest) in verse 1 and ἀρχιερεύς (high priest) in verse 28 suggests that the entire section of chapter 7 is to be considered a unit.[5]

It may be noted that 7:26 uses the expression "such a high priest" (τοιοῦντος . . . ἀρχιερεύς). This is the announcement of what he will develop in chapter 8. In fact, the author employs the same phrase in 8:1 (τοιοῦτον ἔχομεν ἀρχιερέα). In addition, the detailed themes of chapter 8 are also announced in 7:27–28. In these verses the author compares the sacrifices between the heavenly high priest and the earthly

---

[4] Albert Vanhoye, *La structure littéraire de l'Épître aux Hébreux* (Paris: Desclée de Brouwer, 1976), 240; John W. Welch, "Chiasmus in the New Testament," in *Chiasmus in Antiquity: Structures, Analyses, Exegesis*, ed. John W. Welch (Hildesheim: Gerstenberg Verlag, 1981), 125.

[5] Albert Vanhoye, *Structure and Message of the Epistle to the Hebrews*, Subsidia Biblica, vol. 12 (Roma: Editrice Pontificio Istituto Biblico, 1989), 21.

high priests (v. 27) and the different appointment system of the high priest (v. 28).[6] In chapter 8 these ideas are further developed; the former is expressed in verses 2–5 and the latter in verses 6–13.

In what ways, then, are chapter 8 and 9 related to each other? To begin with, in 8:1–2 the author makes a transition between 7:1–28 and 8:3–9:28 by citing the main point of 7:1–10:18 (i.e., we have this high priest who has sat in the right hand of the throne of the Majesty in heaven). This main point then is connected to 8:3 by the explanatory γάρ. Then the author employs another inclusion by the verb προσφέρω (to offer) in 8:3 and 9:28 to indicate that the entire section of chapter 8 and 9 ought to be regarded as a unit.[7] Moreover, the conceptual idea between 8:1 and 9:28 suggests that 8:1–9:28 should be treated as a unit. First, in 8:3 the author states that every high priest is appointed to offer gifts and sacrifices. He closes this thought in 9:28 by describing that Christ, after having been offered once to bear the sins of many, will appear a second time. Next, the conceptual unity is also indicated by the overall content of chapter 8 and 9. In 8:1–13 the author presents that Jesus is a priestly minister and the mediator of a better covenant. This prepares for the discussion of the worship system under the old covenant in 9:1–10 and the new covenant in 9:11–28.[8]

The unity of 10:1–18 is made evident by a series of inclusions throughout the passage. First, the inclusion that encircles the entire section of 10:1–18 is marked by the verb προσφέρω (to offer) in verse 1 and the noun προσφόρα (offering) in 10:18. This section is subdivided by either the verb προσφέρω or the noun προσφόρα. For example, 10:1–10 and 10:11–18 form inclusions by the same words.[9] In addition, the conceptual ideas between 10:1 and 10:18 also indicate a unity. The ideas are antithetical to each other in these two verses: on the one hand, 10:1 shows that the same sacrifices are offered continuously under the law; on the other hand, 10:18 states that, where there is forgiveness,

---

[6] James Swetnam, "Form and Content in Hebrews 7–13," *Biblica* 55 (1974): 334. Swetnam describes this idea in terms of Christ's self-sacrifice (v. 27) and fulfillment (v. 28).

[7] Vanhoye, *Structure and Message of the Epistle to the Hebrews*, 38.

[8] Lane, *Hebrews 1–8*, 203.

[9] Vanhoye, *Structure and Message of the Epistle to the Hebrews*, 40.

there is no longer offering for sin.[10] By these two contrasting ideas the author implies that 10:1–18 forms a literary unit. Then what is the relationship between 10:1–18 and the previous section (7:1–9:28, especially 8:1–9:28)? The reappearance of the words from chapter 8 and 9 in 10:1–18 suggests that they are intimately related to each other. For example, the word σκία (shadow) (8:5) is repeated in 10:1. The term νόμος (law) in 10:1 is already used in 9:19 and 22. The phrase τῶν μελλόντων ἀγαθῶν (good things to come) in 10:1 was already mentioned in 9:11 with reference to Christ.[11] Thus it is obvious that 10:1–18 is the continuation of the discussion in 8:1–9:28. Moreover, the Old Testament quotations between the two sections indicate that they form a unit. The allusion to Psalm 110:1 in 8:1, which speaks of the high priest being seated at the right hand of God, is repeated in 10:12–13.[12] In 8:8–12 the author introduces the theme of the new covenant by making a full citation of Jeremiah 31:31–34; in 10:16–17 he quotes the salient portions of that Old Testament passage.[13]

There is one other structural clue which provides the evidence that 8:3–10:18 forms a literary unit. In verse 3 the word προσφέρω (to offer) is used twice. In 10:18 the author uses the noun form προσφορα (offering). This is another example of inclusion which suggests that 8:3–10:18 forms a literary unit. In 8:3 the author emphasizes the necessity of the heavenly high priest to have something to offer. In between 8:3 and 10:18 he describes the differences of the offering between the heavenly high priest and the earthly high priest. In 10:18 the author explicitly states for the first time that the offering is no longer needed. A brief survey of 7:1–10:18 shows that this long section forms a unit both structurally and thematically. This doctrinal section of Jesus as the high priest of the new covenant is the basis for the exhortation in 10:19–39.

Christological Teaching

As mentioned above, the exposition of 7:1–10:18 is the longest section of all the doctrinal and parenetic divisions in the book of Hebrews.

---

[10] Lane, *Hebrews 1–8*, 258.

[11] Vanhoye, *La structure*, 162.

[12] Lane, *Hebrews 1–8*, 257.

[13] Ibid.

Because of the length of the passage, I will not attempt to have a detailed treatment of many issues involving Christology. Instead, I will
highlight the Christological teachings by summarizing the main points
of each chapter. This summary will be the basis for the discussion of the
parenetic section in 10:19–39. The doctrinal section of 7:1–10:18 can be
divided into four subsections: (1) the high priest after the order of Melchizedek (7:1–28); (2) the high priest of the new covenant (8:1–13); (3)
a comparison of the sacrifices between the two covenants (9:1–28); (4)
the perfect sacrifice of the new high priest (10:1–18).

The High Priest after the Order of
Melchizedek (7:1–28)

To begin with, in chapter 7 the author describes the appointment of
the high priesthood of Christ after the order of Melchizedek. This chapter is the continuation of the discussion which has been set forth in
5:10.[14] As described in the discussion of the literary unit, 7:1–28 may be
divided into two main subsections: the greatness of Melchizedek (7:1–
10) and the superiority of the priesthood of Jesus to that of the Levites
(7:11–28).

The greatness of Melchizedek (7:1–10). The first section (7:1–10)
speaks of the characteristics of Melchizedek and his greatness. The description of his characteristics (7:1–3) is based on Abraham's encounter
with Melchizedek in Genesis 14:17–20, in which he is depicted as a king
of righteousness; a king of Salem (namely, of peace); without father,
without mother, without genealogy, having neither beginning of days
nor end of life.[15] In this sense, it can be said that Melchizedek is made
like (ἀφομοιόω) the Son of God (7:3). In other words, although he is not
exactly the Son of God, he is used as an illustration of the high priesthood of Christ in the Old Testament.[16]

---

[14] George H. Guthrie, *The Structure of Hebrews: A Text-Linguistic Analysis,* Supplements to Novum Testamentum 78 (Leiden: E. J. Brill, 1994), 120.

[15] A careful analysis of 7:1–3 reveals that these verses form one sentence. The subject is οὗτος . . . ὁ μελχισέδεκ and the phrase μένει ἱερεὺς εἰς τὸ διηνεκές (he
remains as a high priest forever) completes the sentence. All the other words between
verses 1 and 3 describe the subject (i.e., Melchizedek).

[16] Lane, *Hebrews 1–8,* 166.

In what ways is the greatness of Melchizedek demonstrated in 7:4–10? His greatness is argued for in three ways. Melchizedek is great because: (1) he received tithes from Abraham (7:4, 6); (2) Abraham was blessed by him (7:6; cf. 7:1); and (3) even the Levites paid tithes to him through Abraham (7:4–10). The μέν . . . δέ construction in 7:5–7 shows the contrast between the levitical reception of tithes from the people and Melchizedek's reception of tithes from Abraham. The logical inference is that since Abraham is greater than his descendants, and since Abraham paid tithes to Melchizedek, Melchizedek must be greater than the levitical high priests. This thought is reinforced by another μέν . . . δέ construction in 7:8 (i.e., mortals vs. the one to whom it is testified that he lives). For this reason the author goes as far as stating that the Levites, who received tithes, paid tithes to Melchizedek through Abraham.[17]

Superiority of the high priesthood of Christ (7:11–28). Then what is the purpose of the discussion of Melchizedek in 7:1–10? It appears that the author's intention is to prepare for the argument in the second section (7:11–28), namely, that "the priesthood of Jesus is superior to and supersedes the priesthood of the tribe of Levi."[18] While the author's exposition of 7:1–10 was based on Genesis 14:17–20, 7:11–18 it is largely based on Psalm 110:4.[19] This section (7:11–28) is further divided into two parts: (1) the imperfection of the levitical high priesthood (7:11–19); and (2) the permanence of the high priesthood of Jesus (7:20–28).

An analysis of 7:11–19 indicates that the author employs a chiasm to explain the imperfection of the levitical high priesthood. It can be illustrated as follows:[20]

---

[17] The phrase "so to speak" (ὡς ἔπος εἰπεῖν) in 7:9 indicates that the verse should be understood typologically, not in a literal sense. With this remark, "the author seems to admit the artificiality of his playful exegesis." See Harold W. Attridge, *The Epistle to the Hebrews,* Hermeneia Commentary (Philadelphia: Fortress Press, 1989), 197.

[18] David Peterson, *Hebrews and Perfection: An Examination of the Concept of Perfection in the 'Epistle to the Hebrews,'* Society for New Testament Studies Monograph Series 47 (Cambridge: Cambridge University Press, 1982), 107.

[19] David M. Hay, *Glory at the Right Hand: Psalm 110 in Early Christianity.* Society of Biblical Literature Monograph Series 18 (Nashville: Abingdon, 1973), 146.

[20] The English text is based on NRSV. I have used the full text of the passage without any alteration of verses for the reader to see the chiastic arrangement of the passage.

A   Εἰ μὲν οὖν τελείωσις διὰ τῆς Λευιτικῆς ἱερωσύνης ἦν, ὁ λαὸς γὰρ ἐπ' αὐ-
    τῆς νενομοθέτηται, τίς ἔτι χρεία κατὰ τὴν τάξιν Μελχισέδεκ ἕτερον ἀν-
    ίστασθαι ἱερέα καὶ οὐ κατὰ τὴν τάξιν 'Ααρὼν λέγεσθαι (Now if perfection
    had been attainable through the levitical priesthood—for the people received the
    law under this priesthood—what further need would there have been to speak of
    another priest arising according to the order of Melchizedek, rather than one ac-
    cording to the order of Aaron?) (v. 11)

B   μετατιθεμένης γὰρ τῆς ἱερωσύνης ἐξ ἀνάγκης καὶ νόμου μετάθεσις
    γίνεται (For when there is a change in the priesthood, there is necessarily a
    change in the law as well) (v. 12).

C   ἐφ' ὃν γὰρ λέγεται ταῦτα, φυλῆς ἑτέρας μετέσχηκεν, ἀφ' ἧς οὐ-
    δεὶς προσέσχηκεν τῷ θυσιαστηρίῳ· (Now the one of whom these
    things are spoken belonged to another tribe, from which no one has ever
    served at the altar) (v. 13).

D   πρόδηλον γὰρ ὅτι ἐξ 'Ιούδα ἀνατέταλκεν ὁ κύριος ἡμῶν, εἰς ἣν
    φυλὴν περὶ ἱερέων οὐδὲν Μωϋσῆς ἐλάλησεν (For it is evident that
    our Lord was descended from Judah, and in connection with that tribe
    Moses said nothing about priests) (v. 14).

D' καὶ περισσότερον ἔτι κατάδηλον ἐστιν, εἰ κατὰ τὴν ὁμοιότητα
    Μελχισέδεκ ἀνίσταται ἱερεὺς ἕτερος (It is even more obvious
    when another priest arises, resembling Melchizedek) (v. 15).

C' ὃς οὐ κατὰ νόμον ἐντολῆς σαρκίνης γέγονεν ἀλλὰ κατὰ δύναμιν
    ζωῆς ἀκαταλύτου (one who has become a priest, not through a legal re-
    quirement concerning physical descent, but through the power of an in-
    destructible life) (v. 16).

B' μαρτυρεῖται γὰρ ὅτι σὺ ἱερεὺς εἰς τὸν αἰῶνα κατὰ τὴν τάξιν Μελχισέ-
    δεκ (For it is attested of him, "You are a priest forever, according to the order
    of Melchizedek") (v. 17).

A' ἀθέτησις μὲν γὰρ γίνεται προαγούσης ἐντολῆς διὰ τὸ αὐτῆς ἀσθενὲς καὶ
    ἀνωφελές- οὐδὲν γὰρ ἐτελείωσεν ὁ νόμος- ἐπεισαγωγὴ δὲ κρείττονος ἐλ-
    πίδος δι' ἧς ἐγγίζομεν τῷ θεῷ (There is, on the one hand, the abrogation of an
    earlier commandment because it was weak and ineffectual [for the law made
    nothing perfect]; there is, on the other hand, the introduction of a better hope,
    through which we approach God) (vv. 18–19).

In this passage the levitical priesthood is contrasted with the priesthood after the order of Melchizedek. Since both concepts run side by
side, it is difficult to make an outline of the passage with a conventional

method. This leads one to think of the possibility that 7:11–19 is arranged in a chiastic manner. Indeed, a detailed examination of the passage indicates that it has an inversion of order at the conceptual level.
The outer sections (A and A') show parallelism with the idea of perfection (τελείωσις in 7:11; τελείωσεν in 7:19). Section A, on the one
hand, speaks of the imperfection of the levitical priesthood by way of a
rhetorical question. Section A' further supplements this idea by way of
affirmation. Sections B and B' are parallel to each other in that while B
speaks of the principle of the change of the law with the change of the
priesthood, B' points to the reality of the change of the priesthood and its
order (i.e., a priest after the order of Melchizedek). Sections C and C'
complement each other in that while C indicates that this new priesthood
belongs to another tribe, C' clarifies that this new order of the priesthood
is not through a legal requirement as in the levitical priesthood. In the
center sections of the chiasm the author intentionally introduces the title
"Lord" (D). By this he makes it plain that this new order of the high
priesthood is none other than Jesus himself. This thought is further explained in section D' (i.e., another priest resembling Melchizedek). This
brief analysis suggests that 7:11–19 is indeed written from a chiastic
point of view. Through this literary device the author re-emphasizes the
imperfect nature of the levitical high priesthood, and the necessity of the
high priest after the order of Melchizedek.

   This idea is further reinforced by another sub-chiastic structure in
7:18–19:

A ἀθέτησις μὲν γὰρ γίνεται προαγούσης ἐντολῆς (There is, on the one hand,
   the abrogation of an earlier commandment) (7:18a)

   B διὰ τὸ αὐτῆς ἀσθενὲς καὶ ἀνωφελές- (because it was weak and ineffec-
      tual) (7:18b).

   B' οὐδὲν γὰρ ἐτελείωσεν ὁ νόμος- (for the law made nothing perfect)
      (7:19a)

A' ἐπεισαγωγὴ δὲ κρείττονος ἐλπίδος δι' ἧς ἐγγίζομεν τῷ θεῷ (there is, on
   the other hand, the introduction of a better hope, through which we approach
   God) (7:19b).

The above structure indicates that a direct contrast is made between
"setting aside (ἀθέτησις) of the previous commandment" and "introduction (ἐπεισαγωγή) of better hope" (A, A'). The μέν . . . δέ con-

struction (B, B') further demonstrates the contrast between the old order of the levitical priesthood and the new order of Jesus' high priesthood. After having described the imperfect nature of the levitical high priesthood (7:11–19), the author moves to an exposition of the permanent nature of Jesus' high priesthood (7:20–28). It should be noted that this section is the continuation of the introduction of a better hope mentioned in 7:19. The permanent nature of Christ's priesthood is demonstrated in three ways.

First, it is shown in terms of the divine oath (7:20–22). These verses are chiastically arranged as follows:[21]

A   Καὶ καθ' ὅσον οὐ χωρὶς ὁρκωμοσίας (This was confirmed with an oath) (7:20a);

B   οἱ μὲν γὰρ χωρὶς ὁρκωμοσίας εἰσὶν ἱερεῖς γεγονότες (for others who became priests took their office without an oath) (7:20b)

B'   ὁ δὲ μετὰ ὁρκωμοσίας διὰ τοῦ λέγοντος πρὸς αὐτόν· ὤμοσεν κύριος καὶ οὐ μεταμεληθήσεται· σὺ ἱερεὺς εἰς τὸν αἰῶνα (but this one became a priest with an oath, because of the one who said to him, "The Lord has sworn and will not change his mind, 'You are a priest forever'") (7:21).

A'   κατὰ τοσοῦτο [καὶ] κρείττονος διαθήκης γέγονεν ἔγγυος Ἰησοῦς (accordingly Jesus has also become the guarantee of a better covenant) (7:22).

The diagram reveals that A and A' complement each other (i.e., to the degree that it was not without an oath . . . to the same degree Jesus became the surety of a better covenant). On the other hand, B and B' show the contrast between the levitical high priesthood which was without oath and Jesus' high priesthood which was with an oath. The μέν . . . δέ construction reinforces the difference between the two priesthoods. Thus the main point of these verses is that Jesus' high priesthood is permanent because it was inaugurated with a divine oath. It has already been revealed from 6:13–17 that God took an oath by himself when he made promises to Abraham and his descendants in order to guarantee the

[21] The English translation is from NRSV.

validity of his word. Likewise, God's oath in Hebrews 7:20–22 discloses the absoluteness and eternal validity of Jesus' high priesthood.[22]
Second, the permanence of Jesus' high priesthood is demonstrated by the eternality of Christ (7:23–25).[23] Again, the author of Hebrews uses the literary device of chiasm (but partially in vv. 23–24) in these verses to accomplish his purpose. It can be illustrated as follows:

A Καὶ οἱ μὲν πλείονες εἰσιν γεγονότες ἱερεῖς (Furthermore, the former priests were many in number) (7:23a),

B διὰ τὸ θανάτῳ κωλύεσθαι παραμένειν (because they were prevented by death from continuing in office) (7:23b);

B' ὁ δὲ διὰ τὸ μένειν αὐτὸν εἰς τὸν αἰῶνα (but because he continues forever) (7:24a).

A' ἀπαράβατον ἔχει τὴν ἱερωσύνην (he holds his priesthood permanently) (7:24b).[24]

In this structure sections A and A' bring out the contrast between the levitical high priesthood and Jesus' high priesthood (i.e., many vs. one). Sections B and B' show the reasons for both the temporary nature of the levitical high priesthood and eternal character of Jesus' high priesthood. These sections also show the contrast between the two high priesthoods. For the author of Hebrews "plurality is apparently a sign of incompleteness and imperfection (1:1ff.; 10:1ff.) and thus the superiority of Christ's priesthood is illustrated in the fact that He uniquely, as an individual, 'continues forever' (7:24)."[25] Thus the contrast between the temporariness of the mortals and the eternality of Jesus proves that Jesus'

---

22 O. Michel, *Der Brief an die Hebräer*, 12th ed. (Göttingen: Vanderhoeck and Ruprecht, 1966), 274. See also see J. Schneider, "ὀμνύω," in *Theological Dictionary of the New Testament*, ed. Gerhard Friedrich, tr. Geoffrey W. Bromiley (Grand Rapids: William B. Eerdmans Publishing Co., 1967), 5:176–185.

23 David John MacLeod, "The Theology of the Epistle to the Hebrews: Introduction, Prolegomena and Doctrinal Center" (Th.D. diss., Dallas Theological Seminary, 1987), 379.

24 The order of the NRSV translation in 7:24 is altered according to the order of the Greek text.

25 Peterson, *Hebrews and Perfection*, 113.

high priesthood is permanent in nature. The inferential conjunction ὅθεν in v. 25 shows that this verse speaks of the consequence of the eternality of Jesus. Because of his function as the eternal high priest, he is able to save those who draw near to God through him.

Third, the permanence of the high priesthood of Jesus can be observed from his character, accomplishment, and status (7:26–28).[26] Although it is not immediately clear, a close analysis of these verses suggests that the author has also arranged this section with a chiastic structure. This can be illustrated as follows:

A Τοιοῦτος γὰρ ἡμῖν καὶ ἔπρεπεν ἀρχιερεύς, ὅσιος ἄκακος ἀμίαντος, κε-χωρισμένος ἀπὸ τῶν ἁμαρτωλῶν καὶ ὑψηλότερος τῶν οὐρανῶν γενόμενος (For it was fitting that we should have such a high priest, holy, blameless, undefiled, separated from sinners, and exalted above the heavens) (7:26)

B ὃς οὐκ ἔχει καθ' ἡμέραν ἀνάγκην, ὥσπερ οἱ ἀρχιερεῖς, πρότερον ὑπὲρ τῶν ἰδίων ἁμαρτιῶν θυσίας ἀναφέρειν ἔπειτα τῶν τοῦ λαοῦ (Unlike the other high priests, he has no need to offer sacrifices day after day, first for his own sins, and then for those of the people;) (7:27a)

B' τοῦτο γὰρ ἐποίησεν ἐφάπαξ ἑαυτὸν ἀνενέγκας (this he did once for all when he offered himself) (7:27b)

A' ὁ νόμος γὰρ ἀνθρώπους καθίστησιν ἀρχιερεῖς ἔχοντας ἀσθένειαν, ὁ λό-γος δὲ τῆς ὁρκωμοσίας τῆς μετὰ τὸν νόμον υἱὸν εἰς τὸν αἰῶνα τετελει-ωμένον (For the law appoints as high priests those who are subject to weakness, but the word of the oath, which came later than the law, appoints a Son who has been made perfect forever) (7:28).

In this structure the center of the chiasm (i.e., B, B') consists of offering up of sacrifices. Level B indicates that Jesus does not need to offer up sacrifices daily as the levitical high priests. The reason for this is expressed in B' (i.e., he did this once for all by offering himself). Levels A and A' are related to each other by the characters of the heavenly high priest; the characteristics described in verse 26 (i.e., guileless, undefiled, separated from the sinners) correspond to the idea of the Son who has been made perfect forever in verse 28. For these reasons it is reasonable to regard 7:26–28 as having a chiastic structure.

26 Ibid., 112.

It is clear that the author describes the character of the heavenly high priest in verse 26, his accomplishment in verse 27 (i.e., offering up sacrifices once for all), and his status in verse 28 (i.e., the Son who has been made perfect forever). In these verses the author shows the contrast between the levitical high priests and the heavenly high priest in their character (i.e., holy vs. sinful, v. 26), the nature of the offering (i.e., once for all vs. every day, v. 27), and the different system of appointment (i.e., the law vs. the word of swearing of an oath, v. 28).

High Priest of the New Covenant (8:1–13)[27]

It has already been revealed from the previous study that 7:26–28 anticipates chapter 8 by comparing the differences between the levitical high priesthood and Christ's high priesthood. In chapter 8 the author expands his exposition of Jesus' high priesthood by emphasizing that he is the high priest of the new covenant. This chapter can be divided into three main sections: (1) the main point (8:1–2); (2) the superiority of Jesus' high priesthood (8:3–6); and (3) the reason for a better covenant (8:7–13).

The main point (8:1–2). The author asserts his main point by the use of the term κεφάλαιον. The word can mean either "summary" or "main point."[28] Since the author repeats in 8:1 τοιοῦτος . . . ἀρχιερεύς from 7:26, it may be said that 8:1–2 is the summary of what has been said in chapter 1–7, especially in chapter 7. Thus the main point of what the author has been trying to convey to the readers is: we have such a high priest who has sat down at the right hand of the throne of the majesty in heaven (8:1). This point is further elaborated in verse 2, which indicates that this exalted high priest is the minister in the sanctuary and in the true tent which is pitched not by humanity, but by the Lord.

The superiority of Jesus' high priesthood (8:3–6). After having stated his main point, the author goes on to describe why the high priesthood of Christ is superior to that of the Levites (8:3–6). First, the new

---

[27] Hebrews 8:1–10:18 is considered by some scholars as the heart of the epistle. See MacLeod, "The Theology of the Epistle to the Hebrews," 389. See also Attridge, *The Epistle to the Hebrews,* 216.

[28] Walter Bauer, *A Greek-English Lexicon of the New Testament and Other Early Christian Literature,* 2nd ed., trans. and adapted by W. F. Arndt, F. W. Gingrich, and Frederick W. Danker (Chicago: The University of Chicago, 1979), 429.

high priesthood is superior because it is based on a better sacrifice (8:3). As the earthly high priest is appointed to offer gifts and sacrifices, this heavenly high priest also needs something to offer. This verse does not specify what this offering is. However, the context makes it clear that it refers to the offering up of himself (7:27). Thus the statement "this one (i.e., Christ) must have something to offer" (7:28) anticipates the details of Christ's offering in the following chapters, especially in chapter 9. The sacrifice of the new high priest is better than that of the levitical high priests because it is the offering up of himself, with his own blood, once for all (e.g., 7:27; 9:12, 14, 25, 26, 28; 10:10; 13:12).

Second, Christ's high priesthood is superior because it is based on a better covenant (8:4–6). An examination of these verses suggests that the author is again developing his thought with a chiastic structure. This may be illustrated as follows:

A   εἰ μὲν οὖν ἦν ἐπὶ γῆς, οὐδ' ἂν ἦν ἱερεύς, ὄντων τῶν προσφερόντων κατὰ νόμον τὰ δῶρα (Now if he were on earth, he would not be a priest at all, since there are priests who offer gifts according to the law.) (8:4)

B   οἵτινες ὑποδείγματι καὶ σκιᾷ λατρεύουσιν τῶν ἐπουρανίων (They offer worship in a sanctuary that is a sketch and shadow of the heavenly one;) (8:5a)

B' καθὼς κεχρημάτισται Μωϋσῆς μέλλων ἐπιτελεῖν τὴν σκηνήν· ὅρα γάρ φησιν, ποιήσεις πάντα κατὰ τὸν τύπον τὸν δειχθέντα σοι ἐν τῷ ὄρει (for Moses, when he was about to erect the tent, was warned, "See that you make everything according to the pattern that was shown you on the mountain.") (8:5)

A' Νυνὶ δὲ διαφορωτέρας τέτυχεν λειτουργίας, ὅσῳ καὶ κρείττονός ἐστιν διαθήκης μεσίτης, ἥτις ἐπὶ κρείττοσιν ἐπαγγελίαις νενομοθέτηται (But Jesus has now obtained a more excellent ministry, and to that degree he is the mediator of a better covenant, which has been enacted through better promises.) (8:6)

In this scheme sections B and B' correspond to each other in that both describe the levitical sacrificial system under the old covenant. The levitical priests serve as a figure and a foreshadow of the heavenly things (B). This point is further explained by God's command to Moses to erect the tent according to the pattern shown to him in the mountain (B'). However, sections A and A' show the contrast between the levitical high priesthood and Christ's high priesthood, which is indicated by a μέν . . .

δέ construction. The second class conditional clause in 8:4 (εἰ . . . ἄν) suggests that "the premise is assumed to be contrary to the fact. The thing in itself may be true, but it is *treated* as untrue."[29] Thus the author's argument is that, if he were on the earth (in fact, he is not), he would not be a priest at all, and consequently, would be less than a high priest (A).[30] There are two implications for this statement. First, the scene of his service must be in heaven and not on earth since Jesus must render high priestly service belonging to the better covenant. Second, two orders of earthly priests cannot exist: the existence of one order on earth excludes the possibility of the coexistence of the other.[31] The contrast between the two types of priests in verse 6 is expressed with νυν[ὶ] δέ: the high priesthood of Christ is superior to that of the Levites because he is the mediator of a better covenant which is legislated on a better promise. His ministry is also superior because he serves in the sphere of the heavenly sanctuary (8:1, 5).

The reason for a better covenant (8:7–13). After the author has announced the theme of a better covenant in 8:6, he goes on to describe the reason that God had to make the first covenant obsolete and institute the new one (8:7–13). Throughout the passage the author stresses the necessity of the new covenant. This section may be divided into three parts: (1) the introduction (8:7), (2) the quotation of Jeremiah 31:31–34 (LXX) (8:8–12), and (3) the conclusion (8:13).

In the introduction (8:7) the necessity of the new covenant is indicated: if the first covenant was faultless, there would have been no place for the second. In the quotation of Jeremiah 31:31–34 (LXX), the author reiterates the point that the new covenant was promised to the people of Israel because God has found fault with the first covenant (8:8–12). That God took the initiative to promise the new covenant with Israel shows that the old covenant was intended to be provisional in character.[32] The

---

29 A. T. Robertson, *A Grammar of the Greek New Testament in the Light of Historical Research* (Nashville: Broadman Press, 1934), 1012.

30 Westcott, *The Epistle to the Hebrews,* 215.

31 Ibid.

32 R. A. Harrisville, *The Concept of Newness in the New Testament* (Minneapolis: Augsburg Publishing House, 1960), 53.

overall emphasis of the quotation of Jeremiah 31:31–34 is to bring out the negative aspect of the old covenant (i.e., the faulty nature of it).[33] However, a detailed analysis of the quotation reveals that the new covenant itself contains positive elements, which can be summarized in two ways; first, the law of this new covenant is not written in tablets, but in the minds and the hearts of the people (vv. 10–11); second, this new covenant will take away the sins of the people forever (v. 12).[34] Through these positive aspects of the new covenant, the negative character of the first covenant is brought out more distinctively. The necessity of the new covenant is also indicated in the concluding remark (8:13). The word καινός (new) is used in verses 8 and 13. The author's use of it in verse 13 calls attention to the beginning of the quotation of the new covenant in verse 8.[35] What is the purpose of mentioning καινός in 8:13? The author indicates that with the emergence of the new one the first one is becoming obsolete. With the use of the verb παλαιόω (to make old), the author makes it clear that God has declared the old covenant to be out-dated and canceled its validity.[36] Throughout the passage the author points out that the new covenant is necessary because the first one was inherently based on a faulty system and is ready to fade away.

Comparison of Sacrifices between the two Covenants (9:1–28)

Although 7:1–10:18 speaks of the high priesthood of Christ as a whole, the previous discussion indicates that each major section has a different emphasis. The emphasis of 7:1–28 was on the appointment of Jesus' high priesthood, namely, that his ministry is according to the order of Melchizedek. In 8:1–13 the author explained the reason for the necessity of the new covenant; it was because of the imperfect nature of the first one. Now in 9:1–28 the emphasis is placed on the sacrifice it-self. In this section the author further elaborates the new covenant by

---

[33] See Vanhoye, *La structure*, 143–44; Lane, *Hebrews 1–8*, 208; Peterson, *Hebrews and Perfection*, 132.

[34] Attridge, *The Epistle to the Hebrews*, 226.

[35] Ibid., 228.

[36] H. Seesemann, "παλαιόω," in *Theological Dictionary of the New Testament*, ed. Gerhard Friedrich, tr. Geoffrey W. Bromiley (Grand Rapids: William B. Eerdmans Publishing Co., 1967), 5:720.

comparing the sacrificial system of the old and the new. Chapter 9 can be divided into two main subsections: (1) sacrifice under the first covenant (9:1–10); (2) sacrifice under the new covenant (9:11–28).

Sacrifice under the first covenant (9:1–10). The author introduces the sacrificial system under the first covenant by stating that it had regulations for worship and an earthly sanctuary (9:1). In 9:2–10 he proceeds to describe both the worship and the earthly sanctuary under the old covenant. However, he does it in an inverted order. First, he elaborates the setting of the earthly sanctuary (9:2–5): the outer tent which is called holy (v. 2) and the inner tent which is called the holy of holies (vv. 3–5). Then he takes up the theme of worship and develops it further (9:6–10). The construction of μέν . . . δέ is used to bring out the contrast between the service of the priests and the high priest (9:6–7). The priests, on the one hand, go into *the first tent* to perform their duties *continually* (9:6). The high priest, on the other hand, enters *the second tent* (i.e., holy of holies), *alone, once a year,* to offer blood for himself and the sins of others (9:7). Then what is the significance of the ritual activities of the levitical priests and the high priests? The author points out that the way into the sanctuary is not yet opened under the Mosaic covenant. The limited entrance to the inner sanctuary (i.e., once a year by the high priest) reveals that "the sacrifices offered under the old covenant did not have an interior effect on the consciences of human worshipers (vv. 8–9), but only concerned fleshly externals (v. 10)."[37]

Sacrifice under the new covenant (9:11–28). In the second major subsection of chapter 9 the author changes the theme to the sacrifice under the new covenant (9:11–28). The conjunction δέ in 9:11 goes back to μέν in 9:1. With the conjunction μέν (9:1), the sacrificial system according to the old covenant is elucidated. With the conjunction δέ in 9:11 the author indicates that he is now shifting his thought to the sacrificial system of the new covenant. This section may also be divided into three parts.

The first part (9:11–14) shows that Christ's entrance into the inner sanctuary resulted in the eternal redemption. An examination of 9:11–12 reveals that these verses are arranged chiastically. This can be illustrated as follows:

---

[37] Attridge, *The Epistle to the Hebrews,* 231.

A Χριστὸς δὲ παραγενόμενος ἀρχιερεὺς τῶν γενομένων ἀγαθῶν διὰ τῆς μεί-
ζονος καὶ τελειοτέρας σκηνῆς (But when Christ came as a high priest of the
good things that have come, then through the greater and perfect tent) (9:11a)

B οὐ χειροποιήτου, τοῦτ' ἔστιν οὐ ταύτης τῆς κτίσεως (not made with
hands, that is, not of this creation) (9:11b)

B' οὐδὲ δι' αἵματος τράγων καὶ μόσχων (not with the blood of goats and
calves) (9:12a)

A' διὰ δὲ τοῦ ἰδίου αἵματος εἰσῆλθεν ἐφάπαξ εἰς τὰ ἅγια αἰωνίαν λύτρωσιν
εὑράμενος (but with his own blood, he entered once for all into the Holy Place,
thus obtaining eternal redemption) (9:12b).[38]

In these verses the ministry of Christ's high priesthood is expressed
both positively and negatively. The center of the chiasm (B and B'), on
the one hand, describes the negative elements, which are in antithesis to
the levitical system of worship and sanctuary. Section B is in direct
contrast to the earthly sanctuary (9:2–5), and section B', to the animal
blood offered by the levitical high priest (9:7). The outer sections (A and
A'), on the other hand, describe the positive elements of Christ's high
priesthood: they indicate that the superior sacrifice of the new covenant
is accomplished by the greater and more perfect tent (i.e., heavenly
sanctuary, 8:2) (A) and his own blood (A').[39] Thus as a result of the better tent and better sacrifice of Christ's high priesthood than those of levitical sacrificial system, Christ secured an eternal redemption (9:12).
The author further elaborates the superior quality of the sacrifice of
Christ by employing an *a fortiori* argument in 9:13–14. The protasis is
indicated by εἰ in verse 13 and the apodosis by πόσῳ μᾶλλον in verse
14. The point of the argument of these verses is: if the blood of the animals and sprinkling of the ashes of the heifer sanctify those who have
been defiled ceremonially, how much more will the blood of Christ . . .
cleanse our conscience from dead works? The point of comparison is

[38] This chiastic structure is observed by Lane (Lane, *Hebrews 1–8*, 237). I added
the rest of the verses in the outer sections (A and A') to complete the chiastic structure in
9:11–12. The order of NRSV translation in 9:12 is altered according to the order of the
Greek text.

[39] For different views on the meaning of the "better and greater tent," see Peterson,
Hebrews and Perfection, 140–44.

between the ceremonial cleansing of the flesh and the cleansing of the conscience. With this argument the author brings home the superior nature of the sacrifice made possible by the work of Christ.

The second part (9:15–28) is related to 9:11–14 by the phrase καὶ διὰ τοῦτο and provides the reason for what has been said: because of Christ's eternal redemptive work by his own blood, he is the mediator of the new covenant (9:15–22). The concept of the new covenant was already introduced in 8:7–13. By reintroducing the word "covenant" (διαθήκη) the author further develops his theme of the new covenant. In 9:15 he states the purpose (indicated by ὅπως) for which Christ is the mediator of the new covenant. The purpose is for those who are called to receive the promise of the eternal inheritance. The participle γενομένου explains the reason why it is possible for them to receive the eternal inheritance; it is because death (i.e., Christ's death) occurred for the redemption of the transgressions under the first covenant. The theme of the new covenant is further explicated by the idea of death (9:16–22). To begin with, the author introduces the general principle that death is necessary for any covenant to take effect (9:16–17). This general principle is applied to the first covenant, namely, the death of animals was necessary for the first covenant to take effect (9:18–22). Then this principle is applied to the new covenant in 9:23–28. In this passage the author reverts to the heavenly sanctuary and the sacrifice of Christ's blood which he discussed in 9:11–14.[40] The imagery of death is clearly brought out by phrases, such as "to offer himself" (v. 25), "his sacrifice" (v. 26), and "having been offered for the sins of many" (v. 28).

An overall analysis of 9:11–28 shows that it forms a unit with a chiastic structure at the conceptual level. Each section of the chiasm may be illustrated as follows:[41]

A Christ entered the sanctuary once through the greater and more perfect tent, not made with hands, but through his own blood, thus securing the redemption (9:11–14)

---

[40] Harold W. Attridge, "The Uses of Antithesis in Hebrews 8–10," in *Christians Among Jews & Gentiles,* essays in Honor of Krister Stendahl on His Sixty-Fifth Birthday, ed. G. Nicklesburg & G. MacRae (Philadelphia: Fortress Press, 1986), 7.

[41] In each section of the chiasm, I have provided my own summary of the verses.

B   Christ is the mediator of the new covenant, in order that those who are called
may receive the promise of the eternal inheritance (9:15-22)

A' Christ entered the heavenly sanctuary once, not into the sanctuary made with
hands, to bear the sins of many. He will appear a second time to save those
who are eagerly waiting for him (9:23-28).

In this scheme it is evident that the author's main point is to present Jesus as the mediator of the new covenant (B). It is also obvious that a
parallel thought is expressed in the outer sections (A and A'): the author
describes in what ways Christ was qualified to become the mediator of
the new covenant. Thus it is reasonable to regard the theme of 9:11–23
as "Christ who is the mediator of the new covenant."

Perfect Sacrifice of the New
High Priest (10:1–18)
It has already been revealed from the survey of 7:1–9:28 that one of
the major emphases in these chapters was the idea of Christ presenting
himself as an offering for the sins of the people once for all (e.g., 7:27;
8:3; 9:12, 14, 23, 26, 28). In 10:1–18, which is the final section of the
doctrinal center of Hebrews, the author brings his theological argument to
a climax by highlighting the perfect and the ultimate nature of the sacrifice of Christ. The emphasis on the sacrifice can be observed from the
frequent use of προσφέρω (10:1, 2, 8, 11, 12) and προσφορά (10:5, 8,
10, 14, 18). This section may be divided into two major parts: (1) the
imperfect nature of the old covenant (10:1–4); and (2) the establishment
of the new covenant (10:5–18).

The imperfect nature of the old covenant (10:1–4). To begin with,
the author launches his discussion with the imperfect nature of the old
covenant (10:1–4). One may observe that this section is also arranged in
a chiastic structure, which may be illustrated as follows:

A   Σκιὰν γὰρ ἔχων ὁ νόμος τῶν μελλόντων ἀγαθῶν, οὐκ αὐτὴν τὴν εἰκόνα
τῶν πραγμάτων, κατ' ἐνιαυτὸν ταῖς αὐταῖς θυσίαις ἃς προσφέρουσιν
εἰς τὸ διηνεκὲς οὐδέποτε δύναται τοὺς προσερχομένους τελειῶσαι
(Since the law has only a shadow of the good things to come and not the true
form of these realities, it can never, by the same sacrifices that are continually
offered year after year, make perfect those who approach.) (10:1)

B   ἐπεὶ οὐκ ἂν ἐπαύσαντο προσφερόμεναι διὰ τὸ μηδεμίαν ἔχειν ἔτι
συνείδησιν ἁμαρτιῶν τοὺς λατρεύοντας ἅπαξ κεκαθαρισμένους; (Oth-
erwise, would they not have ceased being offered, since the worshipers,

cleansed once for all, would no longer have any consciousness of sin?) (10:2)

B' ἀλλ' ἐν αὐταῖς ἀνάμνησις ἁμαρτιῶν κατ' ἐνιαυτόν· (But in these sacrifices there is a reminder of sin year after year.) (10:3)

A' ἀδύνατον γὰρ αἷμα ταύρων καὶ τράγων ἀφαιρεῖν ἁμαρτίας (For it is impossible for the blood of bulls and goats to take away sins.) (10:4)

In these verses the idea of the old covenant is expressed in terms of "the (Mosaic) law" (v. 1) (A) and "the blood of the animals" (10:4) (A'). It may be noted from this chiastic structure that A and A' emphasize that the sacrificial system under the old covenant is not able to take away sins of the people completely. Both sections B and B' explain the reasons for its inability. If the law was able to perfect those who draw near, they would have ceased to offer sacrifice every year because they would no longer have any conscience of sin (v. 2) (B). Consequently, the sacrifice offered once a year on the day of Atonement was the constant reminder that the blood of bulls and goats cannot take away sins (v. 3) (B'). Throughout each section of the chiastic structure the imperfect nature of the old covenant is repeatedly emphasized.

The establishment of the new covenant (10:5–18). After having explained that the law under the old covenant is a shadow of the good things to come (10:1), the author expounds the coming of perfection (i.e., establishment of the new covenant) in 10:5–18. This section can also be divided into two parts: (1) Christ's bodily sacrifice (10:5–10) and (2) the result of Christ's sacrifice (10:11–18).

The first part explains Christ's bodily sacrifice (10:5–10). In this section the author begins the discussion by announcing the coming of Christ into the world (10:5–7). The announcement is made by quoting Psalm 40:7–9 (LXX 39:7–9). A comparison with the Old Testament (both MT and LXX) indicates that the author is closely following the Septuagint.[42] Again, a detailed examination of these verses reveals that they are arranged in a chiastic structure:

---

[42] The only differences are that he changes ὠτία (Psa 37:9 LXX) to σῶμα (Heb 10:5), ᾔτησας (Psa 39:7) to εὐδόκησας (Heb 10:6). The author also changes the word order to ὁ θεὸς τὸ θέλημά σου (Heb 10:7) from τὸ θέλημά σου ὁ θεός (Psa 39:9 LXX).

A Διὸ εἰσερχόμενος εἰς τὸν κόσμον λέγει (Consequently, when Christ came into the world, he said) (10:5a)

B θυσίαν καὶ προσφορὰν οὐκ ἠθέλησας, σῶμα δὲ κατηρτίσω μοι (Sacrifices and offerings you have not desired, but a body you have prepared for me) (10:5b)

B' ὁλοκαυτώματα καὶ περὶ ἁμαρτίας οὐκ εὐδόκησας (in burnt offerings and sin offerings you have taken no pleasure) (10:6)

A' τότε εἶπον· ἰδοὺ ἥκω, ἐν κεφαλίδι βιβλίου γέγραπται περὶ ἐμοῦ, τοῦ ποιῆσαι ὁ θεὸς τὸ θέλημα σου (Then I said, 'See, God, I have come to do your will, O God' [in the scroll of the book it is written of me]) (10:7).

Sections A and A' are parallel with each other by the idea of "coming" (εἰσερχόμενος in A; ἥκω in A') and "saying" (λέγει in A; εἶπον in A'). Moreover, section A' further expresses the purpose of coming (indicated in section A), that is, to do the will of God. Sections B and B' are related to each other by the thought of "sacrifices" even though different words were used to express the idea. After having announced the coming of Christ into the world, in 10:8–10 the author continues to elaborate the will of God which he explained in the previous verses (10:5–7). Then what is the will of God that Christ came to accomplish (specifically mentioned in 10:7)? It is to abolish the first covenant in order to establish the second (10:9). The author further indicates the outcome of his coming: by his will we have been sanctified through the offering of the body of Jesus Christ once for all (10:10).

In the second part (10:11–18) the author further elaborates the result of Christ's sacrifice which he spoke of in 10:10. Again, it may be observed that the thoughts expressed in 10:11–18 are chiastically arranged, which may be illustrated as follows:

A Καὶ πᾶς μὲν ἱερεὺς ἕστηκεν καθ' ἡμέραν λειτουργῶν καὶ τὰς αὐτὰς πολλάκις προσφέρων θυσίας, αἵτινες οὐδέποτε δύνανται περιελεῖν ἁμαρτίας (And every priest stands day after day at his service, offering again and again the same sacrifices that can never take away sins) (10:11).

B οὗτος δὲ μίαν ὑπὲρ ἁμαρτιῶν προσενέγκας θυσίαν εἰς τὸ διηνεκὲς ἐκάθισεν ἐν δεξιᾷ τοῦ θεοῦ, τὸ λοιπὸν ἐκδεχόμενος ἕως τεθῶσιν οἱ ἐχθροὶ αὐτοῦ ὑποπόδιον τῶν ποδῶν αὐτοῦ. μιᾷ γὰρ προσφορᾷ τετελείωκεν εἰς τὸ διηνεκὲς τοὺς ἁγιαζομένους (But when Christ had offered for all time a single sacrifice for sins, "he sat down at the right hand of God," and since then has been waiting "until his enemies would be made a footstool for his feet." For by a single offering he has perfected for all time those who are sanctified) (10:12–14).

B' Μαρτυρεῖ δὲ ἡμῖν καὶ τὸ πνεῦμα τὸ ἅγιον· μετὰ γὰρ τὸ εἰρηκέναι· αὕτη ἡ διαθήκη ἣν διαθήσομαι πρὸς αὐτοὺς μετὰ τὰς ἡμέρας ἐκείν- ας, λέγει κύριος· διδοὺς νόμους μου ἐπὶ καρδίας αὐτῶν καὶ ἐπὶ τὴν διάνοιαν αὐτῶν ἐπιγράψω αὐτούς, καὶ τῶν ἁμαρτιῶν αὐτῶν καὶ τῶν ἀνομιῶν αὐτῶν οὐ μὴ μνησθήσομαι ἔτι (And the Holy Spirit also testi- fies to us, for after saying, "This is the covenant that I will make with them after those days, says the Lord: I will put my laws in their hearts, and I will write them on their minds," he also adds, "I will remember their sins and their lawless deeds no more") (10:15–17).

A ὅπου δὲ ἄφεσις τούτων, οὐκέτι προσφορὰ περὶ ἁμαρτίας (Where there is forgiveness of these, there is no longer any offering for sin) (10:18).

In the above proposed chiastic structure, A and A' are parallel by the idea of offering a sacrifice for sin. However, they are also antithetical to each other: on the one hand, section A expresses that the repeated offer- ing of sacrifice by the levitical priest can never take away sins; on the other hand, section A' indicates that where there is forgiveness of sin, a sin offering is no longer necessary. These two sections clearly contrast the effect of the sacrifice between the old and the new covenant. Middle sections B and B' are parallel with each other in that both describe the sacrifice under the new covenant. Section B points to the finished work of Christ, which is indicated by "for all time" and "a single sacrifice for sin." Moreover, Christ's posture as the seated high priest implies the finality of Christ's sacrifice.[43] The ultimate sacrifice of Christ is further highlighted by the statement that he has perfected for all time those who are sanctified (τοὺς ἁγιαζομένους, 14). In section B' the author brings in the quotation from Jeremiah 31:33–34 to demonstrate that Christ is the fulfillment of the new covenant promised in the Old Testament. It is already revealed that in 8:7–13 the promise of the new covenant in Jeremiah 31 was used to show the imperfect nature of the old covenant. However, in the present context the quotation was used to bring out the positive aspect of the new covenant (i.e., Christ's once for all sacrifice). This is evident from the way the author refines the quotation; the nega- tive aspect is removed (i.e., the removal of Jer 31:31–32) to emphasize the perfect nature of Christ's sacrifice.

43 MacLeod, "The Theology of the Epistle to the Hebrews," 241.

Summary of the Christological teaching

The overall emphasis of 7:1–10:18 is: Jesus, the high priest of the new covenant. A survey of this Christological section reveals that each chapter brings out a different aspect of the high priesthood of Christ. In chapter 7 the author stresses the appointment of Christ as the high priest after the order of Melchizedek. In chapter 8 the emphasis is on the establishment of the new covenant. By an extensive citation of Jeremiah 31:31–34 the author indicates that the new covenant is necessary because of the fault of the first covenant. In chapter 9 the focus of the discussion is on the superior nature of Christ's sacrifice to that of the levitical priests. He brings out his point by comparing the sacrifice between the two covenants. Finally, in 10:1–18 the author brings his exposition to the conclusion by emphasizing the perfect and the ultimate sacrifice of Christ's high priesthood. Again, the perfect character of Christ's sacrifice is shown in comparison with the old covenant. Thus the Christological teaching of the high priesthood is clearly emphasized. Then what might have been the author's purpose of this long doctrinal section? It is apparent that he uses the doctrine of the high priesthood of Christ to exhort the readers to hold fast the confession which they had when they first believed (10:19–39). This aspect will be further discussed in the following section. In order to guide one to follow the exposition of 7:1–10:18 better, the following outline might be helpful.

HIGH PRIESTHOOD OF CHRIST (7:1–10:18)

I. The high priest after the order of Melchizedek (7:1–28)
   A. Characteristics and greatness of Melchizedek (7:1–10)
      1. The description of his characteristics (7:1–3)
      2. Greatness of Melchizedek (7:4–10)
         a. Because he received tithes from Abraham (7:4, 6)
         b. Because Abraham was blessed by him (7:6; cf. 7:1)
         c. Even the Levites paid tithes to him through Abraham (7:4–10)
   B. Superiority of the priesthood of Jesus to that of Levites (7:11–28)
      1. The imperfection of the levitical high priesthood (7:11–19)
      2. The permanence of the high priesthood of Jesus (7:20–28)
         It is demonstrated in three ways:

a. Divine oath (7:20–22)
b. Eternity of Christ (7:23–25)
c. His character, accomplishment, and status (7:26–28)

II. The high priest of the new covenant (8:1–13)
A. The main point (8:1–2)
B. Superiority of Jesus' high priesthood (8:3–6)
  1. Because it is based on a better sacrifice (8:3)
  2. Because it is based on a better covenant (8:4–6)
C. Reason for a better covenant (8:7–13)

III. A comparison of sacrifice between the two covenants (9:1–28)

A. Sacrifice under the first covenant (9:1–10)
  1. Statement of regulation under the first covenant (9:1)
  2. Setting of the earthly sanctuary (9:2–5)
    a. Outer tent (9:2)
    b. Inner tent (9:3–5)
  3. Regulations on worship (9:6–7)
  4. Significance of the ritual activities under the first covenant (9:8–10)

B. Sacrifice under the new covenant (9:11–28)
  1. Christ's entrance into the inner sanctuary (9:11–14)
  2. He is the mediator of the new covenant (9:15–28)
    a. Purpose of Christ being the mediator of the covenant (9:15)
    b. Further explication of the new covenant by the theme of death (9:16–22)
      (1) Principle: the death of animal was necessary for the first covenant to take place (9:18–22)
      (2) Application (9:23–28)

IV. The perfect sacrifice of the new high priest (10:1–18)
A. The imperfect nature of the old covenant (10:1–4)
B. The establishment of the new covenant (10:5–18)
  1. Christ's bodily sacrifice (10:5–10)
    a. Announcement of the coming of Christ (10:5–7)
    b. Purpose of his coming (10:8–9)

c. Result of his coming (10:10)
2. Further elaboration of the result of Christ's bodily sacrifice (10:11–18)

Examination of the Parenetic Section (10:19–39)

The doctrine of the high priesthood of Christ as presented in 7:1–10:18 is an extraordinary exposition as it is. In fact Hebrews is the only book in the New Testament which portrays Jesus as the high priest.[44] In light of this important Christological teaching one needs to ask what the author's real purpose is in setting forth the exposition of the high priesthood of Christ in 7:1–10:18. Did the author intend to provide only a theological treatise for the readers to think about, or did he have another purpose in mind in his exposition of this section? What is his motive in arranging the epistle this way?

It appears that one of the reasons has to do with the audience to whom the author was addressing. It appears that the readers may have been a group of Jewish Christians who had heard the message from the eyewitnesses of the life of Jesus (cf. 2:2–3).[45] Although they began their faith journey well, they are now in danger of falling away from the living God. They were about to abandon their Christian confession and fall into apostasy (i.e., returning to the religious practices of Judaism).

Against this view, Käsemann argues based on the findings he made in 10:19ff., that there is no historically conditioned dispute with the Jewish religion. He asserts that "it is a product of fantasy to read from our letter a judaizing disintegration threatening the Christian community or the danger of apostasy toward Judaism."[46] Käsemann reduces the struggle for faith as the Christian struggle for faith in all ages, and argues against the view that the original readers were those Christians who

---

[44] R. H. Culpepper, "The High Priesthood and Sacrifice of Christ in the Epistle to the Hebrews," *Theological Educator* 32 (1985): 47.

[45] Some scholars who hold this view: George Wesley Buchanan, *To the Hebrews,* The Anchor Bible (Garden City, New York: Doubleday, 1972), 255–67; P. E. Hughes, *A Commentary on the Epistle to the Hebrews* (Grand Rapids: William B. Eerdmans Publishing Co., 1977), 18;

[46] Käsemann, *The Wandering People of God,* 24.

had Jewish background.[47] However, the social and religious background of this community indicates that the original readers were those who were nourished within the Hellenistic-Jewish community. There are at least three reasons why the letter was directed against the Jewish community which was in danger of being apostatized into Judaism. First, their source of authority is the Septuagint rather than the Hebrew text. This is seen from the author's consistent use of the LXX. Second, the audience was familiar with the stories of the Bible. This can be seen from the fact the author refers to certain stories without elaboration (cf. 12:17). Third, the centrality of Moses in the development of Hebrews suggests that the letter was directed toward the Jewish believing community. In the Old Testament Moses is designated a priest only once (Psa 99:6). However, in the Hellenistic-Jewish tradition, Moses is the supreme exemplar of perfection in the sense of immediacy and access to God.[48] These evidences argue against Käsemann's contention that the epistle was not addressed to Jewish Christians. The author is addressing to this group of the Jewish Christian community who was in danger of falling away from faith in Jesus.

With this background in mind, it is easy to see why the author employed the theme of the levitical high priesthood from the Old Testament to explain the doctrine of the high priesthood of Christ in the new covenant. Since it was a familiar concept for them, they were able to realize the significance of the high priest of the new covenant and the terrible consequence of rejecting Jesus. This explains why faith in Hebrews has Jesus as its object even if the author does not use phrases, such as "faith in Jesus" or "believe in Christ." In 10:19–39 the author uses the doctrinal exposition of 7:1–10:18 as a basis to exhort the readers not to forsake their faith in Jesus. In other words, "the scriptural exposition and doctrinal development ultimately have a hortatory aim and an important part of the exhortation derives its force from the doctrinal

---

[47] Ibid., 25. See also Thomas Wiley Lewis III, "The Theological Logic in Hebrews 10:19–12:29 and the Appropriation of the Old Testament" (Ph.D. diss., Drew University, 1965), 15.

[48] The above points are taken from William A. Lane, *Hebrews 1–8*, liv–lv.

156		CHAPTER SIX

or expository development."[49] Since the exhortation follows the doctrine of Christ, it can be said that faith in Hebrews is Christologically motivated. This will become more evident in the analysis of the parenetic section of 10:19–39.

Basis for the Literary Unit

In this section the literary unit of 10:19–39 will be considered in two ways: (1) by examining the relationship between the central exposition (7:1–10:18) and the parenesis (10:19–39), and (2) by examining the literary unit within the parenetic section (10:19–39). The author uses both conceptual and literary clues to show that 7:1–10:18 and 10:19–39 are intricately related to each other. The inferential conjunction οὖν in 10:19 indicates that what follows is the conclusion of the preceding argument.[50] In other words, οὖν goes back to the entire section of the central exposition in 7:1–10:18. This means that what the author is about to say in 10:19–39 is based on the doctrinal teachings in the preceding chapters (7:1–10:18). Indeed, a comparison of the ideas between the two sections reveals that they resemble each other remarkably. The phrase "the entering of the sanctuary" (10:19) is an allusion to 9:8, 12, 24. The reference to "the blood of Jesus" (10:19) is an allusion to "the blood of Christ" (9:14) and "his own blood" (9:12, 18). This expression recalls the means by which Christ entered the true heavenly sanctuary.[51] "A new and living way which he inaugurated for us" (10:20) clearly looks back to "the blood of the covenant which God has ordained" (9:20). The phrase "great priest" (10:21) refers to the high priest of the new covenant which the author has discussed in 7:1–10:18 (e.g., 7:26; 8:1; 9:11). The sprinkling of the heart from an evil conscience (10:22) "recalls the imagery of 9:18–22, in which the sprinkling of the people with blood was associated with the inauguration of the old covenant."[52] The idea of "the sacrifice for sin" (10:26) is the reminder of "the removing of sins

---

[49] Harold W. Attridge, "Paraenesis in a homily (λόγος παρακλήσεος): The possible location of, and socialization in, the 'Epistle to the Hebrews,'" *Semeia* 50 (1990): 211–26.

[50] Bauer, *Lexicon*, 592.

[51] Attridge, *The Epistle to the Hebrews*, 285.

[52] Peterson, *Hebrews and Perfection*, 155.

by the sacrifice of himself (9:26) and "a single sacrifice for sins" (10:12). The illustration of violating the law of Moses (10:28) refers to the first covenant (8:7; 9:1, 15, 18). The phrase "the blood of the covenant" in 10:29 is taken directly from 9:20, which is a clear reference to the new covenant (8:8, 13; 9:15) and a better covenant (7:22; 8:6). A brief comparison between the doctrinal and the parenetic sections supports the argument that parenesis follows doctrine. Thus it may be asserted that 10:19–39 is the summary of the contents presented in 7:1–10:18, and especially in 8:1–10:18. In other words, the author provides in the doctrinal section a firm Christological foundation for the series of admonitions that follow in the parenetic section.[53]

Then what are the clues which suggest that 10:19–39 forms a literary unit? First, it is indicated by the inclusion with the word παρρησία in verse 19 and 35.[54] Since the inclusion is formed between verse 19 and 35, one might argue that the structure unit exists only between 10:19–35. However, the explanatory γάρ in verses 36 and 37 indicates that the thought expressed in verse 35 continues through verse 39. For this reason it is reasonable to conclude that the entire section of 10:19–39 forms a unit. The literary unit of 10:19–39 is strengthened by another inclusion with the word πίστις in verses 21 and 39. It may be argued that this inclusion cannot support the unity of the passage because the word does not appear in 10:19. However, it is to be observed that 10:19–21 is a clause formed by the participle ἔχοντες, which is in turn connected to the main verb προσέρχομαι. In this sense, it may be said that the structural unit of 10:19–39 is solidified by the inclusion of πίστις. Next, the literary unit can be argued from the broader chiastic arrangement of 10:19–39. The chiastic structure is not visible at first glance, but a careful analysis of the passage reveals that the author arranges his argument symmetrically.[55]

A   Since we have Jesus as the high priest over the house of God, let us hold fast the
    confession of our hope without wavering, realizing that the Day is drawing near
    (10:19-25).

---

[53] William L. Lane, *Hebrews 9–13*, Word Biblical Commentary (Dallas: Word Books, 1991), 279.

[54] Vanhoye, *La structure*, 44.

[55] Each section of the chiasm is my own summary of the verses indicated above.

B   If we sin deliberately after having received the knowledge of the truth, there no longer remains a sacrifice concerning sins, but a fearful expectation of judgment, and razing fire which will consume the adversaries (10:26–31).

A' Indeed, you have endured sufferings in the past; therefore, do not throw away the confidence which has a good reward, realizing that the Lord will come and not tarry (10:32–39).

In this proposed construction one can see that sections A and A' express parallel thoughts (e.g., "holding fast" is parallel to "not throwing away the confidence" and "the Day is drawing near" is equivalent to "the Lord will not tarry"). The author appeals to the readers with a positive exhortation in both A and A'. However, his admonition in the center of the chiasm (B) has a negative tone. While the exhortation in A and A' is based on the coming of the Lord, the warning in B is based on the judgment of God. This literary device of alternating the positive and negative thoughts indicates that the author clearly intended the parenetic section of 10:19–39 to be a unit.[56]

Faith and Christology

As mentioned earlier, the discussion of the doctrinal center of Hebrews (7:1–10:18) was carried out by way of summarizing the major parts of section. However, the examination of the parenetic section (10:19–39) will be carried out in a slightly different way. I will analyze the passage with one question in mind: "Is the concept of faith in Hebrews Christologically oriented?" or more specifically, "Is Jesus construed as the object (or content) of faith for believers?" For the purpose of facilitating the discussion this parenetic section can be divided into three parts: (1) exhortation to continue with faith (10:19–25); (2) consequence of disloyalty to Christ (10:26–31); and (3) admonition to persevere in faith (10:32–39). The analysis of these passages will be followed by a summary. In addition the characteristics of faith will also be examined whenever I feel it is appropriate to do so.

---

[56] Bligh also suggests that 10:19–39 is chiastically arranged. His proposed structure has many levels of chiasm. See J. Bligh, *Chiastic Analysis of the Epistle to the Hebrews* (Heythrop: Athenaeum, 1966), 21. Since he does not explain how each detailed level is arranged chiastically, it cannot be confirmed for certain whether it is arranged chiastically. This requires a further investigation.

Exhortation to Continue with
Faith (10:19–25)

In this first section the author of Hebrews uses three independent sentences for the purpose of encouraging the readers to remain in faith. The hortatory nature of this passage is indicated by the use of the subjunctive mood in each of the main verbs (προσερχώμεθα in vv. 19–22; κατέχωμεν in v. 23; κατανοῶμεν in v. 24).[57]

Let us draw near (10:19–22). In the first exhortation (10:19–22) the author expresses faith in terms of drawing near (προσέρχομαι) with a true heart in full assurance of faith. This main point is clearly brought out by the grammatical construction of the passage, which may be illustrated as follows:

(1) Ἔχοντες οὖν, ἀδελφοί, παρρησίαν εἰς τὴν εἴσοδον τῶν ἁγίων ἐν τῷ αἵματι Ἰησοῦ, ἣν ἐνεκαίνισεν ἡμῖν ὁδὸν πρόσφατον καὶ ζῶσαν διὰ τοῦ καταπετάσματος, τοῦτ᾽ ἔστιν τῆς σαρκὸς αὐτοῦ (Therefore, brethren, **having confidence** to enter the holy place by the blood of Jesus, by a new and living way which He inaugurated for us through the veil, that is, his flesh (10:19–20),

(2)   καὶ ἱερέα μέγαν ἐπὶ τὸν οἶκον τοῦ θεοῦ (and **[having]** a great priest over the house of God (10:21),

προσερχώμεθα μετὰ ἀληθινῆς καρδίας ἐν πληροφορίᾳ πίστεως (let us draw near with a sincere heart in full assurance of faith) (10:22a) – **Main clause**

(3)   ῥεραντισμένοι τὰς καρδίας ἀπὸ συνειδήσεως πονηρᾶς (**having** the hearts **sprinkled** clean from an evil conscience) (10:22b)

(4)   καὶ λελουσμένοι τὸ σῶμα ὕδατι καθαρῷ
        (and **having** our bodies **washed** with pure water) (10:22c).[58]

---

[57] The subjunctive mood expresses the hortatory idea in the first person plural. See F. Blass, F. Debrunner, and R. W. Funk, *Grammar of the New Testament and Other Early Christian Literature,* trans. R. W. Funk (Chicago: The University of Chicago Press, 1961), 183.

[58] I have added my own translation of these verses to separate the main clause from the dependent clauses and to emphasize the participles used by the author of Hebrews.

This diagram shows that the sentence structure of this passage is artistically arranged, in such a way that the main point is in the middle, with
two participial clauses before and after it.[59]

In the main clause (10:22a) the author calls for the readers to re-
spond to God by faith: namely, to draw near with a true heart in full assurance of faith. The word προσέρχομαι (to draw near) occurs seven
times in Hebrews (4:16; 7:25; 10:1, 22; 11:6; 12:18; 12:22). It has a
clear reference to salvation in 7:25 and 12:22; however, in the remaining
verses the word has something to do with Christian living (e.g., 4:16,
prayer; 10:1, worship; 11:6, with respect to pleasing God). In 10:22 the
word is used in the context of Christian worship. The author's exhortation "to stimulate one another to love and good works" and "not to forsake their assembling" in 10:24–25 suggests that corporate worship is in
view. However, the word is also general enough to refer to a Christian's
response to the salvation as a whole. In other words, "to draw near"
should be understood "as an expression of the new relationship with God
in Christ."[60] In addition, the phrase πληροφορία πίστεως indicates that
drawing near to God is the response of faith on the part of believers. The
word πληροφορία literally means "supreme fullness."[61] In the Pauline
literature (Col 2:2; 1 Thess 1:5) the word has this sense of meaning.
Likewise, in Hebrews the word is used with reference to "hope" (6:11)
and "faith" (10:22). In these two verses πληροφορία has the meaning of
"full assurance." The phrase "full assurance of faith," along with "full
assurance of hope," is a description of "the certainly and stability that
are created in Christians as a result of the work of Christ and that enable
them to remain loyal to him."[62] As Macrae correctly points out, "the

---

[59] Please note that v. 21 does not have a participle in Greek text. However, it is obvious that the participle ἔχοντες is implied. For this reason I am considering this verse
as a participial clause. The word in the bracket is added to clarify the meaning.

[60] Peterson, *Hebrews and Perfection*, 155.

[61] Gerhard Delling, "πληροφορία," in *Theological Dictionary of the New Testament*, ed. Gerhard Friedrich, tr. Geoffrey W. Bromiley (Grand Rapids: William B. Eerdmans Publishing Co., 1968), 6:310–11.

[62] Lane, *Hebrews 9–13*, 286.

relation of faith to hope is essentially the same."⁶³ While the phrase πληροφορία τῆς ἐλπίδος indicates the goal of the Christian, πληροφορία πίστεως suggests the condition or means for it."⁶⁴ Thus it can be concluded that the author's exhortation to draw near to God is a clear call to be faithful to God.

How is the exhortation to draw near with assurance of faith (10:22a) related to Christology? The proposed structure above reveals that the exhortation is surrounded by the doctrine of Christ's high priesthood in the beginning (vv. 19–21) and the end (v. 22bc). In the beginning part (vv. 19–21), the author provides two reasons for the readers to draw near to God by the use of the participle ἔχοντες.

The first reason is that we have παρρησία in entering the sanctuary by the blood of Jesus (vv. 19–20). Questions are raised as to the exact meaning of this Greek term. Delitzsch understands the word in a subjective sense, rendering it "joyful confidence or feeling of confidence."⁶⁵ However, a mere subjective understanding of the word seems to be inadequate; it also has an objective meaning of an appropriation of something already given.⁶⁶ In other words, "one holds it fast, not merely by holding on as a believer, but by clinging to the presupposition of faith in the promise."⁶⁷ In the present context παρρησία has the meaning of "freedom of access to God, authority to enter the sanctuary."⁶⁸ The

---

⁶³ G. W. MacRae, "Heavenly Temple and Eschatology in the Letter to the Hebrews," *Semeia* 12 (1978): 193.

⁶⁴ Ibid.

⁶⁵ F. Delitzsch, *Commentary on the Epistle to the Hebrews*, trans. T. L. Kingsbury (Edinburgh: T. & T. Clark, 1878), II:170. See also J. Moffatt, *A Critical and Exegetical Commentary on the Epistle to the Hebrews*, The International Critical Commentary (Edinburgh: T. & T. Clark, 1924), 142. Moffatt understands the word as "confident trust, the unhesitating adherence of a human soul to God as its only Master" (142).

⁶⁶ Ernst Käsemann, *The Wandering People of God: An Investigation of the Letter to the Hebrews*, trans. Roy A. Harrisville and Irving L. Sandberg (Minneapolis: Augsburg Publishing House, 1984), 43.

⁶⁷ Ibid.

⁶⁸ H. Schlier, "Παρρησία, παρρησιάζομαι," *Theological Dictionary of the New Testament*, ed. Gerhard Friedrich, tr. Geoffrey W. Bromiley (Grand Rapids: William B. Eerdmans Publishing Co., 1967), 5:884. See also Lane, *Hebrews 9–13*, 273. He translates the word as "authorization," understanding it in the objective sense.

author further indicates that this free access is made possible by the blood of Jesus (ἐν τῷ αἵματι 'Ιησου) (10:19). The preposition ἐν here expresses the idea of cause, thus giving the reason for being able to have access to the sanctuary.[69] Moreover, verse 20 shows that the inauguration of the entrance to the sanctuary was accomplished through the curtain (διὰ τοῦ καταπετάσματος), which is his body. Thus it is evident that the first ground for the exhortation to draw near is Christologically oriented.

The second reason for the readers to draw near is expressed in 10:21, in which the participle ἔχοντες in 10:19 continues with the word ἱερέα in 10:21: we have a great priest over the house of God. The phrase "a great priest" (ἱερέα μέγαν) is a reiteration of "a great high priest" (ἀρχιερέα μέγαν) in 4:14. The phrase "the house of God" is a reminder of the faithfulness of Christ as a Son over the house of God in 3:6. For this reason it is logical to assert that 10:21 is the summary statement of the doctrine of Christ's high priesthood which the author presented in different parts of Hebrews, especially in 7:1–10:18. Thus it may be said with certainty that the second reason for the exhortation to draw near is also based on the Christological teaching of Jesus' high priesthood.

In the closing part of this structure (10:22bc) the author employs two participles to signify that the exhortation to draw near to God (10:22a) is also Christologically oriented. The expression "having our hearts sprinkled (ῥεραντισμένοι) from an evil conscience and having our body washed (λελουσμένοι) with pure water" has its origin in the Old Testament cult.[70] The first participle ῥεραντισμένοι is the perfect tense of ῥαντίζω, which means "to sprinkle."[71] The word is used three times in Hebrews to refer to the Old Testament cult of sprinkling (9:13, 19, 21). However, in 10:22 the word is used metaphorically to refer to the inner cleansing of the heart from an evil conscience, which is equivalent to the "consciousness of sin" in 10:2.[72] It refers to the sprinkling of our hearts

[69] Robertson, *A Grammar of the Greek New Testament*, 532.

[70] C. Hunzinger, "ῥαντίζω, ῥαντισμός," in *Theological Dictionary of the New Testament*, ed. Gerhard Friedrich, tr. Geoffrey W. Bromiley (Grand Rapids: William B. Eerdmans Publishing Co., 1968), 6:979.

[71] Bauer, *Lexicon*, 734.

[72] Attridge, *The Epistle to the Hebrews*, 288.

with the blood of Jesus, namely, the blood of the new covenant.[73] The next participle λελουσμένοι is not related to the blood of Jesus, but instead related to Christian baptism. Whereas the first participle has a reference to the cleansing of the inner heart, the second one refers to the external sign of the inner reality. In other words, the phrase "washing of the body with pure water" refers to the outward application of water as the visible mark of the inward and spiritual cleansing brought about through Christ.[74] The two phrases indicated by the two participles are significant in the present context because they refer to the appropriation of the benefits of Christ's sacrificial death to the believers at some decisive moment in the past.[75] These participles are directly tied to the main verb (προσερχώμεθα) and express the reason that one must draw near to God in full assurance of faith.

An examination of the participial clauses both in 10:19–21 and in 10:22 reveals that they have Christological implications: while the former emphasizes the finished work of Christ as the high priest, the latter stresses the response of believers to the work of the high priesthood of Christ. In this sense, it may be concluded that the exhortation to draw near with a true heart in assurance of faith in 10:22a is Christologically oriented. Even if the author does not use the phrase such as "faith in Christ," the context and the literary structure make it evident that the concept of faith in this passage has Jesus as the object.

Let us hold fast (10:23). In the second exhortation (10:23) faith is expressed in terms of holding fast the confession of the hope without wavering. The word "confession" (ὁμολογία) is used two other times in Hebrews (3:1; 4:14). The meaning of the term was already discussed in chapter four of this book. There I have concluded that it is used to express either the subjective or objective aspect of believers' confession.[76]

---

[73] N. A. Dahl, "A New and New Living Way: The Approach to God according to Hebrews 10:19–25," *Interpretation* 5 (1951): 406.

[74] F. F. Bruce, *The Epistle to the Hebrews,* New International Commentary on the New Testament (Grand Rapids: William B. Eerdmans Publishing Co., 1964), 251.

[75] Lane, *Hebrews 9–13,* 287.

[76] The "objective aspect" refers to some sort of confessional statement or doctrine of faith which believers might have held on to. The "subjective aspect" of ὁμολογία means the confession of faith without any specific reference to a confessional or doctrinal statement.

In 10:23 also the word "hope" may have either subjective or objective element.[77] The objective aspect of the hope is indicated by the genitive τῆς ἐλπίδος, which may be regarded as an objective genitive.[78] This interpretation allows one to understand "hope" as the object of the confession which the community of believers held fast.

Michel goes as far as suggesting that ἐλπίς in 10:23 indicates the object which one confesses, not the act of hope itself.[79] However, it appears that here Michel makes an overstatement. An examination of the use of ἐλπίς in Hebrews indicates that, except for the use in the present context (10:23), the word also denotes a subjective element (i.e., that which one hopes for without necessarily adhering to the doctrinal statement of hope).[80] For this reason Grässer asserts that hope in Hebrews may be both subjective and objective at the same time.[81] It is my opinion that one cannot be certain whether there was an objective creedal statement which was in existence in the community that received the letter of Hebrews because the author is not specific about the content of the confession or that of hope.

However, it is clear that hope has its object of hoping regardless of whether it is subjective or objective. Then what is the object of this hope? Although it is not stated explicitly, the explanatory clause "he who has promised is faithful" (10:23b) suggests that hope is somehow related to the promise of God in Hebrews. The author's use of the noun ἐπαγγέλια (4:1; 6:15; 8:6; 9:15) and the verb ἐπαγγέλλομαι (6:3;

---

[77] Again, the objective use of hope refers to the confessional or the doctrinal statement of hope which believers might have had. The subjective aspect of hope refers to believer's act of hoping for God's promise without any specific reference to the confessional or doctrinal statement.

[78] Michel, *Hebräerbrief,* 347.

[79] Ibid. Likewise, Lane makes the same kind of overstatement: "In Hebrews the term 'hope' always describes the objective content of hope, consisting of present and future salvation" (Lane, *Hebrews 9–13,* 276, 288).

[80] For example, consider the statements such as: confidence of hope (3:6); full assurance of hope (6:11); to seize the hope set before us (6:18); better hope, through which we approach God (7:19). However, in 10:23 the emphasis seems to be more on the objective aspect although the subjective aspect cannot be ignored.

[81] Erich Grässer, *Der Glaube im Hebräerbrief* (Marburg: N. G. Elwert Verlag, 1965), 33, n. 111.

10:23; 11:11; 12:26) indicates that the promise of God refers to the word of God as a whole. More specifically, in 10:23 the promise signifies the word of God which is yet to be fulfilled in the future. It is the promise of entering his rest in the eschatological sense (4:1), an eternal inheritance (9:15), an unshakable kingdom (12:27–28). In other words, the phrase ἡ ὁμολογία τῆς ἐλπίδος refers to "the eschatological elements associated with the confession of one whose lordship is yet to be fully realized."[82]

Grässer recognizes that the object of hope is the possession of salvation which is still open in the future.[83] But he is not willing to recognize that this object of hope is Christologically oriented. He considers that the attitude (or behavior) mentioned in 10:23ff. is merely the Christian ethics in the assembly of believers.[84] Grässer has done well in pointing out the ethical aspect of faith in this passage. Indeed, they are the ethics of the believing community for worship (i.e., holding fast the confession in 10:23; considering one another to love and good words in 10:24). However, as discussed already, the parenetic section of 10:19–39 is based on the Christological teachings in 7:1–10:18. Moreover, in 10:19–25, the three exhortations have a firm basis in the doctrine of Christ's high priesthood. For the author of Hebrews the ethical aspect of faith is not detached from Christology. They go hand in hand: Christology is the foundational element for the ethical concept of faith and faith in Hebrews cannot stand alone without the doctrine of Christ. Thus one may conclude that the exhortation to hold fast the confession of hope (10:23) is Christologically oriented.

Let us consider (10:24–25). It is already pointed out that in the first two exhortations (10:22–23) believers' faith was directed toward God. However, in the third exhortation (10:24–25), the emphasis is changed to one's responsibility to other believers; namely, the author instructs the readers how faith should be exercised toward others in the assembly. In

---

[82] Attridge, *The Epistle to the Hebrews,* 289.

[83] Grässer, *Der Glaube im Hebräerbrief,* 33.

[84] Ibid., 40. According to Grässer, ὁμολογία τῆς ἐλπίδος (confession of hope) is essentially identical to παρρησία καὶ τὸ καύχημα τῆς ἐλπίδος (confidence and the boasting of hope) in 3:6 and πληροφορία τῆς ἐλπίδος (full assurance of hope) in 6:11. He asserts that these phrases show no specific Christological basis for the concept of faith in Hebrews (35).

166 CHAPTER SIX

10:24 faith is described in terms of considering one another to stimulate to love and good works. This main idea is supported by the two participles in 10:25, which explain how the exhortation should be carried out.[85] The first participial clause (μὴ ἐγκαταλείποντες . . .) indicates that stimulating to love and good works should be done by *not neglecting* the gatherings of believers. The second participle (παρακαλοῦντες) denotes that the exhortation must be done by *encouraging* one another to meet together. The author employs these two participles to reinforce the importance of the assembly of believers by bringing together both the positive and the negative exhortations. Immediately, it is not clear whether this exhortation is related to Christology. But the following clause, "all the more that you see the Day drawing near," clearly shows that the exhortation to carry out these Christian conducts is based on the Second Advent of Jesus. Thus the exhortations in 10:24–25 have both Christological and eschatological bases.

In 10:22–25 the author deliberately chooses the words "faith" (v. 22), "hope" (v. 23), and "love" (v. 24) in his exhortation to hold fast the faith. The same words were also used in 6:10–12. These ideas are further developed in the following chapters (i.e., faith in 11:1–40; hope in 12:1–29; and love 13:1–21).[86] The author's use and development of these terms suggest that "hope" and "love" are closely linked to the concept of faith in Hebrews. However, these characteristics are never intended to stand alone merely as ethical qualities. They have Christ as their reference point. These qualities are the outworking of trusting in the high priest of the new covenant, which was elaborated in 7:1–10:18. A survey of the Pauline literature reveals that Paul occasionally uses this triad in writing to different churches (e.g., 1 Cor 13:13; Eph 1:15–18; Col 1:4–5; 1 Thess 1:3; 5:8). A comparison of the usage of these terms between the Pauline epistles and Hebrews suggests that there may not be too much difference in the concept of faith between them. For both authors faith is based on the crucified work of Jesus Christ, however differently it was expressed. For both authors love and hope are the effect of having faith

---

[85] The two participles ἐγκαταλείποντες and παρακαλοῦντες are adverbial participles. Both are used as the participles of manner (i.e., the manner in which the action is carried out). See Blass, Debrunner, and Funk, *Grammar*, 216–7; Robertson, *A Grammar of the Greek New Testament*, 1127).

[86] James Swetnam, "Form and Content in Hebrews 7–13," 339.

in Christ. Thus Grässer's assertion that in Hebrews the specific notion of faith does not have continuation either in the reflective Pauline sense or unreflective Synoptic sense cannot be sustained in light of the evidence that the exhortations using the triad of faith, hope, and love are based on the Christology of Jesus' high priesthood.[87]

Consequence of Disloyalty to Christ (10:26–31)

I have already mentioned in the discussion of the "basis for the literary unit" that 10:19–25 constitutes section A in the overall chiastic structure of 10:19–39, in which the exhortation to remain in faith is described in a positive tone.[88] However, in this second section (10:26–31, which corresponds to section B), faith is described in a negative manner.

The overall structure. Again, in this section (10:26–31) the author utilizes chiasm at the conceptual level to convey the consequence of forsaking Christ. This chiastic structure can be displayed as follows:

A Ἑκουσίως γὰρ ἁμαρτανόντων ἡμῶν μετὰ τὸ λαβεῖν τὴν ἐπίγνωσιν τῆς ἀληθείας, οὐκέτι περὶ ἁμαρτιῶν ἀπολείπεται θυσία, φοβερὰ δέ τις ἐκδοχὴ κρίσεως καὶ πυρὸς ζῆλος ἐσθίειν μέλλοντος τοὺς ὑπεναντίους (For if we willfully persist in sin after having received the knowledge of the truth, there no longer remains a sacrifice for sins, but a fearful prospect of judgment, and a fury of fire that will consume the adversaries) (10:26–27).

B ἀθετήσας τις νόμον Μωϋσέως χωρὶς οἰκτιρμῶν ἐπὶ δυσὶν ἢ τρισὶν μάρτυσιν ἀποθνῄσκει· (Anyone who has violated the law of Moses dies without mercy "on the testimony of two or three witnesses") (10:28).

B' πόσῳ δοκεῖτε χείρονος ἀξιωθήσεται τιμωρίας ὁ τὸν υἱὸν τοῦ θεοῦ καταπατήσας καὶ τὸ αἷμα τῆς διαθήκης κοινὸν ἡγησάμενος ἐν ᾧ ἡγιάσθη, καὶ τὸ πνεῦμα τῆς χάριτος ἐνυβρίσας; (How much worse punishment do you think will be deserved by those who have spurned the Son of God, profaned the blood of the covenant by which they were sanctified, and outraged the Spirit of grace?) (10:29).

A' οἴδαμεν γὰρ τὸν εἰπόντα·ἐμοὶ ἐκδίκησις, ἐγὼ ἀνταποδώσω. καὶ πάλιν· κρινεῖ κύριος τὸν λαὸν αὐτοῦ. φοβερὸν τὸ ἐμπεσεῖν εἰς χεῖρας θεοῦ ζῶντος. (For we know the one who said, "Vengeance is mine, I will repay."

---

[87] Grässer, *Der Glaube im Hebräerbrief,* 79.

[88] Refer to the structure in 157–58.

And again, "The Lord will judge his people." It is a fearful thing to fall into the hands of the living God) (10:30–31).89

In the center of the chiasm (B and B') the author shows the contrast between the judgment under the old covenant and that of the new covenant. The contrast is between the violation under the Mosaic law (B) and the rejection of the Son of God under the new the covenant (B'). The outer sections (A and A') describe the judgment of God. However, the description of sin is more general than that in the center sections (B, B'). Section A' complements section A by confirming the certainty of God's judgment with the citation of the Old Testament passages (Deut 32:35, 36; Psa 135:14, 27). A brief analysis of the passage justifies the contention that the author developed his argument with a chiastic structure in mind.

Faith and Christology. In this section (10:26–31) the author of Hebrews continues to encourage the readers to hold fast the faith which they had when they first believed. However, the exhortation is given from the standpoint of the judgment of God. In other words, he admonishes the readers to continue with faith in God by reminding them of the consequence of forsaking that to which they had once adhered. The question that needs to be answered here is whether or not this calling for the renewal of faith is Christologically oriented. An analysis of 10:26–31 indicates that the passage is full of descriptions of the crucified Son of God. This can be observed in two ways: first, from the definition of sin in 10:26–27; second, from the *a fortiori* argument in 10:28–31.

First of all, the Christological emphasis of faith can be noted from the description of sin in 10:26–27. The author begins 10:26a with the expression "if we continue to sin (ἁμαρτανόντων ἡμῶν) deliberately after having received the full knowledge of the truth."90 The Christological implication of the verse hinges upon the meaning of "the deliberate sin." Which sin does the author have in mind in this verse? Oberholtzer argues that the willful sin refers to not holding fast to the confession and the practice of forsaking the assembly in the immediate context.

89 NRSV translation.

90 The participle of genitive absolute ἁμαρτανόντων in 10:26 expresses the condition. Thus, this clause functions as the protasis in the structure of vv. 26–27. The present tense of the verb justifies translation of "if we continue to sin . . ."

For this reason he argues that the deliberate sin mentioned in 10:26a refers to the sin which does not result in the loss of salvation, but the loss
of means for cleansing of sin.[91] Thus he concludes that the willful sin
does not mean apostasy (i.e., the willful rejection of Jesus Christ), but
that which is severe enough to result in a temporal discipline on the de-
fecting believers.[92]

However, the overall use of the language in 10:26–31 suggests that
the sin is unbelief, namely, the rejection of Jesus.[93] The expression, "after having received the knowledge of the truth" (10:26a), refers to the
enlightenment they received with the reception of the gospel. A similar
phrase is also used in the Pastoral epistles to denote the conversion experience (1 Tim 2:4; 4:3; 2 Tim 2:25; 3:7; Titus 1:1).[94] Therefore, the immediate context reveals that "deliberate sinning" is rejecting the revelation that God provided through Jesus Christ. The consequences of rejecting the truth are described in the apodosis (10:26b–27). The expression, "there no longer remains a sacrifice concerning sins" (10:26b), is
the reflection of the "once for all" nature of Christ's sacrifice for sins
(7:27; 9:12, 26; 10:2, 10). The judgment described in 10:27, "a certain
terrifying expectation of judgment and razing fire are about to consume
the adversaries," speaks of the final outcome of those who reject Christ
willfully after they have received the knowledge of the truth, not temporary discipline for believers. The deliberate sin refers to "a complete
rupture of allegiance to Jesus Christ."[95] Thus it is clear that this warning
has a Christological basis.

Second, the Christological orientation of faith may be observed from
the comparison of the punishment between the old and the new covenant
(10:28–31). The comparison is made by the use of a literary device

[91] T. K. Oberholtzer, "The Warning Passages in Hebrews. Part 4 (of 5 parts): The
Danger of Willful Sin in Hebrews 10:26–39," *Bibliotheca Sacra* 145 (1988): 413.

[92] Ibid, 413, 19.

[93] This idea is described in various ways throughout the epistle, such as "to drift
away" (παραρρέω) (2:1); "to fall away" (ἀφίστημι) from the living God" (3:12); "to
commit apostasy" (παραπίπτω) (6:6); "to sin deliberately" (ἐκουσίως ἁμαρτάνω)
(10:26); "to reject" (ἀποστρέφομαι) him (12:25).

[94] Attridge, *The Epistle to the Hebrews,* 292.

[95] James Kenneth Solari, "The Problem of Metanoia in the Epistle to the Hebrews"
(S.T.D. diss., The Catholic University of America, 1970), 108.

170 CHAPTER SIX

called an *a fortiori* argument. The background of the violation in 10:28 is found in Deuteronomy 17:1–6, which indicates that the sin is referred to as "turning to serve other gods." The implication of the argument is clear: "if the punishment of the offense in the Old Testament was physical death, how much more do you think the spiritual consequence of rejecting the Son of God is?" The consequence of apostasy under the new covenant is far more severe than that under the old covenant.

The characteristics of the one who deliberately sins, as mentioned in 10:26–27, is described in 10:29 with three participial clauses. The first characteristic is described as the one who tramples underfoot the Son of God. The verb καταπατέω is an intensified form of πατέω, meaning either "treading down" literally or "to treat contemptuously" figuratively.[96] In 4:14 the title "the Son of God" was associated with the object of believers' faith. In 6:6 falling away from the "Son of God" is described as crucifying him again. Thus the meaning of trampling underfoot the Son of God may be considered equivalent to re-crucifying him. The second characteristic of the one who willfully sins is described as the one who has profaned (κοινὸν ἡγησάμενος) the blood of the covenant. The verb ἡγέομαι means "to think," "to consider," "to regard," suggesting that it denotes an attitude of the subject.[97] The phrase "the blood of the covenant" (τὸ αἷμα τῆς διαθήκης) is used in 9:20 already. It refers to the better covenant (7:22; 8:6), namely, a new covenant (8:8; 9:5), which was instituted with the blood of Jesus. Thus it can be said that the one who profanes the blood of the covenant has an attitude of unbelief toward Christ. The third characteristic of the one who sins willfully is described as the person who has insulted the Spirit of grace. The Spirit here no doubt refers to the Holy Spirit (2:4; 3:7; 6:4; 9:8). Although this insult is not directly aimed at Christ, the author makes it clear that it is identical to despising the salvific work of Christ because in 9:14 the Holy Spirit is associated with the sacrifice of Christ, and in 10:15, bearing witness to the new covenant. This insult appears to be parallel to the blasphemy of the Holy Spirit in the Synoptic Gospels (Matt 12:31; Mark 3:29; Luke 12:10). The blasphemy against the Holy

---

[96] H. Seesemann, "καταπατέω κτλ.," in *Theological Dictionary of the New Testament*, ed. Gerhard Friedrich, tr. Geoffrey W. Bromiley (Grand Rapids: William B. Eerdmans Publishing Co., 1967), 5:941.

[97] Bauer, *Lexicon*, 343.

Spirit in the Synoptic Gospels is indirectly aimed at the Son of Man; likewise, the insult of the Spirit of grace has an indirect reference to Christ. The *a fortiori* argument in 10:28–29 is strengthened by the next verses (10:30–31), in which the author brings in two quotations from Deuteronomy 32:35–36. In these verses the certainty of divine judgment on those who reject the salvific work of Christ is reiterated.

Summary. An examination of 10:26–31 shows that the willful sin mentioned in 10:26 does not refer to sins in general, but specifically the sin of apostasy, namely, the willful rejection of the Son of God. In this passage the author warns the readers not to commit this dreadful sin by emphasizing the judgment which will come upon them. The idea of judgment is described with words, such as "no more sacrifice for sin" (10:26), "razing fire" (10:27), "how much worse punishment" (10:29), and "it is terrible to fall into the hands of the living God" (10:31). However, that the purpose of employing these negative descriptions is to warn them in such a way that they may continue in the faith which they began with the reception of the knowledge of truth. Moreover, this exhortation to remain in faith is grounded in Christology. The phrase "no more sacrifice for sin" (10:26) is a clear reference to "once for all" sacrifice of Christ. The descriptions such as "trampling underfoot the Son of God," "profaning the blood of the covenant," and "insulting the Spirit of grace" in 10:29 are different ways of expressing not having faith in Jesus Christ, or not trusting Jesus Christ in Pauline language. In this sense, faith in Hebrews is as Christological as in the Pauline literature.

Exhortation to Persevere
in Faith (10:32–39)

The previous discussion showed that the author employed a chiastic structure in arranging the overall structure of 10:19–39. In 10:19–25 the exhortation was given from a positive angle (A). In 10:26–31 (B) it was given from a negative standpoint (i.e., by means of solemn warning). Again, in 10:32–39 the author reverts to a positive exhortation, thus completing the chiasm (A').[98] An examination of 10:19–25 (A) and 10:26–31 (B) has already revealed that faith in Hebrews is closely related to the Christological teaching. Likewise, in this third section

---

[98] Refer to the structure in p. 157–58.

(10:32–39) (A'), faith is grounded in Christology; however, the emphasis is shifted more to the ethical aspect of faith. *The overall structure.* A careful analysis of 10:32–39 reveals that the author arranges his argument by utilizing another chiasm. This may be illustrated as follows:99

A Ἀναμιμνήσκεσθε δὲ τὰς πρότερον ἡμέρας, ἐν αἷς φωτισθέντες πολλὴν ἄθλησιν ὑπεμείνατε παθημάτων (But recall those earlier days when, after you had been enlightened, you endured a hard struggle with sufferings) (10:32),

B τοῦτο μὲν ὀνειδισμοῖς τε καὶ θλίψεσιν θεατριζόμενοι, τοῦτο δὲ κοιν-ωνοὶ τῶν οὕτως ἀναστρεφομένων γενηθέντες. καὶ γὰρ τοῖς δεσμίοις συνεπαθήσατε καὶ τὴν ἁρπαγὴν τῶν ὑπαρχόντων ὑμῶν μετὰ χαρᾶς προσεδέξασθε γινώσκοντες ἔχειν ἑαυτοὺς κρείττονα ὕπαρξιν καὶ μέ-νουσαν (Sometimes being publicly exposed to abuse and persecution, and sometimes being partners with those so treated. For you had compassion for those who were in prison, and you cheerfully accepted the plundering of your possessions, knowing that you yourselves possessed something better and more lasting) (10:33–34).

C Μὴ ἀποβάλητε οὖν τὴν παρρησίαν ὑμῶν, ἥτις ἔχει μεγάλην μισθα-ποδοσίαν (Do not, therefore, abandon that confidence of yours; it brings a great reward) (10:35).

B' ὑπομονῆς γὰρ ἔχετε χρείαν ἵνα τὸ θέλημα τοῦ θεοῦ ποιήσαντες κομί-σησθε τὴν ἐπαγγελίαν. ἔτι γὰρ μικρὸν ὅσον ὅσον, ὁ ἐρχόμενος ἥξει καὶ οὐ χρονίσει· ὁ δὲ δίκαιός μου ἐκ πίστεως ζήσεται, καὶ ἐὰν ὑποσ-τείληται, οὐκ εὐδοκεῖ ἡ ψυχή μου ἐν αὐτῷ (For you need endurance, so that when you have done the will of God, you may receive what was prom-ised. For yet "in a very little while, the one who is coming will come and will not delay; but my righteous one will live by faith. My soul takes no pleasure in anyone who shrinks back") (10:36–38).

A' ἡμεῖς δὲ οὐκ ἐσμὲν ὑποστολῆς εἰς ἀπώλειαν ἀλλὰ πίστεως εἰς περιποί-ησιν ψυχῆς (But we are not among those who shrink back and so are lost, but among those who have faith and so are saved) (10:39).

In this proposed structure sections A and A' are parallel to each other in that both express the thought of salvation; while A describes the initial moment of salvation (i.e., φωτισθέντες in v. 32), A' brings out the idea of eschatological salvation (πίστεως εἰς περιποίησιν ψυχῆς in v. 39).

---

99 The translation is taken from NRSV.

Moreover, A' also points out that those who have endured a hard struggle in the past (A) are identified as the ones who have secured their soul by faith. Sections B and B' are also parallel to each other in that, while the former emphasizes the hardships they had suffered in the past, the latter stresses the need of endurance at the present time. Moreover, the eschatological promise of the reward for endurance in both sections suggests that B and B' are parallel in thought. The center of the chiasm is 10:35 (C), which exhorts the readers not to throw away their confidence. Since there are repetitions of themes between A/B and A'/B', it is reasonable to consider 10:35 as the center of the chiasm.[100] The significance of this center will be explained in the following section. The broad chiastic structure of 10:32–39 may be illustrated as follows:

I   In the past you have endured sufferings after you have been enlightened, realizing that you have a better possession (10:32–34).

II   Therefore, do not throw away your confidence, which has a great reward (10:35).

I'   In the present time you need to have endurance, in order that you may receive the promise of God, after having done the will of God (10:36–39).

This simplified chiastic structure shows that the author makes a contrast between the past and the present spiritual conditions of the readers, with the exhortation not to throw away the confidence in the center section.

Faith and Christology. If this chiastic structure is what the author had in mind, then what might be the significance and the purpose of the exhortation in 10:35? Many scholars agree that the center of chiasm usually forms its climax, indicating the point of the emphasis, whether its significance is ethical or theological.[101] Here in 10:35 the center of the chiasm is important for a theological reason. From the previous discussion of 10:19 it was disclosed that the word παρρησία had Jesus as its object whether it was understood subjectively (i.e., confidence or

---

100 For detailed explanation of the importance of the center of chiasm see C. Blomberg, "The Structure of 2 Corinthians 1–7," *Criswell Theological Review* 4 (1989): 7.

101 Ibid. See also Donald R. Miesner, "Chiasmus and the Composition and Message of Paul's Missionary Sermons" (S.T.D. diss., Lutheran School of Theology at Chicago, 1974), 34.

boldness) or objectively (i.e., the freedom and the authority to enter the sanctuary by the blood of Christ). In that verse it was determined that the emphasis of the word was on the objective meaning. However, in 10:35, the subjective meaning makes more sense because the immediate context (10:32–34) speaks of their enduring public abuse and affliction, and having become the partners with those who are so treated. Here, the author points out that the community's bearing of public hostility is a manifestation of παρρησία.[102] Thus the word παρρησία ought to be translated in a subjective sense as "confidence," or "boldness."

However, I believe that this subjective confidence is Christologically oriented. It denotes "the confident attitude of the person of faith before God and the world."[103] The use of παρρησία in 10:35 goes back to the theme of the sacrificial death and the high priesthood of Christ in 7:1–10:18. It is evident from the author's way of alternating the doctrinal and parenetic section in 7:1–10:39 (7:1–10:18, doctrine; 10:19–39, parenesis). Thus the exhortation not to throw away the confidence is equivalent to not forsaking the high priestly work of Christ, who offered himself up for sins once for all (7:27; 9:12; 10:10) and intercedes for believers (7:24–25). Understanding παρρησία in the broad context allows one to realize that 10:35 is essentially a call to hold fast faith in Jesus Christ. Hebrews' use of παρρησία is not different from that of Paul. Just as Paul's use of the term is closely related to faith in Jesus, Hebrews utilizes it in relation to Christology.[104] In this sense, faith in Hebrews is as Christological as Paul's concept of faith.

---

[102] T. W. Lewis, "'. . . And If He Shrinks Back' (Heb. 10:38b)," *New Testament Studies* 22 (1976): 89.

[103] Lane, *Hebrews 9–13*, 301.

[104] Some examples of Paul's use of παρρησία: (1) access in boldness (παρρησία) and confidence through faith in him (Eph 3:12); (2) with all boldness Christ will be exalted (Phil 1:20); (3) Great boldness in the faith that is in Jesus Christ (1 Tim 3:13); bold enough in Christ to commend you (Philemon 1:8). I am aware that Pauline authorship of Ephesians and the Pastorals is denied by some modern scholars. I affirm that both Ephesians and the Pastorals are written by Paul. For Pauline authorship of Ephesians see: Markus Barth, *Ephesians*, The Anchor Bible (New York: Doubleday, 1974), 36–41; D. A. Carson, Douglas J. Moo, and Leon Morris, *An Introduction to the New Testament* (Grand Rapids: Zondervan Publishing House, 1992), 305–309. Against Pauline authorship of Ephesians see Andrew T. Lincoln, *Ephesians*, Word Biblical Commentary (Dallas: Word Books, 1990), lix–lxxiii; For Pauline authorship of the Pastorals see George W. Knight III, *Commentary on the Pastoral Epistles*, New International Greek Testament

With a Christological exhortation in the center, the author arranges the ethical element of perseverance both in 10:32–34 (A/B or I) and 10:36–39 (A'/B' or I'). As revealed in the chiastic structure, the latter emphasizes the present need of the readers to endure, whereas the former reminds the persevering endurance in the past. Again, it is my conviction that both 10:32–34 and 10:36–39 are arranged symmetrically at the microcosmic level to stress the need for persevering faith on the part of the readers. The chiasm of 10:32–34 may be illustrated as follows:

A   Ἀναμιμνῄσκεσθε δὲ τὰς πρότερον ἡμέρας, ἐν αἷς φωτισθέντες πολλὴν ἄθλησιν ὑπεμείνατε παθημάτων (But recall those earlier days when, after you had been enlightened, you endured a hard struggle with sufferings) (10:32),

   B   τοῦτο μὲν ὀνειδισμοῖς τε καὶ θλίψεσιν θεατριζόμενοι (sometimes being publicly exposed to abuse and persecution) (10:33a),

      C   τοῦτο δὲ κοινωνοὶ τῶν οὕτως ἀναστρεφομένων γενηθέντες (and sometimes being partners with those so treated) (10:33b).

      C'   καὶ γὰρ τοῖς δεσμίοις συνεπαθήσατε (For you had compassion for those who were in prison) (10:34a),

   B'   καὶ τὴν ἁρπαγὴν τῶν ὑπαρχόντων ὑμῶν μετὰ χαρᾶς προσεδέξασθε (and you cheerfully accepted the plundering of your possessions) (10:34b),

A'   γινώσκοντες ἔχειν ἑαυτοὺς κρείττονα ὕπαρξιν καὶ μένουσαν (knowing that you yourselves possessed something better and more lasting) (10:34c).[105]

In this proposed chiastic structure it is obvious that the center sections complement each other; while section C speaks of having been partners of those who are persecuted, section C' explains the reason for their behavior. Sections B and B' speak of the persecution the readers themselves experienced (i.e., B' elaborates in what ways they were pub-

Commentary (Grand Rapids: William B. Eerdmans, 1992), 4–12, 21–45; Against Pauline authorship of the Pastorals see Raymond E. Brown, *An Introduction to the New Testament* (New York: Doubleday, 1997), 653–68.

[105] The translation is taken from NRSV. The chiasm in this passage is also observed by Lane. However, Lane sees the chiastic arrangement only in 10:33a–34b. He fails to observe the chiasm in the entire section of 10:32–34. See Lane, *Hebrews 9–13,* 299. See also Lewis, "'. . . And If He Shrinks Back' (Heb 10:38b)," 89.

licly exposed to abuse and persecution in B). The outer sections (A and A') complement each other in that while A describes hardships after enlightenment, A' explains why they endured persecution and abuse (i.e., they had the knowledge that they had a better and lasting possession in the future). In A and A' the author emphasizes both present and future aspects of eschatology. In this sense, faith in Hebrews has an eschatological orientation. A brief analysis of the above structure provides convincing evidence that the author may well have been thinking chiastically in designing the structure of 10:32–34. In this passage the ethical elements of faith are clearly emphasized. Faith in Hebrews in this section is perseverance (i.e., enduring persecution and hardship). This ethical aspect may be observed from every section of the chiastic structure. However, it should also be remembered that this ethical exhortation has its basis on the Christological orientation of faith in 10:35. For the author of Hebrews Christology is the starting point of faith, and faith does not exist without Christology. This thought will become more evident in the analysis of the parallel passage in 10:36–39.

As mentioned above, a detailed study of 10:36–39 reveals that the author calls the readers to persevere in faith by employing another chiastic structure at the microcosmic level. It may be illustrated as follows:

A ὑπομονῆς γὰρ ἔχετε χρείαν ἵνα τὸ θέλημα τοῦ θεοῦ ποιήσαντες κομίση-
σθε τὴν ἐπαγγελίαν. (For you need endurance, so that when you have done
the will of God, you may receive what was promised) (10:36).

B ἔτι γὰρ μικρὸν ὅσον ὅσον, ὁ ἐρχόμενος ἥξει καὶ οὐ χρονίσει (For yet
"in a very little while, the one who is coming will come and will not delay)
(10:37);

B' ὁ δὲ δίκαιος μου ἐκ πίστεως ζήσεται, καὶ ἐὰν ὑποστείληται, οὐκ εὐδοκεῖ ἡ ψυχή μου ἐν αὐτῷ. (but my righteous one will live by faith. My
soul takes no pleasure in anyone who shrinks back) (10:38)."

A' ἡμεῖς δὲ οὐκ ἐσμὲν ὑποστολῆς εἰς ἀπώλειαν ἀλλὰ πίστεως εἰς περιποίησιν ψυχῆς. (But we are not among those who shrink back and so are lost, but
among those who have faith and so are saved) (10:39).106

---

106 The translation is taken from NRSV.

In this structure the center of the chiasm (B and B') is signaled by the phrases ὁ ἐρχόμενος (B) in 10:37 and ὁ δὲ δίκαιός μου (B') in 10:38. This arrangement becomes obvious when one observes the author's intentional change of the citation of the Old Testament passages. A comparison of 10:37 with Isaiah 26 (LXX) shows that only part of Isaiah 26:20 is quoted (i.e., μικρὸν ὅσον ὅσον), while the expression ὁ ἐρχόμενος ἥξει καὶ οὐ χρονίσει (he who comes will come and will not delay) is inserted intentionally.107 Besides, in quoting Habakkuk 2:4 (LXX) in 10:38, the author intentionally alters the order of the two independent sentences.108 What might have been the reason for this alteration? Although one cannot be dogmatic, it seems that the phrases ὁ ἐρχόμενος and ὁ δὲ δίκαιός μου are arranged closely to each other to show that they form the center of the chiastic structure of 10:36–39. Conceptually, B and B' are parallel because while B emphasizes the future coming of the Lord, B' stresses the necessity of living by faith in the meantime.

Sections A and A' complement each other in that ὑπομονῆς (10:36) stands opposite to ὑποστολῆς (10:39). In addition, the idea of "faith" (πίστις) in 10:39 is closely related to "endurance" (ὑπομονῆς) in 10:36 and "shrinking back" (ὑποστολῆς) in 10:39, which suggests that faith in Hebrews is steadfastness. Furthermore, the parallel thought between A and A' may also be noted from the description of the idea of salvation. In 10:36 "receiving the promise" means the final salvation in the future. This idea is contrasted with the present salvation in 10:39 (i.e., preserving of the soul). Thus it is quite reasonable to conclude that 10:36–39 is arranged in a chiastic manner.

Which aspect of faith is emphasized in this passage? As in 10:32–34 this section also reveals that faith in Hebrews involves the ethical ele-

---

107 Isaiah 26:20 (LXX) reads as follows:

βάδιζε λαός μου εἴσελθε εἰς τὰ ταμίειά σου ἀπόκλεισον την θύραν σου ἀπο-κρύβηθι μικρὸν ὅσον ὅσον ἕως ἂν παρέλθη ἡ ὀργὴ κυρίου. Only the underlined portion is quoted in Hebrews 10:37.

108 Habakkuk 2:4 (LXX) reads:

ἐὰν ὑποστείληται οὐκ εὐδοκεῖ ἡ ψυχή μου ἐν αὐτῷ ὁ δὲ δίκαιος ἐκ πίστεώς μου ζήσεται. In 10:38 the second part of the quotation (i.e., the underlined words) is moved to the beginning of the verse. It is also observed that μου is placed next to δίκαιος in Hebrews 10:38.

ment of steadfastness. This is clearly indicated by the combination of the word πίστις with faith-related terms. For example, sections A and A' reveal that πίστις is equivalent to ὑπομονή (vv. 36, 39). The middle sections (B and B') also show that πίστις is "not shrinking back" in light of the coming of Christ. Hence, Grässer's assertion that faith in Hebrews is "steadfastness" is correct in a sense.[109] However, a critical analysis of 10:36–39 also suggests that this ethical aspect of faith is intimately related to Christology. In the center sections (B and B') the author plainly points out that an exhortation for the righteous one to live by faith (v. 38) is in light of the imminence of the Second Coming of Christ (v. 37). Admittedly, in this passage the author is not explicit about the identity of who "the one who is coming" is. Nevertheless, the broad context (10:19–39) suggests that it has the reference to Christ at his Second Coming. More specifically, 9:28 indicates that Christ will appear a second time to save those who eagerly wait for him. Furthermore, an examination of ὁ ἐρχόμενος in other New Testament literature indicates that the phrase refers to either the First Advent or the Second Advent of Christ. Thus the center of the chiasm makes it evident that an exhortation for the righteous one (i.e., believer) to live by faith is based on the Second Advent of Christ.[110] In other words, it may be asserted that the call to live by faith without shrinking back is Christologically oriented. At the same time, faith in this passage has an eschatological orientation of both present and future. While B focuses on the future, B' has its emphasis on the present aspect. Through this eschatological tension the author brings home the need for the readers not to shrink back (ὑποστέλλω), but to remain faithful through perseverance in the midst of persecutions and trials. Thus the thesis that that the ethical aspect of faith in 10:36–39 is both Christologically and eschatologically oriented has strong support.

---

[109] Grässer, *Der Glaube im Hebräerbrief,* 41–42.

[110] The phrase ὁ ἐρχόμενος is used 17 times in the New Testament. Six times it is used to refer to the First Advent (Matt 11:3; 21:9; Luke 7:19, 20; John. 6:14; 12:13); eight times, the Second Advent (Matt 23:39; Mark 11:19; Luke 13:35; 19:38; Rev 1:4, 8;

Summary and Conclusion

A detailed examination of 7:1–10:39 reveals that the Christological aspect of faith is not lacking. Faith in Hebrews has Jesus as the object of faith for believers, even if it is not expressed in terms of "faith in Christ." The author reminds the readers that the three exhortations (i.e., let us draw near, let us hold fast, let us consider) in 10:19–25 have Jesus as the object of faith because they are based on the teaching of the high priesthood of Christ in 7:1–10:18. In 10:26–31 the author shows the Christological relationship to faith by defining that the deliberate sin is rejecting God's revelation provided through Jesus Christ (i.e., the sin of apostasy) (10:26–27). In 10:32–39 the ethical quality of steadfastness is based on the Christological teaching of not to throw away the confidence. This is essentially equivalent to the expression to continue with faith in Christ. Moreover, the exhortation to have endurance (10:36, 39) is based on the Second Coming of Christ (10:37). In this sense, the author's appeal to be steadfast in their faith is Christological. The above summary makes it clear that the author of Hebrews portrays Jesus as the object of faith for believers without expressing it in terms of "faith in Christ" or "believing in Jesus." Therefore, it may be concluded that faith in 7:1–10:39 is Christologically oriented.

4:8); three times, other than Christ (Luke 6:47; John 6:35; 2 Cor 11:4). This analysis reveals that the phrase is clearly a Christological title.

CHAPTER SEVEN

RELATIONSHIP BETWEEN 11:1–40 AND 12:1–29:
ENDURING FAITH AND DANGER OF
REJECTING GOD'S WORD

An examination of the occurrences of the word πίστις in Hebrews reveals that it is used 32 times throughout the epistle, out of which 25 occurrences are found in 11:1–12:29. This means that the term appears only 7 times outside of this section (4:2; 6:1,12; 10:22, 38, 39; 13:7). The author's frequent use of the term indicates that 11:1–12:29 is a major section for the discussion of the concept of faith. In the larger context the doctrinal (11:1–40) and the parenetic section (12:1–29) form a literary unit from a thematic and a structural standpoint. First, thematically speaking, the author reminds the readers in 10:35–39 that they need to have endurance in the midst of trials that they are facing. In chapter 11 this point is illustrated from a series of the exemplars of faith in the Old Testament. In 12:1–3 the author continues this theme of endurance by exhorting them to consider Jesus who endured the cross. Second, the structural relationship indicates that 11:1–40 and 12:1–29 are related to each other. For example, the reference to ἡμεῖς in 12:1 is related to ἡμῶν in 11:40. The phrase νέφος μαρτύρων in 12:1 refers to μαρτυρη-θέντες in 11:39. In addition, the word τελειωτήν in 12:2 is related to τελειωθῶσιν in 11:40.[1] In this sense, 11:1–12:29 should be considered a literary unit. In this final alternating structure I will examine the relationship between 11:1–40 (doctrine) and 12:1–29 (parenesis) as in the previous chapters to determine whether the concept of faith in this alternating structure is Christologically oriented. At the same time the relationship between faith and eschatology will be dealt with extensively. As for the issue of whether eschatology in Hebrews has a spatial or temporal orientation, it has already been concluded in chapter 2 that the author of Hebrews did not depend on the Hellenistic idea of spatial dualism, or

---

[1] D. A. Black, "A Note on the Structure of Hebrews 12:1–2," *Biblica* 68 (1987): 544.

the Philonic concept of visible and invisible world, but the Jewish temporal idea of eschatology. For this reason I will not interact with the idea of spatial concept in this chapter. I will interpret chapter 11 with temporal eschatology of present and future in mind.

Examination of 11:1–40

The theme of chapter 11 was already announced in 10:38–39 by indicating that the righteous one shall live by faith, and we are not among those who are shrinking back to destruction but those who have secured the soul by faith. In these verses the author emphasizes the necessity of maintaining the steadfastness of faith. Then what is the purpose of chapter 11? Thompson observes that both 10:32–39 and 12:1–11 have a common theme of endurance (ὑπομονή) in the midst of sufferings, and that chapter 11 is in the middle of these two sections.[2] In light of this thematic arrangement it seems that the purpose of chapter 11 is to provide examples of those who have remained steadfast through persecutions and trials.

Basis for the Literary Unit

What evidence does the author provide to warrant that chapter 11 forms a literary unit? Several structural clues suggest that this entire chapter should be regarded as a unit. To begin with, the author employs an inclusion by the words πίστις and μαρτυρέω both at the beginning (11:1–2) and the end of the chapter (11:39–40) to set the boundary for the passage.[3] This overall literary unit is maintained by many scholars.[4]

---

[2] James W. Thompson, *The Beginnings of Christian Philosophy: The Epistle to the Hebrews,* Catholic Biblical Quarterly Monograph Series 13 (Washington, DC: Catholic Biblical Society of America, 1982), 69.

[3] Because of this literary device, some scholars regard 11:1–2 as the introduction, and 11:39–40 as the conclusion. For example, see Paul Ellingworth, *The Epistle to the Hebrews: A Commentary on the Greek Text,* New International Greek Testament Commentary, ed. I. Howard Marshall and W. W. Gasque (Grand Rapids: William B. Eerdmans Publishing Co., 1993), 561. However, it is to be remembered that one cannot depend on the literary form only. The content should be considered along with the form in analyzing the structure. For this reason I maintain that the introduction extends to verse 3. This will become more evident in discussing the chiastic structure of 11:1–3.

A detailed observation of chapter 11 reveals that the middle section (11:3–38) is divided into two main parts. The first part (11:3–31) forms a sub-unit by another literary device called anaphora, which is the repetition of an initial word.[5] In the present context an anaphora is signaled by the dative form πίστει. Moreover, this section is further divided into five parts: (1) the first πίστει series (vv. 3–5); (2) the first interim remark (v. 6); (3) the second πίστει series (vv. 7–12); (4) the second interim comment (vv. 13–16); (5) the third πίστει series (vv. 17–31).[6] The second part (11:32–38) is marked by the end of the anaphora series, which is indicated by the genitive phrase διὰ πίστεως (v. 33).[7] With this expression there follows a rapid series of those who had demonstrated endurance through faith. Hence 11:32–38 may be considered another sub-unit. The chain of thought in 11:32–38 is broken by another use of the genitive form of πίστις in 11:39. This leads to the inference that 11:39–40 serves as the conclusion of the exposition of faith in Hebrews 11.

Teachings on Faith

In the previous discussion it was revealed that in Hebrews an exhortation to remain in faith is always based on certain aspects of the Christological teaching in each of the alternating structures of exposition and parenesis. However, it may be observed that in this final alternating

---

[4] For example see F. F. Bruce, *The Epistle to the Hebrews,* New International Commentary on the New Testament (Grand Rapids: William B. Eerdmans Publishing Co., 1964), 227; D. Guthrie, *The Letter to the Hebrews,* Tyndale New Testament Commentaries (Grand Rapids: William B. Eerdmans Publishing Co., 1983), 59. However, Miller argues that the literary unit of chapter 11 is not complete without the first two verses of chapter 12. See M. R. Miller, "What is the Literary Form of Hebrews 11?," *Journal of the Evangelical Theological Society* 29 (1986): 411–17.

[5] Michael R. Cosby, *The Rhetorical Composition and Function of Hebrews 11: In Light of Example Lists in Antiquity* (Macon, GA: Mercer University Press, 1988), 3.

[6] Ellingworth shares a similar view with me regarding the interim remark of the anaphora. However, he does not consider verse 6 to be the interim remark. Thus he sees only two πίστις series (vv. 3–12 and vv. 17–31). See Ellingworth, *The Epistle to the Hebrews,* 561. I believe that the interruptions of the anaphora are indicated by different cases (i.e., genitive in v. 6, accusative in v. 13), thus making three series of πίστει.

[7] The author indicates the break of the subdivision with the use of different cases of πίστις in chapter 11.

structure (11:1–40 and 12:1–13), there is no specific section devoted to Christological teaching. In what may seem to be the doctrinal section (11:1–40), the author describes only certain aspects of faith. For this reason chapter 11 may be considered expository in form, but parenetic in function.[8] In this section I will demonstrate that the author's eschatological orientation of faith has a forward-looking aspect. Besides, I will set for the argument that this eschatological outlook is directly related to the Christological aspect of faith. It is my conviction that the author of Hebrews deliberately designed chapter 11 chiastically both in its overall structure and many of the subsections to describe what faith is. This structure may be illustrated as follows:

A   Introduction (11:1–3)
  B   Abel's example of suffering on account of faith (11:4)
    C   Enoch's example of triumph through faith (11:5)
      D   Principle of faith: Impossible to please God without faith (11:6)
        E   Example of faith seen through Noah (11:7)
          F   Abraham's faith in obeying God's calling (11:8–10)
            G   Sarah's example of faith in conceiving Isaac (11:11–12)
              H   Middle section: Interim comment (11:13–16)
            G'   Abraham's example of faith in offering up Isaac (11:17–19)
          F'   Examples of faith from Isaac, Jacob, and Joseph (11:20–22)
        E'   Examples of faith seen in the Mosaic era (11:23–29)
      D'   Examples of faith in conquering Jericho (11:30–31)
    C'   Examples of those who had triumph through faith (11:32–35a)
  B'   Examples of those who suffered on account of faith (11:35b–38)
A'   Conclusion (11:39–40)

I will follow this rhetorical structure to examine the concept of faith in chapter 11. The exposition will begin with the center point (11:13–16; H); then each corresponding section will be analyzed to ascertain what aspect of faith is emphasized. In examining each corresponding passage, the basis for the parallel structure will also be established.

Middle Section: Interim Comment (11:13–16; H)

The middle section has caused much difficulty for many scholars. For example, Moxnes states, "the insertion of the author's own comments in 11:13–16 makes it more difficult to see the structure of the un-

---

8 William L. Lane, *Hebrews 9–13*, Word Biblical Commentary (Dallas: Word Books, 1991), 316.

derlying source."9 Michel also recognizes the problem in this passage and asserts that 11:13–16 is an editorial insertion.10 However, these difficulties may be resolved when one realizes that the author placed it intentionally for a rhetorical purpose to make it a center of the chiasm in chapter 11.

Analysis of the structure. As mentioned in the previous discussion, a break of an anaphora, which began in 11:3, is signaled by the accusative use of πίστις with the preposition κατά (i.e., κατὰ πίστιν) in 11:13. The author resumes the faith series by using πίστει again in 11:17. A study of this middle section reveals that it is arranged chiastically, which may be illustrated as follows:11

A Κατὰ πίστιν ἀπέθανον οὗτοι πάντες, μὴ λαβόντες τὰς ἐπαγγελίας ἀλλὰ πόρρωθεν αὐτὰς ἰδόντες καὶ ἀσπασάμενοι καὶ ὁμολογήσαντες ὅτι ξένοι καὶ παρεπίδημοί εἰσιν ἐπὶ τῆς γῆς (All of these died in faith without having received the promises, but from a distance they saw and greeted them. They confessed that they were strangers and foreigners on the earth) (11:13),

B οἱ γὰρ τοιαῦτα λέγοντες ἐμφανίζουσιν ὅτι πατρίδα ἐπιζητοῦσιν (for people who speak in this way make it clear that they are seeking a homeland) (11:14).

B' καὶ εἰ μὲν ἐκείνης ἐμνημόνευον ἀφ' ἧς ἐξέβησαν, εἶχον ἂν καιρὸν ἀνακάμψαι (If they had been thinking of the land that they had left behind, they would have had opportunity to return) (11:15).

A' νῦν δὲ κρείττονος ὀρέγονται, τοῦτ' ἔστιν ἐπουρανίου. διὸ οὐκ ἐπαισχύνεται αὐτοὺς ὁ θεὸς θεὸς ἐπικαλεῖσθαι αὐτῶν· ἡτοίμασεν γὰρ αὐτοῖς

---

9 H. Moxnes, *God and His Promise to Abraham,* Theology in Conflict: Novum Testamentum Supplements 53 (Leiden: E. J. Brill, 1980), 178.

10 O. Michel, *Der Brief an die Hebräer,* 12th ed. (Göttingen: Vanderhoeck and Ruprecht, 1966), 401.

11 The translation is taken from NRSV. Bligh considers that 11:11–17 is the center of 11:1–27. Although he fails to see that 11:13–16 is the center of chapter 11, his observation that this could be the center portion of a major section of the chapter is remarkable. See J. Bligh, *Chiastic Analysis of the Epistle to the Hebrews* (Heythrop: Athenaeum, 1966), 22–23. Lane also recognizes that this section is the center of 11:8–22. In the immediate context his observation is correct; however, he also does not recognize that this is the center of the entire chapter. The author of Hebrews seems to have a broader context in mind. See Lane, *Hebrews 9–13,* 355.

πόλιν (But as it is, they desire a better country, that is, a heavenly one. Therefore God is not ashamed to be called their God; indeed, he has prepared a city for them) (11:16).

In this diagram it may be noted that both A and A' are parallel in thought because the promises that they were greeting from a distance (A) is a heavenly place (A'). Moreover, the reason that they regarded themselves as strangers and exiles on earth (A) is that they reached out to a better city in heaven (A'). Center sections B and B' also share a similar thought: while B mentions that they were seeking a homeland, B' shows what would have happened if they were not seeking a homeland: they would have had opportunity to return. Thus the unified flow of the passage is established.

Basis for the center of the chiasm. In what sense can this section (11:13–16) be considered the center of the chiasm? It is evident from the author's use of the phrase "all these" (οὗτοι πάντες) in 11:13. Whom does the phrase "all these" (οὗτοι πάντες) refer to? Swetnam argues that the phrase refers only to those individuals that appear in vv. 8–12 (i.e., Abraham, Sarah, Isaac, and Jacob) because Enoch is exempted from those who died (v. 5).[12] Attridge also regards that those who died in faith (v. 13) primarily are those who are the patriarchs (i.e., Abraham, Isaac, and Jacob) although he acknowledges that it may refer to all the exemplars of faith mentioned in vv. 4–12.[13] The solutions proposed by these scholars are legitimate because the language of the sojourning and forward-looking in 11:13–16 is clearly parallel to those in 11:9–10. However, I consider that "all these" (οὗτοι πάντες) is broad enough to include all the exemplars of faith mentioned not only in 11:4–12, but also those mentioned in 11:17–38.

Then what is the evidence which indicates that "all these" may include all the exemplars of faith in Hebrews 11? First, it may be detected from the use of the present tenses (i.e., εἰσιν, v. 13; ἐμφανίζουσιν and ἐπιζητοῦσιν, v. 14; ὀρέγονται and ἐπαισχύνεται, v. 16) along with the aorist tenses (ἀπέθανον, v. 13; ἡτοίμασεν, v. 16). The author's in-

---

12 James Swetnam, *Jesus and Isaac: A Study of the Epistle to the Hebrews in Light of the Aqedah.* Analecta Biblica 94 (Rome: Pontifical Biblical Institute Press, 1981), 91.

13 Harold W. Attridge, *The Epistle to the Hebrews,* Hermeneia Commentary (Philadelphia: Fortress Press, 1989), 329. Attridge also recognizes the problem of including all the individuals in vv. 4–12 because of Enoch who did not taste physical death.

terchangeable use of the present and aorist tenses suggests that the expression "all these" (οὗτοι πάντες) may encompass more than the patriarchs mentioned in 11:8–12. The reason for the choice of the present tenses is that the author is identifying the readers with the patriarchs. This observation opens up the possibility that the phrase οὗτοι πάντες should not be limited to those in the immediate context: it may include all the heroes of faith in chapter 11. Second, it may be observed from the theme of the promise of God in chapter 11. It is to be noted that the emphasis of the theme in 11:13–16 is not on "death," but on "the promises of God." In other words, the author's main concern in the middle section is to show that it was in a condition of faith, not of fulfillment, that the Old Testament characters died.[14] In this sense, one may understand that Enoch also did not receive the promise of God until he was taken up into heaven. The emphasis of the theme, "not receiving the promises of God," is further strengthened by the introduction (11:1–3) and the conclusion (11:39–40). In both passages the emphasis is, "having been attested by faith, yet not having received the promise of God." In this sense, it may be said that "all these" in 11:13–16 extends to the exemplars of faith both in 11:1–12 and in 11:17–40, because of its function as the center of the chiastic structure.

   Aspects of faith. Then what aspects of faith are emphasized in the center of the chiasm? What is the purpose that the author of Hebrews places this section in the center of chapter 11? First of all, his intention is to make his readers aware that faith in Hebrews has a future orientation. The expressions such as "not having received the promises," "seeing and greeting them afar," "they were seeking a homeland," "they are reaching out for a better place," "heavenly," and "he has prepared for a city for them" clearly indicate that faith has a forward-looking eschatological outlook. Second, an interchangeable use of the aorist and the present tenses in both 11:13 and 11:16 (i.e., from ἀπέθανον το εἰσιν in v. 13; from ὀρέγονται and ἐπασχύνεται to ἡτοίμασεν in v. 16) indicates that faith in Hebrews also has a present aspect. This tension between "the present and the future," the "already and not yet," can also be found in other parts of the book of Hebrews. For example, one finds in 2:8 that God has already put all things in subjection to Jesus, and crowned him with honor and glory, but 10:13 states that he has to wait until his ene-

---

[14] Ellingworth, *The Epistle to the Hebrews*, 593.

mies should be made a footstool for his feet. Although believers are entering the rest at the present time (4:3), the rest still remains open for the
future (4:1, 6, 9); one must strive to enter the rest.[15] In this sense, it may
be said that faith in Hebrews involves both present and future aspects.

Sarah's Conception and Abraham's Offering up
of Isaac (11:11–12; G//11:17–19; G')

Basis for the chiasm. Abraham's story, which began in 11:8, is interrupted by Sarah's account of conceiving Isaac (11:11–12). This interruption is significant enough for us to ponder the author's motive of doing it. After the interim commentary (11:13–16), the exemplar of faith
by Abraham reappears (11:17–19). In what ways are sections G and G'
parallel to each other? An observation of the passages indicates that they
are related to each other by the reference to Isaac. More specifically,
they are parallel to each other by the idea of the offspring (σπέρματος)
in v. 11; Ἰσαάκ in 11:17) and power (δύναμιν in v. 11; δυνατός in v.
19). Sarah's faith has to do with the birth of Isaac and Abraham's faith,
to the sacrifice of Isaac.

Analysis of the structure. A detailed analysis of section G and G' reveals that each forms a unit by chiasm. To begin with, the structure of G
(11:11–12) may be illustrated in the following way:

> 1   Πίστει καὶ αὐτὴ Σάρρα στεῖρα δύναμιν εἰς καταβολὴν σπέρματος ἔλα-
> βεν (By faith he received power of procreation) (11:11a)[16]

---

[15] For a detailed discussion of the present and the future aspect of the eschatology,
see C. K. Barrett, "The Eschatology of the Epistle to the Hebrews," in *The Background
of the New Testament and its Eschatology,* Essays in Honor of Charles Harold Dodd, ed.
W. D. Davies and D. Daube (Cambridge: Cambridge University, 1954), 363–93; George
Eldon Ladd, *Theology of the New Testament* (Grand Rapids: William B. Eerdmans Publishing Co., 1974), 572–77.

[16] The textual problem involved in this verse is notoriously difficult. For the view
that Abraham is the subject of the verse, see Bruce M. Metzger, *A Textual Commentary
on the Greek New Testament* (New York: United Bible Societies, 1971), 672–73; Ellingworth, *The Epistle to the Hebrews,* 589; Lane, *Hebrews 9–13,* 343. For the view that
the subject is Sarah, see J. H. Greenlee, "Hebrews 11:11–Sarah's Faith or Abraham's?,"
Notes on Translation 4 (1990), 37–42. Greenlee has a convincing argument for Sarah as
the subject. In addition, the intrinsic probability indicates that the subject of 11:11 is
more likely to be Sarah. Throughout Hebrews 11 the author makes it clear who the subject is in the beginning of the verse whenever he introduces the word πίστει (e.g., vv. 4,

2 καὶ παρὰ καιρὸν ἡλικίας (even though he was too old--and Sarah herself was barren) (11:11b),

3 ἐπεὶ πιστὸν ἡγήσατο τὸν ἐπαγγειλάμενον. (because he considered him faithful who had promised) (11:11c).

3' διὸ καὶ ἀφ' ἑνὸς ἐγεννήθησαν (Therefore from one person, descendants were born) (11:12a),

2' καὶ ταῦτα νενεκρωμένου (and this one as good as dead) (11:12b),

1' καθὼς τὰ ἄστρα τοῦ οὐρανοῦ τῷ πλήθει καὶ ὡς ἡ ἄμμος ἡ παρὰ τὸ χεῖλος τῆς θαλάσσης ἡ ἀναρίθμητος ("as many as the stars of heaven and as the innumerable grains of sand by the seashore") (11:12c).[17]

According to this proposed chiastic structure, the center sections (3 and 3') are parallel with each other in that 3' is the result of faithfulness of Sarah in 3. It is also to be noted that while the emphasis of 3 is on Sarah, the focus of 3' is on Abraham (ἀφ' ἑνός). Thus the center sections complement each other by the reference to Sarah and Abraham respectively. Moreover, 3' also indicates that the object of Sarah's faith was God himself (i.e., the one who had promised). As a result of her faith many descendants were born through one man (i.e., Abraham). Sections 2 and 2' are parallel in that while the latter speaks of Abraham's old age, the former refers to the deadness of Sarah's womb because of her old age. The parallelism in these sections reinforces my argument that this section is chiastically designed. Sections 1 and 1' are parallel in that while 1 addresses Sarah's receiving the power to conceive Isaac (which is implied), 1' speaks of the multitude of descendants through Abraham. While the first part (1, 2, 3) refers to Sarah's conception of one seed (i.e., Isaac), the second part (3', 2', 1') speaks of many descendants who will be born through Abraham. This analysis strongly suggests that the author had a chiastic structure in mind in this passage.

Next, the chiastic structure of G' (11:17–19), which is the parallel passage of G (11:11–12), may be illustrated as follows:

5, 8, 17, 23, 30, 31). Because of this consistent authorial style, it seems to be logical to consider Sarah as the subject of 11:11.

[17] The order of translation of NRSV in 11:12 is altered according to the reading of the Greek text.

1   Πίστει προσενήνοχεν 'Αβραὰμ τὸν 'Ισαὰκ πειραζόμενος (By faith Abraham, when put to the test, offered up Isaac) (11:17a).

2   καὶ τὸν μονογενῆ προσέφερεν, ([He] was ready to offer up his only son) (11:17b),

3   ὁ τὰς ἐπαγγελίας ἀναδεξάμενος (He who had received the promises) (11:17c),18

3'   πρὸς ὃν ἐλαλήθη ὅτι ἐν 'Ισαὰκ κληθήσεται σοι σπέρμα (of whom he had been told, "It is through Isaac that descendants shall be named for you") (11:18),

2'   λογισάμενος ὅτι καὶ ἐκ νεκρῶν ἐγείρειν δυνατὸς ὁ θεός (He considered the fact that God is able even to raise someone from the dead) (11:19a),

1'   ὅθεν αὐτὸν καὶ ἐν παραβολῇ ἐκομίσατο (and figuratively speaking, he did receive him back) (11:19b).

In this diagram outer sections 1 and 1' have a parallel thought pattern; while section 1 describes Abraham's offering up of his son, section 1' depicts the result of offering the son by faith: as a result of his faith Abraham received him (Isaac) back. Sections 2 and 2' are similar in that while section 2 speaks of Abraham's dramatic act of offering up his only son, the corresponding section (2') describes the reason behind his willingness to offer up his son; he believed that God was able to raise him (Isaac) from the dead. Center sections 3 and 3' are parallel in that they both emphasize the promise of God: while section 3 speaks of the one who received the promise (i.e., Abraham), section 3' reiterates the content of the promise given to him. Thus it is highly plausible that this section may also have been chiastically arranged by the author.

Aspects of faith. What aspects of faith does the author bring out in these sections? To begin with, these parallel passages emphasize steadfastness of faith, while waiting on the promise of God. Section G (11:11–12) shows Sarah's steadfastness of faith in light of God's promise that he will provide a son to Abraham. The passage indicates that Sarah's ethical aspect of steadfastness is based on the faithfulness of

18 The order of translation of NRSV in 11:17 was altered according to the reading of the Greek text.

God's promise. The forward-looking aspect is certainly present in this
passage, but the emphasis of this section is on Sarah's trust in God's
ability to bring about conception, even when she was in the state of bar-
renness. Likewise, section G' (11:17–19) speaks of Abraham's steadfastness of faith, specifically when he was faced with the test to offer up
his son. As in the case of Sarah, Abraham's faith is also firmly based on
the promise of God. Abraham's dramatic act of offering up his son is
based on believing in God's promise that Isaac will be the heir of the
promise. The promise of God was the object of faith for Abraham.

Next, both sections (G and G') emphasize the concept of resurrection
from the dead. In section G this thought is implied in bringing back
Abraham's physical deadness. In section G' this idea is more explicitly
stated by the thought that God is able to raise up Isaac. The author's use
of παραβολῇ (11:19) suggests that the reference to "raising up from the
dead" encompasses more than bringing back Isaac to life. Ellingworth
notes that there is no reference to the resurrection of Abraham or Isaac
in the Old Testament or other pre-Christian sources.[19] This observation
leads one to consider that the idea of resurrection is the author's reflection upon the Old Testament passage (Gen 22) in light of the new revelation in the New Testament period. Thus it is reasonable to assert that
Abraham's receiving back Isaac is a type of resurrection of believers in
the future.

Moreover, the author's use of τὸν μονογενῆ (the only begotten son)
(11:17) suggests that the reference to Isaac's coming back to life may be
a type of the resurrection of Christ. Thus it is quite possible that the
author has in mind the Christological implication of faith. The exemplars of faith by Sarah and Abraham clearly support the forward-looking
aspect of the Old Testament faith. In this sense, faith in chapter 11 is
eschatologically oriented. However, one should keep in mind that this
future-oriented faith is inevitably related to Christology, which will further be explained later in the discussion.

Examples of Faith in the Patriarchal Period
(11:8–10; F//11:20–22; F')
    Basis for the chiasm. In what sense can F and F' be considered the
counterpart of each other in the proposed chiasm? First, it can be ob-

---

[19] Ellingworth, *The Epistle to the Hebrews,* 602.

served from the chronological order of genealogy. In section F (11:8–10), the author began the forward-looking faith of Abraham. Then, after a brief interruption (11:11–12; 11:13–16; and 11:17–19), he logically continues with the forward-looking aspect of faith from the life of Isaac, Jacob, and Joseph. Next, the parallelism between these two sections is evident from the reference to "Isaac" and "Jacob" in both sections. In 11:9 the author briefly mentions the names of these patriarchs. Then in 11:20–21, he proceeds to explain the detailed account of the forward-looking faith of them, in addition to the faith of Joseph (11:22). Thus it may be said that sections F and F' are parallel to each other.

Analysis of the structure. Again, each of the sections (F, F') is chiastically arranged at the microscopic level. To begin with, section F may be diagrammed as follows:

1   Πίστει καλούμενος 'Αβραὰμ ὑπήκουσεν ἐξελθεῖν εἰς τόπον ὃν ἤμελλεν
    λαμβάνειν εἰς κληρονομίαν, καὶ ἐξῆλθεν μὴ ἐπιστάμενος ποῦ ἔρχεται
    (By faith Abraham obeyed when he was called to set out for a place that he was
    to receive as an inheritance; and he set out, not knowing where he was going)
    (11:8).

2   Πίστει παρῴκησεν εἰς γῆν τῆς ἐπαγγελίας ὡς ἀλλοτρίαν ἐν σκηναῖς
    (By faith he stayed for a time in the land he had been promised, as in a for-
    eign land) (11:9a),

2' κατοικήσας μετὰ 'Ισαὰκ καὶ 'Ιακὼβ τῶν συγκληρονόμων τῆς ἐπαγ-
    γελίας τῆς αὐτῆς· (living in tents, as did Isaac and Jacob, who were heirs
    with him of the same promise) (11:9b)

1' ἐξεδέχετο γὰρ τὴν τοὺς θεμελίους ἔχουσαν πόλιν ἧς τεχνίτης καὶ δη-
    μιουργὸς ὁ θεός (For he looked forward to the city that has foundations,
    whose architect and builder is God) (11:10).

Center sections 2 and 2' are parallel by the idea of dwelling in a foreign land (γῆ and ἀλλοτρίαν in v. 9a; dwelling in a tent in 9b). Moreover, these sections are related to each other by the concept of promise (i.e., land of the promise in v. 9a; same promise in 9b). Section 1 is the summary of Genesis 12:1–4. The Old Testament passage indicates that Abraham departed from Ur in obedience to God's word. The author of Hebrews considers this obedience an act of faith, with which he has been attested by God (11:2, 39). The corresponding section 1' is related to section 1 in that it explains why Abraham was able to obey: it was because he looked forward to the city whose builder and maker is God.

This proposed chiastic structure clarifies that faith in Hebrews involves obedience and a forward-looking attitude (1 and 1'). The emphasis on the promise in the center sections (2 and 2') indicates that the elements of faith expressed in the outer sections (1 and 1') have the promise of God as their object.

Next, the list of exemplars of faith in the patriarchal period, which was interrupted by the story of Sarah, continues in section F' (11:20–22). An analysis of F' suggests that this section is also arranged chiastically. This may be illustrated as follows:

1   Πίστει καὶ περὶ μελλόντων εὐλόγησεν Ἰσαὰκ τὸν Ἰακὼβ καὶ τὸν Ἠσαῦ. (By faith Isaac invoked blessings for the future on Jacob and Esau) (11:20).

2   Πίστει Ἰακὼβ ἀποθνῄσκων ἕκαστον τῶν υἱῶν Ἰωσὴφ εὐλόγησεν καὶ προσεκύνησεν ἐπὶ τὸ ἄκρον τῆς ῥάβδου αὐτοῦ (By faith Jacob, when dying, blessed each of the sons of Joseph, "bowing in worship over the top of his staff") (11:21)

1   Πίστει Ἰωσὴφ τελευτῶν περὶ τῆς ἐξόδου τῶν υἱῶν Ἰσραὴλ ἐμνημόνευ-σεν καὶ περὶ τῶν ὀστέων αὐτοῦ ἐνετείλατο (By faith Joseph, at the end of his life, made mention of the exodus of the Israelites and gave instructions about his burial) (11:22).

In this proposed structure an example of faith by Jacob is naturally in the center section (2) because of the order of the genealogy. Jacob serves as the link between Isaac and Joseph. The twin parts of the outer section (1 and 1') are parallel with each other by the thought of things concerning the future (i.e., blessings for the future in A; the exodus and giving instruction concerning his bones in 1').

Aspects of faith. What aspects of faith are emphasized in these parallel sections? It may be noted that, in section F (11:8–10), the emphasis is on Abraham's forward-looking aspect of faith based on God's promise. The expression "the city which has a foundation; whose builder and the maker is God" (11:10) has a reference to the land of Canaan in the immediate context, in which the descendants of Abraham would inherit 400 years later. However, the descriptions of the city seem to speak of more than the promised land. It is evident that the land of Canaan was not built by God. Here, the author of Hebrews suggests that Abraham looked forward to the eschatological heavenly city.[20] Thus it may be said that Abraham's faith was clearly future oriented. The author continues this forward-looking aspect of faith through the example of Isaac, Jacob, and Joseph in section F' (11:20–22). In Isaac's example (11:20), the future aspect of faith is indicated by Isaac's blessings for the future on Jacob and Esau. As for Jacob's example, it is not immediately clear whether or not his blessing is eschatologically oriented. However, an examination of Genesis 47:29–48:22 makes it evident that the blessing given to both Ephraim and Manasseh involves a future aspect. It is also clear that Joseph's mention of the exodus and the instruction about his burial has to do with the future event. As for the example of faith by Joseph, Wilcox sheds some interesting light concerning the bones of Joseph. By examining Jewish exegetical sources he concludes that Joseph's statement "God shall visit you" (Gen 50:25) not only looks to the exodus event, but also the ultimate redemption of Israel by the Messiah.[21]

> We may thus offer a possible reason why the author of Hebrews chose to refer to Joseph's words recalling God's oath to Abraham and giving instructions about his own bones. It fits at once with the picture found elsewhere in Jewish exegesis of the piety and faithfulness of Joseph, and of the view that the visitation of which he spoke referred not only to Moses and the exodus but also to the final liberation of Israel at the hand of the Second Redeemer.[22]

If this is what the author has in mind, then it can definitely be said that his eschatological outlook has a Christological orientation. This relationship between eschatology and Christology will be developed in later sections of this chapter.

An examination of both F and F' clearly reveals that they have one thing in common: they are related to each other by the theme of forward-looking eschatology. Thus it seems reasonable to conclude that the exemplars of faith by Isaac, Jacob, and Joseph in F' (11:20–22) is the continuation of Abraham's faith in F (11:8–10) with the running theme of

[20] Moxnes, *God and His Promise to Abraham,* 181.

[21] Max Wilcox, "The Bones of Joseph: Hebrews 11:22," in *Scripture: Meaning and Method,* A. T. Hanson Festschrift, ed. Barry R. Thompson (Hull: Hull University Press, 1987), 126.

[22] Ibid.

forward-looking eschatology. The interruption of F and F' by G (11:11–12) and G' (11:17–19) is intentional. It appears that the author inserted these sections in order to develop a different aspect of faith of Abraham and Sarah (i.e., trusting in God's promise).

Examples of Faith Seen through Noah and Moses (11:7; E//11:23–29; E')

Basis for the chiasm. The forward-looking aspect of faith, which was summarized in the center section (11:13–16), continues beyond the examples of faith seen through the patriarchs. According to the proposed chiastic diagram, it may be noted that the story of Noah in 11:7 (E) corresponds to that of Moses in 11:23–29 (E'). Then what is the basis on which these two sections may be regarded as parallel passages in the overall chiastic structure of chapter 11? It appears that both Noah and Moses are related to each other by the experience of water. As Noah and his family were saved from the flood (cf. Gen 6:5–8:22; 1 Pet 3:20; 2 Pet 2:5), so also were Moses and the people of Israel saved through the Red Sea (Gen 14:10–31; 1 Cor 10:2). With the establishment of this initial contact point between the two, I will proceed to examine the details of the parallel passages.

Analysis of the structure. An examination of 11:7 indicates that this verse is arranged in a simple chiastic structure. This may be illustrated as follows:

1. Πίστει χρηματισθεὶς Νῶε περὶ τῶν μηδέπω βλεπομένων, εὐλαβηθεὶς (By faith Noah, warned by God about events as yet unseen, respected the warning)

 2. κατεσκεύασεν κιβωτὸν (and built an ark)

 2' εἰς σωτηρίαν τοῦ οἴκου αὐτοῦ (to save his household);

1' δι' ἧς κατέκρινεν τὸν κόσμον, καὶ τῆς κατὰ πίστιν δικαιοσύνης ἐγένετο κληρονόμος (by this he condemned the world and became an heir to the righteousness that is in accordance with faith).

It may be observed that the center section of this chiastic structure displays Noah's obedience to God's warning; he built an ark (2), and its purpose was for the salvation of his household (2'). The outer sections show parallelism by the idea of faith (i.e., πίστει in 1; δι' ἧς in 1'). In addition, while section 1 speaks of Noah's taking heed to the warning, section 1' states that he became an heir of righteousness which is through faith. In other words while section 1 shows the time of Noah's obedience (χρηματισθείς) and the manner by which the action was carried out (εὐλαβηθείς), section 1' reveals the outcome of Noah's obedient act. Thus this verse makes it clear that faith involves obedience to God's word.

The section on Moses' example of faith (11:23–29; E') may be divided into three subsections: (1) faith of Moses' parents (11:23); (2) Moses' choice to suffer for Christ (11:24–26); and (3) Moses' departure from Egypt (11:27–29). At first glance there seems to be no chiastic relationship among these three divisions. However, a detailed scrutiny of these subsections indicates that they are conceptually chiastical, which may be illustrated as follows:[23]

A By faith Moses' parents obeyed, not fearing the king's edict (11:23).

    B By faith Moses' chose to suffer for Christ, rather than enjoying the fleeting pleasure of sin (11:24–26).

A' By faith Moses obeyed, not fearing the anger of the king (11:27–29).

In this proposed chiasm section B explains the choice that Moses had made for the sake of Christ. The reference to Christ in the center section suggests that Moses' faith has a Christological implication. This will be explained in detail in the discussion of the chiasm in this passage. One may assume that 11:24–26 (B) is the event which had occurred before Moses fled from the presence of Pharaoh. It is true that the decision to endure hardship with the people of God happened before he fled to the land of Midian. However, this passage includes more than a single event in Moses' life. It reflects his attitude toward the people of God throughout his life after he had made that decision. Interpreting this passage as a broad application of Moses' life justifies his sufferings for the sake of God's people in the wilderness. Sections A and A' are related to each other by the theme of obedience. As the act of Moses' parents was done in obedience to faith, so was each activity of Moses in 11:27–29 done in obedience to faith. In addition, in both A and A' similar phrases are used (A: they were not afraid of king's edict; A': not fearing the anger of the king). These similar expressions strengthen the argument that A and A'

[23] Each section of the chiasm is my own summary of the passage.

are parallel to each other. Thus it is reasonable to conclude that 11:23–29 is chiastically arranged.

It is also to be realized that the author employs chiasm in each subsection of 11:23–29. First of all, section A (11:23) may be chiastically arranged as follows:

> 1   Πίστει Μωϋσῆς γεννηθεὶς ἐκρύβη τρίμηνον ὑπὸ τῶν πατέρων αὐτοῦ (By faith Moses after his birth, was hidden by his parents for three months).

> 2   διότι εἶδον ἀστεῖον τὸ παιδίον (because they saw that the child was beautiful);

> 1' καὶ οὐκ ἐφοβήθησαν τὸ διάταγμα τοῦ βασιλέως (and they were not afraid of the king's edict).24

The center section (2) reveals the reason why the parents hid Moses: it was because he was beautiful. Sections 1 and 1' explain why Moses' parents were able to hide him when he was born: they were not afraid of the king's decree. In this verse the emphasis is placed on the faith of Moses' parents.

The second subsection (11:24–26) may also be arranged chiastically:

> 1   Πίστει Μωϋσῆς μέγας γενόμενος ἠρνήσατο λέγεσθαι υἱὸς θυγατρὸς Φαραώ (By faith Moses, when he was grown up, refused to be called a son of Pharaoh's daughter) (11:24),

> 2   μᾶλλον ἑλόμενος συγκακουχεῖσθαι τῷ λαῷ τοῦ θεοῦ ἢ πρόσκαιρον ἔχειν ἁμαρτίας ἀπόλαυσιν (choosing rather to share ill-treatment with the people of God than to enjoy the fleeting pleasures of sin) (11:25),

> 2' μείζονα πλοῦτον ἡγησάμενος τῶν Αἰγύπτου θησαυρῶν τὸν ὀνειδισμὸν τοῦ Χριστοῦ· (He considered abuse suffered for the Christ to be greater wealth than the treasures of Egypt) (11:26a),

> 1' ἀπέβλεπεν γὰρ εἰς τὴν μισθαποδοσίαν. (for he was looking ahead to the reward) (11:26b).

In this chiastic structure the parallelism of sections 1 and 1' may be demonstrated as follows: section 1 affirms that Moses refused to be

---

24 The NRSV translation was arranged according to the order of the Greek text.

called the son of Pharaoh's daughter. Section 1' explains why he refused: it is because he looked to the reward. Thus the two sections complement each other. The center of the chiasm (2 and 2') is indicated by the use of the two participles (ἑλόμενος, v. 25; ἡγησάμενος, v. 26). Section 2 speaks of Moses' choice (ἑλόμενος) to endure hardship with the people of God rather than to enjoy the pleasures of sin in Egypt. The corresponding section (2') describes the reason for his choice: it is because he considered (ἡγησάμενος) the abuse of Christ as greater riches than the treasures of Egypt.[25]

The third subsection (11:27–29) of Moses' example of faith is also arranged chiastically, which may be illustrated as follows:

1   Πίστει κατέλιπεν Αἴγυπτον μὴ φοβηθεὶς τὸν θυμὸν τοῦ βασιλέως· τὸν γὰρ ἀόρατον ὡς ὁρῶν ἐκαρτέρησεν (By faith he left Egypt, unafraid of the king's anger; for he persevered as though he saw him who is invisible) (11:27).

2   Πίστει πεποίηκεν τὸ πάσχα καὶ τὴν πρόσχυσιν τοῦ αἵματος (By faith he kept the Passover and the sprinkling of blood) (11:28a),

2'.   ἵνα μὴ ὁ ὀλοθρεύων τὰ πρωτότοκα θίγῃ αὐτῶν (so that the destroyer of the firstborn would not touch the firstborn of Israel) (11:28b).

1'   Πίστει διέβησαν τὴν ἐρυθρὰν θάλασσαν ὡς διὰ ξηρᾶς γῆς, ἧς πεῖραν λαβ-όντες οἱ Αἰγύπτιοι κατεπόθησαν (By faith the people passed through the Red Sea as if it were dry land, but when the Egyptians attempted to do so they were drowned) (11:29).

To begin with, the outer sections (1 and 1') are parallel by the idea of leaving Egypt: on the one hand, section 1 states that Moses left Egypt without fearing the anger of the king; on the other hand, section 1' further explains the exodus by describing the miracle of passing through the Red Sea.

There is much debate as to which event the author has in mind in 11:27, whether it is the event which took place after slaying an Egyptian (2:11–15) or the exodus event (Exod 14:10–25). Many scholars consider that this verse refers to Moses' departure from Egypt after having murdered an Egyptian because they believe that the author follows the his-

[25] The participle ἡγησάμενος is an adverbial participle, expressing the idea of cause.

torical sequence of events in chapter 11. For example, Lane argues that if verse 27 speaks of the first leaving Egypt, then the order of the event in 11:27 naturally follows that of 11:24–26. He asserts that the latter view requires some explanation for the disarrangement in sequence between verse 27 and verse 28.[26] Likewise, Ellingworth points out that the main argument against the exodus view is that it interrupts the historical sequence of events, which the author is generally careful to follow in chapter 11.[27]

However, an examination of chapter 11 indicates that the author does not always follow the historical sequence of event in his exposition of faith. One may find that the names of Isaac and Jacob are mentioned before the example of Sarah's faith (cf. 11:9, 10–11). It has already been mentioned that 11:13–16 may include all the exemplars of faith in chapter 11. Likewise, in the discussion of 11:24–26, I have argued that Moses' decision to choose to suffer with the people of God is a summary of the attitude his life. Thus it is clear that, in the exposition of faith in chapter 11, the author does not always follow the historical order of events in the Old Testament. This inference opens up the possibility that 11:27 may be a reference to the exodus event rather than Moses' flight to the land of Midian. The main difficulty with considering 11:27 as Moses' first departure from Egypt has to do with the phrase, "not fearing the anger of the king."

This statement is clearly inconsistent with the account in the Old Testament. Exodus 2:15 suggests that Moses left Egypt because he was afraid of being killed by the king.[28] This difficulty will easily be resolved if one considers that the reference to 11:27 is the exodus event in Exodus 14:13–20. The immediate context clearly indicates that the king's wrath involved pursuing after the people of Israel (Exodus 14:1–9). In Exodus 14:13 Moses commands the Israelites not to be afraid of Pharaoh because they will see the salvation of the Lord. This supports

---

[26] Lane, *Hebrews 9–13*, 374–75.

[27] Ellingworth, *The Epistle to the Hebrews*, 615.

[28] For the possible explanation for this problem among those who hold Moses' first departure view, see P. E. Hughes, *A Commentary on the Epistle to the Hebrews* (Grand Rapids: William B. Eerdmans Publishing Co., 1977), 497–501; Bruce, *The Epistle to the Hebrews*, 321–22.

the statement that Moses did not fear the wrath of the king. Thus it is reasonable to regard 11:27 as the exodus event. Then what might be the reason that the author placed the exodus event before the event of keeping the Passover? The answer is simple enough. As it has been noticed to this point in chapter 11, the author's literary style is to arrange each subdivision chiastically. If this is what the author has in mind, then it is natural for him to put the exodus event (11:27, [section 1]) in the beginning of the subsection (11:27–29) because the closing section (11:29, [section 1']) also speaks of the exodus event. In fact 11:29 adds more details of the exodus event by describing that they (i.e., Moses and the people of Israel) crossed the Red Sea, and the Egyptians were swallowed up by the sea. In this sense, it may be said that section 1 (11:27) is parallel to the thought in section 1' (11:29). The middle sections (2 and 2') complement each other in that while 2 describes the institution of the Passover with the sprinkling of blood, 2' explains the reason for it: it was to keep the first-born of Israel from being killed by the destroyer. Thus it is reasonable to consider 11:27–29 as a literary unit by chiasm.

Aspects of faith in Noah's example (11:7; E). What aspects of faith are emphasized through Noah's example of faith? To begin with, Noah's act of taking heed to the warning and building an ark indicates that faith involves obedience to God's word. Next, the text indicates that Noah's faith involved a forward-looking aspect. The phrase "concerning the things not seen" (περὶ τῶν μηδέπω βλεπομένων) refers to the flood which came about 100 years after God had warned Noah about it (Gen 6:1; 7:6), and the promise that he will deliver him and his family from the flood (Gen 6:17–18). This forward-looking aspect of Noah's faith is similar to the theme in the center section (11:13–16). Noah's faith is also a perfect example of the definition of faith described in 11:1 (i.e., faith is the substance of the things hoped for, the proof of the things not seen) because "his action showed that he was convinced of the substantial reality of things still in the unseen future, still in the realm of unfulfilled hope."[29] Moreover, Noah's faith illustrates the nature of faith described in 11:6. Noah was able to take heed to the voice of God and build the ark

---

[29] R. Williamson, *Philo and the Epistle to the Hebrews* (Leiden: E. J. Brill, 1970), 354. It is to be noted that the author uses the same verb (βλέπω) in verses 1 and 7 to refer to the things which will take place in the future.

because "he believed that what God had said He would do—save his household from the flood (Gen. 6:18)—He would do. Despite all the appearances to the contrary Noah put his full trust in God."[30] In this regard one may see that Noah's faith involves trust in God. This trust is also related to the promise of God, which, in turn, involves a forward-looking aspect.

One other issue that is related to the concept of faith is the meaning of the expression, "he became an heir of righteousness according to faith." Attridge argues that, although the phrase appears to be a Pauline expression at first glance, it needs to be interpreted in the context of Hebrews' particular development of common Jewish and Christian themes.[31] For this reason he concludes, "what Noah's story exemplifies is the reverent reliance upon God's promises and consequent faithful action that enables one—in a quite un-Pauline fashion—to do what is righteous."[32] It is true that, in most cases, the word "righteousness" (δικαιοσύνη) is used to refer to the character of a person (e.g., 7:2; 12:11), or the righteous deeds (e.g., 1:9; 11:3) in Hebrews. It is also true that the emphasis of chapter 11 as a whole is on the righteous action done by faith. However, the use of "righteousness" in 11:7 has a different sense. It is qualified by the phrase κατὰ πίστιν, which indicates "the way or the condition by which righteousness is actualized: it describes a righteousness bestowed by God according to the norm of faith."[33] In addition, the verb γίνομαι may have a passive meaning in the middle voice. Thus the phrase may be rendered, "he was made an heir of righteousness according to faith."[34] Understanding δικαιοσύνη in this sense in 11:7 leads to the inference that it is very close to Paul's concept of justification by faith used throughout his epistles.[35] There-

30 Ibid.

31 Attridge, The Epistle to the Hebrews, 320.

32 Ibid.

33 Lane, Hebrews 9–13, 340.

34 Walter Bauer, A Greek-English Lexicon of the New Testament and Other Early Christian Literature, 2nd ed., trans. and adapted by W. F. Arndt, F. W. Gingrich, and Frederick W. Danker (Chicago: The University of Chicago, 1979), 158: 2a.

35 In many instances Paul uses δικαιοσύνη in terms of "the righteousness bestowed by God" (Rom 1:17; 3:21, 22; 4:3, 5, 13; 10:4, 6; 2 Cor 5:21; Gal 3:6; Phil 3:9). It is interesting to note that throughout his epistles he uses the combination of three terms

fore, unlike Attridge's assertion, the phrase "the righteousness according to faith" does have a Pauline ring in some sense. If this deduction is correct, then it is quite possible that the author uses Noah in the Old Testament as a type of Christ in the New Testament. This finding is consistent with the account of Noah in the Synoptic tradition (Matt 24:37–38; Luke 17:26–27). This analysis suggests the real possibility that faith in Hebrews is as Christologically oriented as in the Pauline literature and the Synoptic Gospels. This Christological implication of faith will become more evident in Moses' example of faith in the following section.

Aspects of faith in Moses' example (11:23–29; E'). What aspects of faith are brought out in this passage? The first subsection (11:23) emphasizes the faith of Moses' parents. That his parents were not afraid of the king's edict implies that they obeyed God in the midst of the threat of the king. Their obedience shows their complete trust in God.

The second subsection (11:24–26) describes the choice which Moses had made by faith. Moses' faith involved enduring hardship in that he chose to share ill-treatment with the people of God (11:25). This corresponds to the steadfastness of faith which the author emphasizes throughout the epistle. In this sense, faith in Hebrews is ethically oriented. However, this ethical aspect is not completely detached from Christology. The passage goes on to describe that Moses regarded the abuse of Christ as greater riches than the riches of Egypt (11:26a). Here, the author's use of Χριστός in depicting Moses' example of faith is intriguing. What might be the purpose of including the reference to Christ in 11:26? It appears that his intention is to regard Moses as a type of Christ. A comparison between Moses (11:24–26) and Christ (12:2) indicates that there are similarities between the two. As Moses chose to endure hardship with the people of God rather than the fleeting pleasure of sin, so did Christ choose to endure the cross. As Moses regarded the abuse of Christ greater riches than the treasures of Egypt, so did Christ despise the shame. This comparison indicates that "the choice of Moses

---

(i.e., κληρονόμος, δικαιοσύνη, and πίστις) only once in Romans 4:13. The combination of the same terms are also used only once in Hebrews 11:7. It is also to be realized that Paul's use of δικαιοσύνη is not limited to "the bestowed righteousness from God." As in the case of Hebrews Paul uses the term to refer to the righteous living of a believer (Rom 6:13, 16, 18, 19, 20; 14:17; 2 Cor 6:7; 9:10; Eph 4:24; 5:9; Phil 1:11, 1 Tim 6:1; 2 Tim 2:22; 2 Tim 3:16). In this sense it may be said that Hebrews' use of δικαιοσύνη is not very different from that of Paul.

is not only a model to be imitated, but also the type of the choice of Christ."[36] Thus it may be said that for the author of Hebrews Moses' ethical aspect of endurance is Christologically oriented. There is yet another important element in Moses' example of faith. The context indicates that the reason why Moses refused to be called the son of Pharaoh's daughter is that he looked to the reward that God has stored up for him (11:26). In other words, Moses' faith was eschatologically oriented because it involved the forward-looking aspect as in Noah's faith. This element of faith also corresponds to the theme of 11:13–16, the center section of chapter 11.

The third subsection (11:27–29) further describes the faith of Moses. What aspects of faith may be learned from this passage? To begin with, in all three verses the author points out that faith is a complete trust in and obedience to God. This aspect is shown in Moses' departure from Egypt (11:27): he was able do so because he was steadfast as if seeing the one who is invisible. The fact that Moses instituted the Passover (11:28) and the people of Israel went through the Red Sea (11:29) also shows that faith involves complete trust in and obedience to God. Next, faith in Hebrews is Christologically oriented. The author states that Moses kept the Passover and the sprinkling of the blood (11:28), which may be considered a type of the suffering Christ in the New Testament (cf. 1 Cor 5:7). If 11:28 is intended to be a type, then it is possible that the author may have the Christological orientation of faith in mind in this verse.

Summary of faith from Noah and Moses. An analysis of Noah's and Moses' life indicates that they are indeed similar to each other in the description of faith. In both 11:7 and 11:23–29 faith involves a forward-looking eschatological outlook (e.g., concerning the things not yet seen [11:7]; he looked to the reward [11:26]). In both examples faith entails obedience and trust in God (e.g., "building a boat [11:7]; "leaving Egypt" [11:27]). However, the most important element which brings together these two examples of faith is the author's emphasis on the Christological implication of faith. The references to "heir of righteousness according to faith" for Noah (11:7) and "abuse of Christ" in describing Moses faith (11:26) indicate that the Christological aspect of

---

[36] Mary Rose D'Angelo, *Moses in the Letter to the Hebrews,* Society of Biblical Literature Dissertation Series 42 (Missoula, MT: Scholars Press, 1979), 34.

faith is not absent even in chapter 11. Even though the author does not use the Pauline expression of "trusting in Jesus," he clearly shows that faith in Hebrews has Jesus as the object of faith. This Christological relationship to faith will become even more evident in 12:1–3.

Faith Seen from the Principle of Pleasing God (11:6, D; 11:30–31, D')

Some scholars express the opinion that 11:6 is the continuation of the example of faith by Enoch in 11:5. For example, Attridge argues that "the scriptural datum that Enoch pleased God now provides the basis for the claim that it was because of his faith that the patriarch was translated."[37] However, it is my opinion that 11:6 includes more than Enoch. Just as 11:13–16 should be considered the summary of the exemplars of faith in Chapter 11, the principle of faith in 11:6 applies to all the exemplars of faith in this chapter. Particularly, this verse correlates to 11:30–31 as shown in the proposed chiastic scheme of chapter 11 (D and D'). In this section the basis for the chiasm and aspects of faith will be discussed together in each counterpart of the proposed chiasm.

Principle of faith (11:6, D). Unlike other sections of the chapter this section does not have a chiastic pattern probably due to the brevity of the verse. What principle of faith does the author bring to light in this verse? Here, the author stresses the aspect of believing (i.e., the one who draws near to God must believe). Then what is the content of this belief? The clause with the conjunction ὅτι suggests that faith entails two things. First, it involves believing in the existence of God, which is indicated by the verb ἔστιν. More specifically, faith is not belief in the existence of *a* God, but belief in the existence of *the* God who once made known his will to the fathers through the prophets but in these last days has spoken in his Son.[38] Next, faith encompasses believing in God who rewards those who seek (ἐκζητοῦσιν) him. The word ἐκζητέω literally means "to seek out" or "search for."[39] It denotes "a singular determina-

---

[37] Attridge, *The Epistle to the Hebrews,* 318. See also Bruce, *The Epistle to the Hebrews,* 290.

[38] Bruce, *The Epistle to the Hebrews,* 290.

[39] Bauer, *Lexicon,* 240.

tion to devote oneself to the service of God."⁴⁰ This meaning will take an importance in the comparison between 11:6 and 11:30–31. Moreover, the idea of "reward" implies a forward-looking aspect of faith, which is "a matter of unwavering hope in the God who controls the future. It exhibits the solid faith that is the condition for receiving recompense by God."⁴¹ In this verse one finds the qualities of faith that may be found throughout chapter 11, especially in 11:30–31. In the following section these characteristics of faith will be compared with those in 11:30–31 to ascertain whether the two sections can be considered the parallel passages.

Example of faith in conquering Jericho (11:30–31, D'). In this section a simple chiastic structure can be observed, which may be illustrated as follows:

A Πίστει τὰ τείχη Ἰεριχὼ ἔπεσαν κυκλωθέντα ἐπὶ ἑπτὰ ἡμέρας. (By faith the walls of Jericho fell after they had been encircled for seven days) (11:30).

B Πίστει Ῥαὰβ ἡ πόρνη οὐ συναπώλετο τοῖς ἀπειθήσασιν (By faith Rahab the prostitute did not perish with those who were disobedient) (11:31a),

A' δεξαμένη τοὺς κατασκόπους μετ' εἰρήνης (because she had received the spies in peace) (11:31b).

In this simple chiasm the center section is an example of faith displayed by Rahab. The positioning of Rahab's story in the center of the chiasm suggests that the emphasis of the passage is on her faith. The outer sections (A and A') are connected by the idea of the wall of Jericho. Joshua 2:15 shows that Rahab's house was on the wall of Jericho, which means that the place where Rahab received the spies in peace is the very wall that fell when the people of Israel went around on the seventh day (cf.

---

⁴⁰ Lane, *Hebrews 9–13*, 338.

⁴¹ Ibid., 338–39.

⁴² Bruce, *The Epistle to the Hebrews*, 290.

⁴³ Bauer, *Lexicon*, 240.

⁴⁴ Lane, *Hebrews 9–13*, 338.

⁴⁵ Ibid., 338–39.

Josh 2:1–21). For this reason it is altogether reasonable to consider that 11:30–31 forms a literary unit by chiasm. Then what is the significance of this section (11:30–31) in understanding the concept of faith in chapter 11? What might be the reason that these verses are paired with verse 6? At least two observations may be made. First, 11:30 is significant because it is the story of the second generation of Israel who acted in faith, as opposed to the rebellious first generation. Thus in the gap between verses 29 and 30, the author implies that while the first generation was not able to enter God's rest because of disobedience (3:7–4:13), the second generation did enter the rest (i.e., the land of promise) by faith under the leadership of Joshua. This obedience by the second generation was an act of faith that pleased God, which corresponds to the principle of faith in 11:6. Second, the author's inclusion of Rahab in the list of the exemplars of faith is significant in the discussion of faith in chapter 11. Unlike the people of Israel, Rahab, as a Gentile woman, was the one who became a member of the covenant people of God by faith. The statement of Rahab in Joshua 2:8–14 suggests that she had the same kind of faith as described in 11:6. She came to realize that the God of Israel is the true God by having been informed of the miracles performed by the Lord (e.g., drying up the water of the Red Sea; victory over the kings of the Amorites) (Josh 2:10–11). This corresponds to the principle of faith in 11:6 which states that the one who draws near to God must believe in the existence of God. Moreover, when Rahab realized who the true God was, she received the two spies in peace and pled for her life and the lives of her family (Josh 1:12–14). Her act of faith indicates that she was the one who believed that God is the rewarder of those who earnestly seek out (ἐκζητέω) for him, which corresponds to the second principle of faith discussed in 11:6. Rahab's faith clearly exhibits "a faith that was oriented toward the future and that found specific content in the acts of the God of Israel (Josh 2:11). She was prepared to assume present peril for the sake of future preservation (Josh 2:12–16)."[46] Rahab's faith had God as the object of faith. In this sense, it is logical to state that 11:6 and 11:30–31 are related to each other with regard to the concept of faith.

---

[46] Lane, *Hebrews 9–13*, 379.

Examples of Triumphs and Sufferings through
Faith (11:4–5; B, C//11:32–38; C', B')
The use of anaphora which began in 11:3 with the creation of the
world suddenly ends with Rahab in 11:31. In 11:32–38 the author employs another literary device called asyndeton, which is an omission of
the conjunction.[47] This literary device is often used for emphasis.[48] The
rhetorical function of 11:32–38 is to "bring an already lengthy list to a
conclusion and yet give the impression that the author could go on piling
up ever more examples of similar content."[49] As indicated in the overall
chiastic structure of chapter 11, the author arranged 11:5 (C) to be parallel to 11:32–35a (C'), and 11:4 (B) with 11:35b–38 (B'). What is the
reason for aligning the passages this way? In what way does each corresponding section complement each other in the concept of faith? To answer these questions, I will first argue for the basis of this parallel
structure. Then a comparison will be made between these parallel passages to determine what aspect of faith is emphasized.
    Basis for the chiasm. For the sake of convenience, I will begin with
the discussion of 11:32–38. An analysis of 11:32–38 indicates that it is
divided into two parts. In the first part (11:32–35a), after listing some
exemplars of faith from the Old Testament (i.e., Gideon, Barak, Samson,
Jephthah, David, Samuel, and the prophets), the author proceeds to describe, without specifying the names, certain victories accomplished
through faith. In the second part (11:35b–38), however, the change of
subject is signaled by ἄλλοι δέ . . . ἕτεροι δέ (11:35–36). In other
words, the author intends to show that from this point on he is describing
those who endured sufferings through faith. Thus the two passages
(11:32–35a [C'] and 11:35b–38 [B']) clearly suggest that the same faith

---

[47] Specifically, the literary device of asyndeton is precisely applied in 11:33–34.
However, verses 35–38 are not presented with the same stereotyped clausal structure as
in verses 33–34. The author moves away from this device in verses 35–36, and then continues with the modified asyndeton in verses 37–38 (See Cosby, *The Rhetorical Composition and Function of Hebrews 11*, 59–63).

[48] A. T. Robertson, *A Grammar of the Greek New Testament in the Light of Historical Research* (Nashville: Broadman Press, 1934), 427. See also F. Blass, F. Debrunner, and R. W. Funk, *Grammar of the New Testament and Other Early Christian Literature*, trans. R. W. Funk (Chicago: The University of Chicago Press, 1961), 262 (§ 494).

[49] Cosby, *The Rhetorical Composition and Function of Hebrews 11*, 59.

results in two different effects: on the one hand, it manifests God's power; on the other hand, it allows God's people to endure trials. The themes of triumphs and sufferings are also found in 11:4–5 (B and C). The author uses Abel to illustrate an example of faith through suffering and Enoch to explain an example of faith through triumph.

An examination of these two passages (11:4–5 [B, C]; 11:32–38 [C', B') clearly reveals that they are thematically related to each other. However, one may observe that the themes of sufferings and triumphs are explained in an inverted order. Enoch's victory by faith (11:5; C), on the one hand, corresponds to the exemplars of faith who brought victory in their lives (11:32–35a; C'). Abel's martyrdom because of the act of righteousness by faith (11:4; B), on the other hand, fits well with those who endured sufferings by faith (11:35b–38; B'). Thus it is reasonable to consider that the two passages (11:4–5 and 11:32–38) are parallel to each other thematically.

Aspects of faith in 11:4 (B) and 11:5 (C). Both Abel and Enoch are the exemplars of faith in the antediluvian period. In verse 4 Abel is attested as having been righteous (ἐμαρτυρήθη εἶναι δίκαιος). In what sense is he considered to be righteous? The solution for this problem depends largely on the interpretation of the prepositional phrase δι' ἧς. Grammatically speaking, it is possible for θυσία to be the antecedent of this phrase. However, the context indicates that πίστις is more likely to be the antecedent of δι' ἧς.[50] The importance of πίστις is repeatedly emphasized by the use of different phrases as δι' ἧς and δι' αὐτῆς. This type of literary style is also employed in the discussion of Noah's faith (δι' ἧς, 11:7). If the phrase δι' ἧς goes back to πίστις, then it may be said that Abel's righteousness is that which is bestowed by faith. The passive voice (ἐμαρτυρήθη) further supports the idea that Abel's righteousness is bestowed by God. If this inference is correct, then, as in the case of Noah's faith in 11:7, the author's use of the righteousness by faith in this verse does not differ much from the Pauline concept of righteousness by faith. Abel's martyrdom on account of the righteous offering by faith is a type of those who will be suffering for the sake of righteousness after him. The significance of this point will be discussed later in connection with 11:32–38.

---

50 C. Spicq, *L'Épître aux Hebreux* (Paris: Gabalda, 1952), 2:342; also Lane, *Hebrews 9–13*, 327.

Another issue which is related to Abel's faith is the meaning of the expression "through it (faith), although he is dead, he still speaks" (δι' αὐτῆς ἀποθανὼν ἔτι λαλεῖ). Some scholars argue that it refers to Abel's call for vengeance. For example, Bruce considers that the reference to "he still speaks" is "Abel's appealing to God for vindication until he obtains it in full in the judgment to come."[51] By referring to Hebrews 12:24, which states that Christ's blood speaks better than that of Abel, he contends that the statement "Abel still lives" is a clear reference to Genesis 4:10.[52] However, the context indicates that Abel's speaking is not by his blood as stated in Genesis 4:10, but by faith (δι' αὐτῆς). Moreover, Lane points out that the verb λαλεῖν is never used in Hebrews in addressing God.[53] For this reason it is more likely that Abel's speaking has a reference to his offering in Genesis 4:4. Because of the sacrifice which he offered by faith, he is still speaking to us through the written word of God: he is a living witness to all ages.[54] By making a contrast between "although he died" (ἀποθανὼν) and "he still speaks" (ἔτι λαλεῖ), the author implies that Abel is still living to this day. In other words, Abel's coming back to life from death is a type of those who will be resurrected through Christ in the future. This point will become significant in the discussion of 11:32–38.

Then what aspects of faith are described in Enoch's example of faith? The author's exposition of Enoch's life simply indicates that the reason he was translated was that he was attested as having pleased God. To find out how Enoch pleased God, one needs to go back to Enoch's story in Genesis 5:21–24. In this short account of Enoch's life, it is evident that the reason why God took him is that he walked with God for three hundred years. This fact reveals that Enoch's faith involved obedience to God. The duration of his walk with God for three hundred years also implies that Enoch's faith entailed steadfastness and a forward-looking aspect. Enoch's translation without tasting death shows the tri-

---

[51] Bruce, *The Epistle to the Hebrews*, 286.

[52] Ibid. Genesis 4:10 says, ". . . the voice of your brother's blood is crying to Me from the ground" (NASB).

[53] Lane, *Hebrews 9–13*, 335.

[54] J. Moffatt, *A Critical and Exegetical Commentary on the Epistle to the Hebrews*, The International Critical Commentary (Edinburgh: T. & T. Clark, 1924), 164.

umphant victory he had through faith. He is the first one who experienced the power of resurrection while he was alive. This point will also be important in the discussion of 11:32–38.

Aspects of faith in 11:32–35a (C') and 11:35b–38 (B'). A detailed analysis of the passage reveals that 11:32–38 is arranged chiastically at the conceptual level. This may be illustrated as follows:

I   Further list of the exemplars of faith in the Old Testament (11:32).

II   Exemplars of faith who manifested the power of God though faith (11:32–34).

III   Some women received their dead by the resurrection (11:35a).

III'   Others were tortured in order that they may attain a better resurrection (11:35b).

II'   Exemplars of those who endured sufferings through faith (11:36–37).

I'   Description of those who wandered around the mountains and caves and holes of the earth. The world was not worthy of these exemplars of faith (11:38).

Sections I and I' complement each other for the following reason: while section I lists the names of those who displayed faith in their lives, section I' describes specific incidents of those who endured sufferings by faith. It may be noted that the author of Hebrews especially chooses the life of David in 11:32 and summarizes the manner of his life during the time he endured the trials by faith in 11:38 (cf. 1 Sam 22:1–23; 24:1–22). Sections II and II' complement each other by the contrast of thought: section II illustrates the victory through faith; section II' exemplifies the sufferings and martyrdom through faith. The center section (III and III'), which is the main point of the passage, is parallel to each other by the idea of resurrection. The word ἀνάστασις is used in both sections of the chiasm: on the one hand, 11:35a (III) speaks of the resurrection of those who had victory by faith; on the other hand, 11:35b (III') describes the resurrection of those who went through sufferings and death by faith.

What does the resurrection reveal about the nature of faith of those exemplars in 11:32–38? It shows that faith is directly related to hope, which is repeatedly emphasized throughout the book of Hebrews. This hope of resurrection makes it evident that their faith involved an eschatological, forward-looking aspect. Positively, those who experienced victory by their faith looked forward to the final resurrection (II). Negatively, those who experienced hardships and trials endured through faith because they were looking forward to the same final resurrection (II'). The chiastic structure in 11:32–38 implies that the qualities of faith manifested in the outer sections have their bases on the hope of resurrection in the center sections (III and III'). In this sense, it may be said that the characteristics of faith exhibited by the exemplars of faith in 11:32–38 are eschatologically oriented.

Summary of 11:4–5 (B, C) and 11:32–38 (C', B'). An examination of 11:4–5 and 11:32–38 indicates that the overall emphasis of faith is on triumphs and sufferings on account of the same faith. More specifically, the themes of triumphs and sufferings are directly related to the resurrection. On the one hand, Abel's coming back to life through the Scripture is an example of the resurrection of those who suffered and were martyred for the sake of their faith, which is evident from the reference that Abel is still alive and speaks to us even if he is dead. On the other hand, Enoch's transformation while he was alive may be regarded as an example of the resurrection of those who had victory through their faith. It is noteworthy that the resurrection these women experienced is similar to that of Enoch: both experienced the power of resurrection while they were still alive (cf. 1 Kings 17:17–24; 2 Kings 4:18–37). An observation of the concept of resurrection in both 11:4–5 and 11:32–38 is an additional evidence that these two passages have been arranged chiastically to indicate that they ought to be considered side by side to have a full picture of the concept of faith in these passages.

Introduction and Conclusion
(11:1–3; A//11:39–40; A')

Basis for the chiasm. As one may note from the proposed chiastic structure of chapter 11, the introduction (11:1–3; A) and the conclusion (11:39–40; A') are placed alongside to each other to indicate that they are parallel to each other. What are the clues which may suggest that the introduction and the conclusion are chiastically arranged? First, the context implies that the reference to "the men of old" (οἱ πρεσβύτεροι) in 11:2 corresponds to "they all" (οὗτοι πάντες) in 11:39 (also in 11:13). Second, the introduction is also related to the conclusion by the idea of attestation by faith (ἐμαρτυρήθησαν in v. 2; μαρτυρηθέντες in v. 39). Both the introduction and the conclusion point out that the exemplars of faith in Hebrews 11 were all attested through faith. Third, the use of the verb βλέπω (βλεπουμένων in 11:1; προβλεψαμένου in

11:40) indicates that both sections may be considered parallel to each other. Thus it may be concluded that the introduction and the conclusion are chiastically arranged.

Analysis of the structure. Some scholars consider that the introduction of chapter 11 is limited to the first two verses. For example, Vanhoye argues that 11:1–2 constitutes the introduction because the series of πίστις anaphora begins with verse 3.[55] However, I tend to believe that, despite the literary device of anaphora, the introduction continues to verse 3 thematically and structurally, both of which may be illustrated by a simple chiastic structure in 11:1–3:

1   Ἔστιν δὲ πίστις ἐλπιζομένων ὑπόστασις, πραγμάτων ἔλεγχος οὐ βλεπο-
μένων (Now faith is the assurance of things hoped for, the conviction of things not seen) (11:1).

2   ἐν ταύτῃ γὰρ ἐμαρτυρήθησαν οἱ πρεσβύτεροι (Indeed, by faith our ancestors received approval) (11:2).

1'   Πίστει νοοῦμεν κατηρτίσθαι τοὺς αἰῶνας ῥήματι θεοῦ, εἰς τὸ μὴ ἐκ
φαινομένων τὸ βλεπόμενον γεγονέναι (By faith we understand that the worlds were prepared by the word of God, so that what is seen was made from things that are not visible) (11:3).

It may be observed that the idea of faith is emphasized in each section of the chiastic structure (e.g., πίστις in v. 1; ἐν ταύτῃ in v. 2; πίστει in v. 3). The middle section (2) shows that "faith" is the means by which οἱ πρεσβύτεροι were attested. Sections 1 and 1' are parallel in that 1' is a further explanation of 1: it illustrates how faith is the ὑπόστασις of things hoped for and the ἔλεγχος of things not seen. Especially, the use of the verb βλέπω in both 11:1 and 11:3 substantiates the argument that 1 is parallel to 1'. Lane rightly points out that the logical connection of verse 3 is not verse 2, but verse 1 because it is a statement about faith itself.[56] In this sense, it is quite reasonable to regard 11:1–3 to be a literary unit.

---

[55] Albert Vanhoye, *La structure littéraire de l'Épître aux Hébreux* (Paris: Desclée de Brouwer, 1976), 184. See also Cosby, *The Rhetorical Composition and Function of Hebrews 11*, 25.

[56] Lane, *Hebrews 9–13*, 330.

As in the case of the introduction (11:1–3), the concluding part of chapter 11 is also arranged chiastically, which may be illustrated as follows:

1   Καὶ οὗτοι πάντες μαρτυρηθέντες διὰ τῆς πίστεως οὐκ ἐκομίσαντο τὴν ἐπαγγελίαν, (Yet all these, though they were commended for their faith, did not receive what was promised) (11:39),

    2   τοῦ θεοῦ περὶ ἡμῶν κρεῖττόν τι προβλεψαμένου (since God had provided something better) (11:40a),

1'   ἵνα μὴ χωρὶς ἡμῶν τελειωθῶσιν (so that they would not, apart from us, be made perfect) (11:40b).

In this simple chiasm the center section (2) shows that God had foreseen something better concerning us. The participle προβλεψαμένου (having foreseen) also explains why these exemplars of faith did not receive the promise, even if they had been attested through their faith. The outer sections (1 and 1') complement each other in that section 1' explains the purpose for not having received the promise in section 1: God designed it in such a way that they may not be perfected apart from us (i.e., the people in the new covenant period). This brief discussion permits one to see that the conclusion (11:39–40) forms a structural unit.

Aspects of faith in the introduction (11:1–3; A). Then what principles of faith may be drawn from this passage? An examination of the section of the introduction is necessary to determine which aspects of faith are emphasized. There is an ongoing debate among scholars whether or not the author intended to give a definition of faith in these verses. Some scholars consider that 11:1 is not a formal definition, but a recommendation and celebration of faith, which is the result of the acquisition of life in 10:39.[57] It is true that this passage cannot be considered an exhaustive treatment of what faith is in Hebrews, "but it does provide, in a highly focused and hence somewhat paradoxical way, the

---

[57] Ibid., 328. Likewise, Dörrie asserts that the setting of Hebrews 11:1 has the form of a definition, but does not have a comprehensive validity of definition in any way. See H. Dörrie, "Zu Hebr 11:1," *Zeitschrift für die neutestamentliche Wissenschaft* 46 (1955): 198; Thompson, *The Beginnings of Christian Philosophy,* 70.

essential characteristics that inform our author's understanding."[58] I am inclined to believe that this verse presents one aspect of the definition of faith in Hebrews. This will become evident in the discussion of the two terms, ὑπόστασις and ἔλεγχος, because the meaning of faith in 11:1 is determined largely by how one understands these words.

The difficulty of understanding these terms may be observed from the widely divergent ways they are translated. For example, consider the following translations:

> NRSV – Now faith is the assurance of things hoped for, the conviction of things not seen.
>
> NIV – Now faith is being sure of what we hope for and certain of what we do not see.
>
> KJV – Now faith is the substance of things hoped for, the evidence of things not seen.
>
> Buchanan – Now faith is [the] groundwork of things hoped for, [the] basis for testing things not seen.[59]
>
> Attridge – Faith is the reality of things hoped for, the proof of things unseen.[60]

These examples clearly illustrate the difficult nature of interpreting both ὑπόστασις and ἔλεγχος. An analysis of the above translations shows that the words are understood either subjectively (NRSV, NIV) or objectively (KJV, Buchanan, Attridge). In the following discussion these two terms will be carefully examined to determine which sense is more in line with the author's intended meaning in chapter 11.

A survey of the literature shows that ὑπόστασις may be interpreted in at least three ways. First, the term may be understood in a subjective sense as either "assurance" or "confidence." The proponents of this view consider that this meaning makes sense because the word is used in the same way as in Hebrews 3:14.[61] This subjective meaning is further supported by Paul's use of the word. In 2 Corinthians 9:4 the term is best

---

58 Attridge, *The Epistle to the Hebrews*, 307–8. See also Williamson, *Philo and the Epistle to the Hebrews*, 309.

59 G. W. Buchanan, *To the Hebrews*, Anchor Bible (Garden City: Doubleday & Company, Inc., 1972), 177.

60 Attridge, *The Epistle to the Hebrews*, 305.

61 Bruce, *The Epistle to the Hebrews*, 280; P. E. Hughes, *A Commentary on the Epistle to the Hebrews*, 439.

understood in a subjective way because the context indicates that ὑπόστασις refers to the boasting about the Corinthians' ministry for the saints to the Macedonians (2 Cor 9:1-4). Likewise, in 2 Corinthians 11:17 ὑπόστασις suggests this meaning because it is used in the context of Paul's boasting (2 Cor 11:16-33; 12:5).[62] A subjective understanding of the term is possible in Hebrews 11:1. However, an examination of the exemplars of faith in chapter 11 shows that they had more than a subjective hope; they had an objective hope which they were looking forward to. For this reason a subjective understanding of ὑπόστασις is inadequate in defining faith in chapter 11.

Next, the term ὑπόστασις is understood by some scholars as "foundation." This view takes the word in a literal sense as meaning "standing (στάσις) under (ὑπό)."[63] Lindars argues that the English translation of "assurance" or "confidence" is derived from the literal meaning of "foundation."[64] He asserts that "in the present context faith is the foundation of a positive attitude towards the future, which cannot yet be experienced but has to remain a matter of hope."[65] The word "foundation" emphasizes "the beginning which contains within itself the certainty of completion."[66] This view attempts to interpret the term in a somewhat objective sense. However, the problem with this view, again, is that ὑπόστασις is never used in this sense in the extra-biblical sources. Mathis, for example, surveys both Hellenistic and Greek Patristic literature, and concludes that ὑπόστασις does not mean "founda-

---

[62] On the contrary, Köster considers that ὑπόστασις has the objective meaning of "plan," "purpose," "project." See H. Köster, "ὑπόστασις," in *Theological Dictionary of the New Testament*, ed. Gerhard Friedrich, tr. Geoffrey W. Bromiley (Grand Rapids: William B. Eerdmans Publishing Co., 1972), 8:584-85.

[63] P. E. Hughes, *A Commentary on the Epistle to the Hebrews*, 439. See also Otto Betz, "Firmness in Faith: Hebrews 11:1 and Isaiah 28:16," in *Scripture: Meaning and Method*, A. T. Hanson Festschrift, ed. Barry R. Thompson (Hull: Hull University Press, 1987, 92-113. Betz argues for the "foundation" view by comparing Hebrews 11:1 with Isaiah 28:16.

[64] Barnabas Lindars, *The Theology of the Letter to the Hebrews* (Cambridge: Cambridge University Press, 1991), 110-11.

[65] Ibid. 111.

[66] P. E. Hughes, *A Commentary on the Epistle to the Hebrews*, 439.

tion;" rather, it has the sense of reality.[67] Moreover, translating 11:1 as "faith is the foundation of the things hoped for" does not bring out the sense of eschatological hope which the author stresses throughout chapter 11. There is yet another view which takes ὑπόστασις in an objective sense. Köster, for example, by way of surveying the meaning of the term in Greek literature, the Septuagint, and other Jewish literature, argues that the word is used to denote "reality," "substance," or "actualization."[68] In the present context understanding ὑπόστασις this way makes good sense because "faith lays hold of what is promised and therefore hoped for, as something real and solid, though as yet unseen."[69] This objective understanding of the term is also consistent with an overall emphasis of a forward-looking aspect of faith in chapter 11. The word is used two other times in Hebrews (1:3; 3:14). In both places the objective meaning of "reality" fits the context quite well. In 1:3 Jesus is described as the χαρακτὴρ τῆς ὑποστάσεως αὐτοῦ. His description as the reflection of the glory suggests that ὑπόστασις may be understood as the "reality." Likewise, in 3:14, although it is possible to interpret the word in a subjective sense (i.e., confidence), an objective meaning of "reality" also makes good sense in this verse (i.e., if we hold fast the beginning of the reality until the end). Thus it is reasonable to define ὑπόστασις in 11:1a as the reality of what is hoped for. Faith is "the reality of the *future* blessings that constitute the objective content of hope."[70] This objective meaning allows one to see that faith in Hebrews involves a forward-looking aspect, which is repeatedly demonstrated throughout chapter 11. The participle ἐλπιζομένων in 11:1, along with ὑπόστασις, points to the expectation of a final eschatological event, which is the Second Advent of Christ.[71] Thus it may be said that faith in Hebrews is eschatologically oriented.

---

[67] M. A. Mathis, "Does 'Substantia' Mean 'Realisation' or 'Foundation' in Hebr 11,1?," *Biblica* 3 (1922): 79–87.

[68] Köster, "ὑπόστασις," in *TDNT*, 8:572–89.

[69] P. E. Hughes, *A Commentary on the Epistle to the Hebrews*, 439.

[70] Lane, *Hebrews 9–13*, 328–29.

[71] Thompson, *The Beginnings of Christian Philosophy*, 73.

There is also no unanimity in the interpretation of ἔλεγχος among scholars. Since the word is used in no other place in the New Testament except in 11:1, the exact meaning of the word is difficult to determine. As with ὑπόστασις, the meaning of ἔλεγχος may be interpreted as "conviction" in a subjective sense or "proof" in an objective sense.[72] Among those who takes the subjective view, Bruce asserts that ἔλεγχος means "conviction" in much the same sense as "assurance" in the preceding phrase."[73] Likewise, Moffatt, arguing against the objective understanding of ἔλεγχος, states that "faith is not the ἔλεγχος of things unseen in the sense of 'proof,' which could only mean that it tests, or rather attests, their reality."[74] He asserts that the author of Hebrews "wishes to show, not the reality of these unseen ends of God—he assumes these—but the fact and force of believing in them with absolute confidence."[75]

A subjective understanding of the word is possible here and makes reasonably good sense in the overall context of chapter 11. It may be said that all the exemplars of faith had the assurance of the things of hoped for, and the conviction of the things they had not yet seen. However, since the phrase πραγμάτων ἔλεγχος οὐ βλεπομένων is used to further describe what precedes (i.e., ἐλπιζομένων ὑπόστασις), it seems that ἔλεγχος should also be understood in an objective sense as in the case of ὑπόστασις (i.e., "proof" as opposed to "conviction"). Thompson argues that because of the parallelism between ὑπόστασις and ἔλεγχος the two must be interpreted alongside of each other. Thus he suggests that ἔλεγχος has the meaning of "proof."[76] Interpreting ἔλεγχος in this sense allows one to see that faith in chapter 11 is "an objective reality, so objective that it can be called a 'proof' (ἔλεγχος) of the things which have been and are hoped for by all those involved."[77] Adding the phrase πραγμάτων ἔλεγχος οὐ βλεπομένων establishes the inner right of resting on the thing hoped for (i.e., ὑπόστασις). Un-

---

[72] Bauer, *Lexicon*, 249.

[73] Bruce, *The Epistle to the Hebrews*, 279.

[74] Moffatt, *Hebrews*, 159–60.

[75] Ibid., 160.

[76] Thompson, *The Beginnings of Christian Philosophy*, 70.

[77] James Swetnam, "Form and Content in Hebrews 7–13," *Biblica* 55 (1974): 334.

derstanding ἔλεγχος in a subjective sense breaks down the necessary parallelism of ὑπόστασις and ἔλεγχος in 11:1 and obscures the inner right of the ὑπόστασις.[78] For this reason the objective understanding of ἔλεγχος is more in accordance with what the author has in mind.

If the objective understanding of ὑπόστασις and ἔλεγχος is correct, then the definition of faith stated in 11:1 may be stated as: faith is the reality (or substance) of things hoped for, the proof of things not seen. These two terms clearly indicate that what the author intends to emphasize in chapter 11 is a forward-looking aspect of faith. With this type of faith the men of old (οἱ πρεσβύτεροι) have been attested by God. In the remaining part of chapter 11 he provides exemplar after exemplar of faith who were attested by the forward-looking attitude of faith.

As for 11:3, it has already been pointed out that this verse is structurally parallel to 11:1. An examination of the verse indicates that it is also thematically related to verse 1 in that it further supports the definition of faith which the author sets forth in the beginning of the chapter. Especially, the creation account in verse 3 corresponds to verse 1b (i.e., conviction of things not seen). The expression "what is seen now" (v. 3) is equivalent to "proof" (v. 1b). Moreover, the phrase "not from things visible" (v. 3) is parallel to "not seen" (v. 1b). In this sense, 11:3 may be understood as an illustration that faith is the proof of things not seen in 11:1b. The above analysis provides convincing evidence that 11:3 should be regarded as the continuation of 11:1–2. For this reason my contention that 11:1–3 forms a unit should be given serious consideration.

After having established the basis for the structural unit, the next issue is to decide in what sense 11:39–40 is to be considered the conclusion of chapter 11. This problem can easily be resolved from the structural point of view. In the introduction (11:1–3) (A) the forward-looking aspect of faith is announced: the author clearly defined faith as "the reality of things hoped for" and "the proof of things not seen." Then, after explaining this theme through the exemplars of faith (11:4–12), he restates the forward-looking theme in 11:13–16 (H). Afterwards, he con-

---

78 Friedrich Büchsel "ἔχλγχος," in *Theological Dictionary of the New Testament* , ed. Gerhard Kittel, tr. Geoffrey W. Bromiley (Grand Rapids: William B. Eerdmans Publishing Co., 1964), 2:476.

tinues with the exemplars of faith in 11:17–38. The description in this
center section is general enough to look back to the previous examples
in 11:4–12 and look forward to the examples of faith in 11:17–38. Then
in 11:39–40 (A') the author summarizes the entire chapter by employing
terms and concepts that echo 11:1–3 and 11:13–16. The reference to
"men of old" in 11:1 corresponds to "they all" in 11:13 and 11:39. The
introduction (11:1–3) is also related to the conclusion by the idea of attestation by faith (ἐμαρτυρήθησαν in v. 1; μαρτυρηθέντες in v. 39).
The middle section (11:13–16) is summarized by the entire section of
the conclusion (11:39–40). Ellingworth illustrates the similarity between
11:13 and 11:39 as follows:[79]

v. 13	v. 39
a. Κατὰ πίστιν ἀπέθανον	b. Καὶ οὗτοι πάντες μαρτυρηθέντες
b. οὗτοι πάντες,	a. διὰ τῆς πίστεως
c. μὴ λαβόντες	c. οὐκ ἐκομίσαντο
d. τὰς ἐπαγγελίας	d. τὴν ἐπαγγελίαν

This comparison clearly shows that the idea expressed in 11:13 is
restated in a slightly different way. However, an observation of 11:13–
16 and 11:39–40 reveals that the comparison goes beyond the two verses
mentioned above. In the middle section (vv. 13–16) the present tenses
are used intentionally (εἰσιν, v. 13; ὀρέγονται and ἐπαισχύνεται, v.
16) in describing the exemplars of faith in the past (i.e., in the immediate
context, Abraham, Isaac, Jacob, Sarah). These present tenses correspond
to "concerning us" (περὶ ἡμῶν) and "apart from us" (χωρὶς ἡμῶν) in
11:40. In other words, the author, through these present tenses, is identifying the pilgrimage of the readers with that of the exemplars of faith in
the Old Testament. Moreover, the reference to "God foreseeing something better" in 11:40 corresponds to "the patriarchs reaching out to a
better place" (i.e., the heavenly place), and "God preparing a city for
them" in 11:16. Hence, 11:39–40 may be regarded as the conclusion of
chapter 11.

   Aspects of faith in the conclusion (11:39–40; A'). Then what aspects
of faith can be observed from this concluding section (11:39–40)? The
above comparison makes it clear that the main emphasis of this passage

[79] Ellingworth, *The Epistle to the Hebrews,* 634.

is on the forward-looking aspect of faith. To appreciate how the author summarizes this aspect of faith, several issues need to be discussed. The first issue has to do with the phrase "they did not receive the promise" in 11:39.[80] A survey of chapter 11 indicates that some men and women received what was promised in their lifetime (e.g., Noah, v. 7; Abraham and Sarah, vv. 11–12; the people of Israel, v. 30; Rahab, v. 31; some women, v. 35, etc.). However, 11:39a states that they all did not receive the promise. In what sense did they not receive the promise? To what does the promise refer in this verse? The immediate context does not explain the nature of this promise. However, the parallel passage in the middle section (11:13–16) indicates that the promise that they did not receive is the heavenly place (ἐπουρανίου), the city which God had prepared for them (11:16). In the next chapter the author sheds further light on the heavenly city which the exemplars of faith saw and greeted from afar, without having received the final fulfillment; it is Mount Zion, the city of living God, which is the heavenly Jerusalem (12:22). In this verse the author states that believers in the new covenant have already entered this heavenly city (προσεληλύθατε). In other words, the promise mentioned in 11:39a is an eternal inheritance which is available through Christ, the mediator of the new covenant (9:15).[81]

The next issue which needs to be resolved in this section is the meaning of the phrase κρεῖττόν τι (11:40). What is this "something better" which God had foreseen for us? To answer this question, the interpretation of the ἵνα clause is important. This clause has an epexegetical sense in that it further defines what this "something better" is: it is their denial of perfection without us. That is, it refers to "our inclusion in this people of God for whom the τελείωσις of Christ was destined"[82] It is true that some of the exemplars of faith had experienced fulfillment of God's promises even in this life, but the ultimate promise, in the sense

---

80 D'Angelo suggests that the phrase διὰ τῆς πίστεως can be related to either μαρτυρηθέντες or ἐκομίσαντο. She asserts that this multiplicity of meanings is intentional. See D'Angelo, *Moses in the Letter to the Hebrews*, 23. However, it seems more natural to connect it to μαρτυρηθέντες because of the word order. Moreover, a comparison with 11:2 indicates that this interpretation is more plausible (i.e., the phrase ἐν ταύτῃ refers to πίστις, which is used along with μαρτυρέω).

81 Lane, *Hebrews 9–13*, 392.

82 Moffatt, *Hebrews*, 191.

of the messianic bliss with its eternal life (10:36, 37, cf. 6:17f.) was not granted to them.[83] Their perfection was dependent upon the sacrificial death of Christ. In this sense, their faith was eschatological in that they had a forward-looking orientation of faith. At the same time it is clear that the author connects this eschatological outlook of faith to Christ's sacrificial death. Thus it may be said that the heroes and the heroines of faith in the Old Testament period had a Christological orientation of faith from the author's perspective. However, it is also to be realized that the faith of those who are in the new covenant is both eschatologically and Christologically oriented. On the one hand, it has already been shown from the previous discussion that believers under the new covenant have come to Mount Zion, the city of God, the heavenly Jerusalem, and to Jesus, the mediator of the new covenant (12:22–24). In this sense, the eschatological fulfillment has already taken place. On the other hand, the ultimate eschatological fulfillment has not yet taken place because we are still seeking the city that is to come (13:14). Thus it may be said that the faith of those who are under the new covenant is eschatologically oriented just as those in the old covenant. This forward-looking aspect of faith of those in the new covenant is also closely related to Christology; believers must run the race which lies ahead of them by fixing their eyes on Jesus. This point will become more evident in the discussion of the parenetic section in 12:1–29.

Summary of chapter 11

An examination of chapter 11 reveals much insight into the concept of faith in Hebrews. Analyses of all the corresponding sections, including the center of the chapter (11:13–16), support the argument that chapter 11 is written with a chiastic structure in mind. The primary reason that the author artistically made a chiastic arrangement in writing chapter 11 is to set forth the importance of the eschatological nature of faith (i.e., forward-looking aspect) in Hebrews. This eschatological orientation of faith is introduced in 11:1–3, restated in 11:13–16, and summarized in 1:39–40 by way of conclusion. In between these summary statements, the author brings in examples of faith from the Old Testament to illustrate this forward-looking aspect of faith. In addition, an analysis of chapter 11 reveals that the Christological aspect of faith is

---

[83] Ibid., 190.

not lacking. Several passages in the chapter suggest that this aspect of faith is implied by the author (e.g., the reference to "heir of righteousness according to faith" for Noah in 11:7; "abuse of Christ" in describing Moses' faith in 11:26; institution of the Passover in 11:28). Moreover, the author's references to "God preparing for something better concerning us" and "their denial of perfection without us" (11:40) clearly point to the institution of the new covenant with Christ's sacrificial death on the cross. Thus it is clear that the futuristic outlook of faith (i.e., the forward-looking aspect) by the exemplars of faith in the old covenant is ultimately related to Christ-event in the new covenant. Thus, it may be concluded that faith in 11:1–40 is both eschatologically and Christologically oriented.

Examination of 12:1–29

After an exposition of faith in 11:1–40, the author turns to the final parenetic section of 12:1–29. The change of the literary genre from exposition to parenesis is clearly indicated in this section. This is well pointed out by Lane:

> In 12:1 the writer turns from historical recital (11:1–40) to pastoral exhortation. The previous section was composed entirely in the indicative mood; this unit is marked by the use of the imperative and the hortatory subjunctive. In striking contrast to 11:1–40, where the exposition was carried forward almost exclusively by the use of the third person, the verbs in this section are expressed in the first (12:1, 9) or the second person (12:3, 4, 5, 7, 8, 12, 13). The subject is no longer the attested witnesses of Israel's remote or more recent past but the struggle in which Christians are currently engaged (12:1, 3, 5, 7, 9, 12–13).[84]

As in any other alternating passages, I will first establish the literary unit of 12:1–29, and then proceed to the discussion of the relationship between faith and Christology.

Basis for the Literary Unit

This final parenetic section (12:1–29) may be divided into two main parts: (1) the necessity of endurance (12:1–13) and (2) the danger of re-

[84] Lane, *Hebrews 9–13*, 403.

jecting God's word (12:14–29). In this section I will establish the basis for the literary unit in each of these parts. Then the relationship between these two parts will be discussed.

First, what is the evidence which may support that 12:1–13 forms a unit? To begin with, the literary unit may be argued from the device of inclusion. Vanhoye observes that this parenetic section forms an inclusion by the verb τρέχωμεν in 12:1 and the noun τροχιάς in 12:13.[85] Strictly speaking, the two words are not identical because the former is a verb (to run) and the latter a noun (wheel track course or way).[86] For this reason Swetnam doubts whether τρέχωμεν in 12:1 and τροχιάς in 12:13 form an inclusion.[87] However, a comparison of the meaning of the two words indicates that they are cognate terms. Moreover, 12:13 is an allusion from Proverbs 4:26 (LXX). The author changes the order of words and places τροχιάς in the beginning of the verse.[88] What might be the author's motive for doing this? It appears that his intention is to alert the readers to regard that 12:1–13 is a unit by evoking τρέχωμεν at the beginning of the section (12:1). Thus it is reasonable to consider that this section forms a literary unit by an inclusion. That 12:1–13 is a unit is further supported by the content of the passage. In this context the metaphor of a runner staying on his course and running hard to reach the goal is emphasized.[89] Although this section maintains its unity by the idea of endurance, the content makes it obvious that it is divided into two subsections: (1) exhortation to run the race with endurance (12:1–3) and (2) exhortation to endure discipline (12:4–13). It is my opinion that each of these subsections forms a unit by chiasm, which will be demonstrated in the following section (i.e., Faith and Christology).

Next, the literary unit of 12:14–29 is indicated by an inclusion with the word χάρις in verses 15 and 28. Swetman is doubtful whether even a most alert mind would notice the inclusion by this word.[90] However, the author's use of the word only in these verses in 12:1–29 seems to

[85] Vanhoye, *La structure*, 46.

[86] Bauer, *Lexicon*, 828.

[87] Swetnam, "Form and Content in Hebrews 7–13," 346.

[88] Proverbs 4:26 (LXX) reads, ὀρθὰς τροχιὰς ποίει σοῖς ποσίν . . . .

[89] Buchanan, *Hebrews*, 216.

[90] Swetnam, "Form and Content in Hebrews 7–13," 346.

suggest that he intended to define the limit of the passage by this term. Moreover, the conjunction διό in 12:28 shows that verse 28 is the conclusion, not only of the subdivision of 12:25–29, but also the entire passage of 12:14–29.[91] Third, as for the relationship between 12:1–13 and 12:14–29, there is no structural clue to suggest that these two are related to each other. However, it appears that they are thematically related. Although there is a change of the subject matter from 12:1–13 to 12:14–29, the context also indicates that there is a continuity of thought between the two passages. In 12:13 the author exhorts the readers to lift their drooping hands and strengthen the weak knees to stay on the path of righteous living. Then in 12:14–29 he describes specifically in what ways this principle can be implemented.[92] The author does it by (1) exhorting the readers to pursue peace and not to fail to obtain the grace of God (12:14–17), (2) reminding them that they have come to Mount Zion and to the city of the living God (12:18–24), and (3) warning them not to reject him who speaks to them (12:25–29). The author's appeal in this passage is broader in scope than the exhortation that preceded it. Here, the emphasis is not on the response of the community as it experiences suffering, but on the danger of rejecting the God who continues to speak through his Son and through the Scriptures.[93] The above analysis both from the structural and thematic standpoint suggests that 12:1–29 can indeed be considered a unit composed of two main parts (i.e., 12:1–13 and 12:14–29).

Faith and Christology

As mentioned throughout this book, some scholars do not consider that faith in Hebrews is Christologically oriented. For example, Goppelt asserts that "Christ was not the content, but 'the pioneer and perfecter of our faith' (12:2)."[94] Others maintain that Christ is regarded merely as a

91 Vanhoye, *La structure,* 209–210.

92 D. A. Black, "The Problem of the Literary Structure of Hebrews: An Evaluation and a Proposal," *Grace Theological Journal* 2 (1986): 169.

93 Lane, *Hebrews 9–13,* 445.

94 Leonhard Goppelt, *Theology of the New Testament,* ed. Jürgen Roloff, trans. John Alsup (Grand Rapids: William B. Eerdmans Publishing Co., 1981), 2:263.

model for Christian faith. For example, Lindars argues that faith is primarily a matter of following the example of Jesus."[95] For this reason
faith is reduced to a virtue of endurance or steadfastness without any
reference to Christ being the object of faith for believers. While it is true
that the characteristic of steadfastness is emphasized in 12:1–29, it is
also true that Christ is depicted as a supreme model of faith for believers
in this parenesis. However, it is a considerable mistake to think that faith
in Hebrews does not have Christ as the object of faith merely because it
is not expressed in terms of "faith in Jesus Christ" as in the Pauline literature. Throughout the epistle the author of Hebrews has implied in
various ways that faith is intimately related to the Christ-event. This last
parenetic section (12:1–29) is no exception. A detailed analysis of this
passage demonstrates that faith in Hebrews is Christologically oriented.
The discussion will be carried out in the following order: (1) exegesis of
12:1–3; (2) exegesis of 12:4–13; and (3) exegesis of 12:14–29.

Exegesis of 12:1–3
    The Christological orientation of faith in 12:1–3 can be examined
from the following categories: (1) the chiastic arrangement of the passage, (2) The meaning of ἀρχηγός and τελειωτής, (3) the concept of
endurance, and (4) the concept of hymn.
    The chiastic arrangement. To begin with, the Christological notion
of faith in 12:1–3 may be demonstrated from its literary form. The presence of a chiastic structure in 12:1–2 is recognized by many scholars. I
have already presented Horning's scheme of the chiastic structure of this
passage in chapter two.[96] Horning points out that the first half of the chiasm (i.e., A to D) is focused on "us" while the second half (D' to A') is
on "Jesus."[97] She suggests that the intention of the author is Christologically motivated; namely, it is a challenge for the readers to imitate faith
demonstrated in the sufferings and the death of Jesus.[98] Horning's contribution to the Christological understanding of faith in Hebrews is to be

___

[95] Lindars, *Theology*, 113.

[96] For Horning's chiastic structure, see Chapter Two, 53.

[97] E. B. Horning, "Chiasmus, Creedal Structure, and Christology in Hebrews 12:1–
2," *Biblical Research* 23 (1978): 40–41.

[98] Ibid.

taken seriously. It is quite possible that this may have been the original intention of the author. Her proposed chiastic structure helps one see that Jesus is the very center of focus in believers' race. However, I believe that the chiasm extends to verse 3. This alternative chiastic structure of 12:1–3 may be illustrated as follows:

A   Τοιγαροῦν καὶ ἡμεῖς τοσοῦτον ἔχοντες περικείμενον ἡμῖν νέφος μαρτύρων, ὄγκον ἀποθέμενοι πάντα καὶ τὴν εὐπερίστατον ἁμαρτίαν (Therefore, since we are surrounded by so great a cloud of witnesses, let us also lay
aside every weight and the sin that clings so closely) (12:1a),

B   δι᾽ ὑπομονῆς τρέχωμεν τὸν προκείμενον ἡμῖν ἀγῶνα (and let us run
with perseverance the race that is set before us) (12:1b)

C   12:2
    1   ἀφορῶντες εἰς τὸν τῆς πίστεως ἀρχηγὸν καὶ τελειωτὴν
        Ἰησοῦν (looking to Jesus the pioneer and perfecter of our faith),
    2   ὃς ἀντὶ τῆς προκειμένης αὐτῷ χαρᾶς (who for the sake of
        the joy that was set before him)
        3   ὑπέμεινεν σταυρὸν (endured the cross),
    2' αἰσχύνης καταφρονήσας (disregarding its shame),
    1' ἐν δεξιᾷ τε τοῦ θρόνου τοῦ θεοῦ κεκάθικεν (and has taken his
        seat at the right hand of the throne of God).

B' ἀναλογίσασθε γὰρ τὸν τοιαύτην ὑπομεμενηκότα ὑπὸ τῶν ἁμαρτωλῶν εἰς ἑαυτὸν ἀντιλογίαν (Consider him who endured such hostility
against himself from sinners) (12:3a),

A' ἵνα μὴ κάμητε ταῖς ψυχαῖς ὑμῶν ἐκλυόμενοι (so that you may not grow
weary or lose heart) (12:3b).

In this proposed chiastic structure, outer sections A and A' complement each other conceptually; while section A speaks of being surrounded by so great a cloud of witnesses and putting off the burden and the sin, section A' exhorts the readers not to grow weary or faint-hearted (A'). In other words, section A' shows the reason for the description in section A. The parallelism of sections B and B' may be demonstrated in two ways. First, both sections are related to each other by the idea of endurance (ὑπομονῆς in B and ὑπομεμενηκότα in B'). Second, the thought of "contest" (ἀγῶνα) in section B is parallel to "opposition" (ἀντιλογίαν) in B'.[99] The phrase "the contest which lies before" in B refers to the hardships the readers were facing at the time of writing the letter (cf., 10:32–34). The "opposition" in B' refers to the persecution and the hardship which Jesus endured during the Passion week. This is supported by the explicit mention of σταυρός in 12:2. A comparison of the points between sections B and B' indicates that they may be regarded as parallel passages. Through these parallel thoughts the author indicates that believers must run the race with endurance (B) as they consider the one (i.e., Jesus) who endured such hostility by sinners against himself (B'). In other words, sections B and B' may be considered an appeal for the readers to imitate Jesus who had run the race before them. In this sense, Jesus is regarded as the model of faith for believers.

The center section (C) focuses on Jesus and his accomplishment. After a brief exhortation to fix their eyes on Jesus, the author proceeds to describe who Jesus is, and what he has done for believers.[100] In the proposed chiasm of 12:1–3 I have suggested that the center section (12:2; C) is also chiastically arranged. Sections 1 and 1' complement each other in that the founder (ἀρχηγός) and the perfecter (τελειωτής) of faith (i.e., Jesus) is the one who is seated at the right hand of the throne of God. These outer sections also suggest why the readers must fix their eyes on Jesus: it is because he is at the right hand of the throne of God. Sections 2 and 2' may be considered parallel because 2' (despising the shame) is a further explanation of 2 (instead of the joy set before him).[101] The language used in these sections has a clear reference to the suffering and crucifixion of Jesus. An examination of sections 1/1' and 2/2' indicates that the author considers Jesus as the model and the object of faith. The Christological aspect of faith is more evident in section 3. This middle section, which is the center point of the small chiastic

99 Vanhoye, *La structure*, 197.

100 Lane points out that "the use of the simple personal name 'Jesus' shows that the accent is upon His humanity, and especially His endurance of pain, humiliation, and the disgrace of the cross" (Lane, *Hebrews 9–13*, 410).

101 There are two ways of interpreting ἀντί: (1) for the sake of and (2) instead of. If the prepositional phrase refers to ἐν δεξιᾷ τε τοῦ θρόνου τοῦ θεοῦ κεκάθικεν, then (1) is a better choice. However, if the phrase refers to αἰσχύνης καταφρονήσας as I suggested, then (2) makes a better sense. See N. Turner, *Grammatical Insights into the New Testament* (Edinburgh: T. & T. Clark, 1965), 172–73.

structure in section C, indicates that Jesus endured the cross. It may be said that section 3 is the center of the entire chiastic structure of 12:1–3. The main idea of 12:2 is that believers ought to fix their eyes on Jesus, the founder and the perfecter of faith, who endured the cross. Then what might be the author's purpose in placing the reference to "the cross" in the center of section 12:1–3? It appears that he has a theological motivation in having designed the structure this way. Section C, and more specifically section 3, is placed in the center to imply that Christ and his death on the cross is the basis for the readers to run the race with endurance. Through this literary device the author implies that the exhortation in 12:1–3 is Christologically oriented.

The meaning of ἀρχηγός and τελειωτής. Next, the Christological orientation of faith in Hebrews can be shown from the use of the terms ἀρχηγός and τελειωτής in 12:2. The word ἀρχηγός in the LXX and non-biblical literature has basically two different meanings: (1) leader or ruler; (2) originator, founder, or pioneer (i.e., one who begins something as first in a series to give the impetus).[102] Understanding ἀρχηγός as the former sense leads to the conclusion that Jesus is the model of faith; but taking it in the latter sense, to the conclusion that Jesus is the object of faith.

Hamm argues that ἀρχηγός in 12:2, with the racing image of the context, denotes Jesus as the "leader" as in 2:10. In other words, Jesus is the leader because he is the forerunner as stated in 6:20. For this reason he contends that Jesus is portrayed as the model or the exemplar of our faith.[103] As for the meaning of τελειωτής, Hamm argues that the phrase, "τὸν τῆς πίστεως . . . τελειωτήν" should be translated, not as "perfecter of our faith," but as "perfecter of faith."[104] He believes that while the reference to "perfecter of our faith" is limited to believers in the new covenant, the phrase "perfecter of faith" encompasses the saints both in the Old and the New Testament. In other words, Jesus is the perfecter of faith in the sense that he "models to perfection the imperfect faith exemplified by the ancestors just praised in the previous passage,

---

102 Bauer, *Lexicon,* 112.

103 Dennis Hamm, "Faith in the Epistle to the Hebrews: The Jesus Factor," *Catholic Biblical Quarterly* 52 (1992): 287.

104 Ibid., 280.

who as models of faith, indeed, would not be perfected (τελειωθῶσιν) without us [*sic*] (11:40)."[105] Hamm also argues that the combination of the two words (i.e., ἀρχηγός and τελειωτής) gives the sense that Jesus is the beginner and the finisher of Christian faith, making him to be the enabler of faith.[106] Thus he concludes that Jesus is the model and enabler of faith.

However, an examination of the term ἀρχηγός in Hebrews reveals that Jesus is regarded not only as the enabler and model of faith, but also as the object of faith for believers. The word is used four times in the New Testament (Acts 3:15; 5:31; Heb 2:10; 12:2). An analysis of the context of these passages indicates that the word is always used in association with the salvific work of Christ. It is used in contexts which describe the death and resurrection or exaltation of Jesus.[107] More specifically, in Hebrews the word is used to refer to Jesus not only as the model of faith, but also the founder of salvation (i.e., the object and content of faith). In 2:9 the author mentions that Jesus was crowned with glory because of the suffering of death. This is clearly a reference to the death, resurrection, and exaltation of Jesus in his earthly life. In addition, the use of the word salvation (σωτηρία) in 2:10 further supports that Jesus is viewed as the object of faith. The word σωτηρία occurs seven times in Hebrews (1:14; 2:3; 2:10; 5:29; 6:9; 9:28; 11:7). In 11:7 it is used in reference to the physical deliverance of Noah and his family. However, in the rest of the passages, the word denotes the spiritual salvation. For this reason Scott suggests that the ἀρχηγός of salvation has the sense of the ἀρχηγός of the new age. That is to say, Jesus is the one "through whose sufferings (the 'birth pangs of the Messiah') the new age becomes a reality and whose personal honor and glory, which is shared with 'his sons,' is a major characteristic of it."[108] In this sense, it is reasonable to understand that the phrase "ἀρχηγός of salvation" is the author's way of expressing Jesus as the object of faith for believers, not simply the model of faith.

---

[105] Ibid., 287.

[106] Ibid.

[107] Ellingworth, *The Epistle to the Hebrews*, 160.

[108] J. Julius Scott, "Archegos in the Salvation History of the Epistle to the Hebrews," *Journal of the Evangelical Theological Society* 29 (1986), 50.

The aspect of Jesus being the object of faith can also be demonstrated from the use of ἀρχηγός in 12:1–2. In this passage, the author employs the image of athletes who run the race in the stadium, and exhorts the readers to run the race with endurance. An examination of these verses reveals that Jesus is viewed not only as the enabler and model of faith, as Hamm suggests, but also as the object of faith for believers. One should be reminded that the author has not forgotten the discussion of Jesus' humanity and his high priesthood in the previous chapters. "His attainment of exaltation glory by way of faithful obedience in suffering was unprecedented and determinative."[109] Since Christ has paved a perfect way of faith by his high priestly work, his faith is qualitatively, not simply quantitatively, greater than the faith of the Old Testament saints.[110] This means that, while the author gives examples of faith in chapter 11, he has something else in mind in 12:1–3, in addition to presenting him as the model of faith. The titles of Jesus as ἀρχηγός and τελειωτής circumscribe the dual aspects of the saving work of Jesus Christ: he is the ἀρχηγός (the founder) in the sense that he started eternal salvation for his people; and τελειωτής (perfecter) in that he will see them through to finish the course.[111] Looking at this verse from the soteriological point of view, it can be said that Jesus is the object of faith in Hebrews even if it does not have the Pauline notion of faith (i.e., trust in Jesus for salvation). Moreover, the latter part of 12:2 also supports that the term ἀρχηγός has the idea of Jesus as the object of faith in a soteriological sense. The author uses the word "cross" (σταυρός) in this verse, which is the only explicit reference to this word in Hebrews.[112] Coupled with the use of αἰσχύνης (shame), the author points to the suffering of the death of Jesus. The reference to "seated at the right hand" corresponds to "crowned with glory and

109 Lane, *Hebrews 9–13*, 412.

110 David Peterson, *Hebrews and Perfection: An Examination of the Concept of Perfection in the 'Epistle to the Hebrews,'* Society for New Testament Studies Monograph Series 47 (Cambridge: Cambridge University Press, 1982), 173.

111 William Manson, *The Epistle to the Hebrews: A Historical and Theological Reconsideration* (London: Hodder And Stoughton, 1951), 83.

112 Lane, *Hebrews 9–13*, 414.

honor" in 2:9.[113] In other words, the word ἀρχηγός in 12:2 has the idea of "making the transition from the past to the present and contrasting former suffering with the present honor."[114] The term must be understood in relation to the high priestly doctrine of Hebrews. The description in 12:2 is clearly the expression of humiliation (i.e., in the days of his flesh in 2:7) and exaltation of Jesus, the high priest (i.e., having been made perfect in 2:9). The theme of humiliation and exaltation indicates that Jesus should be taken as the object of faith (i.e., source of eternal salvation, 5:9) as well as the model for imitation.[115]

The concept of endurance. The idea of Jesus being the object of faith can also be demonstrated from the author's use of the concept of endurance in 12:1–3. One recurring idea in 12:1–3 is the thought of endurance (ὑπομονῆς, 12:1; ὑπέμεινεν, 12:2; ὑπομεμενηκότα, 12:3). The endurance exemplified by Jesus is placed side by side with that of the readers. This seems to be intentional: the author deliberately sets the Christological teaching in parallel with the parenesis to indicate that the exhortation to endure trials by faith is Christologically oriented: namely, Jesus is both the model and the object of faith. Even though faith in Hebrews is not expressed in terms of "faith in Jesus" or "trust in Christ," it is so intimately related to the work of Christ that one cannot discuss the concept of faith without dealing with the doctrine of Christology. Faith in Hebrews is directly related to the sacrificial death of Jesus on the cross as in the Pauline literature. Thus it may be argued that, even in Hebrews, Jesus ought to be regarded not only as the model of faith for believers, but also as the object of faith for them.[116]

[113] Thomas Wiley Lewis III, "The Theological Logic in Hebrews 10:19–12:29 and the Appropriation of the Old Testament" (Ph.D. diss., Drew University, 1965), 119.

[114] Scott, "Archegos in the Salvation History of the Epistle to the Hebrews," 50.

[115] Delling also expresses a similar view. He states,

"Yet Jesus is also ἀρχηγός τῆς πίστεως in the sense that as the first man He gave an example of faith in God, that by His death he 'fulfilled' this faith in God's unconditional love and its overcoming of the barrier of sin, and that He thereby gave this love concrete and once-for-all actualisation in the history of salvation." Gerhard Delling, "ἀρχηγός," in *Theological Dictionary of the New Testament,* ed. Gerhard Kittel (Grand Rapids: William B Eerdmans Publishing Co., 1964), 1:488.

[116]For the importance of the chiasm to the theological understanding of Hebrews 12:1–2, see Horning, "Chiasmus," 45–46. Black also, realizing the importance of the structure in the interpretation of this passage, makes note that 12:1–2 "have usually been

The concept of hymn. There is yet another literary form in 12:2 which may also support the claim that faith in Hebrews is Christologically oriented. Some scholars consider the possibility that 12:2a belongs to the category of hymns, which were considered a form of confessional formula that expressed the basic elements of the early church's faith.[117] Gloer nicely compiles the sixteen criteria for determining the presence of hymns in the New Testament.[118] An examination of 12:2b shows that many of these criteria are present in this verse. Some of the examples may be demonstrated as follows: (1) there is a presence of the relative pronoun ὅς: this characteristic is also found in Ephesians 2:14–16, Philippians 2:6, Colossians 1:15, and 1 Timothy 3:16; (2) there is a presence of the participles: in the present verse the author employs two participles (προκειμένης; καταθρονήσας); this style is observed elsewhere in Ephesians 2:14–16, 1 Timothy 3:16; (3) content of material exhibits the basic elements of Christology: incarnation (instead of the joy set before him, cf. Phil 2:6); crucifixion (endured cross, cf. Phil 2:8); shameful death (despising the shame, cf. Phil 2:8); and exaltation (he is seated at the right hand of the throne of God, cf. Phil 2:9–11); (4) there is evidence of chiasm, which I have already demonstrated through a careful analysis.[119]

The identification of the criteria above suggests that 12:2b may have been a creedal statement in the form of a hymn.[120] Then what is the implication of this study? If this verse may be correctly identified as a hymn in the early church, then the author's use of it is significant. His intention may have been to highlight the importance of Christology in the discussion of faith in 12:1–13. This is another piece of evidence

---

interpreted by commentators who were unware of this structure and thus did not ask what it meant." See Black, "A Note on the Structure of Hebrews 12:1–2," 547.

117 W. Gloer, "Homologies and Hymns in the New Testament: Form, Content and Criteria for Identification," *Perspectives in Religious Studies* 11 (1984): 116.

118 Ibid., 124–29.

119 Black identifies nine criteria of hymnal formula in 12:2b based on the work compiled by Groer. See Black, "A Note on the Structure of Hebrews 12:1–2," 548–49. I have identified the four most important criteria with the help of his work.

120 Horning also considers 12:2b to be a creedal formula. See Horning, "Chiasmus," 40.

which strengthens the argument that faith in Hebrews is Christologically oriented (i.e., Jesus is viewed as the object of faith for Christians).

Exegesis of 12:4–13

I am also inclined to consider that the second part of 12:1–13, namely, 12:4–13 has a chiastic arrangement. This may be illustrated as follows:

A   Statement of fact: you have not resisted to the point of shedding blood in fighting against the sin (12:4).

B   The necessity of discipline: the Lord disciplines whom he loves (12:5–6).

C   Discipline for purpose: it is because you are his sons (12:7–8).

D   Comparison between the discipline of the physical father and that of the Father of the spirits (12:9).

C'   The purpose of discipline: it is for the purpose of sharing his holiness (12:10).

B'   The necessity of discipline: it produces peaceful fruit of righteousness for those who have been trained by it (12:11).

A'   Exhortation: therefore, strengthen the weak parts of your body and make straight paths for your feet (12:12–13).

According to this proposed chiastic structure, the center section (D) stresses that the readers must be subject to the discipline of the Father by employing an *a fortiori* argument: if we respected our earthly fathers who trained us, how much more shall we not be subject to the Father of the spirits and live?[121] The expression καὶ ζήσομεν (and shall we live?) emphasizes the importance of willing submission to God.[122] It also recalls 10:38, in which the author states, "but my righteous one shall live by faith." Since both 10:38 and 12:9 are in the context of suffering en-

---

[121] The phrase "the Father of the spirits" (τῷ πατρὶ τῶν πνευμάτων) is a Jewish traditional formula used primarily of God's relationship to the angelic world. However, in the present context it is likely that the formula is used in the anthropological sense. See Attridge, *The Epistle to the Hebrews*, 363.

[122] Lane, *Hebrews 9–13*, 424.

durance by faith, it may be said that discipline is also related to the concept of faith. Sections C and C' show an indication of parallelism because (1) both passages make a comparison between an earthly father and the spiritual Father, and (2) both passages use the word related to "partakers" (i.e., μέτοχοι in 12:8; μεταλαβεῖν in 12:10). An analysis of these two passages suggests what the purpose of discipline is: the readers have become partakers of discipline (C) in order that they may partake the holiness of God (C'). Sections B and B' show the signs of parallelism as follows. First, the description of 12:11 (B') recalls the content of the forgotten aspect of discipline mentioned in 12:5-6 (B). In other words, the forgotten aspect is that every discipline for the present time is not joyful, but sorrowful. Second, the negative aspects of discipline described in 12:5-6 (e.g., ἐκλύω [faint]; ἐλέγχω [reprimand]; μαστιγόω [scourge]) explain why all discipline for the present time does not seem to be joyful, but sorrowful. Third, while section B addresses the negative aspect of discipline, section B' further describes the positive benefit of it (i.e., it yields the peaceful fruit of righteousness for those who have been trained by it). Sections A and A' form the introduction and the conclusion of 12:4-13, respectively. They may be considered parallel to each other because strengthening the weak parts of the body (A') is a necessary part of resisting sin (A).

A brief examination of the structure of 12:4-13 suggests that the passage is to be regarded as a unit. However, one must not forget that 12:4-13 is a continuation of the author's exhortation to endure hardship in the Christian race in 12:1-3. This is indicated by the use of the verb ἐκλύω (μὴ . . . ἐκλυόμενοι, v. 3; μηδὲ ἐκλύου, v. 5).[123] As a sub-unit of the parenetic section of 12:1-13, it further calls for the readers to endure the discipline. While the emphasis of 12:1-3 is on the necessity of endurance in running the race by fixing their eyes on Jesus who endured the cross, the stress of 12:4-13 is placed on the necessity of disciplinary sufferings in the race. Thus it is clear that 12:4-13 speaks of a characteristic of faith: faith involves enduring disciplinary sufferings.

Then how is this characteristic of endurance related to Christ? Is this quality merely an ethical element without any relationship to Christology? An examination of the immediate context of 12:1-3 has already revealed that the quality of endurance is Christologically oriented: Christ

123 Ibid., 417.

is both the object and the model of faith for believers. In addition, a consideration of the broader context of 10:32–12:13 suggests that the aspect of faith described in 12:4–13 (i.e., endurance) is Christologically motivated. This may be illustrated as follows:

A   An Exhortation to endure hardships by faith (10:32–39).

B   Exemplars of faith who endured hardships by faith from the Old Testament (11:1–40).

B'   A supreme example from the founder and the perfecter of faith who endure sufferings on the cross (12:1–3).

A'   An exhortation to endure disciplinary sufferings by faith (12:4–13).

Section A exhorts the readers to endure persecution in two ways: first, by reminding them to recall the former days when they had endured sufferings (10:32–34); second, by pointing out their lack of perseverance at the time of writing the letter (10:35–39). It appears that 10:36–39 corresponds well with 12:4–13 thematically. In fact, the language in both passages are so similar that the letter would proceed quite smoothly even without 11:1–40 and 12:1–3.[124] Vanhoye rightly indicates that 10:36–39 announces the theme that will be discussed in 11:1–12:13.[125] The author especially cites Habakkuk 2:4 (LXX) in 10:38 to set the tone for the following section. The exemplars of faith in 11:1–40 and the supreme example of faith in 12:1–3 are a further explanation of the phrase, "but my righteous one shall live by faith" (10:38a). The exhortation to endure disciplinary sufferings in 12:4–13 is the theme developed from 10:38b, which states, "and if he draws back, my soul will take no pleasure in him." The repeated use of παιδεύω (12:6, 7, 10) and παιδεία (12:5, 7, 8, 9, 11) corresponds to the negative statement in 10:38b. A comparison of sections A and A' makes it evident that the two passages are rhetorically parallel. Both 10:36–39 and 12:4–13 emphasize the necessity for the readers to endure the trials they were facing. As for the center of the chiasm (B and B'), the author illustrates the principle of necessity for endurance through the exemplars of faith in the Old Testament (B). The

[124] Cosby, *The Rhetorical Composition and Function of Hebrews 11*, 85.

[125] Vanhoye, *La structure*, 182.

extended illustration is balanced with the example of endurance displayed by Jesus (B').

It is already revealed from the previous discussion that both 11:1–40 and 12:1–3 show evidence that faith in Hebrews is Christologically oriented, namely, Jesus is portrayed as the model and the object of faith. In the broad structure of 10:32–12:13 the exemplars of faith (i.e., those of the Old Testament and Jesus) are intentionally placed in the center of the structure. What might have been the reason for placing them in the middle section? Again, it is to be remembered that, with the outer sections alone (A and A'), the author could have stressed the importance of accepting suffering because it is the fate of the pilgrim (12:12).[126] However, it looks as though the author intentionally placed 11:1–40 and 12:1–3 in the center (B and B') to imply that the exhortation to endure sufferings in sections A and A' is both Christologically and eschatologically oriented. The exemplars of faith in the Old Testament were able to endure trials, hardships and persecutions because they looked forward to the fulfillment of God's promise (i.e., Jesus). The eschatological outlook of faith finds its fulfillment in Jesus. In other words, their faith was prospective in that they looked forward to the fulfillment of God's promise in Jesus. In this sense, their faith may be regarded as having been Christologically oriented. Likewise, the faith of those who are under the new covenant is retrospective in that they look back to Jesus who endured sufferings. In this sense, it may be said that Jesus is both the model and the object of faith. At the same time, their faith is regarded as prospective because they are still looking forward to the final fulfillment of God's promise in the ultimate sense (12:26–27; 13:14). In light of the eschatological fulfillment of the promise of God, the readers are exhorted to run the race with endurance by fixing their eyes on Jesus, the founder and the perfecter of faith (12:1–3; 4–13). Thus it may be reasonably concluded that faith in 12:1–13 is both Christologically and eschatologically oriented.

Exegesis of 12:14–29

Vanhoye suggests that the parenetic section of 12:14–29 is divided into three subsections: (1) 12:14–17; (2) 12:18–24; and (3) 12:25–29.[127]

---

[126] Thompson, *The Beginnings of Christian Philosophy*, 77.

[127] Vanhoye, *La structure*, 205–210.

Likewise, Lane recognizes these three divisions and proposes that they can be arranged chiastically as follows:

A   Exhortation (12:14–17)
  B   Exposition (12:18–24)
A' Exhortation (12:25–29)[128]

He asserts that these "three paragraphs are unified by a hortatory appeal to material drawn from the OT to warn the recipients of the awful consequences of showing contempt to God."[129] Both Vanhoye and Lane have made helpful observations in recognizing these three divisions. However, a closer look at this passage reveals that section B can be divided into two parts: 12:18–21 and 12:22–24. This division is marked by οὐ in verse 18 and ἀλλά in verse 22.[130] In 12:18–21 the emphasis is placed on drawing near to God under the old covenant; in 12:22–24 the author emphasizes drawing near to God under the new covenant. Lane's proposed chiasm may be modified as follows:

1   Exhortation: Do not fail to obtain the grace of God (12:14–17)
  2   You have not come to Mount Sinai (12:18–21)
  2' You have come to Mount Zion (12:22–24)
1' Exhortation: Do not refuse him who is speaking (12:25–29)

Discussion of the outer sections (1 and 1'). In this proposed chiastic structure I will demonstrate that faith in Hebrews is Christologically oriented. To begin with, section 1 begins with an exhortation to pursue peace with all people (εἰρήνην) and sanctification (ἁγιασμόν) (12:4). Grammatically speaking, both εἰρήνην and ἁγιασμόν are related to the verb διώκετε. Some scholars consider that εἰρήνη is to be understood in a subjective sense as referring to an inner-communal harmony.[131] However, the word has a soteriological sense in Hebrews. For example, the author notes that Rahab received the spies in peace (μετ' εἰρήνης)

128 Lane, *Hebrews 9–13*, 447.

129 Ibid.

130 George H. Guthrie, *The Structure of Hebrews: A Text-Linguistic Analysis*, Supplements to Novum Testamentum 78 (Leiden: E. J. Brill, 1994), 133.

131 Attridge, *The Epistle to the Hebrews*, 367. See also Bruce, *The Epistle to the Hebrews*, 364.

(11:31). Her reception of spies with peace is considered an act of faith. Since Rahab and all her household were delivered because of her act of faith, εἰρήνη here may have a soteriological implication. Likewise, the use of εἰρήνη in 13:20 has a soteriological sense. In that verse the phrase ὁ θεὸς τῆς εἰρήνης is related to bringing back our Lord Jesus from the dead by the blood of the eternal covenant. In the present context also εἰρήνη carries a soteriological meaning. This word is used along with ἁγιασμός. The author indicates that without ἁγιασμός no one will see the Lord. It is not clear whether the Lord here refers to God the Father or Jesus. It is possible that the author has both in mind.[132] In either case ἁγιασμός in association with τὸν κύριον has a soteriological significance. Thus it is reasonable to argue that εἰρήνη in 12:14 has the sense of the eschatological salvation.[133] Moreover, the preposition μετά in 12:14 has the meaning of "in company with."[134] Therefore, this verse should be understood as the author's exhortation to pursue the eschatological salvation along with all believers. The exhortation to pursue peace and sanctification has a Christological implication.

This Christological aspect is further reinforced by the participial clause ἐπισκοποῦντες in 12:15–16, which may be illustrated as follows:

Εἰρήνην διώκετε μετὰ πάντων καὶ τὸν ἁγιασμόν
            οὗ χωρὶς
            οὐδεὶς ὄψεται τὸν κύριον (12:14),
ἐπισκοποῦντες
    μή τις ὑστερῶν ἀπὸ τῆς χάριτος τοῦ θεοῦ,
    μή τις ῥίζα πικρίας ἄνω φύουσα ἐνοχλῇ
            καὶ δι' αὐτῆς μιανθῶσιν πολλοί (12:15),
    μή τις πόρνος ἢ βέβηλος ὡς Ἠσαῦ,
            ὃς
                ἀντὶ βρώσεως μιᾶς
                ἀπέδετο τὰ πρωτοτόκια ἑαυτοῦ (12:16).

132 Ellingworth, *The Epistle to the Hebrews*, 663.

133 W. Foerster, "εἰρήνη," in *Theological Dictionary of the New Testament*, ed. Gerhard Kittel, tr. Geoffrey W. Bromiley (Grand Rapids: William B. Eerdmans Publishing Co., 1964), 2:412–13. See also Lane, *Hebrews 9–13*, 449.

134 Bauer, *Lexicon*, 508.

In this diagram the exhortation to pursue peace and sanctification is expressed in a negative tone, which is indicated by μή τις. Among these
expressions the phrase "grace of God" (τῆς χάριτος τοῦ θεοῦ) is significant. The phrase is similar to the Pauline use. It may refer to either
divine aid that is made available through Christ, or final eschatological
salvation which the readers look forward to in the future.[135] In either
sense, the author's exhortation in 12:14 is Christologically oriented.
Moreover, this Christological emphasis is also suggested by the idea of
apostasy. In 12:16 the author introduces the story of Esau, who sold his
birthright for a single meal. This verse is further explained by γάρ in
verse 17. That is, the experience of Esau described in verse 17 is the
ground of the concern expressed in the previous verse.[136] It is clear that
the illustration of Esau in the Old Testament (cf. Gen 25:33–34; 27:30–
40) is used to warn the readers to guard against sinning. In verses 16 and
17 the author clearly points out that Esau's sin is that of apostasy (i.e.,
he was rejected; he found no chance to repent). For the author not pursuing peace and holiness means falling from the grace of God and ultimately falling into the danger of committing the sin of apostasy. It is
regarded as not trusting Jesus Christ for their salvation. Thus these
verses make it clear that the author has Jesus as the object of faith. In
this sense, it may be said that the faith described in this section has a
Christological orientation.

The idea of apostasy which was introduced in 12:13–17 is more specifically described in 12:25–29 (section 1'). The basic form of 12:25–29
may be classified as parenetic midrash. In this passage the author employs the midrash to materialize the authority of the biblical text for the
readers' situation.[137] Section 1 (12:14–17) is parallel to section 1'
(12:25–29) at the conceptual level. The expression "seeing that no one
comes short of the grace of God" (v. 14) is similar to "watch out that
you do not refuse the one who speaks" (v. 25). Esau's negative example
of having failed to obtain the grace of God in 12:15–17 corresponds to
the peril of falling away from God's grace by the readers in 12:25–29.
From this evidence it is reasonable to conclude that sections 12:14–17

---

[135] Attridge, *The Epistle to the Hebrews*, 197.

[136] Lane, *Hebrews 9–13*, 456.

[137] Ibid., 447.

and 12:25–29 are chiastically arranged. In 12:25–29 the author solemnly warns the readers not to refuse him who is speaking. The imperative form Βλέπετε in 12:25 is also used in 3:12. This use is deliberately intended by the author to call attention to the exhortation in 3:12–19, which warns the readers against falling into apostasy (i.e., falling away from the living God). The verb παραιτέομαι, which is used in 12:19, reappears in 12:25. In verse 19 the word denotes "to ask" or "to request." However, in verse 25 the meaning of the verb is radically different; when this verb is accompanied by a person (with accusative case), it means "to reject or refuse someone."[138] It carries the connotation of a willful and deliberate rejection of the one who speaks. Thus the author clearly indicates that he is warning against the dire consequences of apostasy.

The theme of apostasy is further explicated by reminding them of the severity of God's judgment through the use of an *a fortiori* argument. The author argues that if the wilderness generation was not able to escape the judgment of God, who warned them on earth when they rebelled against him, how much less shall we be able to escape his judgment if we reject him who warns from heaven. The context of 3:7–4:13 makes it clear that the Israelites were not able to enter God's rest because of their unbelief (cf. 3:11, 18, 19; 4:3, 5). The author's use of an *a fortiori* argument is further developed by emphasizing the severity of judgment: from Mount Sinai his voice shook the earth, but in the eschatological judgment he will shake both heaven and earth (12:26–27; cf. Hag 2:6). What then is the implication of the author's argument? He is clearly indicating that the consequence of refusing to listen to God who spoke through his Son under the new covenant (i.e., in these last days) will be much more severe than the consequence of disobedience under the old covenant.

In this final warning section it is not immediately clear whether faith in Hebrews is Christologically oriented because the author does not use obvious terms, such as Jesus, Christ, or the Son. However, the idea of Jesus being the object of faith is expressed in terms of listening to God's word. Throughout the epistle the word of God is considered the object of faith in Hebrews. For example, 1:1–2 mentions that in these last days God has spoken through his Son; in 2:1–4 the readers are warned to pay closer attention to what they heard (i.e., the message of salvation); in 4:12, after exhorting the readers to enter God's rest by reminding them of the consequence of rebelling against God's word, he reiterates the importance of it (i.e., for the word of God is living and active . . .). Likewise, in 10:25–29 the content of faith is expressed in relation to the word of God. Thus it is evident that the exhortation to be obedient to the word of God is the author's way of expressing that faith in Hebrews is Christologically motivated. This point will become more evident in the ensuing discussion of 12:18–24.

Discussion of the center sections (2 and 2'). It has already been revealed from the discussion of the structure of 12:14–29 that 12:18–24 is the center of the chiasm, which indicates that it is the main point that the author wants to emphasize. It is my opinion that the author intentionally placed this passage in the center of 12:14–29 for rhetorical purposes to indicate that the exhortation not to reject God's word both in 12:14–17 (section 1) and 12:25–29 (section 1') is Christologically oriented. This center section reminds the readers of the reality of their spiritual journey; they have not come to Mount Sinai under the old covenant (section 2), but to Mount Zion, the city of the living God under the new covenant (section 2').

The contrast between 12:18–21 and 12:22–24 is signaled by ἀλλά in verse 22. This structural marker clearly shows that the author intends to draw the contrast between coming to God under the old covenant and under the new covenant. Among many counterpoints, there is a contrast of the central figure; in the first half it is Moses and in the second half, Jesus. This fact emerges toward the end in each section (i.e., v. 21 in the first half; v. 24 in the second half).[139] The author intentionally sets these figures toward the end of each section to point out the climax of his point.[140] Then what is the point of this passage? The contrast between Moses and Jesus clearly shows that the central point of discussion of 12:14–29 is none other than Jesus himself. In other words, the chiastic arrangement in 12:14–29 is the author's own way of saying that the exhortations in 12:14–17 (section 1) and 12:25–29 (section 1') are based on Jesus, the mediator of the new covenant. The exhortations such as "pur-

---

[139] Ellingworth, *The Epistle to the Hebrews,* 669.

[140] Ibid.

sue peace and holiness" (12:14), "do not fall short of the grace of God" (12:15), and "do not refuse the one who is speaking" (12:25) are different ways of stating not to forsake Jesus the high priest of the new covenant. Moreover, the expression "sprinkled blood" is a clear reference to the sacrifice of Christ on the cross. In this sense, the concept of faith in 12:14–29 has Jesus as its object. Thus it can be deduced that faith in Hebrews is Christologically oriented.

Summary of 12:1–29

An investigation of Hebrews 12:1–29 reveals much insight into the concept of faith in Hebrews. This passage suggests that in Hebrews Jesus is depicted both as the model and the object of faith for the readers. The author shows the Christological aspect of faith by placing his conceptual ideas in strategic locations of the chiastic structures in different passages to emphasize his main point. This was evident in the examination of 12:1–3. By employing chiasm the author indicates that Jesus is both the model and object of faith by placing the ethical element of faith (i.e., steadfastness) around the sufferings, crucifixion, and the ascension of Jesus. Moreover, an examination of the meaning of ἀρχηγός and τελειωτής, the concept of endurance, and the use of the Christological hymn shows that Jesus is regarded as both the model and the object of faith.

In 12:4–13 the author emphasizes the necessity of disciplinary sufferings in the Christian race. In this section the author does not mention Jesus in describing the quality of enduring disciplinary sufferings. However, the use of chiasm in the broad context of 10:32–12:14 suggests that the exhortation to endure disciplinary sufferings by faith is Christologically oriented. This conclusion is reached because the exemplars of faith from the Old Testament and the supreme example of Jesus are placed in the middle of the conceptual chiasm in 10:32–12:13.

In 12:14–29 the author continues to employ chiasm to emphasize that faith in Hebrews is Christologically oriented. An examination of the outer sections of the chiasm suggests that Jesus is viewed as the object of faith. The exhortation to pursue peace and sanctification (12:14–17) is a warning against apostasy (i.e., exhortation not to forsake Jesus). This idea of apostasy is reinforced by the parallel passage (12:25–29), which is expressed in terms of refusing God's word. In this passage the author indicates that the object of faith is the word of God. In other words, taking heed to God who spoke through his Son is essentially the same as listening to the Son himself. In this sense, it may be inferred that faith in Hebrews is Christologically motivated. Moreover, the center of the chiasm (12:18–24) also shows that the exhortation not to refuse God's word has a Christological basis. In this passage the emphasis is placed on Jesus, the mediator of the new covenant. By using the chiastic structure the author lets the readers know that the exhortation not to reject God's word in the outer sections is identical with the appeal not to reject Jesus, the high priest of the new covenant. In this sense, Jesus may be considered the object of faith for believers.

Conclusion

An analysis of the last alternating structure of doctrine and parenesis (11:1–40 and 12:1–29) reveals that the Christological aspect of faith is not lacking. The Christological aspect of faith is implied by such expressions as "heir of righteousness" in referring to the faith of Noah and "abuse of Christ" regarding Moses' faith. Moreover, the author's description of Jesus as the ἀρχηγός and τελειωτής shows that he is both the model and the object of faith. Furthermore, the exhortation to pursue peace and sanctification must be understood in the context of the warning against apostasy (i.e., the exhortation not to forsake Jesus). Lastly, the warning to take heed to the God who spoke through his Son is equivalent to listening to Jesus himself. Admittedly, faith in Hebrews is not expressed in terms of "faith in Christ" or "to believe in Jesus" as in the Pauline literature. However, this does not mean that faith in Hebrews is replaced by a mere ethical category of steadfastness or endurance as Grässer contends. The author presents abundant evidence throughout this last alternating section that Jesus is both the model and the object of faith for believers. Faith in 11:1–12:29 is Christologically oriented.

CHAPTER EIGHT

SUMMARY AND CONCLUSION

The purpose of this final chapter is to summarize the findings of each chapter and conclude by crystalizing my view of faith in Hebrews. I will also suggest some possible implications of the conclusion to other areas of study in Hebrews.

Summary of the Chapters

Chapter One
Chapter 1 had two purposes in mind. The first was to establish the importance of the study of the concept of faith in Hebrews. I have suggested that the study of faith in Hebrews is important for three reasons. It is needed because of: (1) the difficulty of defining the concept in the overall context of the New Testament; (2) the difficulty in defining the concept within Hebrews itself; and (3) lack of a comprehensive treatment on this subject within the epistle. The second purpose was to lay the foundation for the methodology of the study. The method of developing the thesis was fourfold: (1) exegesis; (2) biblical theology; (3) chiasm; and (4) alternating structure of doctrines and pareneses. I observe that many parts of Hebrews are chiastically arranged. This literary device strengthens the thesis that faith in Hebrews is both Christologically and eschatologically oriented. I have also modified Vanhoye's alternating structure of doctrines and pareneses as follows: 1:1–14 and 2:1–4; 2:5–18 and 3:1–4:16; 5:1–5:10 and 5:11–6:20; 7:1–10:18 and 10:19–39; 11:1–40 and 12:1–13:21. This scheme became the basis for an investigation of the concept of faith in Hebrews.

Chapter Two
In this chapter I have made a detailed analysis of different views on the concept of faith in Hebrews. A careful study of the literature indicates that many different views of faith in Hebrews are caused by different orientations one has toward faith. These orientations of faith can be

classified into three main categories: (1) ethical; (2) eschatological; and (3) Christological.

First of all, the general tendency for those who hold to the ethical view is to de-emphasize the Christological relationship to faith: they contend that in Hebrews, Jesus is not presented as the object of faith. Among the scholars who adhere to the ethical view, Grässer's view is the most extreme of all. According to him, faith in Hebrews is absolutely non-Christological in that it is completely removed from a soteriological, personal reference (i.e., the notion such as "faith in Jesus") into an ethical quality of steadfastness. Next, some scholars consider that faith in Hebrews has primarily an eschatological orientation. A survey of the literature on faith in Hebrews reveals that the eschatological view may be classified into three categories: (1) futuristic in a temporal sense (Longenecker); (2) futuristic in a spatial sense (Käsemann, Thompson); and (3) both present and future in a temporal sense (Lindars). One issue which needed to be addressed in this eschatological view was whether faith in Hebrews is temporally oriented (i.e., present and future) or spatially oriented (visible and invisible). Some argue that the author of Hebrews is influenced by the Hellenistic philosophy of visible and invisible reality (or the Philonic concept of dualism). However, I have demonstrated that it is more likely that the author depends on the Jewish understanding of the temporal idea of present and future. In this eschatological frame, faith functions as the bridge to connect these two aspects together. In other words, trusting in God who is invisible at the present time (11:6, 27) is ultimately linked to trusting in God's promise for the future. As for the characteristics of faith, such as "hope," "endurance," and "confident trust in God's promise," they should be understood within the temporal eschatological frame. Lastly, in contrast to the ethical view, some scholars believe that the concept of faith in Hebrews is Christologically oriented. This view may be classified into two subgroups: (1) Christ as the model of the faith view, and (2) Christ as the object of the faith view. The "Christ the model view" tends to minimize the aspect of Jesus being the object of faith, and instead emphasizes that Jesus is portrayed as the model and enabler of faith for his followers. One of the main arguments of Christ the model view is based on the exegesis of 12:1–2. This view argues that (1) the description of Jesus as ἀρχηγός and τελειωτής indicates that Jesus is the beginner and the finisher of Christian faith, thus making him the enabler of faith; and (2) understanding ἀρχηγος as a forerunner and τελειωτής as a perfecter of faith in the context of the race imagery suggests that Jesus is the model of faith. It is my opinion that the "Christ the model view" is an incomplete representation of Christology in Hebrews. The author of Hebrews depicts Jesus not only as the model of faith, but also the object of faith for believers. "Christ the object of faith view" interprets that the titles of Jesus as ἀρχηγός and τελειωτής in 12:1–2 has the twofold aspect of the saving work of Jesus (12:1–2); ἀρχηγός indicates that he started eternal salvation for his people; τελειωτής shows that he will see them finish the course. In this sense, Jesus is viewed not only as the model of faith but also the object of faith. The characteristics of faith such as endurance, steadfastness, fidelity, obedience must be considered in the context of Christology and eschatology in order to interpret properly the concept of faith in Hebrews.

Chapter Three (1:1–14 and 2:1–4)

The doctrinal section 1:1–14 brings to light two important Christological teachings. To begin with, 1:1–4 emphasizes God's final revelation through the Son. This aspect of Christology is demonstrated by the sentence structure of the passage. The main idea of 1:1–4 is that "God has spoken through his Son (1:1–2a)." The remaining part of the passage (1:2b–4) is a further description about the Son. In this first section, the author points out that the Son is the one through whom God has revealed his final revelation. The second part of the passage (1:5–14) further explains the superiority of the Son to the angels. This point is demonstrated by three rounds of contrast between the Son and the angels. The first round has to do with position (1:5–6); the second, with attributes (1:7–12); and the third, with function (1:13–14). Through these three rounds of contrast, the author shows that the Son is superior to the angels.

In 2:1–4 the author exhorts believers not to drift away from Christian faith on the basis of the Christological teachings he explained in the doctrinal section (1:1–14). A close look at the structure and the content of the parenetic section indicates that the exhortation to remain faithful in 2:1–4 is Christologically oriented. In the first part (2:1) the phrase διὰ τοῦτο looks back to the entire doctrinal section of 1:1–14, and more specifically to 1:1–2. The implication is that since God has spoken to us by his Son in these last days, and the Son is superior to the angels and prophets, we ought to pay closer attention to what we have heard. Moreover, a detailed examination of words such as δεῖ, προσέχειν, ἀκουσθεῖσιν reveals that they are faith-related words. This finding strengthens my position that the exhortation not to drift away is Christologically motivated. In the second part (2:2–4) the author explains why they must pay closer attention to what they have heard by employing an *a fortiori* argument to prove his point. In this context, the question "how shall we escape if we neglect so great a salvation?" implies that there is no possible escape if they do not take heed. A brief summary of 2:1–4 makes it clear that the author's call to pay closer attention to the message they once heard is another way of exhorting the readers to continue to trust in Jesus. Thus it may be concluded along with 1:1–14 that the exhortation in the first parenetic section (2:1–4) is Christologically oriented: Christ should indeed be regarded as the content and the object of faith.

Chapter Four (2:5–18 and 3:1–4:16)

The author again switches from parenesis to doctrine in 2:5–18, which is on the humanity of Christ. The literary analysis of 2:5–18 indicates that the passage is divided into two parts. The first section deals with the humiliation and glory of humankind (2:5–9). This passage argues that man has been destined by God to a glory surpassing that of the angels, even though at the present time he is made lower than they are. The next section is on the solidarity between the Son and humankind (2:10–18). The main point of 2:5–18 is that Jesus is qualified to become a merciful and faithful high priest (2:17–18) because of his identification with humanity as a true human. Again, in 3:1–4:16, the literary genre is changed from doctrine to parenesis. In the immediate context, the conjunction ὅθεν in 3:1 looks back to 2:17–18. However, since 2:17–18 is the conclusion of the exposition for the humanity of the Son in 2:5–16, it may be said that ὅθεν in 3:1 looks back to the entire doctrinal section of 2:5–18. The significance of the relationship between the doctrinal and the parenetic section is that 3:1–4:16 is an exhortation to enter God's rest based on the Christological teaching of the humanity of Christ in 2:5–18. The alternating structure is a clear indication that the qualities of faith described in 3:1–4:16 are Christologically oriented; that is, Christ is to be viewed as the content (or the object) of faith.

More specifically, a close examination of 3:1–4:16 revealed that the author portrays Jesus as both the object and the model of faith. To begin with, there are some clues which suggest that Jesus is described as the object of faith. First, it was demonstrated from the term "confession"

SUMMARY AND CONCLUSION 247

(ὁμολογία) in 3:1. Jesus whom we profess creedally (i.e., objective sense) is also the one whom we confess publicly (i.e., subjective sense). Second, Jesus being the object of faith was also shown from the meaning of the phrase ὁ ἀπόστολος καὶ ἀρχιερεύς (the apostle and high priest) in 3:1. While ἀρχιερεύς refers back to the human aspect of Jesus in 2:5–18, ἀπόστολος shows the divine aspect of Jesus in 1:1–14. In this sense, the words ἀρχιερεύς and ἀπόστολος complement each other in referring to Jesus as the object of faith. Third, Jesus being the object of faith was seen from the phrase, "if we hold firm the confidence and the pride that belong to hope" in 3:6b. In the context of 3:1–6 the content of hope in 3:6 refers to the faithfulness of Jesus and his high priesthood. Thus the phrases "holding fast the confidence" and "the pride of hope" in 3:6 are the author's was of describing Jesus as the object of faith, even if they are described in terms of Christian conduct.

In addition, the author also indicates that Jesus is regarded as the model of faith for believers in 3:1–4:16. First, this idea was perceived from the context of 3:1–6. The overall emphasis of this passage is on the faithfulness of Jesus as the high priest. For this reason the author's exhortation to consider Jesus is his call to imitate the faithfulness of Jesus. Next, a comparison between the faithfulness of Jesus and that of Moses suggested that Jesus is construed as the ultimate model of faith. As Jesus is worthy of more glory than Moses, the readers are to consider the faithfulness of Jesus all the more. In this sense, the exhortation to consider Jesus is equivalent to imitating his faithfulness. The above summary points out that Jesus is not only the object of faith, but also the model of faith for believers. As for the characteristics of faith, it can be defined as trustworthiness, steadfastness, and obedience. However, these ethical qualities must not be understood merely as moral qualities. They must be interpreted in the context of the Christological teaching as set forth by the author to have a proper understanding of faith in Hebrews.

Chapter Five (5:1–10 and 5:11–6:20)
The author again changes from parenesis to doctrine in 5:1–10. In this passage, he emphasizes the merciful aspect of Christ's high priesthood. This section may be divided into two parts: (1) qualifications of the levitical high priesthood (5:1–4) and (2) qualifications of Christ's high priesthood (5:5–10). In this passage the author displays both similarities and differences of the qualifications between the earthly high priests and the heavenly high priest. The structural change from doctrine

(5:1–10) to parenesis (5:11–6:20) already suggests that the exhortation in 5:11–6:20 has a Christological implication. Moreover, the conceptual ideas in this parenetic section demonstrate that Christ is both the object and the model of faith. What are the arguments which support that Jesus is the object of faith? First, it was observed from the meaning of the phrase "elementary teaching of the beginning of God's words" in 5:12. The expression refers to the fundamental doctrines which they received when they first believed. It is equivalent to "the beginning teaching about Christ" in 6:1. These words suggest that Jesus is considered the object of faith, even if the phrase such as "faith in Christ" is not used here. Next, Jesus being the object of faith was also clearly demonstrated from 6:4–8. An examination of the characteristics of those who fall away (6:4–5) suggests that the initial faith of the apostates (whether it is genuine or not) has to do with faith in Jesus. In other words, falling into the apostasy means denying the faith in Jesus Christ. Moreover, the reasons for the impossibility to be renewed again to repentance (6:6) reaffirm that faith in this passage is Christologically oriented. The author shows that the act of apostasy will cause Jesus to be crucified again (ἀνασταυρόω), just as the act of unbelief by the people caused Jesus to be crucified in the Gospels. This idea is illustrated by the agricultural imagery in 6:7–8. In this passage the idea of faith is expressed in negative terms. However, it is clear that the concept of faith expressed in 6:4–8 is notably parallel to Paul's idea of "faith in Jesus Christ."

The parenetic section of 5:11–6:20 also demonstrates that Jesus is to be regarded as the model of faith. In 6:12 the author exhorts the readers to become imitators of those who inherit the promises through faith and perseverance. This point is illustrated by two examples. First, it is brought out by the example of Abraham's steadfastness (6:13–15). The context implies that following the example of Abraham's faith is identical to believing in the promise of God, which is also equivalent to persevering faith in Jesus. Second, it is illustrated by the example of Christ himself (6:19–20). Since Jesus is the forerunner who entered inside the curtain, believers ought to enter in hope as Jesus did. These examples show that Jesus is not only the object of faith, but also the model of faith for believers. The ethical aspect of faith (i.e., the characteristic of steadfastness) must be considered in the context of the author's Christology.

Chapter Six (7:1–10:18 and 10:19–39)
The theme of Christ's high priesthood, which was mentioned first in 2:17, then explained in 3:1–6:20, is fully developed in 7:1–10:18. The main point of this long exposition is: the superiority of Christ's high priesthood to the levitical high priesthood. This section is divided into four different parts. The first part (7:1–28) emphasizes Jesus as the high priest after the order of Melchizedek (7:1–28). In the second part (8:1–13), the emphasis is placed on the establishment of the new covenant. The author states that Jesus' high priesthood is superior because it is based on a better sacrifice (8:3) and a better covenant (8:4–13). In the third part (9:1–28) the emphasis is placed on the superior nature of Christ's sacrifice. The author introduces the sacrificial system under the first covenant (9:1–10), followed by the sacrifice under the new covenant (9:11–28). In the fourth part (10:1–18) the author brings his theological argument to a climax by highlighting the perfect and the ultimate nature of the sacrifice of Christ. It needs to be born in mind that the purpose of the exposition in 7:1–18 is not merely to give a theological treatise for the readers; rather, the author's intention is to use the doctrinal exposition as a basis to exhort the readers not to forsake their faith in Jesus.

A detailed examination of the parenetic section of 10:19–39 revealed that the concept of faith in Hebrews is Christologically oriented: Jesus is indeed regarded as the object of faith for believers. This parenetic section may be divided into three main parts: (1) the exhortation to continue with faith (10:19–25); (2) the consequence of disloyalty to Christ (10:26–31); and (3) the exhortation to persevere in faith (10:32–39). In the first part (10:19–25) the author uses three main verbs to exhort the readers to be steadfast in faith from a positive standpoint. A study of these exhortations, based on three main verbs (προσερχώμεθα in 10:22; κατέχωμεν in 10:23; κατανοῶμεν in 10:24), revealed that faith in Hebrews is Christologically motivated: the exhortations are based on the confession of Christ and the Second Coming of Christ. In the second part (10:26–31), the exhortation to remain faithful is described from a negative standpoint. The author indicates that faith is closely related to Christ by describing that the deliberate sin is rejecting God's revelation provided through Jesus Christ (i.e., the sin of apostasy) (10:26–27). The descriptions of those who commit this sin (10:28–29) show that the sin is none other than a willful rejection of Christ. The author clearly indicates that Jesus is regarded as the object of faith. In the third part (10:32–39) the author again exhorts the readers to remain in faith from a positive standpoint. Here faith is expressed in terms of positive standpoint. Here faith is expressed in terms of the ethical quality of steadfastness. However, this ethical aspect is centered around Christology. This is evident from the overall structure of 10:32–39. The center of chiasm (10:35) is clearly a Christological teaching not to forsake faith in Jesus Christ. Since the ethical element of perseverance revolves around the center (10:35), it may be said that the exhortation to be steadfast in faith is Christologically oriented. In 10:36–39 the Christological aspect of faith was also demonstrated. The exhortation to endure (10:36; 10:39) is based on the Second Coming of Christ (10:37). It is clear that, for the author of Hebrews, faith cannot be separated from Christ; it is inextricably intertwined with the high priesthood of Christ.

Chapter Seven (11:1–40 and 12:1–29)

In the analysis of the previous alternating structures, it was observed that the exposition of the doctrinal sections dealt with certain aspects of Christology. However, in this final alternating structure of doctrine and parenesis, the author does not present any specific new Christological teaching, but instead describes certain aspects of faith. A close examination of 11:1–40 and 12:1–29 indicates that faith in Hebrews is both Christologically and eschatologically oriented. First of all, an examination of chapter 11 reveals that the author arranged the chapter chiastically. In the proposed chiastic structure the eschatological idea is expressed in each section. The primary reason that the author artistically arranged chapter 11 in a chiastic manner is to set forth the importance of the eschatological nature of faith (i.e., forward-looking aspect) in Hebrews. This orientation of faith is stated in the introduction (11:1–3; A), re-emphasized in the center section (11:13–16; H), and reiterated in the conclusion (11:39–40; A'). In between these summary statements the author brings in the exemplars of faith in the Old Testament to illustrate this forward-looking aspect of faith. However, although the author's main emphasis in this chapter is on eschatology, the Christological aspect of faith is not totally absent. The phrases such as "heir of righteousness according to faith" for Noah in 11:7, "abuse of Christ" in describing Moses faith in 11:26, and the reference to the institution of the Passover in 11:28 clearly imply that faith in Chapter 11 is Christologically motivated. A careful look at the eschatological and Christological aspects in Hebrews 11 demonstrates that the futuristic outlook of faith (i.e., the forward-looking aspect) by the exemplars of faith in the old covenant ultimately points to the Christ-event in the new covenant. Thus it was concluded that the concept of faith in Hebrews is both eschatologically and Christologically oriented.

Again, the author returns to another parenetic section (12:1–29) to indicate that Jesus is presented both as the model and the object of faith. The author implicitly suggests this by placing his main ideas in strategic places of the passage to prove his point. This was clearly demonstrated in the first subsection (12:1–3). In the newly proposed alternative chiastic structure, the center section (C) describes the sufferings, crucifixion, and the ascension of Jesus. The implication of this structure is that Jesus is both the model and the object of faith. In 12:4–13 the author continues to emphasize the importance of displaying endurance. However, he shifts his focus to the necessity of disciplinary sufferings in the Christian race. In this section the name Jesus is not mentioned in describing the quality of enduring disciplinary sufferings. However, both the immediate and the broad contexts indicate that the exhortation to endure disciplinary sufferings by faith is both Christologically and eschatologically oriented. As for the concept of faith in 12:14–29, it was revealed that the author also arranged it chiastically to emphasize the Christological aspect of faith. This passage is divided into three main sections and forms chiasm at the conceptual level: 12:14–17; 12:18–24; 12:25–29. In each subsection, the concept of faith is related to Christ. In 12:14–17 (section 1), faith is expressed in terms of pursuing peace and sanctification. This exhortation is contrasted with the idea of apostasy. The theme of apostasy is further developed in 12:25–29 (section 1') by comparing the consequence of rejecting God's word in the old covenant and the new covenant. Here the implication is that taking heed to God who spoke through his Son is equivalent to listening to the Son himself. Thus it may be concluded that faith in Hebrews is Christologically motivated. The center of the chiasm (12:18–24; sections 2 and 2') also has a Christological basis. By employing this chiastic structure, the author indicates that the exhortation not to reject God's word in sections 1 and 1' is essentially the same as the warning not to reject Jesus, the mediator of the new covenant. The above summary reveals that in 12:1–29 Jesus is indeed portrayed as both the model and the object of faith for believers. This section also reiterates that in Hebrews, both Christology and eschatology are intertwined to bring out the concept of faith. Therefore, it may be concluded that faith in Hebrews is both Christologically and eschatologically oriented.

Conclusion and Implications

There is no meaningful dispute among scholars concerning the characteristics of faith. They all essentially agree that faith in Hebrews involves moral qualities, such as faithfulness, trustworthy, steadfastness (or endurance), hope, and confidence in God's promise. However, there is a dispute concerning the nature of these qualities of faith. Grässer indicates that faith in Hebrews is purely ethical in that it is totally removed from the Christ-event into the ethical category of steadfastness. His assertion is that faith in Hebrews is non-Christological, because one cannot find the phrases such as "faith in Jesus Christ" or "trust in Jesus." Grässer's underlying presupposition is that the Pauline soteriological aspect of faith was the normative interpretation in the early church.

However, a careful and extensive examination of the major passages of Hebrews demonstrated that the author's concept of faith is Christological. The alternating structure of doctrines and pareneses is a major clue which helps one to understand that faith in Hebrews has Christ as its content. In other words, the exhortation to be steadfast in faith in the parenetic sections is firmly based on certain crucial Christological teaching set forth by the author. In this sense, Jesus is considered the object of faith, even if the well-known Pauline soteriological and personal expressions such as "faith in Jesus" or "trusting in Jesus as Savior" are absent. Moreover, a detailed exegesis of the parenetic sections revealed that the content is full of the expressions of faith, which suggest that Jesus is viewed as both the object and the model of faith for believers. The author also uses the rhetorical structure of chiasm to emphasize that the ethical elements of faith described in certain passages are Christologically motivated. In this sense, the concept of faith in Hebrews is not significantly different from either the unreflective Synoptic or the reflective Pauline usage. As Paul explicitly indicates that Jesus is the object of faith, the author of Hebrews implicitly shows that Jesus is the object and the model of faith by employing an elegant literary style.

An examination of the major passages of Hebrews also indicated that faith is not only Christological but also eschatological. There is a debate as to whether or not the eschatological outlook in Hebrews is temporal or spatial. It has been made clear through the detailed exegesis that the author of Hebrews is not influenced by the Philonic concept of visible and invisible reality, but the temporal orientation of present and future. More specifically, the eschatological outlook of Hebrews is not simply futuristic; it also involves a present aspect. In this "already and not yet" eschatological frame, the author describes the concept of faith. It is also to be realized that, although the present aspect is not neglected, the emphasis is on the future. The eschatological and Christological teaching must be considered together in discussing the concept of faith in Hebrews. Moreover, the characteristics of faith set forth by the author needs to be interpreted in the context of Christology and eschatology to have a proper understanding of faith as intended by the author.

Then what are the implications for this study? In this final section, I would like to suggest some possible areas of further study which are related to the Christological and eschatological concepts of faith in Hebrews. First of all, this study has suggested that the difference in the concept of faith between Hebrews and the Pauline epistles has been overestimated. A detailed comparative study of the concept of faith between Hebrews and the Pauline literature needs to be done. Second, this study may also lead to the possibility that the author of Hebrews is not far removed from Paul. The similarities of the concept of faith between Hebrews and the Pauline letters suggest that the author of Hebrews may have been a contemporary of Paul. He may have been directly or indirectly influenced by him. Lastly, one needs to reconsider the literary structure of Hebrews. In this study I have observed a consistent use of literary devices by the author of Hebrews while demonstrating that the concept of faith is both Christologically and eschatologically oriented. It has already been established through a careful examination that many of the passages in Hebrews are chiastically arranged. This leads me to consider the possibility that the author of Hebrews may have intended to write the entire letter with a chiastic structuring in mind at the conceptual level. A serious consideration of this broad structure will greatly enhance the understanding of the book of Hebrews as a whole.

There may well be other implications which can lead to further study. However, it is hoped that some of these suggestions would motivate the readers to be engaged in more in-depth study of the book of Hebrews.

BIBLIOGRAPHY

Books

Bauer, Walter. *A Greek-English Lexicon of the New Testament and Other Early Christian Literature*. 2nd ed. Translated and adapted by W. F. Arndt, F. W. Gingrich, and Frederick W. Danker. Chicago: The University of Chicago, 1979.

Blass, F., and F. Debrunner, and R. W. Funk. *Grammar of the New Testament and Other Early Christian Literature*. Translated by R. W. Funk. Chicago: The University of Chicago Press, 1961.

Bligh, J. *Chiastic Analysis of the Epistle to the Hebrews*. Heythrop: Athenaeum, 1966.

Buber, M. *Two Types of Faith*. Translated by N. P. Goldhawk. New York: Harper, 1961.

Bultmann, Rudolf. *Theology of the New Testament*. Translated by Kendrick Grobel. 2 vols. New York: Charles Scribner's Sons, 1951–55.

Coats, George. *Rebellion in the Wilderness: The Murmuring Motif in the Wilderness Traditions of the Old Testament*. Nashville: Abingdon Press, 1968.

Conzelmann, H., and A. Lindemann. *Interpreting the New Testament: An Introduction to the Principles and Method of N.T. Exegesis*. Translated by Siegfried S. Schatzmann. From the 8th rev. German edition. Peabody, MA: Hendrickson Publishers, 1988.

Cosby, Michael R. *The Rhetorical Composition and Function of Hebrews 11: In Light of Example Lists in Antiquity*. Macon, GA: Mercer University Press, 1988.

Cullmann, Oscar. *The Christology of the New Testament*. Translated by Shirley C. Guthrie and Charles A. M. Hall. Revised ed. Philadelphia: Westminster Press, 1963.

D'Angelo, Mary Rose. *Moses in the Letter to the Hebrews*. Society of Biblical Literature Dissertation Series, vol. 42. Missoula, MT: Scholars Press, 1979.

Dey, L. K. K. *The Intermediary World and Patterns of Perfection in Philo and Hebrews*. Society of Biblical Literature Dissertation Series. vol. 25. Missoula, MT: Scholars Press, 1975.

Dodd, C. H. *The Bible and the Greek*. London: Hodder & Stoughton, 1954.

Du Plessis, P. J. *Teleios: The Idea of Perfection in the New Testament*. Kampen: J. H. Kok, 1959.

Dunn, James D. G. *Christology in the Making: A New Testament Inquiry into the Origins of the Doctrine of the Incarnation*. Philadelphia: Westminster Press, 1980.

Dunnhill, John. *Covenant and Sacrifice in the Letter to the Hebrews*. Society for New Testament Studies Monograph Series, vol. 75. Cambridge: Cambridge University Press, 1992.

Dussaut, Louis. *Synopse structurelle de l'Épître aux Hébreux: approche d'analyse structurelle*. Paris: Editions du Cerf, 1981.

Evans, C. F. *The Theology of Rhetoric: the Epistle to the Hebrews*. London: Dr. Williams's Trust, 1988.

Feld, Helmut. *Der Herbräerbrief*. Erträge der Forschung 228. Darmstadt: Wissenschaftliche Buchgesellschaft, 1985.

Filson, Floyd. V. *Yesterday: A Study of Hebrews in the Light of Chapter 13*. Studies in Biblical Theology. Naperville, IL: Allenson, 1967.

Goppelt, Leonhard. *Theology of the New Testament*. Edited by Jürgen Roloff. Translated by John Alsup. 2 vols. Grand Rapids: William Eerdmans Publishing Co., 1981.

Grässer, Erich. *Der Glaube im Hebräerbrief.* Marburg: N. G. Elwert, 1965.

Greer, R. A. *The Captain of Our Salvation: A Study in the Patristic Exegesis of Hebrews*. Beiträge zur Geschichte der biblischen Exegese, vol. 15. Tübingen: J. C. B. Mohr (Paul Siebeck), 1973.

Guthrie, George H. *The Structure of Hebrews: A Text-Linguistic Analysis*. Supplements to Novum Testamentum, vol. 78. Leiden: E. J. Brill, 1994.

Harrisville, R. A. *The Concept of Newness in the New Testament*. Minneapolis: Augsburg Publishing House, 1960.

Hay, David M. *Glory at the Right Hand: Psalm 110 in Early Christianity*. Society of Biblical Literature Monograph Series, vol. 18. Nashville: Abingdon, 1973.

Hofius, O. *Katapausis. Die Vorstellung vom endzeitlichen Ruheort im Hebräerbrief.* Tübingen: J. C. B. Mohr (Paul Siebeck), 1970.

Hughes, G. R. *Hebrews and Hermeneutics*. Society for New Testament Studies Monograph Series, vol. 36. Cambridge: Cambridge University Press, 1979.

Hurst, L. D. *The Epistle to the Hebrews: Its Background of Thought*. Society for New Testament Studies Monograph Series, vol. 65. Cambridge: Cambridge University Press, 1990.

Isaacs, Marie M. *Sacred Space: An Approach to the Theology of the Epistle to the Hebrews*. Journal for the Study of the New Testament Supplement Series, vol. 73. Sheffield: JSOT Press, 1992.

Käsemann, Ernst. *The Wandering People of God: An Investigation of the Letter to the Hebrews*. Translated by Roy A. Harrisville and Irving L. Sandberg. Minneapolis: Augsburg Publishing House, 1984.

Klappert, B. *Die Eschatologie des Hebräerbriefes.* Munich: Kaiser, 1969.

Kosmala, Hans. *Hebräer-Essener-Christen: Studien zur Vorgeschichte der frühchristlichen Verkündigung*. Leiden: E. J. Brill, 1959.

Ladd, George Eldon. *Theology of the New Testament*. Edited by Donald A. Hagner. Rev. ed. Grand Rapids: William B. Eerdmans, 1974.

Laub, Franz. *Bekenntnis und Auslegung: Die paränetische Funktion der Christologie im Hebräerbrief.* Biblische Untersuchungen, vol. 15. Regensburg: Friedrich Pustet, 1980.

Leonard, W. *The Authorship of the Epistle to the Hebrews*. London: Polyglott, 1939.

Lewis, J. P. *A Study of the Interpretation of Noah and the Flood in Jewish and Christian Literature*. Leiden: E. J. Brill, 1968.

Liddell, H. G, and R. Scott. *A Greek-English Lexicon: A New Edition Revised and Augmented Throughout with Supplement*. Revised and augmented by Henry Stuart Jones, with the assistance of Roderick McKenzie, with a Supplement edited by E. A. Barber, 9th ed. Oxford: Clarendon Press, 1968.

Lindars, Barnabas. *The Theology of the Letter to the Hebrews*. Cambridge: Cambridge University Press, 1991.

Loew, W. *Der Glaubensweg des neuen Bundes: Eine Einführung in den Brief an die Hebräer*. Berlin: Akademie, 1941.

Louw, Johannes P., and Eugene A. Nida. *Greek-English Lexicon of the New Testament Based on Semantic Domains.* 2 vols. New York: United Bible Societies, 1988.

Lund, Nils W. *Chiasmus in the New Testament: A Study in the Form and Function of Chiastic Structures.* Chapel Hill, NC: University of North Carolina Press, 1942; reprint, Peabody, MA: Hendrickson, 1992.

Manson, William. *The Epistle to the Hebrews: A Historical and Theological Reconsideration.* 2nd ed. London: Hodder and Stoughton, 1953.

McNeile, A. H. *New Testament Teaching in the Light of St. Paul's.* Cambridge: Cambridge University Press, 1923.

Metzger, Bruce M. *A Textual Commentary on the Greek New Testament.* New York: United Bible Societies, 1971.

Milligan, G. *The Theology of the Epistle to the Hebrews.* Edinburgh: T. & T. Clark, 1899.

Moulton, James H. *A Grammar of New Testament Greek.* Vol. 3, Syntax, by Nigel Turner. Edinburgh: T. & T. Clark, 1963.

Moxnes, H. *God and His Promise to Abraham.* Theology in Conflict: Novum Testamentum Supplements, 53. Leiden: E. J. Brill, 1980.

Neufeld, Vernon H. *The Earliest Christian Confessions.* Leiden: E. J. Brill, 1963.

Oepke, A. *Das neue Gottesvolk im Schrifttum, Schauspiel, bildende Kunst und Weltgestaltung.* Gütersloh: Bertelsmann, 1950.

Peake, A. S. *The Heroes and Martyrs of Faith: Studies in the Eleventh Chapter of the Epistle to the Hebrews.* London: Hodder and Stoughton, 1910.

Perkins, W. *A Commentary on Hebrews 11.* New York: Pilgrim Press, 1991.

Peterson, David. *Hebrews and Perfection: An Examination of the Concept of Perfection in the 'Epistle to the Hebrews.'* Society for New Testament Studies Monograph Series, vol. 47. Cambridge: Cambridge University Press, 1982.

Rissi, M. *Die Theologie des Hebräerbriefes.* Tübingen: J. C. B. Mohr (Paul Siebeck), 1987.

Robertson, A. T. *A Grammar of the Greek New Testament in the Light of Historical Research.* Nashville: Broadman Press, 1934.

Robinson, W. *The Eschatology of the Epistle to the Hebrews.* Birmingham: Overdale College, 1950.

Rose, Christian. *Die Worke der Zeugen: Eine exegetischtraditionsgeschichtliche Untersuchung zu Hebräer 10,32—12,3.* Tübingen: J. C. B. Mohr (Paul Siebeck), 1994.

Rowley, H. H. *The Faith of Israel.* London: SCM Press, LTD., 1956.

Sanders, J. T. *The New Testament Christological Hymns.* Society for New Testament Studies Monograph Series 15 Cambridge: Cambridge University Press, 1971.

Schick, E. *Im Glauben Kraft empfangen Betrachtungen zum Brief an die Hebräer.* Stuttgart: Katholisches Bibel Werk, 1978.

Schlatter, A. *Der Glaube im Neuen Testament.* 5th ed. Stuttgart: Calwer, 1963.

Scholer, John M. *Proleptic Priests: Priesthood in the Epistle to the Hebrews.* Journal for the Study of the New Testament Supplement Series, vol. 49. Sheffield: JSOT Press, 1991.

Sowers, S. G. *The Hermeneutics of Philo and Hebrews: A Comparison of the Interpretation of the Old Testament in Philo Judaeus and the Epistle to the Hebrews.* Richmond: John Knox Press, 1965.

Stauffer, Ethelbert. *New Testament Theology*. Translated by John Marsh. New York: The Macmillan Co., 1955.

Stevens, George Barker. *The Theology of the New Testament*. 2nd ed. Edinburgh: T. & T. Clark, 1918; reprint, 1968.

Swetnam, James. *Jesus and Isaac: A Study of the Epistle to the Hebrews in Light of the Aqedah*. Analecta Biblica, vol. 94. Rome: Pontifical Biblical Institute Press, 1981.

Synge, F. C. *Hebrews and the Scriptures*. London: S. P. C. K., 1959.

Theissen, G. *Untersuchungen zum Hebräerbrief*. Gütersloh: Gütersloh Verlagshaus Gerd Mohn, 1969.

Thompson, James W. *The Beginnings of Christian Philosophy: The Epistle to the Hebrews*. Catholic Biblical Quarterly Monograph Series, vol. 13. Washington, DC: Catholic Biblical Association of America, 1982.

Turner, N. *Grammatical Insights into the New Testament*. Edinburgh: T. & T. Clark, 1965.

Vanhoye, Albert. *La structure littéraire de l'Epître aux Hébreux*. 2nd ed. Paris: Desclée de Brouwer, 1976.

————. *Structure and Message of the Epistle to the Hebrews*. Subsidia Biblica. Vol. 12. Rome: Pontificio Istituto Biblico, 1989.

Volz, P. *Die Eschatologie der jüdischen Gemeinde im neutestamentlichen Zeitalter nach den Quellen der rabbinischen, apokalyptischen, und apokyphen Literatur*. Tübingen: J. C. B. Mohr (Paul Siebeck), 1934.

Williamson, R. *Philo and the Epistle to the Hebrews*. Arbeiten zur Literatur und Geschichte des hellenistischen Judentums, vol. 4. Leiden: E. J. Brill, 1970.

Wolfson, H. A. *Philo: Foundations of Religious Philosophy in Judaism, Christianity, and Islam*. 2 vols. Cambridge, MA: Harvard University Press, 1947.

Zimmermann, H. *Das Bekenntnis der Hoffnung. Tradition und Redaktion im Hebäerbrief*. Cologne: Hanstein, 1977.

Commentaries

Andrew T. Lincoln, *Ephesians, Word Biblical Commentary*. Dallas: Word Books, 1990.

Attridge, Harold W. *The Epistle to the Hebrews*. Hermeneia. Philadelphia: Fortress Press, 1989.

Barth, Markus. *Ephesians*. The Anchor Bible. New York: Doubleday, 1974.

Braun, Herbert. *An die Hebräer*. Handbuch zum Neuen Testament, vol. 14. Tübingen: J. C. B. Mohr (Paul Siebeck), 1984.

Brown, John. *An Exposition of the Epistle of the Apostle Paul to the Hebrews*. Edited by David Smith. 2 vols. New York: Robert Carter and Brothers, 1862.

Brown, Raymond E. *An Introduction to the New Testament*. New York: Doubleday, 1997.

Bruce, F. F. *The Epistle to the Hebrews*. New International Commentary on the New Testament. Grand Rapids: William B. Eerdmans Publishing Co., 1964.

Buchanan, G. W. *To the Hebrews*. Anchor Bible, vol. 37. Garden City, NY: Doubleday & Company, Inc., 1972.

Carson, D. A., Douglas J. Moo, and Leon Morris. *An Introduction to the New Testament*. Grand Rapids: Zondervan Publishing House, 1992.

Davidson, A. B. *The Epistle to the Hebrews.* Edinburgh: T. & T. Clark, 1882.

Davies, J. H. *A Letter to Hebrews.* Cambridge: Cambridge University Press, 1967.

Delitzsch, F. *Commentary on the Epistle to the Hebrews.* Translated by T. L. Kingsbury. 2 vols. Edinburgh: T. & T. Clark, 1878.

Ellingworth, Paul. *The Epistle to the Hebrews: A Commentary on the Greek Text.* New International Greek Testament Commentary. Edited by I. Howard Marshall and W. W. Gasque. Grand Rapids: William B. Eerdmans Publishing Co., 1993.

Guthrie, D. *The Letter to the Hebrews.* Tyndale New Testament Commentaries. Grand Rapids: William B. Eerdmans Publishing Co., 1983.

Hagen, Kenneth. *Hebrews Commenting from Erasmus to Bèze 1516—1598.* Beiträge zur Geschichte der Biblischen Exegese, vol. 23. Tübingen: J. C. B. Mohr (Paul Siebeck), 1981.

Hagner, Donald. *Hebrews.* Good News Commentary. San Francisco: Harper & Row Publishers, 1983.

Hegermann, Harold. *Der Brief an die Hebräer.* Theologischer Handkommentar zum Neuen Testament, vol 16. Berlin: Evangelische Verlagsanstalt, 1988.

Hughes, P. E. *A Commentary on the Epistle to the Hebrews.* Grand Rapids: William B. Eerdmans Publishing Co., 1977.

Jewett, R. *Letter to Pilgrims: A Commentary on the Epistle to the Hebrews.* New York: Pilgrim, 1981.

Kent, Homer A. *The Epistle to the Hebrews.* Winona Lake, IN: BMH Books, 1972.

Kistemaker, Simon J. *Exposition of the Epistle to the Hebrews.* New Testament Commentary. Grand Rapids: Baker Book House, 1984.

Knight, George W., III, *Commentary on the Pastoral Epistles,* New International Greek Testament Commentary. Grand Rapids: William B. Eerdmans, 1992.

Lane, William L. *Hebrews.* Word Biblical Commentary, vol. 47A–B. Dallas: Word Books, 1991.

Michel, O. *Der Brief an die Hebräer.* 12th ed. Göttingen: Vandenhoeck und Ruprecht, 1966.

Moffatt, J. *A Critical and Exegetical Commentary on the Epistle to the Hebrews.* The International Critical Commentary. Edinburgh: T. & T. Clark, 1924.

Morris, Leon. "Hebrews." In *The Expositor's Bible Commentary.* 12:3–158. Edited by Frank E. Gaebelein. Grand Rapids: Zondervan Publishing House, 1981.

Riggenbach, E. *Der Brief an die Hebräer.* Leipzig: Deichert, 1913.

Scott, Ernest F. *The Epistle to the Hebrews: Its Doctrine and Significance.* Edinburgh: T. & T. Clark, 1922.

Snell, A. *A New and Living Way.* London: Faith, 1959.

Spicq, C. *L'Epître aux Hebreux.* 2 vols. Paris: Gabalda, 1952.

Strathmann, Hermann. *Der Brief an die Herbräer.* Das Neue Testament Deutsch, vol. 9. Gottingen: Vandenhoeck, 1935.

———. *Hebrews and the Scriptures.* London: Gabalda, 1935.

Weiß, Hans. *Der Brief an die Hebräer.* 6th. Kritisch-exegetischer Kommentar über das Neuen Testament, vol. 15. Göttingen: Vandenhoeck & Ruprecht, 1991.

Westcott, B. F. *The Epistle to the Hebrews: A Historical and Theological Reconsideration.* London: Macmillan, 1889.

Wilson, R. M. *Hebrews.* New Century Bible. Grand Rapids: William B. Eerdmans Publishing Co., 1987.

Windish, Hans. *Der Hebräerbrief.* Handbuch zum Neuen Testament, vol. 14. Tübingen: J. C. B. Mohr (Paul Siebeck), 1931.

Dissertations

Bateman, Herbert W., IV. "Jewish and Apostolic Hermeneutics: How the Old Testament Is Used in Hebrews 1:5–13." Ph.D. diss., Dallas Theological Seminary, 1993.

Bertsche, George Joseph. "Pistis in the Epistle to the Hebrews." Th.M. thesis, Dallas Theological Seminary, 1957.

Casey, J. M. "Eschatology in Heb 12:14–29: An Exegetical Study." Ph.D. diss., Catholic University of Leuven, 1977.

Cockerill, Gareth L. "The Melchizedek Christology in Heb. 7:1–28." Th.D diss., Union Theological Seminary, 1976.

Darnell, David Rancier. "Rebellion, Rest, and the Word of God (An Exegetical Study of Hebrews 3:1–4:12)." Ph.D. diss., Duke University, 1973.

Dukes, James G. "Eschatology in the Epistle to the Hebrews." Ph.D. diss., The Southern Baptist Theological Seminary, 1957.

Dunham, Duane A. "An Exegetical Examination of the Warnings in the Epistle to the Hebrews." Th.D. diss., Grace Theological Seminary, 1974.

Gordon, Victor Reese. "Studies in the Covenantal Theology of the Epistle to the Hebrews in Light of Its Setting." Ph.D. diss., Fuller Theological Seminary, 1979.

Greer, Rowan Allen. "The Antiochene Exegesis of Hebrews." Ph.D. diss., Yale University, 1965.

Guthrie, George Howard. "The Structure of Hebrews: A Text-Linguistic Analysis." Ph.D. diss., Southwestern Baptist Theological Seminary, 1991.

Lehne, Susanne. "The Concept of the New Covenant in Hebrews." Ph.D. diss., Columbia University, 1989.

Lemmon, Eric Gregory. "The Nature of Biblical Faith: a Philosophical, Historical, Philological and Theological Survey." Th.M. thesis, Fuller Theological Seminary, 1968.

Leschert, Dale Frederick. "Hermeneutical Foundation of the Epistle to the Hebrews: A Study in the Validity of Its Interpretation of Some Core Citations from the Psalms." Ph.D. diss., Fuller Theological Seminary, 1991.

Lewis, Thomas Wiley, III. "The Theological Logic in Hebrews 10:19–12:29 and the Appropriation of the Old Testament." Ph.D. diss., Drew University, 1965.

MacLeod, David John. "The Theology of the Epistle to the Hebrews: Introduction, Prolegomena and Doctrinal Center." Th.D. diss., Dallas Theological Seminary, 1987.

Maxwell, Kenneth Leroy. "Doctrine and Parenesis in the Epistle to the Hebrews, with Special Reference to pre-Christian Gnosticism." Ph.D. diss., Yale University, 1953.

McCown, Wayne Gordon. "Ο ΛΟΓΟΣ ΤΗΣ ΠΑΡΑΑΛΗΣΕΩΣ: The Nature and Function of the Hortatory Sections in the Epistle to the Hebrews." Th.D. diss., Union Theological Seminary in Virginia, 1970.

Mercado, Luis Fidel. "The Language of Sojourning in the Abraham Midrash in Hebrews 11:8–19: Its Old Testament Basis, Exegetical Traditions, and Function in the Epistle to the Hebrews." Ph.D. diss., Harvard University, 1967.

Miesner, Donald R. "Chiasmus and the Composition and Message of Paul's Missionary Sermons." S.T.D. diss., Lutheran School of Theology at Chicago, 1974.

Miller, Merland Ray. "The Theological Argument of Hebrews 11 in Light of Its Literary Form." Th.D. diss., Concordia Seminary, 1984.

Price, B. J. "Paradeigma and Exemplum in Ancient Rhetorical Theory." Ph.D. diss., University of California, Berkeley, 1975.

Prince, Andy. "An Investigation into the Importance of Perseverance in the Christian Life as Presented in Five Warning Passages in Hebrews.." Ph.D. diss., Southwestern Baptist Theological Seminary, 1980.

Rathel, Mark Anthony. "An Examination of the Soteriological Terminology in the Epistle to the Hebrews." Th.D. diss., New Orleans Baptist Theological Seminary, 1988.

Sanford, Carlisle, Jr. "The Addresses of Hebrews." Th.D. diss., Dallas Theological Seminary, 1962.

Solari, James Kenneth. "The Problem of Metanoia in the Epistle to the Hebrews." S.T.D. diss., The Catholic University of America, 1970.

Staples, Austin F., Jr. "The Book of Hebrews in Its Relationship to the Writings of Philo Judaeus." Ph.D. diss., The Southern Baptist Theological Seminary, 1951.

Stine, Donald Medford. "The Finality of the Christian Faith: A Study of the Unfolding Argument of the Epistle to the Hebrews, Chapters 1–7." Th.D. diss., Princeton Theological Seminary, 1964.

Taylor, Spartan Wallace. "A Study of Philo and in the Epistle to the Hebrews." Ph.D. diss., Emory University, 1965.

Tetley, Joy D. "The Priesthood of Christ as the Controlling Theme of the Epistle to the Hebrews." Ph.D. diss., University of Durham, 1987.

Tymeson, Gale Ellis. "The Material World in Gnosticism and the Epistle to the Hebrews." Ph.D. diss., University of Pittsburgh, 1975.

Worley, David Ripley. "The Hortatory Use of Commissive Language in Hebrews." Ph.D. diss., Yale University, 1981.

Essays

Attridge, Harold W. "The Uses of Antithesis in Hebrews 8–10 [Heb 10:1–18]." In *Christians Among Jews & Gentiles*. Essays in Honor of Krister Stendahl on His Sixty-Fifth Birthday, ed. G. Nicklesburg & G. MacRae, 1–9. Philadelphia: Fortress, 1986.

Barrett, C. K. "The Eschatology of the Epistle to the Hebrews." In *The Background of the New Testament and its Eschatology*. Essays in Honor of Charles Harold Dodd, ed. W. D. Davies and D. Daube, 363–93. Cambridge: Cambridge University Press, 1954.

Barth, M. "The Old Testament in Hebrews: An Essay in Biblical Hermeneutics." In *Current Issues in New Testament Interpretation*. Festschrift for O. Piper, ed. W. Klassen and G. F. Snyder, 53–78. New York: Harper & Row, 1962.

Bauernfeind, Otto. "πρόδρομος." In *Theological Dictionary of the New Testament*, ed. Gerhard Friedrich, tr. Geoffrey W. Bromiley, 8:235. Grand Rapids: William B. Eerdmans Publishing Co., 1972.

Behm, Johannes. "γεύομαι." In *Theological Dictionary of the New Testament*, ed. Gerhard Kittel, tr. Geoffrey W. Bromiley, 1:675–77. Grand Rapids: William B. Eerdmans Publishing Co., 1964.

Betz, Otto. "Firmness in Faith: Hebrews 11:1 and Isaiah 28:16." In *Scripture: Meaning and Method*. A. T. Hanson Festschrift, ed. Barry R. Thompson, 92–113. Hull: Hull University Press, 1987.

Black, M. "Critical and Exegetical Notes on Three New Testament Texts: Hebrews xi.11, Jude 5, James i.27." In *Apophoreta*, ed. W. Eltester, 39–45. Berlin: A. Töpelmann, 1964.

Blackman, E. C. "Faith, Faithfulness." In *The Interpreter's Dictionary of the Bible*, ed. George Arthur Buttrick, 2:222–34. New York: Abingdon Press, 1962.

Bock, D. "Introduction." In *A Biblical Theology of the New Testament*, ed. Roy B. Zuck and D. Bock, 11–17. Chicago: Moody Press, 1994.

Boman, T. "Hebraic and Greek Thought-Forms in the New Testament." In *Current Issues in New Testament Interpretation*. Festschrift, Written in Honor of O. A. Piper, ed. W. Klassen and G. F. Snyder, 1–22. New York: Harper and Row, 1962.

Braumann, G. "κράτος." In *The New International Dictionary of New Testament Theology*, ed. Colin Brown, 3:716–18. Grand Rapids: Zondervan Publishing House, 1978.

Bromiley, G. W. "Faith." In *The International Standard Bible Encyclopedia*, ed. Geoffrey W. Bromiley, 2:270–73. Grand Rapids: William B. Eerdmans Publishing Co., 1982.

Buchanan, G. W. "The Present State of Scholarship on Hebrews." In *Christianity, Judaism and Other Greco-Roman Cults*. Festschrift Morton Smith, ed. J. Neusner, 299–330. Leiden: E. J. Brill, 1975.

Büchsel, Friedrich. "ἔλεγχος." In *Theological Dictionary of the New Testament*, ed. Gerhard Kittel, tr. Geoffrey W. Bromiley, 2:476. Grand Rapids: William B. Eerdmans Publishing Co., 1964.

Bultmann, Rudolf, and K. Rengstorf. "ἐλπίς, ἐλπίζω." In *Theological Dictionary of the New Testament*, ed. Gerhard Kittel, tr. Geoffrey W. Bromiley, 2:517–33. Grand Rapids: William B. Eerdmans Publishing Co., 1964.

———. "Πιστεύω κτλ." In *Theological Dictionary of the New Testament*, ed. Gerhard Kittel and Gerhard Frederick, tr. Geoffrey W. Bromiley, 6:174–228. Grand Rapids: William B. Eerdmans Publishing Co., 1968.

Caird, George B. "Son by Appointment." In *The New Testament Age: Essays in Honor of Bo Reicke*, ed. William C Weinrich, 1:73–81. Macon, GA: Mercer University Press, 1984.

———. "The Development of the Doctrine of Christ in the New Testament." In *Christ for Us Today*, ed. W. Norman Pittenger, 66–80. London: SCM Press, 1968.

Carlston, C. E. "The Vocabulary of Perfection in Philo and Hebrews." In *Unity and Diversity in New Testament Theology*, ed. R. A. Guelich, 133–59. Grand Rapids: William B. Eerdmans Publishing Co., 1978.

Conzelmann, Hans. "φῶς κτλ." In *Theological Dictionary of the New Testament*, ed. Gerhard Friedrich, tr. Geoffrey W. Bromiley, 9:310–58. Grand Rapids: William B. Eerdmans Publishing Co., 1974.

Delling, Gerhard. "πληροφορία." In *Theological Dictionary of the New Testament*, ed. Gerhard Friedrich, tr. Geoffrey W. Bromiley, 6:310–11. Grand Rapids: William B. Eerdmans Publishing Co., 1968.

———. "τέλος, κτλ." In *Theological Dictionary of the New Testament*, ed. Gerhard Friedrich, tr. Geoffrey W. Bromiley, 8:49–87. Grand Rapids: William B. Eerdmans Publishing Co., 1972.

Eichler, Johannes. "κλῆρος." In *The New International Dictionary of New Testament Theology*, ed. Colin Brown, 2:295–303. Grand Rapids: Zondervan Publishing House, 1975.

Ellingworth, P. "New Testament Text and Old Testament Context in Heb. 12.3." In *Studia Biblica 3*, ed. E. A. Livingston. JSNT Supplement Series 3, 89–96. Sheffield: Journal for the Study of the Old Testament Press, 1980.

Fanning, Buist M. "A Theology of Hebrews." In *A Biblical Theology of the New Testament*, ed. Roy B. Zuck and D. Bock, 369–415. Chicago: Moody Press, 1994.

Fiorenza, E. S. "Der Anführer und Vollender unseres Glaubens: Zum theologischen Verständnis des Hebräerbriefes ." In *Gestalt und Anspruch des Neuen Testaments*, ed. J. Schreiner, 261–81. Würzburg: Echter, 1969.

Fitzmyer, J. A. "Habakkuk 2:3–4 and the New Testament." In *To Advance the Gospel: New Testament Studies*, 236–46. New York: Cross Road, 1981.

Frost, Stanley. "Who were the Heroes? An Exercise in Bi-testamentary Exegesis, with Christological Implications." In *The Glory of Christ in the New Testament: Studies in Christology in Memory of George Bradford Caird*, ed. L. D. Hurst and N. T. Wright, 165–72. Oxford: Clarendon Press, 1987.

Fuchs, A. "βέβαιος." In *Exegetical Dictionary of the New Testament*, ed. Horst Balz and Gerhard Schneider, 1:211. Grand Rapids: William B. Eerdmans Publishing Co., 1990.

Gaffin, R. B. "A Sabbath Rest Still Awaits the People of God." In *Pressing Toward the Mark*, ed. C. G. Dennison and R. C. Gamble, 33–51. Philadelphia: The Orthodox Presbyterian Church, 1986.

Grundmann, Walter. "δεῖ, δέον ἐστί." In *Theological Dictionary of the New Testament*, ed. Gerhard Kittel, tr. Geoffrey W. Bromiley, 2:21–25. Grand Rapids: William B. Eerdmans Publishing Co., 1964.

Hauck, F. "ὑπομένω, ὑπομονή." In *Theological Dictionary of the New Testament*, ed. Gerhard Kittel, tr. Geoffrey W. Bromiley, 4:581–88. Grand Rapids: William B. Eerdmans Publishing Co., 1967.

Héring, J. "Eschatologie biblique et idéalisme platonicien." In *The Background of the New Testament and Its Eschatology*, ed. W. D. Davies and D. Daube, 444–63. Cambridge: Cambridge University Press, 1954.

Hoffmann, E. "Hope, Expectation." In *The New International Dictionary of New Testament Theology*, ed. Colin Brown, 2:238–44. Grand Rapids: Zondervan Publishing House, 1986.

Hunzinger, C. "ῥαντίζω, ῥαντισμός." In *Theological Dictionary of the New Testament*, ed. Gerhard Friedrich, tr. Geoffrey W. Bromiley, 6:976–84. Grand Rapids: William B. Eerdmans Publishing Co., 1968.

Hurst, L. D. "The Christology of Hebrews 1 and 2." In *The Glory of Christ in the New Testament: Studies in Christology in Memory of George Bradford Caird*, ed. L. D. Hurst and N. T. Wright, 151–64. Oxford: Clarenden Press, 1987.

Köster, H. "ὑπόστασις." In *Theological Dictionary of the New Testament*, ed. Gerhard Friedrich, tr. Geoffrey W. Bromiley, 8:572–89. Grand Rapids: William B. Eerdmans Publishing Co., 1972.

Lincoln, A. T. "Sabbath, Rest and Eschatology in the New Testament." In *From Sabbath to Lord's Day: A Biblical, Historical and Theological Investigation*, ed. D. A. Carson, 197–220. Grand Rapids: Zondervan Publishing House, 1982.

Michaelis, W. "μετριοπαθέω." In *Theological Dictionary of the New Testament*, ed. Gerhard Friedrich, tr. Geoffrey W. Bromiley, 5:938. Grand Rapids: William B. Eerdmans Publishing Co., 1967.

———. "ὁδός." In *Theological Dictionary of the New Testament*, ed. Gerhard Friedrich, tr. Geoffrey W. Bromiley, 5:42–96. Grand Rapids: William B. Eerdmans Publishing Co., 1967.

———. "παραπίπτω, παράπτωμα." In *Theological Dictionary of the New Testament*, ed. Gerhard Friedrich, tr. Geoffrey W. Bromiley, 6:171–72. Grand Rapids: William B. Eerdmans Publishing Co., 1968.

Michel, O. "Faith, Persuade, Belief, Unbelief." In *The New International Dictionary of New Testament Theology*, ed. Colin Brown, 1:587–606. Grand Rapids: Zondervan Publishing House, 1975.

———. "ὁμολογέω κτλ." In *Theological Dictionary of the New Testament*, ed. Gerhard Friedrich, tr. Geoffrey W. Bromiley, 5:199–220. Grand Rapids: William B. Eerdmans Publishing Co., 1967.

Moody, Dale. "Faith." In *Mercer Dictionary of the Bible*, ed. Watson E. Mills, 289–93. Macon, GA: Mercer University Press, 1990.

Nicole, R. "Some Comments on Hebrews 6:4–6 and the Doctrine of the Perseverance of God with the Saints." In *Current Issues in Biblical and Patristic Interpretation*, ed. G. F. Hawthorne, 355–64. Grand Rapids: William B. Eerdmans Publishing Co., 1975.

Niebuhr, R. R. "Archegos. An Essay on the Relation Between the Biblical Jesus Christ and the Present-Day Reader." In *Christian History and Interpretation. Studies Presented to John Knox*, ed. W. R. Farmer, 79–100. Cambridge: Cambridge University Press, 1967.

Rad, Gerhard von. "There Still Remains a Rest for the People of God: An Investigation of a Biblical Conception." In *The Problem of the Hexateuch and other Essays*, 94–102. Edinburgh: Oliver & Boyd, 1966.

Schlier, H. "βέβαιος κτλ." In *Theological Dictionary of the New Testament*, ed. Gerhard Kittel, tr. Geoffrey W. Bromiley, 1:600–603. Grand Rapids: William B. Eerdmans Publishing Co., 1964.

———. "παραδειγματίζω." In *Theological Dictionary of the New Testament*, ed. Gerhard Kittel, tr. Geoffrey W. Bromiley, 2:32. Grand Rapids: William B. Eerdmans Publishing Co., 1964.

———. "παρρησία, παρρησιάζομαι." In *Theological Dictionary of the New Testament*, ed. Gerhard Friedrich, tr. Geoffrey W. Bromiley, 5:871–86. Grand Rapids: William B. Eerdmans Publishing Co., 1967.

Schneider, J. "ὀμνύω." In *Theological Dictionary of the New Testament*, ed. Gerhard Friedrich, tr. Geoffrey W. Bromiley, 5:176–185. Grand Rapids: William B. Eerdmans Publishing Co., 1967.

Schoonhoven, Calvin R. "The Analogy of Faith and the Intent of Hebrews." In *Scripture, Tradition and Interpretation*. E. F. Harrison Festschrift, ed. W. W. Gasque and

W. S. Lasor, 92–110. Grand Rapids: William B. Eerdmans Publishing Co., 1978.

Seesemann, H. "καταπατέω κτλ." In *Theological Dictionary of the New Testament*, ed. Gerhard Friedrich, tr. Geoffrey W. Bromiley, 5:940–41. Grand Rapids: William B. Eerdmans Publishing Co., 1967.

———. "παλαιόω." In *Theological Dictionary of the New Testament*, ed. Gerhard Friedrich, tr. Geoffrey W. Bromiley, 5:720. Grand Rapids: William B. Eerdmans Publishing Co., 1967.

Trilling, W. "Jesus der Urheber und Vollender des Glaubens (Hebr. 12, 2)." In *Das Evangelium auf dem Weg zum Menschen*, ed. O. Knoch, 3–23. Frankfurt am Main: Knecht, 1973.

Verhey, A. D. "Faithful; Faithfulness." In *The International Standard Bible Encyclopedia*, ed. Geoffrey W. Bromiley, 2:273–75. Grand Rapids: William B. Eerdmans Publishing Co., 1982.

Walter, Nikolaus. "'Hellenistische Eschatologie' im Neuen Testament." In *Glaube und Eschatologie*. Festschrift für Werner Georg Kümmel, ed. E. Grässer and O. Merk, 335–56. Tübingen: J. C. B. Mohr (Paul Siebeck), 1985.

Warfield, B. B. "Faith." In *Dictionary of the Bible*, ed. James Hastings, 1:827–38. Edinburgh: T. & T. Clark, 1951.

Welch, John W. "Chiasmus in the New Testament." In *Chiasmus in Antiquity: Structures, Analysis, Exegesis*, ed. John W. Welch, 211–49. Hildesheim: Gerstenberg Verlag, 1981.

Wilcox, Max. "The Bones of Joseph: Hebrews 11:22." In *Scripture: Meaning and Method*. A. T. Hanson Festschrift, ed. Barry R. Thompson, 114–30. Hull: Hull University Press, 1987.

Periodicals

Adams, J. C. "Exegesis of Hebrews vi.1f." *New Testament Studies* 13 (1967): 378–85.

Albani, J. "Hebr. V,11–VI,8." *Zeitschrift für wissenschaftliche Theologie NF* 12 (1904): 88–93.

Allen, E. L. "Jesus and Moses in the New Testament." *Expository Times* 67 (1955–56): 104–6.

Anderson, C. P. "The Epistle to the Hebrews and the Pauline Letter Collection." *Harvard Theological Review* 59 (1966): 429–38.

Arden, Eugene. "How Moses Failed God." *Journal of Biblical Literature* 76 (1957): 50–52.

Arowele, P. J. "The Pilgrim People of God (An African's Reflections on the Motif of Sojourn in the Epistle to the Hebrews)." *Asia Journal of Theology* 4 (1990): 438–55.

Attridge, Harold. W. "'Let Us Strive to Enter That Rest': The Logic of Hebrews 4:1–11." *Harvard Theological Review* 73 (1980): 279–88.

———. "New Covenant Christology in an Early Christian Homily." *Quarterly Review* 8 (1988): 89–108.

———. "Paraenesis in a homily (λόγος παρακλήσεως): The possible location of, and socialization in, the 'Epistle to the Hebrews'." *Semeia* 50 (1990): 211–26.

Auffret, P. "Essai sur la structure littéraire et l'interprétation d'Hébreux 3.1–6." *New Testament Studies* 26 (1980): 380–96.

Bacon, B. W. "The Doctrine of Faith in Hebrews, James and Clement of Rome." *Journal of Biblical Literature* 19 (1900): 12–21.

Barber, C. J. "Moses: A Study of Hebrews 11:23–29a." *Grace Journal* 14 (1973): 14–28.

Barth, G. "Pistis in hellenistischer Religiostät." *Zeitschrift für die neutestamentliche Wissenschaft* 73 (1982): 110–26.

Bartlett, R. E. "The Cloud of Witnesses: Heb. 12.1." *Expositor 1st Series* 5 (1877): 149–53.

Bauer, J. B. "Kain und Abel." *Theologisch-Praktische Quartalschrift* 103 (1955): 126–33.

Benetreau, S. "La foi d'Abel: Hebreux 11/4." *Etudes theologiques et religiueuses* 54 (1979): 623–30.

Black, D. A. "A Note on the Structure of Hebrews 12:1–2." *Biblica* 68 (1987): 543–51.

———. "Hebrews 1:1–4: A Study in Discourse Analysis." *Westminster Theological Journal* 49 (1987): 175–94.

———. "The Problem of the Literary Structure of Hebrews: An Evaluation and a Proposal." *Grace Theological Journal* 2 (1986): 163–77.

Bligh, J. "The Structure of Hebrews." *The Heythrop Theological Journal* 5 (1964): 170–77.

Blomberg, C. "The Structure of 2 Corinthians 1–7." *Criswell Theological Review* 4 (1989): 3–20.

Brady, C. "The World to Come in the Epistle to the Hebrews." *Worship* 39 (1965): 329–39.

Brandenburger, E. "Pistis und Soteria: Zum Verstehenshorizont vom 'Glaube' im Urchristentum." *Zeitschrift für die neutestamentliche Wissenschaft* 85 (1988): 165–98.

Brawley, Robert L. "Discoursive Structure and the Unseen in Hebrews 2:8 and 11:1: A Neglected Aspect of the Context [table]." *Catholic Biblical Quarterly* 55 (1993): 81–98 .

Bream, N. "More on Hebrews 12.1." *Expository Times* 80 (1968–69): 150–51.

Bronson, D. "Review of 'Der Glaube im Hebräerbrief' by E. Grässer." *Journal of Biblical Literature* (1965): 458–59.

Brooks, C. L. "The Choice of Moses (Heb. 11:24)." *Methodist Quarterly Review* 55 (1929): 463–72.

Brown, Raymond. "Pilgrimage in Faith: The Christian Life in Hebrews." *Southwestern Journal of Theology* 28 (1985): 28–35.

Bruce, F. F. "Recent Contribution to the Understanding of Hebrews." *Expository Times* 80 (1969): 260–64.

———. "Recent Literature on the Epistle to the Hebrews." *Themelios* 3 (1966): 31–36.

———. "Structure and Argument of Hebrews." *Southwestern Journal of Theology* 28 (1985): 6–12.

Buchanan, G. W. "The Use of Rabbinic Literature for New Testament Research." *Biblical Theology Bulletin* 7 (1977): 110–22.

Bue, Francesco Lo. "The Historical Background of the Epistle to the Hebrews." *Journal of Biblical Literature* 75 (1956): 52–57.

Burch, V. "Factors in the Christology of the Letter to the Hebrews." *Expositor, 8th series* 21 (1921): 68–79.

Burtness, J. H. "Plato, Philo and the Author of Hebrews." *Lutheran Quarterly* 10 (1958): 54–64.

Caird, G. B. "Just Men Made Perfect." *London Quarterly and Holborn Review* 35 (1966): 89–98.

———. "The Exegetical Method of the Epistle to the Hebrews." *Canadian Journal of Theology* 5 (1959): 44–51.

Campbell, J. C.. "In a Son: The Doctrine of Incarnation in the Epistle to the Hebrews." *Interpretation* 10 (1956): 24–38.

Carlston, C. E. "Eschatology and Repentance in the Epistle to the Hebrews." *Journal of Biblical Literature* 78 (1959): 296–302.

Cavallin, H. C. C. "The Righteous Shall Live by Faith." *Studia Theologica* 32 (1978): 33–43.

Chavasse, C. "Jesus Christ and Moses." *Theologia* 54 (1951): 244–50.

Clark, D. J. "Criteria for Identifying Chiasm." *Linguistica Biblica* 5 (1975): 63–72.

Cleary, M. "Jesus, Pioneer and Source of Salvation. The Christology of Heb. 1–6." *Bible Today* 18 (1973): 1242–48.

Conner, C. "Hebrews XI.1." *Expository Times* 3 (1891–92): 373.

Coppens, J. "Les Affinites qumranienes de l'Epître aux Hebreux." *Nouvelle Revue Theologique* 84 (1961–62): 128–41; 257–82.

Cosby, Michael R. "The Rhetorical Composition of Hebrews 11." *Journal of Biblical Literature* 107 (1988): 257–73.

Crosby, H. "Hebrews 10:26–27." *Journal of Biblical Literature* 7 (1887): 1–2.

Culley, R. C. "Structural Analysis: Is It Done with Mirrors?" *Interpretation* 28,2 (1974): 165–81.

Culpepper, R. Alan. "A Superior Faith: Hebrews 10:19–12:2." *Review and Expositor: A Baptist Theological Journal* 82 (1985): 375–90.

Culpepper, R. H. "The High Priesthood and Sacrifice of Christ in the Epistle to the Hebrews." *Theological Educator* 32 (1985): 46–62.

Dahl, N. A. "A New and New Living Way: The Approach to God according to Hebrews 10:19–25." *Interpretation* 5 (1951): 401–12.

Daly, R. J. "The Soteriological Significance of the Sacrifice of Issac." *Catholic Biblical Quarterly* 39 (1977): 45–75.

Dautzenberg, Gerhard. "Der Glaube im Hebräerbrief." *Biblische Zeitschrift* 17 (1973): 161–77.

Dhotel, J. C . "La 'sanctification' du Christ d'après Héb. II.11. Interprétation des Pères et des scolastiques médiévaux." *Revue des Sciences Religieuses* 47 (1959): 515–43.

Dörrie, H. "Zu Hebr 11:1." *Zeitschrift für die neutestamentliche Wissenschaft* 46 (1955): 196–202.

Downing, J. "Jesus and Martyrdom." *Journal of Theological Studies* 14 (1963): 279–93.

Duke, Jimmy. "The Humanity of Jesus in Hebrews." *Theological Educator* 32 (1985): 38–45.

Durnbaugh, Donald F. "Go Forth in Faith: Qualities of Faith from Hebrews 11–12." *Brethren Life and Thought* 35 (1990): 160–67.

Ebert, D. J. "The Chiastic Structure of the Prologue to Hebrews." *Trinity Journal* 13 (1992): 163–79.

Ellingworth, Paul. "Jesus and the Universe in Hebrews." *Evangelical Quarterly* 58 (1986): 337–50.

Emerton, J. A. "The Textual and Linguistic Problems of Habakkuk 2:4–5." *Journal of Theological Studies n.s* 28 (1977): 1–18.

Fenton, J. C. "The Argument in Hebrews." *Studia Evangelica* 7 (1982): 175–81.

Ferris, T. E. S. "A Comparison of 1 Peter and Hebrews." *Church Quarterly Review* 3 (1930–31): 123–27.

Fichtner, J. "Zum Problem Glaube und Geschichte in der israëlitisch-jüdischen Weisheitsliteratur." *Theologische Literaturzeitung* 76 (1951): 145–50.

Fischel, H. A. "Martyr and Prophet." *Jewish Quarterly Review* 37 (1946–47): 265–80, 363–86.

Garvey, A. E. "In Praise of Faith: A Study of Hebrews 11.1, 6; 12.1, 2." *Expository Times* 26 (1914–15): 199–202, 278–81, 328–31.

———. "The Author and Finisher of Faith: Lenten Meditations." *London Quarterly and Holborn Review* (1940): 184–94.

———. "The Pioneer of Faith and of Salvation." *Expository Times* 26 (1914–15): 502–4, 546–50.

Giblet, J. "Exegesis in Hebr. 11,1–2." *Collectanea Mechliniensia* 33 (1948): 285–88.

Glasson, T. F. "'Plurality of Divine Persons' and the Quotations in Hebrews 1:6ff." *New Testament Studies* 12 (1965–66): 271–2.

Gleason, Randall C. "The Old Testament Background of the Warning in Hebrews 6:4–8." *Bibliotheca Sacra* 155 (1998): 62–91.

Gloer, W. "Homologies and Hymns in the New Testament: Form, Content and Criteria for Identification." *Perspectives in Religious Studies* 11 (1984): 115–132.

Goldstein, J. A. "Creatio Ex Nihilo: Recantations and Restatements." *Journal of Jewish Studies* 38 (1987): 187–94.

———. "The Origins of the Doctrine of Creatio Ex Nihilo." *Journal of Jewish Studies* 35 (1984): 127–35.

Gourges, M. "Remarques sur la 'structure centrale' de l' Épître aux Hébreux. A l'occasion d'une réédition." *Revue Biblique* 84 (1977): 26–37.

Grässer, E. "Das wandernde Gottesvolk: Zum Basismotiv des Hebräerbriefes." *Zeitschrift für die neutestamentliche Wissenschaft* 77 (1986): 160–79.

———. "Der Hebräerbrief 1938–1963." *Theologische Rundschau* 30 (1964): 138–236.

———. "Exegese nach Auschwitz? Kritische Anmerkungen zur hermeneutischen Bedeutung des Holocaust am Beispiel von Hebr. 11." *Kerygma und Dogma* 27 (1981): 152–63.

———. "Mose und Jesus. zur Auslegung von Hebr. 3:1–6." *Zeitschrift für die neutestamentliche Wissenschaft* 75 (1984): 2–23.

———. "Neue Kommentare zum Hebräebrief." *Theologische Rundschau* 56 (1991): 113–39.

Grayston, K. "Obedience Language in the New Testament." *Epworth Review* 2 (1975): 72–80.

Greenlee, J. H. "Hebrews 11:11—Sarah's Faith or Abraham's?" *Notes on Translation* 4 (1990): 37–42.

Grogan, Geoffrey W. "Christ and His People: An Exegetical and Theological Study of Hebrews 2:5–18." *Vox Evangelica* 6 (1969): 54–71.

Gyllenberg, Rafael. "Die Christologie des Hebräerbriefes." *Zeitschrift für systematische Theologie* 11 (1934): 662–90.

Haacker, Klaus. "Der Glaube im Hebräerbrief und die Hermeneutische Bedeutung des Holocaust." *Theologische Zeitschrift* 39 (1983): 152–65.

Hamm, Dennis. "Faith in the Epistle to the Hebrews: The Jesus Factor." *Catholic Biblical Quarterly* 52 (1990): 270–91.

Hanson, A. T. "Rahab the Harlot in Early Christian Theology." *Journal for the Study of the New Testament* 1 (1978): 53–60.

Harris, Murray. "The Translation and Significance of ὁ θεός in Hebrews 1:8–9." *Tyndale Bulletin* 36 (1985): 129–62.

Harrison, E. F. "The Theology of the Epistle to the Hebrews." *Bibliotheca Sacra* 121 (1964): 331–40.

Hayes, D. A. "Jesus the Perfecter of Faith (Hebr 12,2)." *The Biblical World* 20 (1902): 278–87.

Healon, F. A. "Hebrews XII,2." *Theology* 2 (1930): 43–44.

Hillmann, W. "Glaube und Verheissung: Einführung in die Grundgedanken des Hebräerbriefes 10:32–13:25." *Bibel und Leben* 1 (1960): 237–52.

Hoekema, A. A. "The Perfection of Christ in Hebrews." *Calvin Theological Journal* 9 (1974): 31–37.

Hohenstein, H. H. "A Study of Hebrews 6:4–8." *Concordia Theological Monthly* 27 (1956): 433–44, 536–46.

Holtz, T. "Einführung in Probleme des Hebräerbriefes." *Zeitshrift für Katholische Theologie* 23 (1969): 321–27.

Honeycutt, Roy L. "Hebrews." *Review and Expositor* 82 (1985): 317–440.

Horning, E. B. "Chiasmus, Creedal Structure, and Christology in Hebrews 12:1–2." *Biblical Research* 23 (1978): 37–48.

Hughes, P. E. "Hebrews 6:4–6 and the Peril of Apostasy." *Westminster Theological Journal* 35 (1972–73): 137–55.

———. "The Blood of Jesus and His Heavenly Priesthood in Hebrews (Part II: The High-Priestly Sacrifice of Christ)." *Bibliotheca Sacra* 130 (1973): 195–212.

———. "The Blood of Jesus and His Heavenly Priesthood in Hebrews (Part III: The Meaning of 'True Tent' and 'The Greater and More Perfect Tent')." *Bibliotheca Sacra* 130 (1973): 305–14.

———. "The Blood of Jesus and His Heavenly Priesthood in Hebrews (Part IV: The Present Work of Christ in Heaven)." *Bibliotheca Sacra* 130 (1974): 26–33.

———. "The Blood of Jesus and His Heavenly Priesthood in Hebrews (Part I: The Significance of the Blood of Jesus)." *Bibliotheca Sacra* 130 (1973): 99–109.

———. "The Christology of Hebrews." *Southwestern Journal of Theology* 28 (1985): 19–27.

———. "The Doctrine of Creation in Hebrews 11:3." *Biblical Theology Bulletin* 2 (1972): 64–77.

Hutton, W. R. "Hebrews iv.11." *Expository Times* 53 (1940–41): 316–17.

Huxhold, H. N. "Faith in the Epistle to the Hebrews." *Concordia Theological Monthly* 38 (1967): 657–61.

Irwin, J. "The Use of Hebrews 11:11 as Embryological Proof-Text." *Harvard Theological Review* 71 (1978): 312–18.

Jobes, K. H. "Rhetorical Achievement in the Hebrews 10 'Misquote' of Psalm 40." *Biblica* 72 (1991): 387–96.

Johnsson, W. G. "Issues in the Interpretation of Hebrews." *Andrews University Seminary Studies* 15 (1976–77): 169–87.

————. "The Pilgrimage Motif in the Book of Hebrews." *Journal of Biblical Literature* 97 (1978): 239–51.

Johnston, G. "Christ as Archegos." *New Testament Studies* 27 (1981): 381–85.

Jones, J. Estill. "Now Faith is Hope." *Review and Expositor* 52 (1955): 508–30.

Jones, P. R. "A Superior Life: Hebrews 12:3–13:25." *Review and Expositor* 82 (1985): 391–405.

Kaiser, Walter C., Jr. "The Old Promise and the New Covenant: Jeremiah 31:31–34." *Journal of the Evangelical Society* 15 (1972): 11–23.

————. "The Promise Theme and the Theology of Rest." *Bibliotheca Sacra* 145 (1973): 135–150.

Kent, Homer A. "The New Covenant." *Grace Theological Journal* 6 (1985): 289–98.

Klappert, B. "Die Eschatologie des Hebräerbriefes." *Theologische Existenz Heute* 156 (1969): 11–61.

Koch, D. A. "Der Text von Hab 2,4b in der Septuaginta und im Neuen Testament." *Zeitschrift für die neutestamentliche Wissenschaft* 68–75 (1985): 68–85.

Kolenskow, A. B. "The Genre Testament and Forecasts of the Future in the Hellenistic Jewish Milieu." *Journal for the Study of Judaism in the Persian, Hellenistic and Roman Period* 6 (1975): 57–71.

Küster, Otto. "Konkreter Glaube." *Zeitschrift für Theologie und Kirche* 48 (1951): 101–14.

Lane, W. L. "Hebrews: A Sermon in Seach of a Setting." *Southwestern Journal of Theology* 28 (1985): 13–18.

————. "Unexpected Light on Hebrews 13:1–6 from a Second Century Source." *Perspectives in Religious Studies* 9 (1982): 267–74.

Langkammer, H. "Der Ursprung des Glaubens an Christus den Schöpfungsmittler." *Studii biblical franciscani liber annuus* 18 (1968): 55–93.

Lewis, T. W. "'. . . And If He Shrinks Back. . (Heb. 10:38b)." *New Testament Studies* 22 (1976): 88–94.

Lindars, B. "Review of Attridge." *Biblica* 72 (1991): 286–90.

————. "The Rhetorical Structure of Hebrews." *New Testament Studies* 35 (1989): 382–406.

Lloyd Neeley, Linda. "A Discourse Analysis of Hebrews [charts]." *OPTAT* 3–4 (1987): 1–146.

Loader, William R. G. "Christ at the Right Hand: Ps. CX. 1 in the New Testament." *New Testament Studies* 3–4 (1978): 199–217.

Lohse, E. "Emuna und Pistis-jüdisches und urchristliches Verständnis des Glaubens." *Zeitschrift für die neutestamentliche Wissenschaft* 68 (1977): 147–63.

Lombard, H. A. "Κατάπαυσις." in the Letter to the Hebrews." *Neotestamentica* 5 (1971): 60–71.

Longenecker, Richard N. "'The Faith of Abraham Theme' in Paul, James and Hebrews: A Study in the Circumstantial Nature of New Testament Teaching." *Journal of the Evangelical Theological Society* 20 (1977): 203–12.

Lührmann, Dieter. "Pistis im Judentum." *Zeitschrift für die neutestamentliche Wissenschaft* (1973): 19–38.

Lund, N. W. "The Presence of Chiasmus in the New Testament." *Journal of Religion* 10 (1930): 74–93.

————. "The Significance of Chiasmus for Interpretation." *Crozer Quarterly* 20 (1943): 105–23.

Luter, A. Boyd and Michelle V. Lee. "Philippians as Chiasmus: Key to the Structure, Unity and Theme Questions." *New Testament Studies* 41 (1995): 89–101.

Mackay, C. "The Argument of Hebrews." *Church Quarterly Review* 168 (1967): 325–38.

MacLeod, D. J. "The Doctrinal Center of the Book of Hebrews." *Bibliotheca Sacra* 146 (1989): 291–300.

———. "The Literary Structure of the Book of Hebrews." *Bibliotheca Sacra* 146 (1989): 185–97.

———. "The Present Work of Christ in Hebrews." *Bibliotheca Sacra* 148 (1991): 184–200.

Macrae, G. W. "Heavenly Temple and Eschatology in the Letter to the Hebrews." *Semeia* 12 (1978): 179–99.

Man, R. E. "The Value of Chiasm for New Testament Interpretation." *Bibliotheca Sacra* 141 (1984): 146–57.

Manson, T. W. "Martyrs and Martyrdom." *Bulletin of the John Rylands University Library of Manchester* 39 (1956–57): 463–84.

Marshall, I. Howard. "The Problem of Apostasy in New Testament Theology." *Perspectives in Religious Studies* 14.4 (1987): 65–80.

Massa, G. W. "The Fearful Results of Faith (Hebrews 10:19–39)." *Princeton Seminary Bulletin* 61 (1968): 55–59.

Mathis, M. A. "Does 'Substantia' Mean 'Realisation' or 'Foundation' in Hebr 11,1?" *Biblica* 3 (1922): 79–87.

McCullough, J. C. "Some Recent Developments in Research on the Epistle to the Hebrews." *Irish Biblical Studies* 2 (1980): 141–65.

———. "Some Recent Developments in Research on the Epistle to the Hebrews: II." *Irish Biblical Studies* 3 (1981): 28–45.

———. "The Impossibility of a Second Repentance in Hebrews." *Biblical Theology Bulletin* 24 (1974): 31–37.

McKnight, S. "The Warning Passages of Hebrews: A Formal Analysis and Theological Conclusions." *Trinity Journal* 13 (1992): 21–59.

Meier, J. P. "Structure and Theology in Hebrews 1:1–14." *Biblica* 66 (1985): 168–89.

———. "Symmetry and Theology in the Old Testament Citations of Heb 1:5–14." *Biblica* 66 (1985): 504–33.

Melbourne, B. L. "An Examination of the Historical-Jesus Motif in the Epistle to the Hebrews." *Andrews University Seminary Studies* 26 (1988): 281–97.

Mercado, L. J. "The Language of Sojourning in the Abraham Midrash in Heb. XI,8–10: Its Old Testament Basis, Exegetical Traditions and Function in the Epistle to the Hebrews." *Harvard Theological Review* 59 (1967): 494–95.

Michel, O. "Zur Auslegung des Hebräerbriefes." *Novum Testamentum* 6 (1963): 189–91.

Miller, M. R. "Seven Theological Themes in Hebrews." *Grace Theological Journal* 8 (1987): 131–40.

———. "What is the Literary Form of Hebrews 11?" *Journal of the Evangelical Theological Society* 29 (1986): 411–17.

Minear, P. S. "Ontology and Eschatology." *New Testament Studies* 12 (1966): 89–105.

Moloney, Francis. "The Reinterpretation of Psalm VIII and the Son of Man Debate." *New Testament Studies* 27 (1981): 656–72.

Moule, C. F. D. "Review of Grässer, Der Glaube im Hebräerbrief." *Journal of Theological Studies n.s.* 17 (1966): 147–50.

Mugridge, A. "Warnings in the Epistle to the Hebrews: An Exegetical and Theological Study." *Reformed Theological Review* 46 (1987): 74–82.

Murillo, L. "Does 'Substantia' Mean 'Realization' or 'Foundation' in Hebr. 11,1?" *Biblica* 3 (1922): 87–89.

Nardoni, E. "Partakers in Christ (Hebrews 3:14)." *New Testament Studies* 37 (1991): 456–72.

Nisius, J. B. "Zur Klärung von Hebr 12,2." *Biblische Zeitschrift* 14 (1917): 44–61.

O'Neill, J. C. "Hebrews 2:9." *Journal of Theological Studies* 17 (1966): 79–82.

Oberholtzer, T. K. "The Warning Passages in Hebrews. Part 1 (of 5 parts): The Eschatological Salvation of Hebrews 1:5–2:5." *Bibliotheca Sacra* 145 (1988): 83–97.

———. "The Warning Passages in Hebrews. Part 3 (of 5 parts): The Thorn-Infested Ground in Hebrews 6:4–12." *Bibliotheca Sacra* 145 (1988): 319–28.

———. "The Warning Passages in Hebrews. Part 4 (of 5 parts): The Danger of Willful Sin in Hebrews 10:26–39." *Bibliotheca Sacra* 145 (1988): 410–19.

———. "The Warning Passsages in Hebrews. Part 2 (of 5 parts): The Kingdom Rest in Hebrews 3:1–4:13." *Bibliotheca Sacra* 145 (1988): 185–96.

———. "The Warning Passages in Hebrews. Part 5 (of 5 parts): The Danger of Willful Sin in Hebrews 12:25–29." *Bibliotheca Sacra* 146 (1989): 67–75.

Omark, Reuben E. "The Sayings of the Savior: Exegesis and Christology in Hebrews 5:7–10." *Interpretation* 12 (1958): 39–51.

Parsons, Mikeal C. "Son and High Priest: A Study in the Christology of Hebrews." *Evangelical Quarterly* 60 (1988): 195–215.

Pelser, G. M. M. "A Translation Problem. Heb. 10:19–25." *Neotestamentica* 5 (1974): 43–53.

———. "The Concept Archegos in the Letter to the Hebrews." *Hervormde Teologiese Studies* 28 (1972): 86–96.

Perkins, D. W. "A Call to Pilgrimage: The Challenge of Hebrews." *Theological Educator* 32 (1985): 69–81.

Peterson, D. G. "The Situation of the 'Hebrews' (5:11–6:12)." *Reformed Theological Review* 38 (1976): 14–21.

Pretorius, E. A. G. "ΔΙΑΘΗΚΗ in the Epistle to the Hebrews." *Neotestamentica* 5 (1971): 22–36.

Reicke, B. "Glaube und Leben der Urgemeinde. Bemerkungen zu Apostelgeschichte 1–7." *Abhandlungen zur Theologie des Alten und Neuen Testaments* 32 (1957): 152–57.

Rice, G. E. "Apostasy as a Motif and Its Effect on the Structure of Hebrews." *Andrews University Seminary Studies* 23 (1985): 29–35.

———. "The Chiastic Structure of the Central Section of the Epistle to the Hebrews." *Andrews University Seminary Studies* 19 (1981): 243–46.

Richardson, Alan. "Whose Architect and Maker Is God." *Theology Today* 8 (1951): 155–56.

Rissi, Mathias. "Die Menschlichkeit Jesu nach Hebr. 5:7–8." *Theologische Zeitschrift* 11 (1955): 28–45.

Roehrs, W. R. "Divine Covenants: Their Structure and Function." *Concordia Journal* 14 (1988): 7–27.

Rose, C. "Verheissung und Erfüllung. Zum Verständnis von Epaggelia Im Hebräerbrief." *Biblische Zeitschrift* 33 (1989): 60–80.

———. "Verheissung und Erfüllung. Zum Verständnis von Epaggelia Im Hebräerbrief." *Biblische Zeitschrift* 33 (1989): 178–91.

Ross, J. "Two Aspects of Faith (Heb. XI.1)." *Expository Times* 23 (1911–12): 182–83.

Rowell, J. B. "Exposition of Hebrews Six: 'An Age-Long Battleground.'" *Bibliotheca Sacra* 94 (1937): 321–42.

Rusche, H. "Glaube und Leben nach dem Hebräerbrief." *Bibel und Leben* 12 (1971): 94–104.

Schmitt, A. Von. "Struktur, Herkunft und Bedeutung der Beispielreihe in Weish 10." *Biblische Zeitschrift* 21 (1977): 1–22.

Scott, J. J. "Archegos in the Salvation History of the Epistle to the Hebrews." *Journal of the Evangelical Theological Society* 29 (1986): 47–54.

Sharp, J. R. "Philonism and Eschatology of Hebrews: Another Look." *East Asia Journal of Theology* 2 (1984): 289–98.

Siebeneck, R. T. "May Their Bones Return to Life—Sirach's Praise of the Father." *Catholic Biblical Quarterly* 21 (1959): 144–28.

Silva, M . "Perfection and Eschatology in Hebrews." *Westminster Theological Journal* (1976): 60–71.

Smalley, S. S. "Atonement in Hebrews." *Evangelical Quarterly* 33 (1961): 126–35.

Smith, T. C. "An Exegesis of Hebrews 13:1–17." *Faith and Mission* 7 (1989): 70–78.

Sproule, J. A. "Παραπεσόντας" in Hebrews 6:6." *Grace Theological Journal* 2 (1981): 327–32.

Swetnam, James. "Form and Content in Hebrews 1–6." *Biblica* 53 (1972): 368–85.

———. "Form and Content in Hebrews 7–13." *Biblica* 55 (1974): 333–48.

———. "Jesus and Logos in Hebrews 4:12–13." *Biblica* 62 (1981): 214–24.

———. "On the Literary Genre of the 'Epistle to the Hebrews.'" *Novum Testamentum* 11 (1969): 261–69.

Thompson, James W. "Structure and Purpose of the Catena in Heb. 1:5–13." *Catholic Biblical Quarterly* 38 (1976): 352–63.

Thurston, R. W. "Philo and the Epistle to the Hebrews." *Evangelical Quarterly* 58 (1986): 133–43.

Tietjen, John H. "Hebrews 11:8–12." *Interpretation* 42 (1988): 403–407.

Todd, Virgil H. "Biblical Eschatology: An Overview." *Cumberland Seminarian* 22 (1984): 3–16.

Tongue, D. H. "The Concept of Apostasy in the Epistle to the Hebrews." *Tyndale Bulletin* 5–6 (1960): 19–26.

Toussaint, Stanley D. "The Eschatology of the Warning Passages in the Book of Hebrews." *Grace Theological Journal* 3 (1982): 67–80.

Vanhoye, Albert. "A Situation et signification de Hébreux V. 1–10." *New Testament Studies* 23 (1976–77): 445–56.

———. "Discussions sur la structure de l'Épître aux Hébreux." *Biblica* 55 (1974): 349–80.

———. "Longue March ou access tout proche? Le contexte biblique de Hébreux 3:7–4:11." *Biblica* 49 (1968): 9–26.

Vorster, W. S. "The Meaning of ΠΑΡΡΗΣΙΑ in the Epistle to the Hebrews." *Neotestamentica* 5 (1971): 51–59.

Waal, C. Van der. "The People of God in the Epistle to the Hebrews." *Neotestamentica* 5 (1971): 83–91.

Weeks, Noel. "Admonition and Error in Hebrews." *Westminster Theological Journal* 39 (1976): 72–80.

Widdess, A. G. "A Note on Hebrews 11:3." *Journal of Theological Studies* 10 (1959): 327–29.

Wikgren, A. "Patterns of Perfection in the Epistle to the Hebrews." *New Testament Studies* 6 (1960): 159–67.

Williamson, R. "Philo and New Testament Christology." *Expository Times* 90 (1970): 361–65.

———. "Platonism and Hebrews." *Scottish Journal of Theology* 16 (1963): 415–24.

———. "The Background of the Epistle to the Hebrews." *Expository Times* 87 (1976): 232–37.

Wolterstorff, Nicholas P. "The Assurance of Faith [Are Calvin, Locke, and Heb. 11 Compatible?]." *Faith and Philosophy* 7 (1990): 396–417.

Wood, J. E. "Isaac Typology in the New Testament." *New Testament Studies* 14 (1967–68): 583–89.

Wright, A. G. "The Literary Genre Midrash." *Catholic Biblical Quarterly* 28 (1966): 105–38, 417–57.

INDEX OF AUTHORS

Adams, J. C., 113–14
Attridge, H. W., 33–35, 74–76, 84, 89, 92, 95, 98, 104, 118–19, 121, 124, 127, 135, 141, 144–45, 147, 156, 162, 165, 169, 185, 200, 203, 213, 232, 236, 238

Barrett, C. K., 5, 51, 187
Barth, M., 174
Bateman, H. W., 68, 70
Bauer, W., 47, 73, 74, 88, 97, 106, 113, 141, 156, 162, 170, 200, 203–4, 216, 222, 227, 237, 239
Betz, O., 214
Black, D. A., 17, 19–21, 23, 26, 180, 223, 230–31
Blackman, E. C., 36
Blass, F., 112, 159, 166, 206
Bligh, J., 26, 91, 158, 184
Blomberg, C., 15–16, 173
Bock, D., 12–13
Braumann, G., 88
Braun, H., 21, 76
Brown, J., 18, 36, 88, 93, 175
Bruce, F. F., 21–22, 67, 82, 104, 110, 163, 182, 198, 203, 204, 208, 213, 216, 236
Buchanan, G. W., 213, 222
Büchsel, F., 43, 217
Bultmann, R., 2–3, 36–38, 57, 125

Caird, G. B., 83
Carson, D. A., 174
Conzelmann, H., 116
Cosby, M. R., 182, 206, 211, 234
Culpepper, R. H., 154

D'Angelo, M. R., 94, 202, 219
Dahl, N. A., 75, 163
Dautzenberg, G., 38, 77
Debrunner, F., 112, 159, 166, 206
Delitzsch, F., 87, 161

Delling, G., 160, 230
Dörrie, H., 212

Ellingworth, P., 5, 11, 19–21, 26–27, 50–51, 60–61, 81, 90, 92, 94–95, 105–6, 110, 117–18, 123, 128, 181–82, 186–87, 190, 198, 218, 228, 237, 240

Fenton, J. C., 28
Foerster, W., 237
Fuchs, A., 76
Funk, R. W., 112, 159, 166, 206

Gleason, R. C., 120
Gloer, W., 231
Goppelt, L., 3–4, 13, 223
Gordon, V. R., 8
Grässer, E., 29–32, 35, 37–39, 56, 62, 72–73, 77, 112, 123, 129, 164–65, 167, 178, 242, 244, 252
Greenlee, H., 187
Grundmann, W., 74
Guthrie, D., 19–20, 77, 182
Guthrie, G. H., 18, 20, 22–23, 76–77, 80, 84–85, 95, 101, 110–11, 134, 236
Gyllenberg, R., 87

Hagner, D., 3, 21
Hamm, D., 52–57, 62, 95, 128, 227, 229
Harrisville, R. A., 40, 87, 116, 143, 161
Hay, D. M., 135
Herodotus, 127
Hoffmann, E., 93
Hofius, O., 97
Horning, E. B., 53, 224, 230–31
Hughes, G. R., 4, 29, 38, 60, 120, 124
Hughes, P. E., 19, 89, 104, 113, 118, 120, 154, 198, 213–15

Hunzinger, C., 162
Hurst, L. D., 10, 50, 52, 60, 83

Josephus, 105, 121

Käsemann, E., 9, 39–42, 45–49, 87, 98,
    116, 154, 161, 244
Kent, H. A., 19
Knight, G. W., III., 174
Köster, H., 215

Ladd, G. E., 3, 13, 187
Lane, W. L., 26, 52, 61–62, 67, 73–75,
    81, 83, 94–95, 102, 110, 118, 124,
    126–27, 130, 132–34, 144, 146,
    155, 157, 160–61, 163–64, 174–75,
    183–84, 187, 198, 200, 204–5, 207–
    8, 211, 215, 219, 221, 223, 226,
    229, 232, 236–38
Leonard, W., 5
Lewis, T. W., 8–9, 40, 155, 174–75,
    230
Liddell, H. G. & Scott, R., 14
Lincoln, A. T., 174
Lindars, B., 11, 32–33, 35, 44–45, 214,
    224, 244
Longenecker, R. N., 39, 244
Lund, N. W., 14–16, 103
Luter, A. B. & Lee, M. V., 15

MacLeod, D. J., 108, 139, 141, 151
Man, R. E., 82–83, 171
Manson, W., 87, 229
Maxwell, K. L., 74, 76–78
Meier, J. P., 69–70
Mercado, L. F., 7
Metzger, B. M., 187
Michaelis, W., 105, 119
Michel, O., 1–2, 36–37, 68, 81, 88, 98,
    118, 139, 164, 184
Miesner, D. R., 15, 173
Miller, M.R., 57–59, 182
Moffatt, J., 82, 104, 109, 121, 161,
    208, 216, 219
Moo, D. J., 174

Morris, L., 21, 174
Moule, C. F. D., 30–31
Moulton, J. H., 123
Moxnes, H., 183, 184, 193
Mugridge, A., 121

Neufeld, V. H., 61, 62, 89
Nicole, R., 117, 120
Nida, E. A., 64

Oberholtzer, T. K., 168–69

Peterson, D., 88, 103–4, 135, 139, 144,
    146, 156, 160, 229
Polybius, 127

Rissi, M., 6
Robertson, A. T., 67, 143, 162, 166,
    206
Rowell, J. B., 120

Schlier, H., 76, 92, 121, 161
Schoonhoven, C. R., 56
Scott, J. J., 228, 230
Seesemann, H., 144, 170
Solari, J. K., 169
Spicq, C., 73, 90, 207
Sproule, J. A., 115
Stevens, G. B., 3
Stine, D. M., 8
Swetnam, J., 25–26, 82, 90, 102, 109,
    111, 124, 132, 166, 185, 216, 222

Thompson, J. W., 6, 42–49, 181, 193,
    212, 214–16, 235, 244
Toussaint, S. D., 120
Turner, N., 123, 226

Vanhoye, A., 14, 23–27, 66, 71, 80–81,
    85, 97, 107–110, 131–33, 144, 157,
    211, 222–23, 226, 234–36, 243

Westcott, B. F., 59, 61, 104, 130, 143
Wilcox, M., 193
Williamson, R., 49, 122, 199, 213

INDEX OF SUBJECTS

a fortiori, 76, 79, 146, 168, 170, 232, 239, 246
a minori ad majus, 76
Abraham, 7, 39, 48–49, 55, 110–11, 123–24, 126–28, 134–35, 138, 152, 183–85, 187–193, 218–19, 248
alternating structure, 12, 17, 56, 63, 180, 183, 242–43, 246, 250, 252
anaphora, 33, 182, 184, 206, 211
announcement of the subject, 23, 26
ἀπαύγασμα, 67, 68
ἀπιστία, 2, 11, 46, 64, 97–99, 110
apostasy, 1, 10, 21, 47, 86, 116, 119, 121–23, 154, 169, 170–71, 179, 238–39, 241–42, 248–49, 251
apostates, 116, 119–22, 125–26, 128, 248
apostle, 60, 86–87, 89–92, 94–95, 100, 129, 247
ἀρχηγός, 230
ἀρχιερεύς, 22, 27, 85, 87, 89–90, 100, 102, 130–31, 140–41, 247

baptism, 116, 163
better covenant, 21, 132, 138, 142–43, 153, 157, 170, 249
blood, 60, 84, 105, 142, 145–47, 149, 156, 159, 161, 163, 167, 170–71, 174, 197, 199, 202, 208, 232, 237, 241

change in genre, 22, 24
characteristic terms, 24
characteristics of faith, 10, 29, 35, 45, 49, 52, 63, 86, 96, 100–101, 112, 129, 158, 204, 210, 244, 247, 252, 253
chiasm, 12–16, 19, 28, 53, 67, 71–72, 102, 135, 137, 139, 140, 146–47, 157–58, 167–68, 171–73, 175, 177–78, 184–87, 190, 194–97, 199, 203–4, 206, 209–10, 212, 222, 224, 226, 230–31, 234, 236, 240–41, 243, 250–52
Christ's high priesthood, 14, 22, 63, 101–2, 106–8, 130, 142, 146, 152, 161–62, 165, 247, 249
Christ's superiority, 82
Christological, 4, 8, 10–11, 17, 29–30, 32–37, 52–55, 57–59, 62–63, 66–67, 69–70, 72–75, 77, 79, 82, 84, 86, 89–90, 100, 102–3, 108–13, 115, 121–25, 128, 131, 133–34, 152, 154, 157, 162–63, 165–66, 168–69, 171, 174, 176, 178–79, 182, 190, 193, 195, 201–2, 220, 224, 226–27, 230, 237–38, 241–42, 244–48, 250–53
Christology, 6, 28, 53, 63, 66, 70, 83, 86, 100, 109, 112, 115, 129, 131, 134, 161, 165–68, 171–74, 176, 178, 190, 193, 201, 220, 221–22, 224, 230–31, 233, 245, 248, 250–51, 253
concept of faith, 1–12, 14–15, 18, 28–29, 31–40, 42, 45–46, 49, 52–53, 57, 62–63, 72, 77–78, 87, 99, 111, 125, 128, 131, 158, 163, 165–66, 174, 180, 183, 200, 205–6, 210, 220, 230, 233, 241, 243–44, 248–49, 251–53, *See also* faith in Hebrews
confession, 27, 38, 56, 60–61, 63, 75, 85–92, 94–95, 100–101, 152, 154, 157, 163–65, 168, 246, 249
confidence, 3, 8, 16, 37, 44, 47–48, 56–57, 60–61, 63–64, 86, 90–92, 94, 96, 100, 110, 113, 158–59, 161, 164–65, 172–74, 179, 213–16, 247, 252
content of faith, 4, 29, 32–33, 35, 60–62, 64, 123, 228, 240, *See also* object of faith
creedal statement, 164, 231

cross, 9, 53–54, 59, 63, 180, 201, 221, 225–27, 229–31, 233–34, 241

David, 18, 20, 206, 209
deceitfulness of sin, 93, 98
different views of faith, 29, 243
disobedience, 2, 71, 96, 98–99, 205, 239
doctrinal section, 11, 19, 27, 65, 70, 72, 82, 86, 90, 99, 108, 130–31, 133–34, 152, 157, 183, 245–46
doctrine, 5, 8, 11–12, 24, 27–28, 63–64, 71, 75, 79, 84, 90, 103, 109–11, 114, 125, 130, 152, 154–55, 157, 161–63, 165, 174, 180, 230, 242, 246, 247, 250

endurance, 3, 7, 9, 24, 44–47, 49, 52–53, 57, 79, 172–73, 176–77, 179–82, 202, 221–22, 224–27, 229–30, 233–35, 241–42, 244, 251–52
Enoch, 183, 185–86, 203, 207–8, 210
ἐπαγγελία, 40, 142, 172, 176, 184, 189, 191, 212, 218
Esau, 192–93, 238
eschatological, 5–7, 10–11, 29–32, 34, 38–39, 41–45, 49, 51–52, 62–63, 77, 122, 165–66, 172, 176, 178, 183, 186, 193, 202, 209, 215, 220, 235, 237–39, 244, 250, 252–53
eschatology, 1, 5–6, 10, 16, 28, 30, 39–42, 44–45, 49–52, 62–63, 74, 86, 176, 180, 187, 193, 245, 250–51, 253
ethical, 4, 6, 10, 16, 29–33, 35, 37–39, 44, 52, 62–63, 72–73, 77, 79, 100, 112, 129, 165–66, 172–73, 176–77, 179, 189, 201, 233, 241–42, 244, 247, 248, 250, 252
evil heart of unbelief, 98
exaltation, 19, 34, 48, 68–69, 84, 228, 229, 231
exemplar of faith, 4, 35, 56, 187, 217
exemplars of faith, 45, 180, 185, 190, 192–93, 198, 203, 205–7, 209–10, 212, 214, 216–19, 221, 234–35, 241, 250

faith in Christ, 5, 10, 30, 57, 64, 79, 92, 94, 99, 114, 120, 125–26, 128, 163, 167, 179, 242, 248
faith in Hebrews, 1, 4–10, 12–13, 16, 29–30, 32–35, 37–39, 42–44, 46–50, 52, 54–59, 62–63, 72, 77–79, 99–101, 112, 114, 116, 121, 124–25, 128, 131, 155, 165, 171, 174, 176–77, 182, 185–86, 192, 201–3, 210, 213, 215, 223–24, 227, 229–32, 235–36, 239, 241–44, 247, 249–53, See also concept of faith
faithful high priest, 86, 101, 130
fidelity, 3, 33–35, 38, 62–63, 245
firmness, 31–33, 110
forerunner, 127–28, 227, 244, 248
forward-looking aspect, 7, 39, 48, 183, 190–194, 199, 202, 204, 208–9, 215, 217, 219, 220, 250
founder, 226–29, 234–35

gifts and sacrifices, 104
Gnostic, 40
God's promise, 10, 34, 48, 50, 52, 54, 63, 124–25, 127, 164, 189, 192, 194, 235, 244, 252, See also promise
God's rest, 20, 86, 93, 96, 99–100, 205, 239, 240, 246
God's word, 77, 94, 96, 118, 191, 195, 199, 222, 239–40, 251

Hellenistic, 7, 10, 25, 31, 36, 41–42, 49–50, 52, 62, 92, 155, 180, 214, 244
hendiadys, 46, 112, 123
high priest, 4, 18, 19, 21–22, 24, 60, 85–87, 89, 90–92, 94–95, 100–109, 127, 130–34, 137, 140–43, 145–46, 151–57, 162–63, 166, 230, 241–42, 247, 249
high priesthood of Christ, 1, 8, 10–11, 21, 56, 60, 101, 111, 130, 134, 135, 141, 143–44, 152, 154–55, 163, 174, 179, 250
Holy Spirit, 71, 115, 117–20, 151, 170
hook words, 24

hope, 3, 7–10, 33, 37–38, 44–45, 47–
    52, 56–59, 61, 63, 86, 90–92, 94,
    96, 100, 111, 126–27, 136–38, 157,
    160, 163–66, 199, 204, 209, 213–
    15, 244, 247–48, 252
humiliation, 20, 22, 82, 84, 90, 121,
    226, 230, 246
humiliation and exaltation, 230
humiliation of Christ, 84, 90
hymn, 224, 231, 241

imitation, 127, 230
immaturity, 109
inclusion, 25, 27, 66, 71, 80–81, 85,
    97, 102, 110, 126, 131–33, 157,
    181, 205, 219, 222
Isaac, 48–49, 82, 111, 123–124, 183,
    185, 187–93, 198, 218

Jacob, 49, 183, 185, 191–93, 198, 218
Jesus, 3–5, 8–9, 18, 20, 22, 24, 29, 32–
    37, 40, 45, 52–64, 68–69, 72–73,
    75, 77–79, 81–96, 99–109, 111–14,
    116, 118, 120–35, 137–44, 148,
    150, 152–59, 161–63, 166, 169–71,
    173–74, 179–80, 185–86, 203, 215,
    220, 224–30, 232–33, 235, 237–42,
    244, 246–49, 251–52
Jewish, 3, 7, 25, 36, 38, 50, 52, 62, 68,
    70, 92, 154, 181, 193, 200, 215,
    232, 244

καύχημα, 48, 91, 92, 165

levitical high priesthood, 102–3, 107–
    8, 130–31, 135, 137–39, 142, 152,
    155, 247, 249
literary device, 12–14, 71, 76, 80, 85,
    103, 111, 137, 139, 158, 169, 181–
    82, 206, 211, 227, 243
LXX, 31, 35, 54–55, 82–83, 96, 124,
    143, 149, 155, 177, 222, 227, 234,
    See also Septuagint

mediator, 18–19, 61, 132, 142–43,
    147–48, 153, 219–20, 240, 242, 251
Melchizedek, 21, 24, 25, 102, 107–9,
    127, 130–31, 134–36, 144, 152, 249

merciful and faithful high priest, 84,
    86, 90, 101–2, 130, 246
model of faith, 10, 29, 52, 54–55, 59–
    60, 62–63, 86, 94–96, 100, 111–12,
    126–29, 131, 224, 226–30, 234,
    245–48, 252
Mosaic covenant, 145
Moses, 18–19, 33, 48–49, 54, 59–60,
    76, 90–91, 94–96, 100, 136, 142,
    155, 157, 167, 193–99, 201–2, 219,
    221, 240, 242, 247, 250
Mount Sinai, 236, 239–40
Mount Zion, 40, 219, 220, 223, 236,
    240

new covenant, 8, 10–11, 32, 55, 59, 72,
    127, 132–34, 143–49, 151–53, 155–
    56, 163, 166, 168–69, 212, 219–20,
    221, 227, 235–36, 239–40, 242,
    249–51
New Testament, 1–5, 10, 12–16, 19,
    21, 30, 32, 35, 36, 38, 39, 43, 47,
    50–51, 57, 59, 64–65, 67, 73–74,
    76–77, 82–83, 88–89, 92–93, 103–
    6, 110, 112–13, 116–17, 119, 121,
    123–25, 127, 135, 139, 141, 143–
    44, 154, 159–163, 166, 170, 174,
    178, 182, 187, 190, 200–202, 206,
    214, 216–17, 223, 226–31, 237, 243
Noah, 48, 183, 194, 199–200, 202,
    207, 219, 221, 228, 242, 250
νωθροί, 110

obedience, 7–8, 34, 37, 45–47, 55–57,
    63, 93, 96–100, 108, 191, 194–95,
    199, 201–2, 205, 208, 229, 245, 247
object of faith, 5, 9–10, 32, 35–36, 52,
    56–63, 65, 73, 75, 77–79, 86, 90,
    92–94, 99, 112–13, 116, 121, 123–
    26, 128, 179, 190, 203, 205, 224,
    226–230, 232, 235, 238–39, 241–
    42, 244, 246–49, 251–52, See also
    content of faith
old covenant, 71, 76, 104, 132, 142–
    45, 148–49, 151–53, 156, 168, 170,
    220–21, 236, 239–40, 250–51
Old Testament, 3, 7–9, 31, 35, 37, 40,
    58–59, 68–70, 76, 93, 103–4, 120,

133–34, 149, 151, 155, 162, 168, 170, 177, 180, 186, 190–91, 198, 201, 206, 209, 218, 220, 229–30, 234–35, 238, 241, 250
ὁμολογία, 63, 165

παραπικρασμός, 96–97
parenesis, 11–12, 18, 24, 27–28, 64, 71, 79, 101, 109, 111, 156, 174, 180, 182, 221, 224, 230, 242, 246, 247, 250
parenetic section, 19, 27–28, 70, 72, 74, 84, 86, 89, 96, 100–101, 109–10, 113, 130, 134, 156, 158, 165, 174, 180, 220–24, 233, 235, 245–46, 248–49, 251
παρρησία, 47–48, 60, 91, 92, 157, 159, 161, 165, 172, 173, 174
Passover, 197, 199, 202, 221, 250
Pastoral epistles, 169
patriarchs, 185–86, 191, 194, 218
Pauline concept of faith, 35
Pauline epistles, 78, 125, 166, 253
Pauline Epistles, 4, 36
perfecter, 32, 34, 53, 223, 225–27, 229, 234–35, 244
Philo, 7, 30–35, 42, 44, 49–50, 122, 199, 213
Philonic concept, 39, 49, 52, 181, 244, 252
pioneer, 4, 32, 53, 83, 223, 225, 227
πιστεύω, 2, 11, 64
πιστός, 2, 31, 64, 94–96
πίστις, 32, 46–47, 57, 64, 112, 124, 211
Platonic, 42, 49
present and future, 5, 10, 44, 49, 52, 61–62, 164, 176, 178, 181, 187, 244, 253
promise, 3, 9, 40, 45, 47–48, 50–52, 58–59, 93, 98, 111, 123–24, 126, 128–29, 143, 147–48, 151, 161, 164, 173, 177, 186, 189, 191, 199, 205, 212, 219, 235, 244, 248, See also God's promise
προσφέρω, 107, 132–33, 148, 150
πρόδραμος, 127–28
qualifications of a high priest, 103

Rahab, 204–6, 219, 236
reliability, 33, 35, 63
resurrection, 93, 114, 190, 209, 210, 228
rhetorical structure, 13, 183, 252
righteousness, 36, 93, 134, 194, 200–202, 207, 221, 232–33, 242, 250

Sabbath rest, 1, 5, 10, 20, 51, 86
sacrifice, 8, 19, 21, 32, 61, 132, 134, 142, 144–54, 156, 158, 167, 169–71, 187, 208, 241, 249
sacrifices, 104–8, 131–32, 134, 140–42, 145, 148–50
salvation, 3, 9, 19, 24, 30, 32, 36, 38, 45, 48, 62, 69, 71–73, 75, 77, 79, 80, 82–83, 87, 93–94, 108, 112, 116–118, 120, 160, 164–65, 169, 172, 177, 194, 198, 228–30, 237–38, 240, 245–46
Samuel, 206
sanctuary, 21, 127, 141–47, 153, 156, 161, 174
Sarah, 48, 183, 185, 187–90, 192, 194, 198, 218, 219
semantic borrowing, 111

Septuagint, 92, 119, 123, 149, 155, 215, See also LXX
sonship, 1, 10, 56, 61
soteriological, 3–4, 30, 35–36, 77, 120, 229, 236, 244, 252
spatial concept, 10, 30–31, 49, 181
spatial dualism, 6, 49, 52, 180
steadfastness, 10, 30–31, 35, 38, 47, 62–63, 77, 79, 96, 100, 112, 123–24, 126, 128–29, 177–79, 181, 189, 201, 208, 224, 241–42, 244, 247–48, 250, 252
superiority of Christ, 10, 20, 22–23, 66, 139, 249

τελειωτής, 54, 224, 226–27, 229, 241–42, 244
transcendent reality, 6, 39, 42–45, 49
trust in God, 8, 10, 52, 58, 190, 200–202, 244

unbelief, 2, 11, 85, 93, 97–99, 110,
121–22, 169–170, 239, 248
ὑπομένω, 46
ὑπομονή, 46, 178

wandering motif, 40

warning passage, 113, 115
word of God, 5, 41, 54, 58, 76, 86, 93–
94, 96, 99–100, 102, 113–14, 117,
120, 123, 125–26, 128, 165, 208,
211, 239, 241

www.ingramcontent.com/pod-product-compliance
Lightning Source LLC
Chambersburg PA
CBHW070910100426
42814CB00003B/123